# On Loving, Hating, and Living Well

Monograph Series of the
Ralph R. Greenson
Memorial Library of the
San Diego Psychoanalytic
Society and Institute

Monograph 2

# On Loving, Hating, and Living Well

## The Public Psychoanalytic Lectures of Ralph R. Greenson, M.D.

*Edited by*

**Robert A. Nemiroff, M.D.**
**Alan Sugarman, Ph.D.**
**Alvin Robbins, M.D.**

INTERNATIONAL UNIVERSITIES PRESS, INC.
MADISON, CONNECTICUT

Acknowledgment is also made to MacGibbon & Kee, an imprint of HarperCollins Publishers Limited, for permission to reprint xaipe by e.e. cummings.



**Library of Congress Cataloging-in-Publication Data**

Greenson, Ralph R., 1911–
On loving, hating and living well: the public psychoanalytic lectures of Ralph R. Greenson, M.D./ edited by Robert A. Nemiroff, Alan Sugarman, Alvin Robbins.
p. cm.— (Monograph series of the Ralph R. Greenson Memorial Library of the San Diego Psychoanalytic Society and Institute: 2)
ISBN 0-8236-3790-5
1. Psychoanalysis. I. Nemiroff, Robert A. (Robert Allen) II. Sugarman, Alan. III. Robbins, Alvin. IV. Title. V. Series.
[DNLM: 1. Greenson, Ralph R., 1911– . 2. Emotions. 3. Psychoanalysis. 4. Psychoanalytic Interpretation. WM 460 G814o]
RC509.G74 1992
616.89'17—dc20
DNLM/DLC
for Library of Congress 92-1438
CIP

Manufactured in the United States of America

# Dedication

This book is dedicated to the memory of Ralph R. Greenson, M.D., extraordinary clinician, creative scholar, and inspiring teacher; and to his family: his beloved wife Hildi and their children, Daniel and his wife Barbara and Joan and her husband Andy, who keep the memory of this unique man vital for all of us.

# Table of Contents

# Acknowledgments

We deeply appreciate and take this opportunity to acknowledge the considerable help we received in the preparation of this book. Foremost, of course, was the invaluable contribution of Hildi Greenson, who provided us with beautifully edited transcripts of the lectures themselves and many hours of inspiration as well as assistance with proofreading and correction of biographical facts. Daniel Greenson too was especially generous with his time and thoughtful advice.

The style and cohesiveness of our words benefited immeasurably from the editorial skills of Barbara Blomgren, whose help we and other colleagues at The University of California, San Diego (UCSD), have appreciated over the years. Phyllis Baumgart, administrative coordinator of psychiatric residency training at UCSD, graciously coordinated many aspects of manuscript preparation. Joyce Harding, administrator of the San Diego Psychoanalytic Institute, kindly provided access to important

Institute resources. Last, but by no means least, Emanuel Lippett and Barbara Nemiroff read the entire manuscript, making useful suggestions and providing ongoing encouragement.

# The Man and His Life

Ralph R. Greenson practiced and taught psychoanalysis in Los Angeles, California, from 1936 to 1979. To many who knew him he was a remarkable man, one of the most exceptional psychoanalysts of his generation, combining the gifts of sensitive and perceptive clinician, creative and prolific scholar, inspiring and challenging teacher, dedicated and loving husband and father, an original and unforgettable personality.

In this volume we have the pleasure of presenting "Romi" Greenson, as he was known by those who loved and admired him, in one of the roles he enjoyed most, communicating to a lay audience his understanding of people and life and his insights about the science and art of psychoanalysis. No matter how large the audience, listening to Greenson lecture was having him share with you his deeply felt, meaningful, and accurate interpretations of your own as well as the human condition.

Before introducing the public lectures, we shall set the stage by telling you something about the life and work of this very special man.

Ralph Greenson was born on September 20, 1911, in the Brownsville section of Brooklyn, New York, the first of a set of fraternal twins born to Joel O. and Kathrine Greenschpoon. Family lore says that it was Papa Greenschpoon, a romantic at heart, who chose the names Romeo and Juliet. Growing up in Brooklyn with the name of Romeo presented the kind of problem to which Romi wryly ascribed his becoming a psychoanalyst. Unknown to his parents, when he was in the fifth grade, he changed his name to Ralph, after a hero he was reading about in *Ralph of the Roundhouse*. Romi and Juli and their sister and brother grew up in a warm and volatile family. Both parents were Russian Jewish immigrants who were striving to make a place for themselves and their children in America. When Romi and Juli were born, their father was a first-year medical student preparing to become a family physician. During the early years, their mother Kathrine, who had been schooled as a pharmacist, supported the family. A woman of indomitable energy, she created an environment of Yiddish culture and prompted the children's musical development. Romi took to the violin, and evenings spent playing in chamber music with friends eventually became a regular, cherished custom in his own home.

In 1914 Papa Greenschpoon graduated from medical school. In a short period of time he became a well-respected and dedicated physician. Frequently Papa would take Romi, still a small child, on house calls. It was surely those experiences and his love and respect for his father that led Romi to declare early on that he too would be a doctor. He later described three indelible impressions left with him from those days: first, his father, the doctor, could see naked ladies when he wanted; second, he seemed unafraid when everyone else was frightened; and third, and best of all, he made those people better.

As a youngster and adolescent, Romi attended public elementary and high school in Brooklyn and completed his undergraduate and premedical studies at Columbia University. In those days a quota system was applied to Jewish applicants to American medical schools, so Romi enrolled at the University of Berne, Switzerland. There he quickly learned German, it being the language of instruction. It was in Switzerland to his considerable good fortune that he met the great love of his life and his lifelong companion, Hildi. Eventually Hildi and Romi had two children. Their son Daniel was to become a physician and is now a training and supervising psychoanalyst at the San Francisco Psychoanalytic Institute. Their daughter Joan is an artist. A delightful extended family was created for the Greensons by Daniel, his wife Barbara, and their children as well as by Joan and her husband Andy Aebi and their children.

Romi completed his medical training at Cedars of Lebanon Hospital in Los Angeles and studied psychoanalysis in Vienna with the imaginative but sometimes erratic William Stekel. Greenson then entered private practice in Los Angeles and engaged in formal psychoanalytic training at the new Los Angeles Psychoanalytic Institute. Fortunately for Romi, Otto Fenichel had just arrived. He would become Romi's inspiration, trusted mentor, colleague, and friend. The scholarly, disciplined Fenichel was just the right counterpoint to the brilliant but unpredictable Stekel. Fenichel and Greenson had an excellent working relationship, and taught one another much, although they had very different styles. Fenichel's approach to the unconscious was quite systematic, while Greenson's was more intuitive and empathic. To Fenichel's great credit, after noting that his student was slavishly trying to imitate him, he declared that it would be "better to be a first rate Greenson than a second-rate Fenichel." Fenichel's untimely death in 1946 was a severe blow to the psychoanalytic community and a deeply felt, disturbing loss to Greenson.

Having completed his training analysis with Otto Fenichel and become a graduate psychoanalyst, Romi entered the United States Army in 1942. There he discovered that he had a gift for teaching and hugely enjoyed lecturing. He began giving seminars to psychiatrists, psychologists, social workers, chaplains, and other medical personnel on how to treat war neurosis and to understand the war casualties. Leo Rosten's popular book, *Captain Newman, M.D.*, and the film based on it are largely modeled on Captain Greenson's wartime experiences. Rosten captures Greenson's remarkable ability to stimulate and influence others and his efforts to humanize the care of psychiatric casualties in an impersonal military setting. Rosten described Captain Newman (Greenson) as follows: "The mannerisms he had always displayed, that unpredictable interplay between the wry, the weary, the impatient, the disenchanted—he was spilling over with responsiveness. . . . His seminars were jammed, from the beginning, and they were about as lively, unorthodox, and illuminating as any I ever heard of. He loved to teach. He loved to perform" (p. 219).

The war years were kind to Romi, not only because he remained in the United States, but because he gained invaluable knowledge and experience in a relatively short period of time. His compassion for the soldiers knew no bounds, and when he returned to Los Angeles he realized that the years of witnessing so much suffering needed distilling and clarification. He started his second analysis with Frances Deri. His psychoanalytic practice flourished; he taught seminars, wrote scientific papers, and started to give the public lectures now collected in this volume. Success and popularity came quickly as the public and professional worlds recognized a marvelous clinician and educator in their midst, always ready to share his experiences and inspire his listeners. He soon became a training analyst and later served as president and dean of the training school at the Los Angeles Psychoanalytic Institute. Over the years he played many important roles in the American Psychoanalytic Association and the American Psychiatric Association. Particularly important to him was his appointment as clinical professor of psychiatry at the University of California, Los Angeles School of Medicine, where he taught medical students and psychiatric residents. In addition, he was active as a clinician and lecturer at The Reiss-Davis Child Guidance Clinic, The Center for Early Education, and for The California Chapter of the Anna Freud Foundation, of which he was the honorary president.

It is not widely realized that the mass of Greenson's contributions to psychiatry and psychoanalysis came after his heart attack in 1955 at the age of forty-four. Although he had to change his lifestyle (no more smoking and less rigorous exercise), he continued to practice, teach, and write creatively for the next twenty-four years.

In 1970, Romi received a diagnosis of heart block and was given his first pacemaker. Four years later, during his fifth pacemaker revision, he suffered a calamitous embolus that left him aphasic. Not being able to communicate orally was a terrible blow to this great teacher. For a number of weeks he could not read, write, or speak, and he, who found his dreams so useful to his creativity, even stopped dreaming. With the courage and will that had been the hallmarks of his life, he fought back. He underwent intensive speech therapy and with remarkable determination taught himself once more how to read, write, and finally to speak in public.

Greenson knew he would be able to resume professional life when one morning he awoke and remembered that he had dreamed. He returned to the fray. Although his speech was never again quite as eloquent as before, he bravely gave public presentations. The last two lectures in this book, "Beyond Sexual Satisfaction . . . ?" and "People in Search of a Family," were given in San Diego after Romi had recovered from his aphasia.

Despite valiant efforts, eventually the generous heart gave out, and after numerous hospitalizations, Romi Greenson died of heart failure on November 24, 1979.

## Scientific Achievements

Ralph Greenson's writings in the areas of theory and clinical practice have earned him a place among the immortals in psychiatry and psychoanalysis. His textbook, *The Technique and Practice of Psychoanalysis*, first published in 1967, is a classic and central reference for students of psychotherapy and psychoanalysis around the world. Undergoing many printings, it has been translated into German, Italian, French, Spanish, and Dutch. In 1978, a collection of thirty-two scientific articles was published under the title *Explorations in Psychoanalysis*. Their titles alone suggest Greenson's versatility and the range of his talent for interweaving clinical observation and theoretical explanation, for example: "The Mother Tongue and the Mother" (1950), "The Struggle Against Identification" (1954), "Forepleasure: Its Use for Defensive Purposes" (1955), "Empathy and Its Vicissitudes" (1960), "On Enthusiasm" (1962), "The Working Alliance and the Transference Neurosis" (1965), "That 'Impossible Profession' " (1966), "Disidentifying from Mother: Its Special Importance for the Boy" (1968), "The Exceptional Position of the Dream in Psychoanalytic Practice" (1970), "The 'Real' Relationship between the Patient and the Psychoanalyst" (1971), "Loving, Hating and Indifference toward the Patient" (1974). Despite the great range of Greenson's scientific interests and contributions, a central theme emerges from his work. As Robert J. Stoller, a particularly close and valued colleague, wrote for Greenson's obituary in the *International Journal of Psycho-Analysis* (1980):

> He knew—and so much enjoyed knowing it—that the central feature of psychoanalysis is the relationship between patient and analyst. From that awareness, that organic commitment, came his therapeutic brilliance, innovative techniques, contributions to analytic theory, and his unparalleled clinical descriptions. He was not only sure that a psychoanalytic report has no anchor unless it is clinically true, but he also was blessed with the capacity to transmit his data to us by means of his words. He wrote to reveal, not hide, clinical reality, and his explorations were powered by intense and compassionate empathy, not by dogma and disquisition. The record of his life shows that he knew how to search and where to find, and then, respecting the value of what he found, he could easily share [pp. 001–002].

Joshua A. Hoffs, psychoanalyst and good friend of Greenson, in an obituary note in the *Bulletin of the Southern California Psychoanalytic Institute and Society*, also described how Greenson's work focused on the special and unique relationship of patient and psychoanalyst. Hoffs stated that Greenson's writing in this area "produced a tangible, direct, and specific beneficial shift in the way psychoanalysts practiced. It has restructured the psychoanalytic situation." With his brilliant descriptions of the complex interplay among the real relationship, the therapeutic alliance, and the transference, Greenson taught us how to orient ourselves in our behavior to our patients, not only using and imparting the necessary emotional insight, but using the experience of the interaction between patient and analyst as curative. In "The 'Real' Relationship between the Patient and the Psychoanalyst" (1971), he wrote:

> My clinical experience leads me to believe that the final resolution of the transference neurosis depends to a great extent on the transference neurosis being replaced by a real relationship. I do not share the traditional psychoanalytic point of view that interpretation alone can resolve the transference neurosis. Interpretation has to be supplemented by a realistic and genuine relationship to the person of the analyst, limited though it may be, for the transference neurosis to be replaced [p. 439].

Greenson's theoretical concerns about the doctor–patient relationship were rendered in striking clarity by the clinical descriptions in his public lectures. His special capacity to care for his patients singled him out. Morton Shane, current director of the Los Angeles Psychoanalytic Institute, has said, "I know no patient who emerged from an interview with him unimpressed with his interest, empathy, and intense wish to help, always disciplined by knowledge of the limits of the therapeutic relationship he knew so well."

Greenson's gift for empathy in interpersonal relations was evident early in his career. Al Goldberg, a close psychoanalytic colleague of Greenson, tells a story about Romi in his medical student days which foreshadowed his later capacities for clinical observation and compassion:

> Romi came under the influence of Professor Klaesi and I am told that Klaesi did not like foreign American students. He did not hold them in high regard. One day the professor brought a patient into the amphitheater and started calling on students to come down and interview the patient. He called on one student, a Swiss, who came down and asked the patient what his name was. Klaesi dismissed him immediately. Another student came down and asked him where he was from. He also got dismissed immediately. Finally he got to Romi. Romi came down and (I can see it. I have watched him in similar situations) turning gently to the patient, said, "You're very sad, aren't you?" Whereupon, Klaesi said, "You know what I think of American students, but this one is going to be a psychiatrist." I tell this story not only because Klaesi had an eye for a good psychiatrist, but that was typical of Romi, to zero in immediately on the most important aspect, which, in this case, had to do with sadness or the mood of the patient. His early papers

> are all about that . . . apathy, boredom and depression. His papers, the clinical vignettes, the stories he told, the examples he chose in the literature were full of those moods and how he helped the patient to understand [1963, pp. 27–28].

Finally, Bess Kaufman, a dear friend of the Greensons, put Romi's unique clinical ability in this way: "He seemed able to peel away surface layers and reach down intimately and knowingly into the real person. At such times the recipient of his attention would feel very special, loved, attractive, and well-understood." He was "a man to whom you could bring your most private and innermost thoughts . . . he would treat each idea as a jeweler examining a fine stone."

# The Public Lectures

The lectures contained in this volume spanned the years between 1955 and 1978. We count it our misfortune that before 1955 many went unrecorded. Greenson's lectures were given to a variety of lay audiences, including nursery schools, temple groups, university forums, mental health associations, and radio listeners. It was a period during which there was a great thirst for information about the new science and practice of psychoanalysis. This was due to the considerable value psychoanalytic theory and principles had in helping psychiatrists and other physicians understand and treat war neurosis during World War II and its psychological aftermath. There was no better spokesman for psychoanalysis than Ralph Greenson. Never would he talk down to his audience; he always conveyed information with great charm and respect for his listeners and the clinical situations he was portraying.

Before each lecture we have provided an introduction describing the setting in which it took place and some of the social circumstances that prevailed at the time. Reading these talks now is like reading a chronicle of the great psychosocial issues of the last thirty-five years. Our efforts were helped immeasurably by the clear and informative notes provided by Hildi Greenson. Even though some of the social issues are no longer current, the basic human concerns that Greenson addresses with psychoanalytic understanding, such as love and emotional involvement, hate, aggression and war, masculinity, femininity, and sexuality, jealousy, envy and possessiveness, and the vicissitudes of child rearing and family development are the timeless and universal concerns of the human condition. On reading these lectures we are impressed with not only the wisdom they offer for our current concerns, but how revolutionary and prophetic his thinking was. His public lectures profoundly influenced countless numbers of professional workers and lay people alike. Mardi Horowitz, an eminent psychoanalytic clinical scholar, describes how hearing Ralph Greenson's public lectures was instrumental in his eventual choice of psychiatry and psychoanalysis as a career. In his book, *Introduction to Psychodynamics: A New Synthesis*, Horowitz writes:

> One's fascination with psychodynamics grows from observation of people, and deepens with concern for helping them resolve their conflicts and develop to their maximum potential. My own interest began during the 1950s, when I heard Ralph Greenson speak on the radio. At the time I was an undergraduate at the University of California at Los Angeles, and he was a psychoanalyst who spoke to the public on such topics as "People Who Hate." He vividly described neurotic behavior and unconscious mental processes and linked psychodynamic theory directly to everyday life. Hearing him both made me a better observer of personality traits and gave me more understanding of people who were repeating self-impairing behavior [1988, p. 3].

We have told you some things about the origins and achievements of Ralph R. Greenson, M.D., and we have outlined the scope of the twenty-four public lectures collected for you here, each a gem of wisdom and humor. Try to picture the man as he approaches the lectern: confident, strong, with an energetic gait. There is a wry, knowing smile on his face; he is already making emotional contact with his audience. From his first words you will feel he wants to talk directly to you and impart his knowledge and experience to help you. As you read these unique and entertaining lectures, let Ralph Greenson enter your heart and mind. You won't be sorry.

## References

Goldberg, A. (1963), Memorial Tribute for Ralph R. Greenson. Psychoanalytic Society and Institute, *Mimeo*. (Unpublished.)

Greenson, R. (1978), *Explorations in Psychoanalysis*. New York: International Universities Press.

Horowitz, M. (1988), *Introduction to Psychodynamics*. New York: Basic Books.

Rosten, L. (1956), *Captain Newman, M.D.* New York: Harper and Brothers.

Stoller, R. (1980), Obituary, Ralph R. Greenson. *Internat. J. Psycho-Anal.*, 61:001–002.

# 1 Misunderstandings of Psychoanalysis (1955)

*This was one of many lectures that Greenson gave at the School for Nursery Years, now The Center for Early Education in Los Angeles. Among his many interests and involvements, none was more important to him than early childhood education and the problems of parents and children. He believed fervently in the importance of parental education for the prevention of emotional problems in children. In his engaging and forthright way, he began this talk by admitting that since he had been the speaker on so many occasions, he supposed that he was "also responsible for much of the misunderstanding."*

*Among the misunderstandings that Greenson described was the mistaken charge that psychoanalysis encouraged the excessively permissive, nonauthoritarian parent, or that psychoanalysis advocated the unbridled expression of instincts on the part of children to the exclusion of parental authority when it recognized parents and children as "equal." He described how that attitude, on the contrary, leads to an increase in guilt, confusion, and low self-esteem in children, and he advocated instead the principle of "limits being love." Further, he described how the excessively permissive parent does not realize that one of the most important aspects of maturing, in fact one of the most crucial signs of being an adult, is the capacity to bear tension, to be able to wait or postpone.*

*Child analysts currently describe how parents are still struggling with the problems of permissiveness in child rearing. Parents report considerable confusion in such areas as parental nudity, whether to allow children to call them by their first names, or the limits that should be set regarding behavior involving sex and drugs.*

*Greenson described how another misunderstanding of psychoanalysis in relation to child rearing is manifested by parents who "interpret" instead of reacting normally to their children. By not reacting, in Greenson's opinion, such parents are avoiding normal emotions. "People get the idea that it is wrong for a parent or friend to be annoyed, to love, to be angry, to be envious, to be miserable, to be depressed. . . . And I say to you, it is right to be miserable and angry and annoyed and loving when the situation calls for it." Greenson went on to say, "the parents I have seen who were good parents, were not parents who read the most, but parents who had this kind of trust in their basic, everyday reactions and impulses. These were parents who could have emotions and impulses. These were parents who could have emotions, who could love, who could be angry, who could reward and punish and hug and kiss and slap their kids. And these kids felt loved and grew up pretty well." Thus, in this lecture Greenson addressed in a moving and profound way many of the issues that torment and confuse the contemporary parent. His message that children want and need to look up to strong and consistent parents, who can relate to them with genuine and spontaneous emotional responses, rings very true for the parent of today.*

Ladies and Gentlemen.

That was very impressive, the introduction by Dr. Hanna Fenichel. In a way I suppose I am responsible for all these lectures, and I suppose I am also responsible for much of the misunderstandings. However, I will not take the full responsibility. Later on I will explain to you why I think you are to blame, for part of the misunderstandings, anyway.

I thought it would be a good idea to talk about misunderstandings of psychoanalytic lectures because again and again I have heard people discuss psychoanalytic principles or raise questions about problems related to psychoanalysis, and they have given me the unmistakable impression that they fail to grasp the essential aspects of psychoanalytic thinking. It is astonishing because these people who come to lectures are eager to learn. One of the most flagrant examples of this concerned a lady at a lecture which I had given four or five times—you know, about the various stages and phases of development of children. I noticed her in the audience and after I finished speaking she came over to me and said, "Dr. Greenson, that was wonderful!" And I said, "You know, you look familiar to me." She answered, "Yes, well I come to every lecture." And I said, "Well, the same lecture?" "Oh, yes, I don't pay much attention to what you are saying, but I like the way you express yourself."

Well, what is it that people misunderstand in a psychoanalytic lecture? I would like to discuss this, and then later, discuss, why do they misunderstand.

The most frequent misunderstanding of psychoanalysis today, where parents are concerned, is their belief that psychoanalysts are in favor of complete instinctual satisfaction for children. People who hear psychoanalysts speak come away with the impression that the psychoanalyst said, "All instincts of children should be gratified as quickly as possible." If you give a talk, for example, about "mothering," the early oral phase of development, and the importance of mothering for the child, there are people in the audience who think you mean that the mother is to be a slave to the child; that every cry, every whimper, every sign of restlessness means take out the breast or the bottle and shove it in the kid's mouth. They have the idea that any pain or frustration damages the child. If you give a lecture on toilet training, problems of toilet training, there are mothers and fathers in the audience who will come away with the notion that the analyst said to let the child wet and let the child soil, that there is no reason to train them, and if they get to be ten or eleven and twelve, so what. Eventually they will get fed up with the mess and train themselves.

There are people who attend psychoanalytic lectures about the phallic phase, where children four, five, six become interested in sexuality, masturbation, curiosity about the parents, who come away from such lectures with the idea that their children should be permitted all kinds of sexual satisfaction. They should be allowed into the bedroom and one should walk around nude. If your little girl comes to join you in the bathroom and says, "Daddy, what is that?" And you say, "Why, this is my penis." And if she says, "I would like to hold it." You say, "Hold it, go ahead." Yes, these parents feel that masturbation should be permitted at any time, at any place, in front of strangers, or company, or on the street.

I give rather crass examples, but they are by no means rare of what people think psychoanalysis advocates. The same is true about aggression. Their child beats the neighbor's child and they consider this healthy. Let out your aggression! Or, the child kicks the father or the mother, this is healthy too. Just let out your aggression! Well, I gather from your laughter that you agree with me. That this is a misunderstanding. But why? Why is it wrong to permit immediate satisfaction of all instincts? Why? What harm does it do?

The excessively permissive parent, in a way, fosters excessive gratification. If you permit children to get immediate, instantaneous satisfaction, these children are apt to become fixated to this form of instinctual satisfaction. There are two attitudes which are responsible for keeping a child fixated on a certain level of development. Excessive frustration is one. The other, is excessive gratification. It is particularly unfortunate that the so-called progressive parent who wants to undo the tyranny of his own upbringing, is in turn responsible for the excessive gratification of his child, which leads to the fact that these children don't progress, don't mature. They stay on this level of infantile development, way beyond their years. An added complication due to excessive gratification is that the child has no motivation and no incentive to grow up. The mother who instantly recognizes the child's every need, by the tone of its cry, by his expression, anticipates everything it wants, is apt to have a child who doesn't learn to speak. I have seen such children, I have seen such mothers—who don't wait for the child to express dissatisfaction or some frustration, but instantly want to satisfy a need, even before that need becomes very obvious. I think retardation of development as far as speech, walking, motility, and as far as toilet control are concerned as well as fixating children to parents, all this comes about from the fact that the parent is under the impression that it must gratify every instinctual need of the child all the time and instantly. They forget to realize that one of the important aspects of maturing, of growing up, perhaps the most crucial signs of being adult, is the capacity to bear tension—the capacity to wait, to postpone. Infantile people cannot wait, cannot bear tension nor postponing. These parents, who are so quickly ready to gratify, who are nothing but the bearers of supplies, are parents who bring up children who never learn the capacity to postpone gratification, i.e., to grow up. This is my first point about misunderstandings of psychoanalytic lectures.

My second point is very similar. People who go to psychoanalytic lectures often get the impression the psychoanalyst is against all authority. The psychoanalyst is against all force and coercion and discipline. These people have the notion that in bringing up children you ought to maintain that we are all equal. You call your child Johnny, and Johnny calls you Joe, or whatever your first name happens to be. His friends call you by the first name and you call them by their first name, and we are all equal. Oh, I may be bigger and taller, but we are really the same. They get the idea that this is what psychoanalysis tries to teach.

You know, it is important to remember some of the history of the development of psychoanalysis. Freud, in the 1880s and 1890s, when he first began to write psychoanalytically, wrote about the fact that most of his neurotic patients were the victims of straitlaced, severe, cruel parents. His first case history had to do with the effects of tyrannical parents on helpless children. Therefore, in the first psychoanalytic writing, this point was stressed again and again: how a cruel, stern, sadistic father had produced a neurosis in a little child. Similarly, the first analytic writings about the problems of sexual development, showed how in a strict, straitlaced Victorian upbringing, children became neurotic when they were not able to discharge their tensions and get satisfaction for their instinctual needs. Therefore, the early psychoanalytic writings stressed these points. However, now I think, partly because of Freud, times have changed. People seem to be going to the opposite extreme, where they bring up children in this so-called pseudodemocratic way in which we are all equal, and we vote on everything. So they say to a child, "You must do this." And the child says, "No, I don't want to." And they respond with "okay, let's vote" or something like it. I think parents have the right and duty to be the ones who make certain important decisions. It makes sense that parents are supposed to know more, and have more experience, and be wiser. And maybe we could vote on whether a child gets a piece of candy or not, but there are many more vital issues upon which there is no voting. I think it is hypocrisy and delusional to let children grow up with the notion that they are the equal of the parent.

I have seen mothers and fathers who go out of their way to be buddy-buddy with their children. Though analysts are generally in favor of some *quasi-equal* relationship while playing, fishing, or reading to a child, treating children as complete equals is going too far. They are not ready for this kind of premature equality, which only brings on guilt, anxiety, and confusion. I think this behavior by the parents is in part due to the fact that many of them were products of a strict authoritarian upbringing, and now want to undo this, and give their children those liberties that they never enjoyed themselves.

I see this fear of being authoritarian as a fear of creating guilt feelings. There are parents who, after hearing psychoanalysts speak, or reading a psychoanalytic book, draw the conclusion that you should bring up children without guilt. Don't make the child feel guilty. That is damaging! I have seen instances of this upbringing where the mother always minimized the transgression. I know of a little girl who stole. She stole a bracelet from another little girl. She was six years old. She stole it because she liked it. She stole it because she was envious of the other girl. She stole it because she was miserable, resented the little girl, and so she stole it. The teacher found it and told the mother. And then the mother said, "I know you didn't mean to steal it." However, she did mean to steal it! She wanted to steal it! But the mother made any response impossible for the child. Instead of making her less guilty, she made her feel much more guilty. This overly solicitous mother doesn't even let her child feel appropriately guilty or angry. If this mother had cracked her one and said, "How terrible to have stolen!" the little girl at least could have hated her mother. Now all she could do was keep it in and feel terribly unworthy.

Or, take the example of the child who beats the little baby sister, and the mother with this phony smile says, "I know you did not mean to hit her." Sure he meant to hit her; he probably would have liked to kill her. But the mother prevents the child from recognizing that people have such impulses. What happens as a consequence of this? First of all, there is complete confusion about what is real. If you hit out of jealousy and rage, and mother, who is the authority, says, "You didn't mean it," then your own emotions cannot be real; they are strange and unique. What can you trust, what mother says, or what you feel? These permissive parents, with their Pollyanna attitude—you didn't mean this, I know you didn't have any such impulse or thought in you—foster confusion and added guilt.

Similarly, parents who once heard a lecture about children's fears, try to calm a child who is, let us say, afraid of an elephant in his room at night, by saying: "I'll get rid of the elephant. Go away, elephant! Go away, elephant!" Maybe this helps the child for a moment, but what about the ego of this child which is trying to establish some principles of reality? What is real and what is not real?

Another consequence of this kind of misunderstanding is to be seen in the deformities of conscience that children develop who were brought up by excessively permissive nonauthoritarian parents. You would think that if you have such an easy-going attitude the child will grow up easy-going too. This is not true. If your easy goingness is excessive, you will see certain pathological formations in the children. They may develop a severely strict conscience because you were not firm enough to serve as a model for them.

One of the most masochistic persons I ever treated was the child of a psychiatrist whose father never punished him, he only interpreted. When anything was wrong, the father said, "This means you wanted to do X," or "This means you are hostile against your mother," or this means this and this means that. Brought up in this so-called tolerant atmosphere, this boy developed the most severe self-torturing conscience that I ever saw clinically. Not only are you apt to get a severely strict conscience from this easy-going attitude, but you are also apt to get defects in conscience formations, in the form of delinquency.

These children now, because they never had any models to go on, to incorporate, to make part of themselves, pick up models someplace else, and these models are often delinquent, defective models. All kinds of distortions of conscience stem from this namby-pamby attitude about what is right and what is wrong.

I think it is important to recognize that in growing up, children need models for right and wrong, better and worse, fair and unfair, just and unjust. They need these models because the child can then take these models and make them part of his own conscience. Remember, children need to form ideals. Part of the formation of ideals is based on the feeling that you, the parent, are strong and mighty. They would like to impart some of this within themselves, and strive to live up to it. By not being strong or forceful or authoritative, you make it impossible for them. There are still other important consequences from the lack of authority and the lack of discipline. The fact is that the child is looking to you for help in his struggle with his own instincts. If a child is overwhelmed with strong aggressive impulses to beat, to hit, to hurt, and if you permit it, because of some mistaken idea that he should act it out, it scares him. He is much more reassured if you grab him and stop him, than if you let him alone. Any of you who have children, you know that time and time again, children want to be controlled because they don't feel they have as yet this control apparatus within them. It is your duty to control them. To say, "No," or to grab or to hold them back. This is their way of learning to gain mastery over their own instincts. You make it impossible when you refuse to control and just sit there waiting for these emotional storms to go on their way.

Finally, evasion of authority brings about the problem that children get to feel that all conflicts are to be avoided. There are parents who have the notion that if you act as an authority and say, "No! I forbid! I prohibit" it will bring the child into a conflict, and that this is bad. Again, this is a misunderstanding. Conflict, though it brings trouble, pain, and anguish, is also a means of contending with the world. All of living is tied up with conflict in one form or another. Our children must learn not to avoid conflicts, but to handle them, to meet them. The overprotective point of view leads children to adopting a passive, submissive attitude whenever there is trouble.

I have so far tried to describe to you two important kinds of misunderstandings that people who attend psychoanalytic lectures tend to have. Now I would like to answer the question of how people should feel in bringing up their children.

What does the psychoanalyst means when he lectures or talks about a child's need for instinctual satisfaction? What does he mean when he talks about the child's need for freedom, and then also talks about the child's need for discipline and authority? Well, it was much easier to tell you what not to believe than what you should believe. Nevertheless, I would like to express some ideas. Psychoanalysis and Freud recognized that children have, from birth on, important and imperative instinctual needs, and that these needs require a certain amount of satisfaction. However, Freud later on recognized that in the course of development the child must learn not only how to gratify his impulses, but how to curb them, how to master them, how to cope with them. Part of growing up is dependent upon the child's developing a set of inner controls which would replace the external controls of the parent; this is essential for maturation.

Psychoanalysis teaches that human behavior can only be understood if you recognize that the human being has a certain psychic structure which is influenced by various psychic forces. The ego, the thinking, acting, deliberating part of the personality structure, is surrounded by different forces, and it is the task of this ego to decide, to try to relate these opposing forces, in order to get both satisfaction and also security—security meaning freedom from fear and guilt. It is the task of the ego to cope with the instinctual demands, as well as with the conscience, which has its demands, and those of the external world. It is the aspiration of the human being to live happily within himself and with people in the world. Psychoanalysis tries to indicate complications in this achievement, how excessive frustrations and satisfactions produce complications.

I want to mention here another troublesome misunderstanding of what psychoanalysts lecture about. People get the impression that by constantly trying to understand what happens in children and adults, we also approve of the behavior. We explain and demonstrate and lecture in order to teach something about human behavior. But this does not mean that because we try to understand, we think an act is okay. It is not true that understanding is synonymous with excuse, except in psychoanalytic treatment, and that is something else, that is different from ordinary life. This is an understatement, I realize it. But, I do want to say that the psychoanalyst, when he is a therapist, is there only to understand.

Misunderstanding of understanding has brought about this notion, that if you can describe a piece of behavior, or talk about a piece of behavior, it is cured, it is over, it is changed. Since analysts are always trying to understand, give explanations and insights, you too, at home with your child (and it does not have to be a child, it could be your husband or wife, or even a friend) should interpret and explain. When a transgression of some kind occurs, let us say, the child hits the little baby in the crib over the head with the bottle, and you say to the child, "This is due to the fact that you envy your little brother, isn't it?" Now you are contented that you have handled the situation. Yes? Or the child breaks something in the dining room, or soils, or has a temper tantrum and screams when you have company, and you say to the company, "This is due to the child's envy, or the child is constipated, this is something anal." Or you say it to the child, which is worse: "I know what this is, this is your frustration at having had to move your bowels this morning."

In other words, there are people who get the impression that the way to live with children or with people is to be a kind of junior psychoanalyst. After having been exposed to a few analytic lectures or books, they decide now everything has to be verbalized, everything has to be talked about. They never react to a child, they don't get mad, they don't get glad, they don't kiss or hug a child—they interpret. They say, "Oh, you want me to kiss you," but don't kiss. "You want me to hit you," but don't hit. They interpret, they don't react. Perhaps I exaggerate a little, but I do it in order to make you aware of this danger. By not reacting, emotions are now avoided. People get the idea that it is wrong for a parent or a friend to be annoyed, to love, to be angry, to be envious, to be miserable, to be depressed—that is wrong. And I say to you, it is right to be miserable and angry and annoyed and loving when the situation calls for it. There are so many which call for it. And it is wrong just to interpret them or put them into words. Feelings are the reality. This is what matters—not words, not interpretations.

An extension of this idea is that words now replace gestures. There is no more preverbal or nonverbal communication. You don't hug someone impulsively. You don't push someone in anger. You don't, you explain. And you talk and talk, and you never smack a child, scream at a child, or even laugh at a child. You are calm—dead and calm. When relationships are built on this kind of constant compulsive incessant thinking, all you are is a thinking machine with answers instead of reactions. I would even go further and say that parents who think they understand something about analysis, feel they are not permitted to *mis*understand their child, they are never to be confused. How wrong! Even an analyst will tell you how much they don't understand. It is permissible not to understand. And it is permissible to be confused, and not to know an answer right away. You can say, "I don't know," to a child or to a friend, even a husband. Just say, "I don't know. I'm mixed up. Don't ask me now, I'll tell you tomorrow." There used to be a time when parents thought this was the only answer they had to give, but now I think they have gone to the other extreme and feel they owe their children answers, interpretations instead of real and genuine emotional responses.

What is the result of this kind of misuse of insight, and misuse of communication, and misuse of understanding? In my opinion, it brings about a misuse of the intellect in children. Instead of using the intellect to bring satisfaction, to give pleasure, it becomes an end in itself; becomes a defense; becomes a way of living. You see children who are bright, quick, verbal, but are they happy? Most of them I've had occasion to see are not. I watch these tense little faces that are so quick, so bright, and I see how this intellect developed at the cost of their emotional development. These children grow up to have a contempt for anything emotional, they consider it weak, dirty, and vulgar.

What does analysis really try to convey about communication and understanding? I've given you quite a blast about the misuse of understanding, but please remember, I am very much in favor of understanding, and children need to be understood. But they must be understood in the right way, not only in the intellectual way. It is so much better to demonstrate understanding to a little child by a look, by an affectionate glance, or grabbing and holding the child, than by words. It is so much more efficacious than always having to resort to words. I think this is also true for adults. The child has to be understood, but in its proper time and place, when anger has passed. How confusing to the child if you grit your teeth, hold yourself tense and taut, and then try to say some words of explanation, or interpret a piece of behavior. What should he believe—your jaw, which hates him, or your kind words? How can he cope with you? I think it is much better if you are angry and cannot simply express it, not to talk, to wait until you are calm. Then try to understand. I think yes, in general, understanding should be added, but not in the heat of emotional situations. In retrospect when things are quieter, perhaps to talk about it then. Children need to feel the spontaneity in their parents because we hope they will be spontaneous. We hope they will be flexible, not rigid, not machines, not thinking machines. I think psychoanalysts stress understanding, but this doesn't mean just verbal understanding, it means emotional understanding. What good is it if you've only got the right words for what the kid is feeling, if you didn't capture the feeling?

Another misunderstanding that you get from psychoanalytic lectures is the fact that people, after they hear lectures, and I must say, after they have heard some of my lectures, have said, "Well, you listen to Greenson and you get the idea—kids are hopelessly complicated. It's impossible to be a parent." Freud once wrote that there are three impossible professions: one, bringing up children; two, being a leader of a nation; and three, being a psychoanalyst. You see how tough it is when you are two of the three.

At any rate, children are complicated and people are complicated. But I don't feel it is hopeless at all. I think children are complicated, and people are complicated when you're in trouble, when things are going poorly. Suddenly everything takes on this enormously complicated view. But when things are peaceful you get sometimes the impression that things are relatively simple. It is true that we psychoanalysts do go with microscopic detail into the behavior and motivations of different aspects of people's behavior; but as far as living is concerned I think analysis indicates few basic principles about living which, if they are achieved and mastered, make life relatively simple.

The combination of giving a child love and at the same time giving it a good representation of reality which is not in contradiction to everything else that is going on in the world around this child, that is of central importance. I think if parents can trust their own basic response, not from books or an analyst, if they love their child and feel they are in good contact with reality, I think bringing up a child is *not* an overwhelmingly complicated task. Of course, few people have this kind of composure, that they trust their own impulses. I think there are many complicated reasons for their lack of trust, but the parents I have seen who were good parents, were not parents who read the most books, or not parents who had the most analytic information, but were parents who had this kind of trust in their basic, everyday reactions and impulses. These were parents who could have emotions, who could love, who could be angry, who could reward and punish and hug and kiss and slap their kids. And these kids felt loved and grew up pretty well.

I have heard it said, and this is another misunderstanding of psychoanalysis, that healthy people conform. Sheer nonsense. There is no such an idea that conformity is what the analysts think is healthy. By no means. I think every analyst is too well aware of the miseries in the world today to ask people to accept this pleasantly. Sometimes it is necessary to accept misery and injustice and tyranny, but not to like it, and not to accept it blindly. I think a healthy person is a person who can also rebel, complain, squawk, and fight, and not one who is in line with everyone and is the same as everyone. The healthy human being is flexible and part of being mature is feeling able to disagree. Children who conform and never make trouble are limited in their full emotional development. Of course, here the matter of degree is very important, and some can go to an extreme.

Another aspect of this problem is tied up with the idea that analysts teach, that if you're healthy, you won't have emotional problems. This is very far from the truth. It is inevitable in growing up and in being grown-up, for emotional problems to develop. We don't want people to live without problems. You can live in a cell and someone will give you three meals a day and you will have no problem, but you will agree, that is not living. Of course, what is crucial is how you handle the problem, how you meet it, how you resolve it and attack it—this is what makes you either a healthy person or not a healthy person. There are all kinds of problems in this world which we have to meet, and not merely avoid. Now, what analysis does try to do is to make it possible for persons to live to the fullest extent of their abilities without guilt and unreal anxieties.

There are many real miseries in the world, and many real causes for anxiety. The real anxiety, real danger is usually much easier to handle than unreal, neurotic anxiety. I should not say "unreal." That does the neurotic anxiety injustice, due to the kind of terror neurosis brings.

I want to come now to the last part of my talk. Why are psychoanalysts misunderstood and what is the reason for people misunderstanding psychoanalytic lectures? I have thought about this, having lectured so often and having also been misunderstood. Why? First, why do people come to a psychoanalytic lecture? Often they come, not to learn, but to be reassured. They come out of some anxiety, some problem, and they hope I will say something like: "See, it is all right, perfectly all right to do what you are doing." They do not hear all that I say, only that part which agreed with what they were doing. I think this is one of the answers.

Another, I think, has to do with the fact that they come with a certain amount of unconscious defenses, and they hope by coming, not to learn, but to get some kind of treatment from the lecture. They come out of some sense of guilt, of having done wrong to their children, and they don't want to listen in order to learn to do better, but to change the guilty feeling. It is the feeling they want changed. And thus, they don't listen to the content, but rather try only to perceive or gather something which will change this ill feeling. I would say they come to be treated in a way, in this kind of mass therapy, instead of to listen and to learn.

# 2 Apathy, Boredom, and Miltown (1958)

*The subjects of apathy and boredom held great interest for Greenson, and in this lecture he offered illuminating clinical examples of the distinction between the two states. After pointing out the usefulness of the psychoactive drugs for agitated and highly disturbed patients, including how the drugs make patients more accessible for treatment intervention and are thereby potentially life saving, Greenson described the dangers of the abuse of medication in misguided attempts to solve the everyday problems of existence, a prophetic warning for our pill-dominated society of the 1990s. He said, "It appears to me that there is a definite trend in our society to seek easy and quick peace of mind. Miltown is a peace of mind tablet. Unfortunately, it does not really bring genuine peace of mind. No, instead, Miltown brings rose-colored boredom or a kind of sugar-coated apathy." He spoke out strongly against the mindless search for peace of mind and asserted that living means a struggle to contend, to accomplish, and to endure and, in so doing, to find satisfaction and happiness. As did Freud, he felt that we must replace neurotic misery with facing real misery and that good living is hard work.*

*With biologic psychiatry adding the antidepressants and lithium to the major and minor tranquilizers of which Greenson spoke in 1958, we have witnessed a tremendous increase in the use and abuse of these substances. Psychoanalysts report how patients who are treated by narrow-minded biological psychiatrists, who militantly eschew psychotherapy or psychoanalysis, come to their offices with a tremendous need to talk and process their problems. Greenson's prophetic warning that we must use these substances very carefully and not allow them to substitute for living life as fully as possible, has become even more urgent today. Although he speaks of Miltown, we can easily substitute the name of Valium or Xanax and a score of other substances that are being abused and actually lead to addiction. While psychopharmacology has considerably helped the treatment of our seriously ill patients, as Greenson pointed out, there is the danger that it can be misused to numb our minds as well.*

Apathy and boredom are relatively obscure phenomena. We do not know a great deal about them, and most people are not particularly interested in them. Clinically, apathy is usually a sign of some overwhelming, catastrophic illness, organic or mental. We know that children who become apathetic are usually critically ill and often die. The same is frequently true with adults. Boredom is ordinarily not considered a sign of illness. Patients who come for psychiatric treatment on their own volition, by and large, are not apathetic or bored; otherwise they would not actively seek help.

However, in recent years there has been a change in this situation. More and more patients come into treatment complaining of boredom. They complain that they are "Not with it," "Out of it." They frequently complain of a feeling of emptiness. In addition, we see indications of latent and masked forms of boredom. It becomes apparent in recent years that many people spend a great deal of their free time seeking, rather frantically, for distractions rather than satisfactions. They apparently look for diversions rather than real enjoyment. This becomes a serious problem when you realize that there is a tendency in our society to make available for more people, more and more leisure. The

---

School for Nursery Years, Lecture Series, 1958, Los Angeles.

imminence of greater leisure suggests the probability that there will be more boredom.

In the past, psychiatrists often noted the Sunday neuroses. They were people who seemed to be adjusting adequately during the week when they were busy, but on Sundays would become depressed, agitated, discontent, and unhappy. With the increase of leisure we have noticed not merely Sunday neuroses but weekend neuroses. If leisure still increases we can expect three-day, four-day leisure neuroses. It is characteristic for bored people to be agitated rather than active, and to go through a lot of motions without real emotion.

Miltown belongs in this discussion in a way which will be indicated later on. Let me hasten to state that I used the concept of Miltown rather than the name Miltown. I am referring to the whole group of tranquilizing drugs or ataraxic drugs; in short, these refer to those chemical compounds which are administered to the patient in the hope that they will bring with them some kind of peace of mind and tranquility. The tranquilizers are worthy of our attention. It has been estimated that in 1957 approximately 35 million prescriptions for tranquilizers were written by physicians.

It is a curious observation that in years past, physicians prescribed many more stimulants like dexedrine and benzedrine; whcrcas now they seem to be prescribing more tranquilizers. Why? What is happening in our socicty? What is happening to us which would explain such a change?

## Apathy

Apathy means the lack of emotion, affectlessness, the absence of drive. Apathy means indifference to stimuli, no reaction. The apathetic person appears to be slowed down, his face has a masky quality, the eyes particularly seem to have a dullness about them. Such people stare, they are compliant, passive, and they do not complain.

Apathetic patients are seen in severe catatonic schizophrenia, in the psychotic depressions and melancholia, in long, severe, chronic organic illnesses, in starvation. By and large, apathy is seen as a reaction to catastrophic and overwhelming events, whether physical or emotional, internal or external.

My experience with apathy was gained during the war [World War II] in studying and treating former prisoners of war. Generally these patients were neglected on the ward because they caused no trouble, they were quiet, they did not complain. Often I would find them lying on their beds, quietly, as if asleep, with their eyes wide open, staring. They were uncommunicative and did not tell their story or participate actively in the bull sessions of the other men. Very often they were diagnosed as schizophrenics or melancholia cases, which they were not. During World War II, we often treated our patients by injecting sodium pentothal intravenously in order to recover the past traumatic war experience, so that the patient could, in this reliving, master the painful situations. Usually this was quite a dramatic recital of terribly dangerous, violent experiences. It was quite different with the apathetic patient.

As an example I would like to quote a pentothal interview of an apathetic patient who had been a prisoner of war of the Japanese for four years. He was given 10cc of a 5 percent sodium pentothal solution. He promptly fell asleep and then was aroused. He began then to chant rather mournfully, "I wanna go home, I wanna go home, I wanna go home, I wanna go home." I injected some more pentothal in order to get him deeper to sleep. He slept. I aroused him once more. I shook him. Slowly and mournfully he began, "I wanna go home, I wanna go home, I wanna go home, I wanna go home." Again I injected more pentothal to get him still deeper. He was extremely difficult to rouse, and he would mutter the same mournful chant, "I wanna go home, I wanna go home, I wanna go home." It was obvious that for this man the whole world had shrunk into very little. The only residue that mattered, the only thing he thought about, was concerned with, was home.

As was my custom, the next morning I interviewed this man and told him what he spoke about under the pentothal. I said to him that I felt he should be discharged from the Army and that I was going to send him home. He looked at me quietly, with no emotion, and said slowly, and somewhat sadly, "Doc, I have no home." Only then did I realize that this man was brought up in an orphan asylum. He had joined the regular Army at eighteen. This leads me to what I consider to be the crucial etiological factor in producing states of apathy. By and large, apathy is a reaction to deprivation, to deprivation of staggering proportions. Apathy results from long periods of loneliness, monotony, starvation. Patients do not start their illness by becoming apathetic. Apathy is an end reaction to a long sequence of events. Ordinarily in the history of the apathetic patient you will find first anger and rage reactions, then depression, and after a prolonged period of depression, apathy.

It was interesting to find that even in former prisoners of war the sequence of events went something like this: At first, in the early months after their capture, there was a lot of sex talk, pornography, prayer, and hopefulness. Then they stopped praying, they stopped hoping. As one of my patients put it, "I put my mind in neutral." He began to hibernate and vegetate. He became only interested in food and eating, and later on, thinking about food and thinking about eating, or looking at pictures of food. They waited. The prisoners themselves knew or learned that those who were angry, furious, enraged, died. The depressed ones who wept and cried, died. Only the apathetic ones seemed to survive.

Apathy may be looked upon as dying a little, a kind of partial dying. It can be explained perhaps theoretically as a defense mechanism of the ego which blocks perception when perception will only bring pain and frustration. The simplest example of this defense would be fainting where one is suddenly confronted by an extremely painful stimulus. Apathy may be considered a relatively successful defense. As I mentioned earlier, orphans who later became soldiers would develop apathy instead of the fatal rage or depression which occurred in the prisoners of war. When the world is overwhelming, the ego retreats by restricting its perceptions and its reactions to perceptions. The prisoners of war hated the world, were not ambivalent because they felt justified in hating the world. Therefore, they did not internalize their rage and become depressed like other depressives do. They waited.

One finds similar clinical pictures when there has been organic disease of long duration or where there has been chronic hunger and poverty. One sees similar pictures in the schizophrenias or in the melancholias where the painful mental stimuli of many years duration force the ego to retreat so that there is only a little island of living left in which there is little hope, and waiting, either for rescue or for death. The treatment of the apathetic patient essentially is to give them food, love, tenderness, and time. In the Army we were ill-equipped for this treatment and often sent these patients home. The sad part of the story is that many had no homes, but we felt they had a better chance to get the treatment they needed in civilian life.

## Boredom

Boredom can be described as follows: There is the coexistence of dissatisfaction with a disinclination to action. This is an unusual combination because ordinarily dissatisfaction leads to action. In boredom there is a longing, and an inability to designate what is longed for. Boredom comes with the sensation of emptiness. There is a passive, expectant attitude. The bored person looks toward the external world to tell him what it is he wants or needs. There is a distortion of the sense of time in boredom. In German the word for boredom is *Langeweil*. Boredom is seen in healthy people as a transient state. In neurotics, boredom is extremely rare, since most neurotics used to be full of anxiety, phobia, frustration, obsessions, and depressions. In recent times more and more patients complain of boredom and emptiness. Essentially there are two different types of boredom, one the apathetic or calm boredom, the other an agitated or excited boredom. However, in each and both there is the same essential pathological structure and dynamics.

The outstanding feature in the clinical picture of boredom revolves around the feeling of emptiness, unpleasant emptiness. The bored person may have thoughts or memories, but the feelings which ordinarily accompany thoughts and memories are absent. Their thoughts and memories and ideas seem trivial to them and insignificant. They are searching for something meaningful, zestful, real. They long to be active but do not know what to do. Very frequently their activities concern eating, drinking, looking at pictures, picture magazines, TV, etc. There is this curious tension of emptiness. Ordinarily emptiness is a pleasurable sensation after satisfaction. In the bored person, emptiness is felt as tension and is unpleasant, and one can complain of being full of emptiness. Their urge is to fill up the emptiness; therefore, they undertake many activities of an oral, incorporative nature.

The bored person wants to kill time, not spend it. Time is torturesome, it never seems to pass, which is characteristic for people in states of frustration in which they feel unable to contend with it. The bored person searches for distractions rather than indulging in real thinking. The key to understanding the problem of boredom concerns the pathology in thinking and in memory. It is characteristic for bored persons to have an absence of fantasies. Bored people have no real imagination at the time of their boredom.

Their fantasies are blocked and inhibited. Their fantasies do not lead to any meaningful ideas or actions. There is no link between their state of dissatisfaction to either their wishes or drives or significant feelings and memories. In states of boredom, even sexual activity is boring. They do not know what to think about during sexual activities. They do not know what to feel. Boredom is a defense against real feelings, and above all seems to attack the link to real feelings, namely the fantasies. Essentially boredom indicates a restriction in ego functions. The sensation of emptiness seems to be derived from this loss of ego functions, the loss of meaningful human relations during this period. It also stems from the denial of bad feelings in human relations. The emptiness also reflects hunger for meaningful people or activities. In a sense, in boredom the sensation of emptiness has replaced a fantasized object.

Theoretically one might say that boredom comes about as the result of a self-administered deprivation, particularly directed against fantasies and feelings. Bored people are hungry for stimuli but are blocked. They seek diversions which will divert them from what is feared or frightening. Boredom is an intrapsychic phenomenon. Others may frustrate you; you, however, bore yourself.

Apathy comes from massive deprivations, external or internal. Boredom is localized apathy and always comes about from internal sources. The apathetic patient has given up hope and waits. The bored still hopes and searches. In both of them we have the giving up of ego functions, the renunciation of thinking, contending, struggling, and, above all, fantasy. In both apathy and boredom we have the regression to a state of partial oblivion.

## Miltown

The tranquilizers or the ataraxic drugs are an extremely valuable medical adjunct in the treatment of a great variety of mental and emotional disorders. They consist essentially of two large chemical groups, the chlorpromazine group and the reserpine group. Most drugs are either derivatives of these two groups or resemble in their action these basic divisions. This is no place to go into detail about the action of these compounds, but suffice it to say that they act on specific parts of the brain, namely the hypothalamus, rhinencephalon, and midbrain, and do not act upon the cortex. In their effects these medications combat and attack either the emotional tone or the disturbed thinking processes of the patient.

Essentially, as a result of these interactions, there is a diminution in fantasy production or a lessening of the reaction to fantasy. The tranquilizers calm down painful emotion, frightening emotion, or dangerous emotion; or calm down the production of fantasies which might stir up these violent emotions. The ataractics are extremely valuable for dealing with combative, assaultive, pugnacious patients. They are extremely helpful in dealing with the acutely suicidal patient, or patients whose irritability and agitation make them uncontrollable.

In general, the greatest use is that with the aid of these drugs it makes patients who are inaccessible to treatment accessible. It is extremely valuable for patients who are disabled by either anxiety or stress. It is an invaluable preparation for sick patients who need treatment and who are untreatable. These are a relatively new group of drugs and we do not know too much about them; however, and this should be underlined, they are not for everyday use unsupervised. And, above all, they should not be used by patients to deny their illness, or by those who want to use it for denying that they have problems or painful, stressful situations. Tranquilizers are helpful for patients who know they are sick and who are being treated, but they are harmful for patients who use them in order to deny that they are sick.

It is important to recognize that pain and fear are useful emotional signals and responses. Both pain and fear have an extremely valuable warning or signal function. The person who feels or perceives pain or fear in any form is being given an important signal, a chance to prepare, to fight, to contend, to struggle with some impending danger.

Pain and fear are indications of conflict, are indications of stress and problems. However, growth and maturity depend upon resolving problems and not in avoiding problems. The avoidance of problems leads to stagnation or to regression, again a form of partial living. It is a function of the human mind to feel and to think. If you numb the mind you are living less. Drugs which numb any important function of the mind do not bring peace of mind but peace of mindlessness.

I do not believe that one can successfully pursue peace of mind directly. Peace of mind can only be the indirect result of accomplishment, of struggle, of overcoming pain, of obtaining satisfaction. Peace of mind does not come from evasion or diversions or distractions and, above all, peace of mind is not fun and should not be confused with fun.

It appears to me that there is a definite trend in our society to seek easy and quick peace of mind. Miltown is a peace of mind tablet. Unfortunately, it does not really bring genuine peace of mind. No, instead, Miltown brings rose-colored boredom or a kind of sugar-coated apathy.

It is very striking how the youth of today has changed certain basic attitudes and values. They seem to want to start their careers retired. They are not ambitious or zealous or eager to work. Ambition is considered queer or neurotic. The youth today, it seems to me, is much more interested in security. They are much more prone to conformity than to rebellion. I remember in my youth, the youth was told to get the lead out of its tail. Today they seem to be told, or seem to be eager to get lead into their tails. There is an atmosphere of peace at any price, even at the price of vegetating. Don't perceive, don't imagine, don't fantasize, don't think. Be safe, be secure, be peaceful, be a turnip. There is a dangerous tendency to the degradation of fantasy and imagination. The prevalence of prefabricated, ready-made fantasies ready for you with which you do not have to think or create or imagine, is vividly demonstrated by the great consumption of television.

I am not sure how one can explain this difference in the youth of today, but I believe in part it has to do with the great passivity that many parents inflict on their children. In the olden days, children had to find groups for themselves to play with. Children walked or rode their bicycles. Today we have arranged play groups artificially for them. In the olden days if there were three or four pictures in a book, you were delighted. Today our youth grow up on comic books, illustrated magazines, and television. The taking in of pictures is quite different psychologically from the reading of words. It is much more passive and requires much less mental effort than the reading of words. Furthermore, there seems to be a tendency to blame all of this on world conditions, and I am not sure that this is not right. However, blaming the world leads nowhere except in the general direction of taking pills in order to cure one's dissatisfaction with life.

I am sure many people believe that peace of mind is one of the essential and, perhaps, the most vital goals of life.I do not happen to be of this opinion. Living means a struggle to contend, to accomplish, and to endure and, in so doing, to find satisfaction and happiness, but the substance of life is the struggle and the contending. Quick and easy peace of mind is a poor substitute for living. They all represent a regression into a partial oblivion. True, the Miltown will make the boredom or the apathy rosy-colored and give it a sugary coating, but, nevertheless, it is still apathy and boredom and in that sense, it is still oblivion.

# 3 People Who Hate (1960)

*This was a very popular lecture given over Pacifica Radio, KPFA, Berkeley. Eventually the radio station produced a promotional record called Pacifica Sampler in which they included a segment from Greenson's lecture. The program notes read in part, "it can be broadcast repeatedly without ever stemming the tide of requests for re-broadcasts." In the lecture Greenson tried to show how a psychoanalyst understands people who hate and what he saw in people who hate; more than that, how he viewed hate itself and people who do not even know that they hate.*

*In describing how hate develops, he paid particular attention to the important step of ambivalence, describing how in childhood there is a good mommy and a bad mommy, but mom she is, and how it could be that to feel simultaneously love and hate for the same object is an achievement in development. The discussion includes definitions of greed, envy, contempt, and their relationships to hate, as well as a description of guilt as self-hate.*

*Finally he described how to hate well; he believed that it is important to respect hate because there are many things worth hating. In his electrifying style he implored his audience: "the perpetrators of injus-*

*tice, hate them; tyrants and all tyranny, warmongers, people who like war, hate them; people who seem to want poverty and bring about poverty—hate poverty, hate ignorance, hate disease, hate all of these things . . . above all, when you hate, be willing to act upon it and do something, and if you will do that, you will not hate yourself."*

*Greenson delivered this lecture at the height of the Cold War and America's preoccupation with the threat of Russian attempts at world domination. Even though the Cold War has now ended, the universality of his thoughts about hatred and aggression are valuable insights in understanding the continuing hatred, intolerance, and racism of contemporary society. The tensions and hatred current in the Middle East demonstrate how central aggression is in the human condition.*

I would like to portray for you how a psychoanalyst looks upon people who hate, and what he sees in people who hate; and more than that, how he sees hate and people who do not know they hate.

I will begin by describing a few of the characters who I will try to analyze a little bit for you tonight. I will start with some kind of person I am sure you will recognize, or at least have read about: for example, a murderer. A man who cold-bloodedly murders his wife, a man who plans it, cleverly, carefully, and has thought about it.

Another character in this gallery: a man who didn't plan it, but got drunk and got into a fight, and in this fit of frenzy, killed someone, let's say, his wife. I know you will feel for the subject matter.

A third character among people who hate is a man I saw last week in a locked ward in a hospital; when I asked him what was bothering him, he said, "Well, he had a red spot on his wrist that bothered him." He was worried if that was an infection. And when I looked at his wrists I saw two thick scars, one on each wrist, and I said to him, "What happened?" And he said, "Well, you know, I was full of bad, bad feelings. I'm no good, and didn't want to be a burden to anybody, so I did a foolish thing—I cut my wrists." He belongs also in our gallery of people who hate.

---

Broadcast on KPFA-FM, Berkeley, California. First broadcast on April 22, 1960. Recorded at the Los Angeles School for Nursery Years Lecture Series on February 12, 1960.

I will mention to you a fourth, a woman this time, who goes from doctor to doctor, and they cannot find anything wrong with her. She doesn't hate anybody; she likes people. But, she has terrible, terrible pain in her abdomen, and colitis, and it becomes clear she doesn't hate anyone, but her gut hates her. She also suffers from hatred, sick hatred.

I could add a fifth person, a Southerner, an upstanding citizen of Little Rock, who hates Negroes, believes that there is good reason for lynching. He belongs in this group.

A sixth is a delicate, tender little lady, fragile, who cannot kill a fly, cannot stand the sight of blood, but is mean and cruel to her children. You know the type. She belongs here too among the people who hate.

A seventh is a woman who complains about her bad luck. Married three times and strangely and unexpectedly always ends up married to the same drunken brute that she first divorced. Bad luck pursues her, she is accident-prone. So, let's add her to this group.

An eighth member should be the alarmists who are sure the Russians are going to destroy us. They know it, they have inside information from the neighbor next door. They believe the only thing to do is start a preventive war and kill millions of them. Let's add them to our group.

Unfortunately, I think, to sort of round out the picture I must look to my own profession, pick out a psychiatrist who loves to do shock therapy, who enjoys it and thinks this is the best kind of treatment. And if he has to take out a little piece of brain, well, he thinks that serves a useful purpose too. Let me add him to our group of people who hate.

Put together, it is quite a collection of characters. They all suffer, every one of this group, from pathological hatred. They are complicated, and they're all different, and they have to be understood. Some of them hate consciously; some of them don't know they hate, they hate only unconsciously. Some hate others, some hate only themselves or mainly themselves. Some hate actively, they go out and do damage and others seem to be pursued by hate. In some the hate is transformed and what you see is not hate, but exaggerated, distorted pity or overconcern. Some apparently hate what they fear, and some fear what they hate. It is a very complex picture that I present here, but what all have in common is that they are sick in the way they hate. All these ways of hating that I have described are pathological ways of hating, are the result of distortions in the development of a person. However, everybody hates, it's true; more than that, hate is contagious. It is a curious thing, love is not contagious. Partly, of course, one does not love publicly, but hate publicly we all do. How easy it is to get supporters whenever you hate anything. How readily one can rouse a group of people, or a mob of people, to hate. To love? That is boring. Hate is inevitable. I'll go further and say hate is necessary, it is all over, we all have it, and I want to clarify that.

It is necessary to hate for good mental health. Good mental health does mean to love, but it also means to hate, but to hate well. The cases I have described, these nine different types, are sick, not just because they hate, but in the way they hate, how they hate and why they hate. I think it is my task tonight to try to explain to you the basis of pathological hatred, how to hate better.

I would like to begin by going back to the origins of hate. I said a few moments ago, that we all hate, but I want to add to that statement: we are not born with hate. We have to learn to hate, we have to grow into it, mature into it. In a strange way we have to become civilized into hating. By that I mean the following. Basically and essentially we are born with instincts, vital bodily instincts, the sexual, that is, bodily pleasure instincts, and the aggressive instincts. We are born with this. Freud believed that the bodily pleasure instincts, the sexual instincts, had to do with love. He called this whole group of instincts Eros, and then he described another group of instincts which he attributed to the death instinct. Freud believed in his later writings that all of us are born with an instinct that drives us to die. We seek death from birth on. This theory has been contested. Many do not agree with it, I am not sure I agree with it. But one thing is clear, just as sexuality is parallel to the love instinct, so is aggression and destructiveness parallel to the so called death instinct. Perhaps there isn't a drive to die, but a drive to hurt, to destroy, certainly exists. There are analysts who will say, that this only comes about from pain and frustration. Perhaps, but since life begins with pain and frustration, and being born is painful, it is already there at birth. No matter how you see it, the newborn starts life already with a great deal of aggressive drive and instinct. It is striking that already at birth the newborn has inborn mechanisms to express his aggression and hostilities. All newborn children can express rage, fury, anger. They do not have to be taught that at all. You can see typical emotional reactions, bodily reaction, and above all, violent muscular reactions, with rage and fury.

It is very significant that all of us are enraged and infuriated as infants in this same way. There is no difference, rich or poor, white or black, peasant's child, psychoanalyst's child, all are enraged and infuriated in the same way. We are also infuriated and enraged by the same thing, namely pain. Anything which causes pain, and so everything frustrating, enrages and infuriates us. This is impersonal and indiscriminate. Rage, fury, anger, exist before hate. They are the forerunners, they are the substance from which hate later develops. If you observe a child as it grows, as the ego develops, you will see the intensity of the rage begin to diminish, controls begin to develop, and as thinking commences the capacity to wait grows, the ability to postpone. Rage changes, it is directed from the pain itself to the situation which causes the pain, and from the situation which causes the pain to the person who causes the pain. Only when it is directed toward a person can we really strictly talk about hate. When a child who is enraged at his hunger pangs and at his stomach eventually stops hating his hunger and his stomach and hates his momma who doesn't bring him the bottle instead, that's when he has advanced to hate. Roughly, if you watch children you will see somewhere between one and three (the smarter ones earlier), they develop this capacity to hate instead of just being infuriated or enraged. I think it is interesting to recognize that at first hate is preambivalent. That is to say you hate something or somebody, but the person you hate is very different from the person you love, even though the person who brings you the pleasure and the person who brings you the pain is the same one.

It is very curious to notice when children hate the mommy who frustrates them and does not give them what they want, she stops being mommy. She is a witch, or a step-mommy, but not mommy, mommy is synonymous with good mommy. All fairy tales are built on this, to separate the good and the bad mother; they are not the same, one is mother and one is a false mother, a witch. But, as the child's thinking, judgment, perception, develop, he recognizes that the same mommy who brings him the milk is also the mommy who sometimes doesn't bring the milk. And he hates mommy. There is a good mommy and a bad mommy, but mommy it is. This is a big step in development. He has reached ambivalence. The ability to feel simultaneously love and hate for the same object is an achievement. Very sick people cannot do that. They always split objects apart, and the ones they hate are very different from the ones they love. It is a real problem. But from here on, hate becomes controllable. The intensity diminishes, it is no longer overwhelming, you don't have purposeless tantrums, explosions of wasted rage, because hate brings with it the need for action. I will come back to this point when I talk about the value of hate. Let me only say, as the child develops and his ego develops, he can differentiate various forms of hate, like aversion, resentment, dislike, annoyance, repugnance, disgust, all varieties of hate. Now hate becomes controllable, hate becomes discriminatory. It is attached to people for definite reasons, causes, and it leads to purposeful actions, purposeful in terms of the child, of course.

One of the basic principles in understanding problems of hate is to realize that all uncontrolled, primitive hate, is a regression back to early childhood forms of rage, and is very frightening, not to the outsider alone, but to the person who feels it. Primitive hatred is perceived as a danger. It is a threat to one's own existence. We even say, one is eaten up with rage, bursting with hate, or full of poison, venom, consumed with hate. And all these phrases describe how primitive hate is a danger to the self. The man with the slit wrists was full of hate. He was full of bad feelings, and he believed he was full of rottenness and poison. He wanted to get rid of himself. I have seen a man, some time ago, who was tied in a bed. I was asked to see him by his dermatologist because this man had a terrible dermatitis which did not yield to treatment. In his sleep he tore his flesh to ribbons and was bleeding. Nothing restrained him, and when they gave him sedatives he even got worse. When I talked to him for some time, I discovered all of this began shortly after the death of his father for which he felt guilty because he had been negligent. And every night, when he became unconscious, he hated himself, and he tore at his flesh, and ripped off his skin again and again to pay in this primitive way. It scared him to feel such primitive hate.

The more aggression, the more the self is in danger. Hatred has to be controlled for it always is a danger to the self. How we do this I will try to describe briefly, later. So much for a brief outline, insufficient, but all I can say here about the origin of hate. Let me go on to a new subject, a new aspect about factors which influence the development of hate.

Now that one has achieved the capacity to hate, what influences the development of hate in a person? Let's try to understand the characters described earlier, the murderer, the lady who can't kill a fly, the depressive, the phobic, the one who wants to bomb Russia. What happened? What factors influenced them? Certainly constitutional factors must play a role, and I would agree people vary in their temperament, in their basic aggressiveness or destructiveness, in their potential for hate. I would agree that there is some difference; but that this ever makes the difference between normal and pathological hate, I wouldn't agree. I have never seen anybody where I felt satisfied the difference was constitutional. But maybe we do not know enough about constitutional factors, and someday we will learn. There are constitutional factors, admitted, but I put them in secondary position.

The first important factor which influences the development of hate is the amount of frustration and deprivation which one has to endure in early childhood. As I have said, rage and hate are responses to pain, a response which means ill-will, an urge to destroy the pain or what causes it. Satisfactions make it possible for frustrations to be bearable. Above all, the sense of being loved makes it possible for a child to tolerate a good deal of frustration. But if there is a great deal of frustration and pain, and little or no love and satisfaction, you will get repeated reactions of rage and hate. Obviously excessive frustrations will produce excessive rage and hate. Unreliable satisfaction, plus frustration, will do the same thing. In the history of people who hate pathologically, you will always find excessive frustration, little love, or if there was love it was unreliable, undependable.

I want to talk about greed as a second developmental factor

which influences what happens to hate. Greed is one of the first manifestations of what later becomes pathological hate. Greed has to do with the state of being insatiable, to want more and more, because one can never get enough and one does not trust that what one has gotten will ever come back again. If one only expects deprivation and frustration, one has to take in more and more in order to try to achieve some satisfaction. But this is done with rage, and what one takes in, one also hates, and because one hates it, one destroys it. So, there is never enough. I am describing, I hope, an infant, a disturbed infant, but I think I could be describing lots of other people.

I mentioned to you in my gallery of people who hate, a lady who didn't hate anybody, but her guts hated her. This is a lady who was greedy. She became richer and richer and it was never enough. She used to say, "Whatever I eat turns to poison." She hated everything she ate and she hated to spend for what she ate; it turned to poison and it hated her and she hated it. She never had enough, she wanted more and more possessions. Whatever is accumulated out of hate will turn against you, will even haunt you.

Next, what develops out of greed is envy: to want what someone else has, and to hate him for having it; to feel constantly like a have-not, and to hate everyone who has what you want, that is envy. This is not a desire to be an equal, oh no, but to take away what someone else has, so that he becomes a have-not and you instead will be the owner. This is envy. To have something for yourself, and if possible, to have it all to yourself, and alone. Some amount of envy is in all of us, but I must say, in my experience, it is more prominent in women than in men. Partly because our society gives so many more favors to men, but partly, I think, for pure reasons of physiology and anatomy, where women feel they were deprived of this marvelous male organ, and they have something less. They resent it, and hate men for it, belittle them, and if they had the chance, would castrate them. Not all women, please, I do not mean all women feel that way. Someone said, "Thank God." I find envy a very common trait, and I do find it more pronounced in women, probably for this reason.

But, I want to mention to you a relative of envy: contempt. How often you see people who do not seem to suffer from envy, but are full of contempt, ready to belittle and despise. You realize, of course, that contempt is more palatable than envy. Envy is painful, one is ashamed to admit being envious; it is embarrassing, it is childish. But, contempt is grown-up, it is respectable. To have contempt is superior. But, did you ever try to study people who are full of contempt? What goes on? A crass example of this is to be seen in people who are prejudiced, who are fanatically prejudiced, against Jews, Negroes, Catholics. They have contempt for these "inferior" people. Consider Jews dirty, greedy, ambitious, and cunning. Negroes they consider lazy, oversexed with brute strength. This contempt may be partly a projection. They project their own impulses onto the Jew or the Negro. But, wait. Did you not hear in every attack on the Jew or the Negro, by the fanatically prejudiced person, something that sounded like envy? I did. The Jew is ambitious, clever, successful. The Negro is oversexed, but potent. Do you hear under the contempt the repressed envy that all prejudiced people have for the object of their prejudice? Contempt is one of the derivatives of hate. I do not want to pick only on the prejudiced ones, in this regard I'm broadminded. I will pick on other fanatics as well. You know all kinds of people who love mankind but hate people. There are many. Mankind is great, but for people they have contempt. That was certainly true for the fanatical communists.

We have talked of greed, envy, contempt. Now I want to talk about guilt, and the relationship between guilt and hate. Actually if you think about it a moment, guilt is self-hate. If you do something for which you feel guilty, you come away with the thought, "I hate myself for doing it." You know the cliché, "I will hate myself in the morning," after having done something for which you feel guilty. Technically, guilt is the reaction to tension between the superego and the ego, the conscience and the ego. But, where does hate come in? The conscience, the superego, is derived and built up on hate. (Not *only* hate, I stress hate for tonight's discussion.) Isn't it strange how much more often our conscience is cruel and mean and demanding, and how rarely kind and good-natured? Let me explain this briefly, simply, oversimply.

Basically, conscience is formed roughly between the ages of three to six years, during the period we call the oedipal phase (i.e., the triangle, child, mother, and father). The child loves the parent of the opposite sex and feels rivalry, jealousy, hate, and love for the parent of the same sex. I will take the boy as my example, it is simpler. He loves mother, sexual feelings are involved, loves father but also hates him and is jealous and frightened of him. How does he resolve this kind of an oedipal conflict? The resolution of this basic, nuclear conflict comes about by the child internalizing part of his father. In order to cope with this man, this big, gigantic, frightening, lovable man who also is the object of his hatred, he has to take part of this father into himself and internalize this childish conception of his father. Now he has something in him with rules, values, standards of his father. This transformation is done primarily out of fear and hate, and I think this is why so much of the conscience is full of hate. Of course, it will depend a great deal on how much love there was to the father, how brutal the father really was, how frightening, how cruel, how mean he was. That certainly plays a role. But the gentlest fathers, the most considerate fathers, will still have children who will build up a conscience which will have a good deal of hate, and in fact, too gentle a father can have the same kind of a result as a brutal father. In emotional development, extremes are very close to each other.

When the conscience finally is developed, this internalized version of the parent with its hate, the hate is now directed toward the self and toward the ego. This is a step in development. We have now, in addition to fear, reaction in the form of, "I will be punished by the parent." Something new, an internalized fear and guilt, a new emotion, self-hate. Now the father does not have to punish the child, nor does the mother. He punishes himself. When a child punishes himself, he has learned guilt. I described several instances: the man who tore his flesh, the woman who married three times and always somehow the same drunken brute. What motivated them? Guilt. And, why guilt? Because there is only one way to get rid of guilt and that is to suffer. Guilt demands pain, suffering, punishment. It makes a lot of difference how you do this, whether you consciously decide, "Yes, I have been guilty and I want to pay," do it correctly, rationally, reasonably, intelligently. Or like people I described who pay unconsciously and much too high a price. Unconscious guilt is irrational and terrible. The only way ever to get rid of guilt is by suffering, but one can suffer intelligently.

In the Army I saw this again and again. In the Air Force many of my soldiers were guilt-laden: they had run away from a burning plane and did not help the pilot, and the plane exploded, and they felt guilty. You can understand that. I certainly could. But what did this soldier do now? On the basis of his guilt, he got into trouble. He fought the MPs, he beat up an officer, he ran away from the camp and he was sentenced to ten years in prison in a federal penitentiary. Who did that help? No one. What good did it do, this pain, this suffering? When I saw this man in the psychiatric ward, which used to serve as the prison ward of the hospital, I would talk to him and say, "All right. You feel guilty, you should be guilty. I don't disagree. But pay intelligently. This man was killed and you feel guilty. Be smart, don't go to prison for ten years. Find out, does he have a wife, does he have a family? Take a year of your earnings, send it to them. They will benefit from it. You will feel better. Ten years in the penitentiary does nothing." I saw many such problems with guilt in the Army. I am reluctant to go on to the next chapter without mentioning a few interesting types Freud described. There are guilt-ridden types of people who may escape your notice. Those wrecked by success. You know the people who as long as they have adversity, they have a bad job, they complain about the boss, they complain cheerfully and go on working. When they become boss, they have a nervous breakdown. People who can always be vice-president and complain, but as president they have a depression and have to resign from the job. The suicide attempts you read about in the paper are often after a man has been given a promotion. Guilt cannot stand success.

The Sunday neuroses afflict people who cheerfully complain during the week. Sunday without work, no suffering means instant misery. There are criminals from a sense of guilt. I once had to see a man in jail. I was asked by his brother to see him. He had just gotten out of the Army, a young man from a good family, intelligent and reasonable. To everybody's amazement, he went and held up a liquor store, and robbed the man of, I don't know, some thirty or forty dollars. When I talked to him, I asked him, "How did you get caught?" He said, "Well, it's funny, you know, after I held up that store, I was very curious about what was going to happen, so I got in my car and I rode around the block." This man literally rode around the block again and again, waiting for the police. The police were slow but he waited patiently. Finally, he got tired and double-parked. When the police came, saw a car double-parked, they went over to him and he said, "Yes, I did it," and they arrested him. I was puzzled and said, "Well, why did you do it?" He said, "I don't know. I've been so depressed and so restless since I got out of the Army. I don't know what to do with myself. I don't want to go to work. I can't settle down to anything." I said, "Well, what gave you the idea to rob?" He did not know. He thought of it, it came to his mind, he read it in the paper and he thought of it and he did it. I said, "Tell me something. Where were you, in the Army or the Air Force, or where?" Then he tells me in five minutes the story, the crux of the story. He was a flyer. He was shot down over Germany and was captured, and he was in a prisoner-of-war camp. There was an opportunity to escape, and he escaped. He could have told another person about it, there were just a few of them in on this escape route, but he didn't. And he had this terrible sense of guilt, that he didn't tell his friend to escape. This friend died, he found out later, and he always thought, "I killed him." I say to you, he had to rob, he had to go to prison because, unconsciously, he had to pay. How wrong and stupid and ignorant and destructive a way to pay. He was a criminal from a sense of guilt. Many of the organ neuroses (the so-called psychosomatic illnesses, in which an organ in the body becomes a scapegoat for hatred and now torments the bearer) have this quality of hate, internalized hate, and that is what guilt is.

So many people hate and don't know they hate. In some it is unconscious, as I have described. Why is it unconscious? Because hate is objectionable, one does not even like to use the word. In ordinary society you rarely say, "I hate," unless it is about something innocuous like, "I hate mushrooms." You don't ordinarily say, "I hate so-and-so." You may say, "I dislike him," if you are particularly bold, but you usually say, "I'm not crazy about him," which means, "I despise and hate this man." In psychoanalytic circles you don't say that. You say, "I have negative feelings about him." Real elegant, huh? But meaningless, sterile, and hypocritical. You don't like to admit you hate. Why? I cannot answer that completely. I can give you some ideas why.

First of all, hate is closely related to fear and dread. Particularly, primitive hate is frightening. Hate is not only destructive outwardly, but it is also a threat to the self. Whatever one hates, one is scared of, and whatever is frightening, is also painful, and pain is hateful, and then you get into this vicious cycle. You hate what you fear and you fear what you hate, and back and forth. Then, too, hate brings the innate response to destroy, to get rid of what you hate, and that brings about the fear of retaliation. If I destroy, I will be destroyed. That is not pleasant either. But on top of all of that, hate is related to love, and this complicates matters enormously, because, think a moment, to love means, among other things, to be vulnerable to the person you love, which means to be accessible to being hurt, and that brings with it, again, this innate basic reflex, hate, and one wants to avoid it. One does not admit to hating one's wife ordinarily because she hurt your feelings. Instead of being angry, you drop the platter of cocktail things on the living room floor, by accident of course. But, underneath it, there is hate. Combatted, distorted, camouflaged, hidden, but hate. We fight it in many ways, and some of the people I described to you have worn the disguises of hate.

Let us look at some of the disguises of hate. The reaction formations of hate. You know, where hate is disguised by reversing it. The people who hate hate. Remember the I can't hurt a fly lady? She could not stand the sight of blood. But to her children, she was cruel, mean, and cold. Why? The hate is hidden, but comes out in overconcern. She was always worrying about them, and taking them to the doctor or taking their temperature and dressing them warm and giving them diets and food they hated, but it was for their own good! The hate creeps in, and she manages to make their lives miserable. I am reminded of the pacifist who will kill you gladly if you disagree with him.

Another category are those people who project hate. "I don't hate. They hate me." The Russians, they are barbarians, brutes, ready to kill us. Out of pure self-defense, with the best motives in the world, let's destroy ten million of them tomorrow. It's not I, it's them who hate. Paranoid reactions of all kinds are based on this. They are obvious and I think that you know that's so pathological and clear I don't have to stress it. The prejudiced ones I described, hate the Negro or the Jew for qualities they project onto that group.

There's one whole other group who hate, and vent their hate, not upon themselves, not upon certain people or groups of people, but who vent it on society at large. The whole group of delinquents who are children who hate. Teenagers between the ages of ten and eighteen, who did not internalize their hate and develop guilt and conscience pangs because they did not have the models for it. Their parents were either corrupt, people with no moral character, or parents who pretend to be moral and are hypocrites. Look into the study of delinquency and you will always find obviously demoralized or hypocritically pretentious parents who have latent delinquent tendencies, which their kids pick up.

I want to come to the conclusion of this talk by reminding you that though I said pain brings hate, pain also brings wakefulness, alertness. Satisfaction brings sleep. It is very pleasant. But pain brings weakness, thoughtfulness, action. People who work at maximum efficiency in their thinking or in their occupations, the really successful people, who are expert, and have mastered their field, they hate well. They think well, and they work well, because pain and the handling of hate make for this. It is only people who can sublimate their hate, who can use it effectively by doing, thinking, who become successful, because hate becomes turned into mastering difficulties, attacking problems, overcoming obstacles. This is the benign hate in healthy people. Good natured, satisfied people, are wonderful to have around but they do not necessarily make the greatest workers or thinkers. Though hate energies can be harnessed for work, please don't get the idea that if you do this, then you stop hating. There is plenty left over, as much as you will sublimate it and put it into work and thinking, there's still more. Drive along Wilshire Boulevard sometime. Look at the people in the cars and how they drive. Try once, to slow down two miles an hour slower than the guy behind you and you'll be destroyed. You rarely meet a good-natured driver.

Since not all our hate can be channeled, some has to come out in other forms. You know we have all kinds of harmless ways, like sports, go to the baseball game and "Kill the Umpire." There are good, clean ways of expressing aggression.

How do people develop the capacity to sublimate their hate? Briefly, with a goodly amount of predictable, reliable love in childhood, moderate, not excessive, frustrations, and permissive expressions of hate which is not too destructive. Lots of large muscle activity, but physical restraint when outbursts of violent rages and hatred occur. The child must know that you are strong enough to control his terrible hate and that it does not overwhelm you. I said restraint, not necessarily punishment.

What do you do with adults who hate? That is much harder. Many of them do not know they are sick, this is the problem. The prejudiced ones; many of the jinxed people who feel it is just bad luck; the delinquents who feel society is at fault, they have to be made aware they are sick. If prejudiced people realized that prejudice is a sign of envy, I think it would make them neurotic, which is an improvement, because if they are neurotic they can be treated. It is important to treat the sick who hate, they do well with all kinds of insight.

In general I would like to say that it is important to respect hate. We must realize that some healthy hates which are clear, undistorted, specific, appropriate, and reasonable are necessary in order to function successfully. Hates, of course, which are either harmless or which have to do with issues about which we are willing to take a stand. I would like to say to you something you may not agree with. I think intelligent and active people ought to be willing to have enemies. I decry this quest for universal popularity. I think a person who is really worth something in a community ought to be hated by a few people. Besides, there are so many things that are worth hating. I mean this very seriously and this is what I want to close with. I would like to remind you where it is worth hating, if you are worried about what to do with hatred. Please: the perpetrators of injustice, hate them; tyrants and all tyranny, warmongers, people who like war, hate them; people who seem to want poverty and bring about poverty—hate poverty, hate ignorance, hate disease, hate all of these things. But above all, when you hate, be willing to act upon it and do something, and if you will do that, you will not hate yourselves. Thank you.

# 4 The Conflict Between Psychoanalysis and Religion (1960)

*In her notes, Hildi Greenson tells the following story about this lecture, which illustrates Greenson's wonderful sense of humor and how quickly he was able to respond in front of an audience. Some weeks prior to this lecture, he had participated in a University of California, Los Angeles (UCLA), symposium at Lake Arrowhead called "The Good Life." He was joined on the program by three speakers with predictably differing points of view: a Catholic priest, a Protestant minister, and a rabbi. During one of their heated debates a terrifying thunderclap and instant power failure occurred. Fearful of some disaster, or maybe God's wrath, everybody jumped to his feet. However, when the lights came on again, Greenson calmly observed, "Please note, I am the only speaker still sitting down." His self-assurance had scored a point for psychoanalysis.*

*Greenson chose to discuss the conflict between psychoanalysis and religion because he felt there was a growing tendency among religious leaders and also among psychoanalysts to deny some of the basic conflicts between the two schools of thought. As he did frequently, he began developmentally, describing how children invent God out of their need to be helped and rescued; turn in their need for salvation to parents who become godlike; and then turn to God who becomes parentlike. However, his problem with worship, faith, prayer and obedience is they could impair eventual intellectual development and that such activity "impedes and eventually crushes the child's curiosity which is essential for intellectual growth."*

*Psychoanalysis is not amoral, as is charged by some religionists, but it has a concept of morality that differs from that of organized religion. For the psychoanalyst, morality has to develop from the person's own experience. Greenson explained, "the only reliable self-esteem, the only kind of self-esteem that stays with us, is the one we have built up in relationship toward our own conscience, toward our own ideals. We will never have a reliable and secure sense of self-esteem as long as it is dependent on God, church, or any other organization."*

*In this lecture Greenson also spoke out against the practice of "thought control" practiced by many religions where the thought is held to be equal to the deed. He described one of the most important clinical issues with which we must help our patients, namely, that thoughts and deeds are very different: "Our clinical findings certainly do not agree with the notion that it is harmful or wicked to have hostile, aggressive, sexual, forbidden thoughts. Having these thoughts and recognizing them gives us a much better chance of dealing with them. Repressing them only makes us more prone to become a victim of them in some form or other."*

*In drawing sharp distinctions between religion and psychoanalysis in this lecture, perhaps Greenson was most troubled by dogma and the sense of religious intolerance that flares up from time to time in America. He closed the lecture by saying "we all have a right to our own illusions, but none of us, in my opinion, has the right to impose his illusions upon man."*

I have chosen to discuss "The Conflict Between Psychoanalysis and Religion" at this time because I have found that there is a growing tendency among religious leaders and also among psychoanalysts to deny that there is a basic conflict between these two schools of thought. In the past, religious leaders have freely attacked psychoanalysis as immoral, sinful, and a menace to mankind. I remind you of the many remarks by

From a public lecture given under the auspices of the School for Nursery Years, Los Angeles, October 18, 1960.

Bishop Fulton Sheen on this subject. Freud was quite outspoken in his opposition to religion. Two of his works are devoted almost exclusively to this subject, "The Future of an Illusion" and "Civilization and Its Discontents." He maintained that religion is a mass neurosis and harmful to mankind. Today many religious leaders maintain there is no fundamental conflict between psychoanalysis and religion. Certain analysts have also come out with a similar position, namely, Gregory Zilboorg, who converted to Catholicism before his death, and Erich Fromm, who believes that certain democratic religions are in accord with psychoanalytic principles. I think the time is ripe, therefore, to once more try to clarify whether or not there is a conflict and if so, what is the nature of the conflict between psychoanalysis and religion.

First I would like to attempt to define what I mean by religion. A religion is a system of worship of a God. The deity varies from religion to religion. He may be regarded as Jehovah, or Jesus Christ, or Buddha, but in all events this Godlike figure is omnipotent, omniscient, perfect, and unchanging. In all religions God is supernatural, beyond the realm and condition of man, and this God requires obedience and unquestioning submission to his laws and dogmas. Different religions perform different rituals in order to establish communication with their God, but all religions contain these two elements: (1) the belief in a supernatural deity, and (2) the requirement of worship.

It may be argued that this conception of religion is limited to the very orthodox and that there are more abstract and less personified ways of considering God and worship, but I maintain that all religions, if they are truly religions and not merely a code of ethics or a code of humanitarian principles, contain these two elements.

Now I would like to try to define psychoanalysis. Psychoanalysis is an attempt to systematize, classify, and formulate our knowledge about human behavior. There are some six basic elements in the psychoanalytic approach which Freud has postulated and which are considered essential for psychoanalysis. I shall only mention a few to illustrate. There is the genetic point of view which means that our present-day behavior is determined by our past experiences, and that we are the product of experiences and events which impinged upon our anatomical and physiological constitution. There is the topographical point of view which states that our behavior is not only determined by our conscious thinking, wishes, and impulses, but much more importantly, by our unconscious desires, wishes, and impulses. The dynamic point of view attempts to understand our behavior as the consequence of conflicts between instincts impelling us in one direction and defenses counteracting those instincts. It is not possible in a brief period of time to adequately amplify this definition, but essentially all these basic elements are dedicated to the proposition that psychoanalysis is an attempt to classify, organize, systematize, and formulate our findings about human behavior.

I would like to stress at this point, that psychoanalysis is a scientific discipline and, therefore, very different from a religion. In a science it is permissible to dispute, to modify and to change different hypotheses. It is not necessary to accept any statement as being beyond a doubt. For example, there is a great difference of opinion among analysts about the existence of a death instinct, which Freud postulated, but one can be considered a psychoanalyst and not be "decouched" if one doubts or disbelieves in the death instinct. Freud, as brilliant as he was, and the genius that he was, could be wrong, and he was in certain places, and he has to be modified and changed; but if Freud were considered infallible, and if you had to follow out every one of the prescribed techniques that he advocated, then you would be practicing a religion and not a science. There are some so-called analysts who are Freud worshippers, but they cannot be considered scientists. Only those analysts are scientists who are not true believers, who dare to doubt, to question, to study in our attempt to better understand human behavior.

Let us get down to one of the central points of the conflict between psychoanalysis and religion, namely, the existence of God and his relationship to man. According to most of the major religions, God created the universe and also created man. We psychoanalysts believe that all phenomena have causes and we, therefore, feel it is a proper question to ask who made God, where did God come from, and our psychoanalytic answer is precisely this: God did not make man. Man made God. Not even that; not men, but children made God. God was created by children. All children make gods; all children need gods; all children believe in gods; all children are religious. Even if you do not teach it to them, even if you don't believe in it. In fact, particularly the children of nonbelievers are religious. In our study and observations of children, we find it again and again, it is universally present, the belief children have in God and their tendency to be religious. If they grow up, if they mature, they can get over it. Otherwise they never do.

But let me go a little slowly and explain this. How is it that children create God? God begins with the need for God. The longing for God begins with the fact that the human child is the most helpless of all newborn creatures in this world. No other mammal is so ill-prepared to survive as the human child. He is born helpless and at the mercy of his environment. The child very early becomes aware of its helplessness and also very early becomes aware of his salvation, of his rescuers, the parents. It is this alternation between helplessness and salvation which is the forerunner of the belief in God and religion. To the child, the ones who save him from despair, destruction, annihilation, desertion, torture, are the parents. And he later transforms or imbues these parents with godlike qualities: the first Gods are his parents.

And it should be remembered that the way a child thinks is quite different from the adult mature-thinking grown-up. Children's thinking is full of magic; children believe that their wishes are known without utterance, without speaking. Children believe that there are all-powerful, all-knowing creatures who can do everything and anything and who know everything and anything. Children have difficulty in distinguishing self from nonself and very often and typically project what is going on in them onto others and find it going on in others. Children, in order to comprehend the universe and nature in which they live, personify everything because it gives them a method of coping with it, of understanding it. And to a child, for example, thunder is understood as a loud, angry voice; that is the only comparable experience a child has had that can help him understand such a phenomenon as thunder. Thunder is personified, "parentalized," deified.

And with this kind of thinking and with the dependency on the parent, the parent is given magical qualities. But you see what later happens in the child's development, somewhere between ages six and nine we have the beginning of the dethronement of the parents; the latency phase of development. Normally, the child gets sexually and erotically involved with one parent and feels hatred, jealousy, and envy toward the other in the earlier oedipal phase of his development. In his attempt to resolve this terrifying conflict, the child internalizes some of his parental images, and develops a conscience. There is a resultant devaluation of the parents and the parents stop being gods. But now the child out of his continuing helplessness, out of his anxiety, out of his insecurity, looks for something to replace the godlike parents and now finds other gods, particularly in a society which has them made to order. We hand it to them: This is God! And the child now displaces what he felt toward the parent onto this new figure which becomes idealized, idolized, and partly embued with all of the projections of the child's primitive, powerful impulses; all are put onto this God so that this God is an angry God, a jealous God, a vengeful God, and also a protecting God. The intensity of the child's instincts and emotions are projected onto this God and all kinds of other phenomena are personified and connected up to it and the thunder is God's voice and the lightening is God's punishment. Of course it is aided and abetted by a society which teaches this in Sunday Schools, or on the radio or television. And, like the parent, God can reward, as well as punish. God is very powerful. My essential point is: children in their need to be helped and rescued, in their need for salvation, turn to the parents who become godlike and then turn to God who becomes parentlike.

Let me give you a clinical example to show you how one can see this in a patient during psychoanalysis. This is not only true of patients, but it so happens I know more about patients than I know about people. Many years ago I treated a young man, a very bright, capable man who had one major symptom that bothered him severely—sudden attacks of anxiety. He would get attacks of fear which came up at particular times; the worst attacks were accompanied by a sensation of suffocation. Upon certain occasions when he relaxed and was daydreaming, he would suddenly become seized by a feeling of suffocation. Worst of all, in his sleep he would be awakened in terror by the sensation of suffocation.

Consciously he was not a religious man and had been brought

up by rather progressive, healthy neurotic people. He did not believe in religion or God particularly; although he admitted it was true he had certain superstitions, and little compulsive rituals. He had to wash his hands three times before he did certain kinds of things in order to be sure that he would be successful. Now this was not religious, but it is true he remembered hearing that in certain religious practices one had to wash one's hands before doing certain things. There were also certain foods he avoided, not because he was Jewish, but it so happened that he was allergic to ham, he thought. It was also true he had certain other eccentricities which he had to repeat which might seem to be connected to religion, but they were not, he claimed, because he did not consciously believe in religion and prayer and he certainly did not believe in God. He thought he was unlucky and fate, not God, was against him. So, he maintained he was not religious, only superstitious—a frequent state of affairs in many so-called progressive people.

Anyway, I want to tell you about his attacks of suffocation, which I tried to understand and analyze. One day he told me he had a terrible attack of suffocation; he awoke from a deep sleep terrified, sweating, trembling, choking, blue, breathless, almost on the verge of fainting. He was very shaken. When he came to see me and told me this, I asked him if he remembered what he had been dreaming. He was startled and replied that the dream just occurred to him now. He had dreamt that somebody was choking him; in fact, now he was reporting the dream, he remembered a painting in which God was depicted and he realized that the person who was choking him was God. As he told me this he became more convinced; yes, that was the dream, the dream was that God was choking him. When he talked on a bit, he then remembered peculiarly a detail of God's face; there was a mole on God's cheek; and that struck him because startlingly he now recalled that he once knew a man who had exactly such a mole but he could not place him. After struggling with his memory a bit more, it occurred to him that his father had such a mole when the patient was a little boy and later this mole had been removed. And so we could trace the picture of this godlike figure who was strangling him to his father as he existed in this boy's life when he was under five.

Still another detail emerged. He remembered that the hands that were choking him seemed to have a ring on one finger of the right hand. As he described it to me he touched the finger on his own right hand on which he had a ring, and he realized that the hands that were choking him were just like his own. He now remembered this ring was given to him when he had been confirmed—about to become a man. He also recollected a terrible fight with his younger brother; how he had hit him and cut him severely with this ring. Now it became rather clear to me what was involved in this figure of God. The God who was strangling him was his childhood picture of father, but imbued with the hostility, rage, and jealousy of a rejected little boy; this is what was suffocating him.

Although I make a rather elaborate explanation of it, let me tell you this is no unusual description of the origin and the beginnings of the notion of God as it arises in childhood. If you want to trace God back, here is where it always ends. You start with God and eventually, sooner or later you will get to the parents and sooner or later you will get not only to a parent, but to the infantile instinctual life of the child projected onto these parents. This is how God is made.

But let me go on. Religious people call God "our Father" and we are to be considered his children. This is everyday language—father, children. I seemed to stress in my example, that God is a wrathful creature. I want to point out to you that according to the church, God also protects. This is another very important aspect of God. He protects. But here the analyst would say, "Yes, he protects, but at what price?" "What price do you pay for God's protection?" This is an important question because the price you pay is worship, obedience, faith. And we psychoanalysts say, "That is too high a price!" Why? I must go over it briefly, because I think it is important to make clear why this is too high a price to pay. Because worship makes you, the worshipper, insignificant. The greater God is, the lowlier is the worshipper. He who worships is always lowly. The more perfect God is, the more defective you are. The more wonderful and pure God is, the more evil and sinful you are. Worship makes for servility, a feeling of unworthiness, and a need for conformity. By elevating anything to godlike proportions, you degrade the worshipper. To recognize that we are relatively insignificant creatures in the universe—fine, that is realistic. But to glorify this kind of relationship, to revere this insignificance, to make this situation holy and sacred, this smacks of masochism and self-destruction.

Faith, a few words about faith. It is comforting to have faith. But is it really? To believe without evidence; that is what faith is. To believe without the use of intelligence and knowledge is wishful thinking. It is belief in illusion. That is faith. True, we all had faith once and it remains in all of us in our unconscious mind, ready to pop up in times of stress. But I don't make this a virtue. I am not proud of it and I would not try to sell it to you. I recognize it for what it is: weak, fragile, magical, fun, pleasurable. Above all, childish. It exists within us but I would never suggest it to you in place of thinking, knowledge, reason, and intelligence.

Prayer is a direct communication with God. I would not be so presumptuous; I don't even talk to Freud. Ambrose Pierce, who wrote a delightful book called *The Devil's Dictionary*, defined prayer: "To ask that the laws of the universe be annulled on behalf of a single petitioner, confessedly unworthy." We all occasionally resort to this kind of thinking, including me, granted. But, to elevate this infantile thinking to some kind of exalted communication and great virtue—no.

Aside from faith and prayer, organized religion requires unquestioning obedience, and that impairs the intellectual development of man. Let us be very clear about this. It is one of Freud's major points in his critique of religion. It impedes and eventually crushes the child's curiosity, which is essential for intellectual growth. You are not going to get children who will fully develop intellectually if you stifle their curiosity by demanding faith and obedience. Children have to be encouraged to doubt, to question, not only "Where do babies come from?" but "Where does God come from?" All such complex questions cannot be answered by referring to God's inscrutable ways. It is a harmful explanation for intelligent people to give. I think it is much better to say, "I don't know," than to explain it as God's doing. That is cowardly or dishonest.

I want to go on. Let us talk about morality. You know in the major religions—the orthodox religions—all of them more or less claim that their morality stems from God's laws as revealed to his apostles. Man, to them, is essentially sinful and can only be saved by adherence to dogma, ritual, and so on. Sin is of central importance to all religious morality. Now sin is not just error, but error in accordance with God's laws, God's dogma; this is a special kind of error. Religious morality is based essentially on avoidance of sin and paying for sin.

Bertrand Russell pointed out in one of his many works written on the subject: "Relatively little importance and merit is given to what you accomplish; you may have made the greatest discoveries in science or art; but if you committed a sin, you die a sinner." This kind of emphasis is typical for the morality of religion. The concept of eternal punishment in Hell is used to keep you from sinning, and the concept of Heaven and immortality is the reward if you don't. This epitomizes religious morality, although I grant you it is a rather one-sided, orthodox view of religious morality. But I chose it deliberately because it is present to some degree in all morality derived from God.

What about the analyst? Do we believe in morality? Of course we do, but not in the above-mentioned kinds of morality. Why not? Let me tell you why. First of all, this kind of morality, this belief that right and wrong can be decided not within you, but externally, we consider a regression. This is a childish system of morality. These are childish standards. It is a retreat back to something primitive that most children have overcome by the time they are nine or ten years of age, we hope, or at least have begun to overcome. When children at seven, eight, nine, or ten develop a conscience and develop ego ideals, these are internalized conceptions of right and wrong. Surely it began once from an outside authority, from the parents, who determined what was good or bad. Believing in God's morality and God's punishment is a retreat back to seeking the standards for right and wrong outside of yourself.

Yes, psychoanalysts believe in morals, but not in those rigidly determined by God or by churches or any other organization. It is your own sense of right and wrong that has to develop from your own experiences. Only in this way can it develop as we grow and mature. Religious conceptions based on God are relatively static and unchangeable. The concept of what is right and what is wrong and who is bad or who is virtuous changes as your wisdom and knowledge increases. Yes, we believe we must live with our own standards, our own ideals. Man needs these, by all means, but let them be those he has chosen and worked out for himself and not ideals imposed upon him from without. The only reliable self-esteem, the only kind of self-esteem that stays with us, is the one we have built up in our own relationship toward our own conscience, toward our own ideals. We will never have a reliable and secure sense of self-esteem as long as it is dependent on God, church, or any other organization. This kind of morality that God is watching and God will punish, or the church is watching or the church will punish, is a regression, a going back to the notion of a sort of celestial policeman who is watching over us—this is another form of bogeyman.

The concept of sin compounds and complicates the child's sense of guilt. It only adds to the child's own guilt and his own conscience, which can be severe and strict enough. The idea that sinful thoughts are as bad as sinful acts (which is a typical religious notion), is absolutely contradicted by the findings of psychoanalysis. The people who do good in this world are not people who never had a wicked thought; quite the contrary. The really dangerous people are the people who repress their evil thoughts, then one day, boom, a murder. I exaggerate to make my point. But let me assure you, a death wish a day keeps the analyst away, as well as the policeman. I oversimplify. It takes more than this to keep an analyst away; you know that. Nevertheless, our clinical findings certainly do not agree with the notion that it is harmful or wicked to have hostile, aggressive, sexual, forbidden thoughts. Having these thoughts and recognizing them gives us a much better chance of dealing with them. Repressing them only makes us more prone to become a victim of them in some form or other.

The concept of Hell, not typical for all religions, but for many, is to my mind one of the most amazingly sadistic creations I have ever encountered. I don't know how this could be conceived as any form of morality, something as cruel and vicious as eternal punishment. Think of it for a moment. To live with this threat, one either must be terrified or cynical. On the other hand, promises of immortality and Heaven, I wonder is this not a bribe? Everybody is afraid of death; we don't know anything about death. The fear of it is certainly present in all of us and the belief in Heaven and immortality would certainly be a relief. I admit that if a person is desperate or dying he would in all likelihood grasp at it; but I do not admit, in fact I would disagree, that this notion of immortality and the belief in Heaven is a good idea to live with. To die with, yes. Yes, to die with; not to live with. I think we all are afraid of death, but I think the best guarantee of facing death decently is to live well. I believe a person who has lived well and has had a good and rich life can face death; I don't say enjoy death, but face it, bear it, go through with it, and die decently. Yes. I think the only kind of immortality that there is any evidence of is the immortality of being remembered by people. This is all. No other immortality exists, only the immortality of being remembered. I think anything more than this is an illusion, if not a delusion.

Again I want to say that man needs morals and man needs ideals, but ideals in terms of man and in terms of mankind. I want to ask you: Are any of the major religions in the forefront consistently fighting against war? Or the testing of the H-bombs? Morality and morals, yes; but based on reasoned, sober values of right and wrong. Think of all the crimes committed in the name of moral fervor. Every witchhunt, every gas chamber, every pogrom was committed by people who felt morally justified, morally superior to everyone else. The biggest danger of the communists is not that they have another system of economic philosophy; the danger is that they have become fanatic religionists who feel morally superior and worship their God, Marx. This is the great danger; they have become fervently moralistic and want to wage a crusade and convert the whole world to communism. Just a belief in another kind of economic system would be little danger to us all.

I want to go to another area and this is a basic one about man's instinctual life. The major religions, all of them I believe, neglect sex and only accept it for purposes of procreation. They consider sexual satisfaction, sensual pleasure as either sinful, or at best, as a necessary evil. I stress this because it is an important area and source of man's conflicts. How does the analyst look at it? We feel it was an amazing step forward when man, unlike his animal predecessors, faced his sexual object, knew his sexual object, liked his sexual object and loved it. We thought that was wonderful. Animals who mount their sexual counterpart from behind merely respond at certain designated times to glandular activity, that's all. We thought: what a piece of progress humanity has made! You knew and looked at what you were loving, you were not only passionate and lustful, but affectionate and tender. This psychoanalysis considers mature sexuality. Is the use of sex for reasons of procreation very different from our animal predecessors?

Let's talk about another basic instinctual drive: aggression. Here the situation is much more complicated because some religions seem to take a very contradictory position. On the one hand the cruel concept of sin and Hell and on the other hand you read in the Bible: "Love thine enemies." I must admit I have trouble enough loving my friends—or at least strangers. But my enemies? How many of you love thine enemies? I think this is an impossible demand made on mankind and calculated to confuse and confound man and make him feel guilty and unworthy.

Yes, we analysts recognize that man is full of feelings of destructiveness; and, of course, we know it has to be dealt with, but not by denying it, not by trying to cover it up, nor by turning it into its opposite, love. Such love is thin, false, and unreliable. It makes a mockery of love. Destructiveness has to be tamed, harnessed, sublimated, all of that; but it will not be done by denying it or repressing it. Above all, sexual frustration and instinctual deprivation make people cruel, not kindly. Asceticism generally does not make gentle, docile, kindly people. Instinctual satisfaction does. Hate is a harsh word, but hating the right people and the right things for the right reason is a virtue and a necessity. Tyrants, disease, and poverty deserve to be hated.

I have talked long but I have to make a few more points. Religion has been and still is a very powerful force and there is in all of us a need in this direction. Religion tries to give us answers, clear-cut, definite answers about what to believe, how to believe, and why to believe. From a psychoanalytic point of view, those answers are unrealistic, regressive, fantastic, neurotic, and harmful. Yes, I would agree with Freud's statement, "Religion is like a mass neurosis." It may save the individual from an individual neurosis, but it is neurotic to try to solve man's problems by asking him to regress back to childhood levels of thinking and operating without facing reality.

All right, but man needs something, doesn't he, something to believe in, particularly when there is anxiety and uncertainty. I agree. Do you remember that saying during World War II? "There are no atheists in foxholes." Granted, when anybody is in a state of panic he reaches desperately for something or somebody to hold on to, like God or momma. Panic makes us all children; please remember this. We can all become overwhelmed under certain circumstances and then like children look to something godlike for protection. But life is not a foxhole and as uncertain as things are today, there is a big difference between living in a foxhole and living with uncertainty. I want to submit to you the idea that as long as man is panicky he will try to reach out for godlike magical solutions. But once he becomes secure, he does not need them. Man prays for his daily bread as long as he is not sure of getting it or as long as he feels unworthy for having gotten it. Give man a chance to feel sure and worthy of getting his daily bread, he won't pray, but he will be grateful to the society which made it possible.

You know we have to deal with a lot of uncertainty and one is always tempted to reach for absolute and complete answers. I cannot offer you as a psychoanalyst any neat, simple, unified answer. What will replace religion? Part of the answer will come when we have helped man overcome his sense of helplessness and when we have helped him in his fight against the irrational, regressive anxieties. This will lessen the need for any kind of religion. In its place we should offer man more knowledge, more information, a greater respect for reason, the mind, and intelligence. The scientific attitude of establishing limited certainties, not absolute, magical certainties, shall slowly and surely prevail. The quest for truth, the truth about man, about the world and the universe, will supplant the belief in childish, magical, perfect answers. The voice of the intellect is soft, said Freud, but if properly developed, eventually demands a hearing. This, I believe, is one part of mankind's greatest hopes for the future: the freedom from irrational anxiety and the development of knowledge, reason, and the mind.

But all of this is not enough, because man needs more in order to attain a good life. Man must have ideals which are bigger than himself. He must have goals which are beyond him but not impossible. Man must have the capacity to love something more than himself. The emphasis in religion has always been on ideals so sublime and so completely unattainable that man could only feel hopelessly inadequate or cynical. Man must have ideals to strive for, but these ideals should be based on man's relationship to man and to mankind rather than on obedience to a god and his dogma. If we free man from his fantastic anxieties and feelings of unworthiness, and if we free his mind from impossible ideals, if we give him an opportunity to learn and to struggle with the destructive forces within him and outside of him, his desire to love and to work and to do good will be increased.

The psychoanalyst does not have the right to impose any brand of morality or values of any kind upon his patient. It is our duty only to free the patient from his irrational unconscious and tyrannical past. If we succeed in doing this and our patient has achieved some maturity, he should be free then to chose the kind of morality, standards, and values that suit him. The analyst only brings insight and understanding which then leads to freedom to make one's own choices.

I have now reached the end of this discussion and I want to leave with a final point. I have placed great emphasis on reason and knowledge and the mind, and you might now ask me, is there no place for illusion and fairy tales in this world that I strive for? Of course there is room for it. We all have our faith and illusions, whether consciously or unconsciously, in one thing or another. We all hold on to magical ideas, whether we believe in luck or fate or God, whether we consciously realize it or not. My only point is that we should recognize this for what it is, unreliable, fragile, and irrational. We all have a right to our own illusions, but none of us, in my opinion, has the right to impose his illusions upon man.

# 5 Sleep, Dreams, and Death (1961)

*During the early 1960s the country was in the grips of great anxiety about the hydrogen bomb and the situation in Berlin. Fallout shelters and death seemed to be on the collective American mind. Greenson's motivation in this talk was to try to make attitudes about death more understandable. He said, "If I can do that, perhaps I can also make it not as terrifying, or as frightening as it is to most of us." First he discussed sleep and dreaming from the point of view of the need to regress: "Above all, sleep gives us a chance for emotional and psychological rest. When we sleep we have a chance not merely to get away from the demands and the frustrations of civilized life, but more than that, we have a chance to go back to some of the basic, primitive satisfactions which we once knew in childhood and which are so necessary for us today in order to endure adult life."*

*He then turned to the different meanings that humans project onto death. For some, dying and death are awful and tortuous because of the fear of being helpless. For others, death means the ultimate loss of control, which means being at the mercy of terrible instincts or being overwhelmed by shameful impulses. For still others, dying and death mean destruction of the body and may be related to castration anxiety. Many people anticipate death as a great abandonment; those are the people who do not have the capacity to be alone. Greenson demonstrated how, in any such instance, some childhood dread, some childhood anxiety has been displaced onto death.*

> *All these terrors can be condensed into the following. Either they are due to magical animistic thinking and feeling sorry for oneself, or death has become personified into the grim reaper, the devil and witches one had in childhood. These anxieties are displaced and become now remobilized as the fear of death. All this is loaded with hostility. Death has become aggressified; dying has become aggressified. All kinds of destructive impulses are displaced onto death and dying by people who fear punishment for their hostile and sexual impulses. They are loaded with unresolved hostilities, have little capacity for love, which would neutralize their fear of death.*

*Greenson contrasted that with a healthier, more realistic attitude toward the inevitability of dying and death, encouraging the audience to be able to face death but to be able to push it away at the same time. He said, "face it when there is a reason to face it, when death is imminent; somebody's death or your own, or society's. But not to live with it as your constant companion . . . to be able to forget it . . . to repress it . . . to suppress it. Not to deny it or glamorize it. Death is unpleasant, it is painful, it is sad, to say the least. But neither dying or death has to be a sheer terror. It should not and does not have to be unbearable. One should be able to die as a human being, decently. That is enough."*

*His clear thinking about death and dying in this lecture is helpful to us today with respect to controversies surrounding the issue of quality of life and whether one has the right to choose when to die, especially in light of medicine's ability to prolong life. By understanding the emotional meanings we attach to death and dying, we can better sort out the irrational in our dealing with these most complex issues.*

I would like to begin by explaining to you how I came to select these topics; sleep, dreams, and death. Above all, I had

---

From a public lecture given under the auspices of the School for Nursery Years, Los Angeles, October 11, 1961. Broadcast on KPFA-FM, Berkeley, and KPFK-FM, Los Angeles.

wanted to talk to you about death, and I thought there were many reasons, important reasons, to talk about death. First of all, the H-Bomb panic that is sweeping the United States, the question of Berlin, shall we have a war and if we have a war, *what kind of war*? A small war? A big war? People are frightened about dying, not only frightened, but panicky, irrationally afraid of dying, and this influences their thinking. They come to all kinds of conclusions on how to avoid death rather than to be intelligent, correct, moral, or honest. Furthermore, I thought about this question that is sweeping the country, the question of fallout shelters, private fallout shelters, and I must say I resent this. I resent the fact that people who have enough money can build fallout shelters and save themselves and those who don't, cannot, and, therefore, will not be able to save themselves. And, it occurred to me that what would happen at a dinner party on a Saturday night if you had, let us say, twenty people for dinner, and all you have room for in your shelter is six people. How do you decide whom you will let die? Yes, this is what concerns me, bothers me. And this is why I chose this topic.

But there are other reasons for my wanting to talk about death. I saw *La Dolce Vita*, which is also about death, but another form of death. This is about animated boredom which I consider to be another aspect of death. Then I saw *Breathless*, a French film version of *La Dolce Vita*, which was shorter, but also concerned people who, to me, seemed to be dead, who didn't care about living, who didn't love, who were detached, and dead, and moving around, but nevertheless, dead. I saw *Krapp's Last Tape*, and again I was struck how the central character in this play is a man who is dead and empty. The same with *The Balcony* or *Endgame* or *The Iceman Cometh*. These are all about dead people. So it occurred to me that it is time that one ought to talk about death and try to explain something about it rather than merely glamorizing it, or enacting it, or denying it, or pretending it is not there or is not very important. I think it is time one talked seriously about death.

All these are rational reasons for talking about death and you know a psychoanalyst is never content with merely the rational, there must be other than rational reasons for talking about death. Here I suppose I must admit that the older you get, and the closer to death you get, the more you are concerned about death. People around you, your friends, your relatives, begin to die. This makes you ruminate more about it, makes you wonder about it. There is something mysterious and fascinating about death because we know so little about it. I suppose what finally made me decide to talk about death was the strange coincidence that my last birthday happened to fall on Yom Kippur, which is the Day of Atonement. The previous talk I gave on this program was on "The Conflict Between Psychoanalysis and Religion." Now in that particular talk I spoke in no uncertain terms about my opposition to the concept of God, and worship, and religion. How strange, how curious, in fact, how odd of God to make my birthday fall on Yom Kippur! So I have many reasons for talking about death. I would like to do so realistically, without glamorizing death, without beautifying it, making it seem even better than life, which I would call the "Forest Lawn" approach to death. I would like to make our attitude about death and dying more understandable. If I can do that, perhaps I can also make it not as terrifying, or as frightening as it is to most of us.

Let me explain how I came to add the topics sleep and dreams. The closest that we come to anything resembling death comes from our experience of deep, dreamless sleep. Again, I must preface this by saying we know so little about death, but the little we do know seems to indicate that there is a relationship between deep, dreamless sleep and death. There are different kinds of sleep and there are different kinds of dreams. The dreamless sleep is the deepest. But the dream performs a very important function in preserving and protecting our sleep. Freud said the dream is the guardian of our sleep. By that he meant that when our sleep is threatened to be disturbed, when certain stimuli impinge upon our sleep, it could awaken us. The dream comes and helps protect us in such a way that we continue sleeping by dreaming. Freud himself struggled with these three subjects (sleep, dreams, and death) from the very beginning to the very end of his work in psychoanalysis.

The first major psychoanalytic work Freud wrote was *The Interpretation of Dreams*, which was published in 1900. And his last contributions concerned the importance of the death instinct. But here I must add that neither Freud nor I were alone in bringing these three subjects together. Shakespeare had done it a long time before, in 1604 to be exact. Let me quickly quote from Hamlet [Act III, Scene 1]:

> "To die: to sleep;
> No more; and by sleep to say we end
> The heart-ache, and the thousand natural shocks
> That flesh is heir to, 'tis a consummation
> Devoutly to be wish'd. To die, to sleep;
> To sleep: perchance to dream: ay there's the rub;
> For in that sleep of death what dreams may come,
> When we have shuffled off this mortal coil,
> Must give us pause: . . ."

Here you have it, sleep, dreams, and death beautifully joined together.

I do not hope or expect to be able to describe, either poetically like Shakespeare or with Freud's genius, the relationship between sleep, dreams, and death. But I would like to try to present to you systematically the relationship between these three. I know this is an enormous task and I cannot hope to possibly cover all the many connections among them. But I would like to try. Let me begin my talking first about sleep.

I believe today you would accept the idea that the need to sleep is a basic bodily need, is one of man's bodily necessities, and, therefore, can be considered an instinct. Recently this has been confirmed in many different ways by various experiments. For example, by disturbing the sleep of healthy people for long periods of time, it was very easy to demonstrate that profound disturbances in various basic functions would occur. People whose sleep had been disturbed suffered from disorders in perception, thinking, suffered from delusions, hallucinations, fatigue, exhaustion, loss of control, and above all, eruptions of aggression and hostility. Furthermore, I think it is a well-known fact that difficulty in sleeping, insomnia, is a more and more frequently found symptom among people in our so-called Western civilization. More and more people are taking sleeping pills, or following one or another special routine or practice, in order to try to get a half-way decent night's sleep. By far the most popular means has to do with the taking of sleeping pills or alcohol. There are those who find it easy to fall asleep, but sleep for only a few hours, and those who find it difficult to fall asleep and then cannot get up in the morning. More and more people seem to have lost their natural capacity to fall asleep, to sleep deeply, and to awaken refreshed. Then there is an entirely other group of people who cannot stop sleeping, they are usually depressed, and take tranquilizers to keep themselves partly asleep all day long in order to survive. These people I would classify along with the television addicts who also cannot bear life except if they are constantly being distracted from the real world. The main difference is the tranquilizer people take their medicine by mouth and the others take it through the eyes, but in either case, perceptions, thoughts, fantasies and imagination are dulled and they sort of sleepwalk their way through life.

The fact that people try too desperately to sleep and are constantly seeking different ways of helping themselves fall asleep and stay asleep, indicates that the need to sleep is basic. I would like to spend a little time discussing some aspects of the importance of sleep. First of all, if you observe the newborn infant, you will instantly recognize that the newborn baby spends a goodly portion of his time asleep, if he is happy and healthy. The only time he is awake is when he is in pain. The newborn baby who is warm, well-fed, and comfortable, sleeps on and off almost constantly. This is a rather important observation. It indicates a certain quality which exists throughout life, namely the relationship between pain, perception, thinking, and activity on the one hand, and satisfaction, bliss, comfort, and sleep on the other hand. This duality exists in one form or another all through life. The more satisfied you are, the more ready you are to sleep. Satisfaction of various kinds always brings sleep with it. Pleasurable and satisfying eating experiences, drinking experiences, working experiences, and especially sexual experiences, always end up in sleep. It is as though you don't need the outside world when you are satisfied. What keeps you awake is a sense of frustration, hunger, dissatisfaction, the need for the external world. I must add parenthetically here that although complete satisfaction makes for good sleep, the people who accomplish the most in this world are not necessarily the good sleepers. The thinkers, the doers, the accomplishers are not people who find it easy to attain that blissful state of satisfaction, or satiation, or contentment.

It seems as though one has a choice. One either sleeps well or works well. Although that is too much of a simplification to be true. But, let us now go back to the question: why do we sleep at all? Why is sleep necessary? As you know, an analyst rarely answers a question directly. And I will not attempt to answer this question directly, but rather ask you to try to follow me in my train of thought. Let us observe people who sleep, particularly the newborn. What seems to be happening to a newborn infant as he sleeps? First of all the posture is very striking. This posture is also seen in adults when they sleep. They are not only reclining, but they are curled up, curled up in a typical fetal position. The eyes are shut; they apparently do not see. They apparently do not seem to be hearing. Every form of external stimulus seems to be shut off. A sleeping person hardly moves. He is very quiet. This is another outstanding characteristic of sleep, the restriction of locomotion.

But these are only the obvious visual indications of what happens during sleep. If you explore a bit further you will see that other changes take place during sleep. Your thinking changes. You think differently while you are fully awake. As you become sleepy you begin to think in visual images, in pictures. Your thinking is without logic and without order. It is full of emotion. There is no sense of time; and contradictions do not neutralize each other. The most vivid thinking which occurs in sleep, occurs in the form of dreams. As you know, dreams consist primarily of visual images without order in time, without logic; they are full of contradictions. The most peaceful sleep is dreamless sleep, but even here I suspect that one has blank dreams, a notion which has been put forth by Lewin.

Now if you add up all these observations, posture, the lack of motility, the lack of response to external stimuli, the regression in thinking, I believe it is fair to assume that, above all, sleep is a regressive state. In sleep we retreat, we go back to a time of early infancy, perhaps to a time which resembles the womblike state, the curled-up position, the shut eyes, the lack of reaction to stimuli, primitive thinking—all of this sounds as though it could resemble a state of being in the womb. Freud was very much of the impression that the human infant is born when he is not quite fully ready to be born. And he stated that he thought the need to sleep is based partly on the fact that the newborn child is not ready to face the external world and has to retreat back to his womblike state in order to recuperate so that he can return to the external world. Although this may be true of the newborn, I think to some extent, it is also true in adults. Only the proportionate need is different. Adults, too, in order to endure being civilized, in order to be able to live in this world of ours, need to spend approximately one-third of their lives in this regressed womblike state, sleep.

In other words, we need to sleep because we need to regress. Sleep does this in a variety of ways, partially it does so by giving us a purely physical chance to rest; it refreshes and gives us a chance to recoup our energies. But the most important function of sleep is not merely the requirement of physical rest. Above all, sleep gives us a chance for emotional and psychological rest. When we sleep we have a chance not merely to get away from the demands and the frustrations of civilized life, but more than that, we have a chance to go back to some of the basic, primitive satisfactions which we once knew in childhood and which are so necessary for us today in order to endure adult life.

There are several outstanding points which must be remembered about what makes sleep so important. You can only sleep when you feel safe. (There is one exception to this, namely that you can sleep when you are utterly physically exhausted or on the verge of despair.) The most important function of sleep is the opportunity it gives us to dream. The need to sleep and the need to dream are very closely related to each other, just as the inability to sleep and fear of dreaming are related to each other. I will get on to that subject later. Now, only a few more points about sleep.

The need to sleep varies from person to person, and in each particular person how much sleep is required depends upon many conditions. It has been more or less established that adults require roughly some six hours of sleep per night. Some people require more, some less. It is very interesting to notice that some people sleep more when they are happy and content, and some sleep more when they are depressed, or in pain, or worried. Some people cannot sleep when they are worried or depressed. Others cannot sleep when they are happy. The basic question realy boils down to: What does sleeping mean to an individual? This is an extremely personal question and depends on one's history and experiences. The analogy to this question would be, what does wakefulness mean to a particular person? Does being awake mean misery, frustration, suffering, or does being awake mean satisfaction, pleasure, happiness? Is sleep the end of pleasure or is sleep an escape from pain? All these questions are very vital to try to understand a person's need for sleep. However, I think it is important to indicate there are different kinds of sleep. Sleep varies in depth: there is light sleep which resembles wakefulness, and, there is deep sleep which gets very close to complete unconsciousness or stupor.

I think at this point it would be worthwhile to make it clear that when you sleep you are never totally unconscious. Complete unconsciousness is called stupor. When you sleep, no matter how deeply you may be asleep, you are partially awake. It can be demonstrated by pointing out that you can always awaken a sleeper. For example, a person may be in a deep sleep, but if you flash a bright light into the eyes of the sleeper, you will awaken him; if you make a sudden, loud noise the sleeper will awaken; if you pinch him or stick him with a pin he will feel it and awaken. In other words, all these sensory functions and perceptions are going on in sleep although they are diminished. If that person were in a stupor you could not awaken him. Let me illustrate the relationship between sleep and stupor and even death by a clinical example which occurred many years ago during my Army service in the war.

A soldier was brought to my hospital ward who had been unconscious for four days. They had brought him in from the neurological ward where he had been a patient because he appeared to be in a stupor. They had given him a spinal tap but could find nothing positive and there was nothing they could do to make him regain consciousness. Since all the physical findings were negative, they thought he must be a psychiatric patient and sent him to the psychiatric ward. At that particular time I was the chief of the combat fatigue section in the convalescent hospital. They brought this patient in, put him in a bed, and, as was customary during the hectic days of the war, I did not have an opportunity to examine him that day. I went home and the next morning returned when the nurse told me that this patient could not be awakened. I went to examine him, shook him, jostled him, pinched him, but could not awaken him. I then looked at his chart and found that he had been brought to the hospital in this condition four days ago. There were no physical findings that would indicate any organic or neurological illness of any kind. I looked at him; he seemed to be blissfully, but deeply asleep. I looked at his chart and saw that he had been brought to our hospital from a small town where he had been on leave. He had become unconscious at home, was brought to a hospital there, and then transferred to an Army hospital. I noticed that his name was something like James Smith. I had no real idea what I should do for this man. Purely on the basis of some kind of hunch, purely intuitively, I went over to him and sat on the side of the bed, took his hand, and quietly said to him, almost whispered into his ear, "Jimmy, Jimmy, come on Jimmy boy, it's time to get up. Jimmy, wake up Jimmy." Softly, quietly, I repeated it many times. To my amazement he woke up. He looked at me and said, "Hi, what am I doing here? Who are you?" Then he bolted upright and said, "Please excuse me," and ran to the bathroom. When he returned I talked to him. All he could tell me was the following:

About two weeks previous his uncle had died. The patient had gone to the funeral. He remembered feeling rather sad and sleepy after the funeral and went to his parents' car, lay down, and fell asleep. That is the last thing that he could remember. Apparently he had been asleep for almost two weeks and now had just awakened. The thought that this incident occurred at the funeral of his uncle, the fact that his sleep was more like a stupor, more like a deathlike state, immediately made me wonder if there wasn't some connection with death. So I took the time to talk and I asked him, "What have you done on overseas duty?" He replied, "I was a tail gunner." I asked him, "How many missions did you fly?" He said, "I flew about 50 missions." I asked him, "Did you have any trouble?" He said, "Yes, we were shot down over Germany and I was a prisoner of war. But it was for a short time and I was liberated." When he told me this, he seemed quite depressed.

I decided not to press him any further, but he spontaneously continued the story. "You know, Captain, we were shot down from the rear and I was a tail gunner and I always had the feeling it was my fault." I said nothing. He continued, "After I had completed about 25 missions, I got the peculiar idea that what determined whether I lived or died, was not my skill with a machinegun but by God, and I got to thinking that since God was going to decide whether I would live or die, what's the use of even shooting this gun, what's the use of even looking for the enemy. I then decided, to heck with it. And when we went on a mission I would curl up and go to sleep. Well, on this particular mission, I fell asleep and the enemy came in from the rear and we were shot down. Three of my buddies were killed. I woke up, bailed out, and I was a prisoner of war. Maybe I am to blame because my buddies were killed when I was asleep."

Now I had some understanding about his very pathological symptoms. His sleep was actually a form of dying, a form of death. This was his way of paying for the fact that he had slept and caused some of his buddies to be killed. He was now punishing himself by acting as though he were dead. And this whole experience was triggered by going to the funeral of his uncle. Interesting thing about this man, nobody else could get him to wake up except me. Although the nurses heard me talk to him and heard how I called to him in order to awaken him, they were unable to waken him when I was not on the post. For example, when I left on Friday for the weekend, he would be asleep until I came back. The nurses tried to imitate me. They would say, "Jimmy, Jimmy. It's time to wake up." But he would never wake up. But when I would wake him and say the same thing, "Jimmy, come on Jimmy boy, wake up," he would wake up. This puzzled all of us. After some time I asked him, "How is it that when the nurses call to you and tell you to wake up, you won't wake up?" He looked at me long and thoughtfully and answered, "You know it's funny, I hear all of you, I hear the nurses and I hear you. The only difference is that when you say 'Jimmy boy, wake up,' you mean it and they don't."

I think this story indicates some of the relationships between sleep, stupor, and death, and above all, it indicates that in sleep, we think, we feel, we hear but all in a very primitive and diminished way.

There are variations in the depth of sleep and in the quality of sleep. There are good sleeps and bad sleeps, refreshing sleep, and exhausting sleep. Partly this depends on the length of time we sleep but that is not an absolute criteria. Very often it depends on other things. The quality of a good sleep depends essentially on the quality of the dreams or the ability to reach a dreamless sleep. There are some people who are afraid to dream. There are other people who are afraid to reach that dreamless, blank-dream state. Above all, a long sleep or a short sleep does not necessarily equal a refreshing or nonrefreshing sleep. For example, there are some people who can sleep a long time and when they awaken they are exhausted. There are others who nap for 10 or 15 minutes and wake up refreshed. There are two central issues here, one is one's attitude toward losing consciousness (i.e., letting oneself dream), and another factor is one's attitude toward a dreamless state: there are some people who long for it, there are others who are afraid of it. We will return to this later.

Another important consideration about sleep is one's willingness, or unwillingness to give up the external world. It is very hard for frustrated people who are hungry for stimuli to renounce the external world. They stay awake and want to keep awake constantly searching for satisfaction. It is much easier for satisfied people to give up the external world, to renounce it, and to retreat back to their internal world. Frustrated people, hungry people, ambitious, discontented people, sleep poorly. Satisfied people, smug people, resigned people, apathetic people, sleep better. What matters is the willingness to be passive. To be able to sleep you must be willing to be passive. One cannot make oneself sleep, only let oneself sleep. It is very similar to doing free association or having an orgasm. You cannot make it happen, you can only let it happen. This is an extremely important point. People who have a fear of being passive find it very hard to sleep. People who are suspicious, or impatient, or impulsive, and who equate passivity with femininity are afraid of being passive. They will unconsciously fight against sleep. It is relatively easy for people who are essentially feminine and passive and dependent, and who are naive and optimistic and trustful to sleep. To be able to sleep means to be willing to give up your control, willing to trust your unconscious mind, and not only your own unconscious mind, but to trust the world around you. When you sleep you are vulnerable. You are exposed.

If you live in a hostile world, if you are full of suspicion and mistrust, if you are afraid that you will be killed or attacked, or that you will lose control and soil and wet, you will also have difficulty sleeping. Guilt laden people who fear punishment, particularly from God or from the superego, have a hard time giving up control. Macbeth [Act II, Scene 2] said:

> "Me thought I hears a voice cry, 'Sleep no
> more! Macbeth does murder sleep' the innocent sleep,
> Sleep that knits up the raveled sleave of care."

For people who are relatively free of neurotic or real guilt and who are free of shame it is easy to sleep and to be at peace with themselves. To be able to sleep you must be willing to be alone; though I must modify that. In sleep you are with your past feelings, memories, and past object relations. In the regression of sleep you give up all external people. You may start out by holding onto something but you give up this external holding on, and go through a phase when all you have is what is inside you, the memories of past relationships. Therefore, no one ever really sleeps alone, only in death are we alone.

When we sleep we not only give up external relationships to people and go back to memories, but we go back to the *earliest* memories. In a sense, one returns to the earliest memories of childhood. People who have had terrible childhood experiences have difficulty in sleeping unless they have overcome them. Above all, in sleep one returns to the memories of the earliest mothering object, and if one has had some loving object in early childhood and one is able to let oneself regress to the memories of that object, one will be able to sleep.

As you fall asleep you regress step by step. In every phase of the mind's activities, you go from the highest to the lowest. The most recent acquisitions leave you and you go to the more primitive, through every earlier phase of development, and you end up with no more than a sensation. The dreamless sleep is a sleep full of only a sensation. A blank dream is whatever you want to call it. This is what dreamless sleep is all about. Many people are afraid of this deep dreamless sleep, or they are afraid of the dreaming part of sleep and they take pills, alcohol, drugs, to neutralize one or another aspect of sleep. They want to skip it or to go past the dream very quickly.

Now, about dreams. You know Freud considered his book, *The Interpretation of Dreams*, his greatest contribution. It was published in 1900. And he himself said about that book, "insights such as this, fall to one's lot only once in a lifetime." It is one of the two books he edited again and again. All the rest he wrote and never reedited. This book he constantly changed. He started writing it in 1896 when he was forty years old. It was shortly after the death of his father, which upset him mightily. And in trying to analyze himself, Freud used his dreams and *The Interpretation of Dreams* was the result. I might add a historical note: he finished it in 1899 but the publisher thought it would be a bigger success if it was published in 1900, so they waited a few months and published it in 1900. It sold 351 copies in six years, for which Freud received in total $209.00.

Let me give you some of the main points about dreams. First of all, the dream is the guardian of sleep. It protects the sleeper from disturbing stimuli, external or internal. Example: You sleep and the blanket falls off. If you are able to dream, you dream something like you are ice skating, there is a brisk wind, but it is invigorating, you are with a charming woman, etc. And there you are ice skating and you are cold and you continue sleeping. But if you don't dream, you wake up; where is the blanket? It is a simple example but it is pertinent. What is the function of the dream? To protect the sleeper from disturbing stimuli. That was an external stimulus, but it also protects you from internal stimuli. Now let me give you an example of how a dream protects you from disturbing internal stimuli. I will take an example from some years ago.

A woman patient of mine, who had been in analysis a short time, six or nine months, told me the following dream: She is going to a doctor because her feet hurt her. And especially one foot hurts her in the back of the foot. She goes to this doctor who is a kindly old doctor. He examines her foot very carefully. But it is peculiar how he does it. He is very tender and gentle and never takes her shoes off. Then he says to her, "Oh, it is nothing to worry about. All you have is Hodges' disease." That was her dream.

Now, in associating or letting her thoughts drift about the dream, let me tell you something of what came out. The kindly doctor, well, she once had or knew such a kindly doctor in her childhood. He was an older man; he is now dead. He was an old-fashioned man, and he had an old-fashioned office. It was sort of sloppy and disheveled. "Not like your office, Doctor Greenson, not so modern and 'ritzy,' and cold; but warm and friendly. And the way he treated me, kindly, gentle, not like you. You are cold, icy." That was the first group of thoughts. Then: "I never had trouble with my feet. I had trouble with lots of other things but my feet, in fact, I'm proud of. I have beautiful feet. I don't know if you ever noticed it, doctor. But I am proud of my feet. And you know I am also very ticklish on my feet. And I remember now a game I played with my brother in which we used to tickle our feet and it was very funny, he used to be overbearing. He was older than I and he took advantage of me and he pushed me around. (The back of her foot hurt her, i.e., that heel, her brother.) That sickness, Hodge's disease, it's a funny thing I saw a television show," she said. "And there I saw a woman and she had some terrible disease, and she was dying from that disease. It was incurable and it sounded something like Hodge's disease." And I said, "It wasn't Hodge's disease, it was Hodgkin's disease. And what you left out, what you censored was the *kin*, Hodg-kin disease." The disease that she suffers from is a disease of her kin, her relatives, her brother.

Do you see what the dream did? Here was a woman resenting her doctor. So she dreams about a nice kindly old-fashioned doctor, who doesn't even examine her beyond her shoe. However, what really bothers her is her whole life situation, her soul, her emotional life. The dream says, "No, it is just your foot." And then the dream says the people you cannot bear are nothing to you, "It's only Hodges' disease." When in reality her brother, the heel, and her father, mother, all her kin are killing her. Note how the dream tried to make these painful stimuli, painless, and how it succeeded. She dreamed and she slept because the dream protected her sleep. How, asked Freud? By wish fulfillment. By taking painful stimuli and by transforming them into something pleasurable, or endurable, or at least sleepable.

Freud said much more about dreams, such as in order to understand the wish fulfillment of a dream you have to hear the patient's associations. Dreams never concern trivialities. The ego functions continue in dreams although diminished. There is still censorship and defenses only less severe, less strict. There are distortion and disguise like condensation, symbolization, and so on. There is always, or almost always, some awareness of dreaming. Ninety-nine times out of a hundred you know you are dreaming. It is a rare time when you wake up and think: Well, it's only a dream. Most of the time you wake up and you know you were dreaming. Sometimes one dreams of having a dream, yet goes on sleeping because it is only a dream. But above all, Freud stressed the regression in the thinking and the ego functions.

We dream every night as part of the process of falling asleep but we tend to forget our dreams. We forget them because so often they are painful to remember when we awake. This is a very crucial point; the attitude toward our bad dreams not our good dreams. And I say to you, a person who dares to remember his bad dreams can generally forget his psychoanalyst. Why do we have painful dreams? We may dream painful dreams because of our wish or our need to be punished, out of a sense of guilt, or out of a masochistic need. But sometimes dreams fail to fulfill their wishful function. The dream tries to make a disturbing stimulus pleasurable, it fails and you wake up with a nightmare. Another category of painful dreams are the dreams about traumatic events. You have an accident; you go to bed and you dream about the accident. Why? Wishful or punishment? Not necessarily. Freud puzzled and puzzled about this type of dream, the dreams of trauma, the dreams of shock. Why do we repeatedly have them? I will come back to what he answered finally many years later.

In the meantime, let me add some recent work on dreams which is very interesting. In the last few years a group of workers, Kleitman, Dement, and others, did experiments by attaching an electroencephalogram apparatus to the heads of sleeping volunteers and found that they could determine when these people were deeply asleep without dreams or when they were dreaming, by studying their electrical wave patterns. That experiment made it very clear that everyone who slept dreamt many times every night, between four and seven times. But even more interesting, they then went on and awakened people when they started to dream. (They could tell that by the electroencephalographic patterns or by the ocular movements under the eyelids.) They woke them everytime they began to dream; interrupted the dream, and then let them go back to sleep. Everytime they dreamt, they woke them. They found, amazingly, that if you did this, these people became extraordinarily disturbed. Like I described sleep deprivation, you saw dream deprivation. These people developed difficulty in their thinking, perceptions, and concentration. They developed hallucinations and pathological outbursts of aggression. Once the experiment was stopped, they dreamed two or three times as much as they would have normally. As though they had a dream hunger or a dream deficit. However, the question arose, how do we know that this isn't caused by the sleep being disturbed rather than the dream? So they did the same experiment again, interrupting the sleep of their subjects not when they were dreaming, but when they were not dreaming. There was no trouble; they had none of the symptoms that I described above. The crucial pathology of sleep is dream pathology.

There are many other interesting things about dreams. Just a word or two about that. Dreams and schizophrenia, Rosen's idea that schizophrenics are really in a dream state. Lewin's work about dreams of depressives and the question of an unconscious relationship to the mother's breast. Color in dreams, some interesting ideas of Calif, Linn, and others about people who occasionally dream in color. I have found that painters always dream in colors; in fact, they look at you and say, "Well, don't you?" And I have come to a conclusion, a temporary conclusion, that everybody dreams in colors every night and it is washed out and filtered out in the process of waking up. Like when you say, "Oh, I dreamt there was this blood," and you may wonder how did you know it was blood. I think you knew it was blood because it was red. There was color but you censored the color, repressed it, as you woke up. A man named Blank did some interesting work on blind people's dreams and found it fascinating. Blind people do not dream in visual images, but in sounds, in touch, in temperature, in movement.

I want to go back to Freud who was struggling with "why do we dream traumatic dreams?" Freud struggled with the problem from 1899 to 1920. Why this repetition of painful dreams? In 1920 he wrote a book, *Beyond the Pleasure Principle*. He had postulated before that the search for pleasure is a basic drive and now he made an important amendment. Something else, another kind of a drive, beyond pleasure, has to do with the need to repeat and repeat. A repetition compulsion. And what is that urge to repeat? He said it is derived from a deep-seated instinctual drive which propels all living creatures to return to what they originally were: inanimate, inorganic, dead. He felt there was a death instinct driving man and all living creatures to die.

Freud offered these ideas rather modestly. He considered them speculations, hypothesis. "I do not urge you to agree, I only urge you to pay attention." He predicted that these ideas would be most unpopular. The psychoanalysts themselves never fully accepted these ideas. I would say today only a minority accept the notion of a death instinct.

What does this mean? To be brief, there are two sets of instincts, said Freud. One, the life instincts represented by love, sex, self-preservation. The aim of this group of instincts, is to form close units, relationships, to build higher and higher, bigger and bigger combinations of units. These are the life instincts. There's another set, the death instincts, which are relatively mute but which are manifested by sadism, by hate, by this compulsion to repeat, and, later on, Freud added, by all the destructive urges of aggression and hostility. These are the manifestations of the death instinct. What is their aim? Not pleasure, but the return to a tensionless state of unanimation or inanimate being—back to an inorganic, old state from which we once came, when we were inorganic matter, dead.

All of life, Freud said, is a compromise between these two conflicting forces; forces to live, love, preserve, versus forces to destroy and to die. These instincts fuse together and that's how they manage to hold each other in check, and when they defuse and separate, then you get the real morbid pathology. What was his evidence for these theories? He admitted it was flimsy.

Freud found clinically deep masochistic urges originating seemingly from early childhood on, in those unconsciously guilty people who seem driven to hurt themselves or kill themselves in one form or another. He found it in the paranoids, the severe obsessionals, and in the negative therapeutic reactions of some patients who go for years and years in analysis and instead of improving, only get worse. He thought perhaps it was not only the fault of the analyst, but also the need of some people to be miserable, to suffer and to die. He considered the fact that certain animals, certain fish, will travel hundreds and thousands of miles to get to certain places in order to spawn and die; certain birds who seem driven to die in a certain way, in a certain place. Other animals die after sexual satisfaction. For some human beings the pleasurable sensation after full sexual satisfaction is often described as resembling death, a pleasant death. Freud said, look, these are speculations, but he felt he had touched on something important.

My own position about this, I must say, is uncertain. I am more and more inclined of late to accept the theory of a death instinct, because I have been terribly impressed by the overwhelming prevalence of destructiveness and hostility in all people. I am struck by the fact that the more infantile people are, the more regressed, the more deadly, the more destructive, the more self-destructive they become. I am more and more convinced that the only thing that has a chance to keep people from killing themselves and others is to have some deep experience of being loved by somebody, and that if children do not have this experience early, they die or become psychotic. If people do not have it later on in life they too will either die or kill somebody—in some form or other.

With all this I still want to say I'm not altogether convinced about a death instinct. Much of the pathology could be explained on the basis that there are destructive drives which start out with external hating of those people who hurt and frustrate you. When these frustrations arise you become afraid of destroying the people who you also love and need and as a defense against those impulses the destructiveness becomes internalized. That is how you get a destructive instinct originating from external sources rather than an originally internal death instinct.

Let me go on with this discussion of death. What is the fear of death all about and what can we do about it? And now I speak for myself alone.

Part of the difficulty is that people confuse the two components of death: death and dying. They are to be separated. Although both are unpleasant and frightening, people fear each of them differently. To some people, dying is terrible. And death is not so bad, and visa versa. Montaigne, you known, said "It is not death but dying that alarms me." On the other hand, I read a poem by e.e. cummings, whom I admire, who said exactly the opposite. Let me mention it briefly:

dying is fine)but Death

?o
baby
i

wouldn't like

Death if Death
were
good:for

when(instead of stopping to think)you

begin to feel of it,dying
's miraculous
why?be

cause dying is

perfectly natural;perfectly
putting
it mildly lively(but

Death

is strictly
scientific
&artificial&

evil & legal)

we thank thee
god
almighty for dying

(forgive us,o life!the sin of Death)

The only thing e.e. cummings capitalizes is Death. I must say I disagree with him wholeheartedly. I think what is great is when you are far away from dying. But, the closer you get it becomes quite evident that dying is the more frightening, though both are no bargain.

Well, what is frightening about it? Let me say we know much more about dying than about death. We know about dying from people who have been close to dying and we know something of their experiences, and of their fantastic notions about it. But about death we know little. We have never been dead and at the same time conscious, thinking, and perceptive. Recently I read a book by Feifil which contains very interesting ideas about death and which prompted me to talk about this. Freud's notion was that when we were children we had no conception of death, that people live and go on living. The only conception of death a child has is that somebody is gone or absent. And, in fact, in dreams the symbol for death is somebody goes on a trip or is away or is missing. All death notions occur late in childhood, usually four, five, six, somewhere in there, if not later. But what we do find is childhood anxieties getting displaced later onto death. Let me mention a few neurotic, unrealistic fantasies about dying. I want to underline: these are unrealistic and neurotic. For many people death and dying means torture. Now this is strange because actually in most instances of dying, today with modern medicine, modern drugs and modern surgery, there is relatively little torture. You find that when a person really goes through a closeness to death, the perception, the thinking, all of this is diminished, and if you talk with people who have made a suicide attempt and have recovered (if it wasn't swallowing some corrosive poison, but let's say, taking sleeping pills) it is interesting how rarely they experienced this as something horrible.

The closest picture we can get to what death is like, and this is purely an approximation and perhaps some wishful thinking, is that it is like sleep, the dreamless blank sleep, even deeper. But, again I say we have little evidence. This is pure speculation. But the tortures, what are all the tortures people imagine about death that make them so panicky? If you study this you get some very interesting fantasies. Let me point them out to you.

For many people death and dying is awful and torturesome because of being helpless. Now why is helplessness equated with torture? Again, it's like what we talked about with sleep. Why is passivity so terrifying? Yes, if you live in a world full of monsters, then helplessness and passivity is terrifying. Or, death and dying means loss of control. Which means being at the mercy of terrible instincts or being overwhelmed by shameful impulses and so forth. Or, death and dying means body destruction either on the level of castration or on another level of body damage, of complete bodily obliteration and extinction. In all these fantasies there is some childhood dread, some childhood anxiety that has been displaced onto death.

The fear of the unknown is also claimed to be terrifying. But, why must the unknown always be terrible and awful? Unless we project all kinds of terrifying things onto the unknown, the fear of nothingness, fear of loss of identity, extinction, obliteration of the self. But, wait a minute. If you are dead you are not perceiving this. You cannot have it both ways; now you are dead and now you say, look at me, poor me, dead without any identity. A real distortion here of feeling sorry for yourself, and a kind of animistic thinking. You still imagine that you are dead, but think at the same time, 'I am alive,' which cannot be true.

A man who had an identity when he was alive, has an identity when he is dead. He cannot be aware of it, but others are. And, if he had none, if he was a glob when he was alive, then he is a dead glob. Let me be clear, I do not mean that a man has to have fame or fortune or popularity, please no. Only an identity, he was a person, he had characteristics, and you could tell him apart from him or her or it. Others say that death is frightening because it is lonely; that, too, is animistic thinking. If you are dead, you are not thinking, and if you are not dead, what are you worrying about? This whole idea of, I am dead but I want togetherness, is a childhood conception of abandonment now projected onto death. I am dead, poor me, all alone. These people who do not have the capacity to be alone without getting lonely.

All these terrors can be condensed into the following. Either they are due to magical animistic thinking and feeling sorry for oneself, or death has become personified into the grim reaper, the devil, and witches one had in childhood; these anxieties are displaced and become now remobilized as the fear of death. All this is loaded with hostility. Death has become aggressified, dying has become aggressified. All kinds of destructive impulses are displaced onto death and dying by people who fear punishment for their hostile and sexual impulses. They are loaded with unresolved hostilities, have little capacity for love which would neutralize their fear of death.

There are other problems. I maintain that you cannot properly handle the fear of death by the following maneuvers; these are points I want to attack. Fear of death cannot be handled by denying it; nor by believing in immortality, which the religions try to offer you. Religious people for the most part fear death more than unreligious people. I believe it is too high a price to pay to be an orthodox religious person in order to gain some belief in immortality. The whole notion of the soul was invented to belittle physical death and promote some notion that the mind has a separate existence; I do not believe it, although I wish it were true. I think this is some form of a bribe to accept some kind of religious worship. I do not believe in glorifying death and making life all the more drab, and that is what they try to do. The more you glamorize death and immortality and the hereafter, the more drab and unimportant and degraded is life. I do not believe that death is a fulfillment or that it is the beginning of eternity, or what the existentialists and Zen Buddhists seem to be saying that the only way to really get the quintessence of living is by dying. I would lump them all together as some kind of escape from life, an attempt to deny that there is death. All denial mechanisms are unreliable, fragile devices that take tremendous effort to maintain, and they usually fail.

Neither do I believe that the way to handle the fear of death is to be in a state of vigilance, devoting your life to various safety measures. I do not believe the safety seekers are ever better prepared. Quite the contrary, people who devote their life to safety are constantly living with death. That is their companion, not you, or me, husband, wife, child—death is their constant companion. These people live very little with other human beings and have little happiness. These frightened ones who are being vigilant and are striving for security, they are the ones, paranoid in their basic makeup, suspicious and obsessed with ideas of death, who want to drop H-bombs, have private shelters, and want to renounce living to save their miserable lives. I do not want to live in a fallout shelter. I do not think that is much of a life. I do not want to die either, but I am not ready to be on perpetual alert.

It is interesting how many people who are so afraid of dying will kill themselves to avoid dying. Many suicides are committed by people who are terrified of dying in one way but will kill themselves in order to die in their own way.

Just as I do not approve of the safety addicts, I also do not believe in a third group, the death seekers. They are the ones who, instead of being afraid of death, are always going out with open arms to woo death, to get close to it. You know, the impulse ridden, counterphobics, psychopaths; the addicts who are constantly searching for some kind of oblivion. They really are seeking some kind of death, a peaceful nothingness. The Miltown eaters, the alcohol addicts, all belong to the oblivion-seeking people. They have perhaps given up living, and have already started dying, only a little bit is still alive. I do not believe any of these methods succeed in handling the fear of death.

Now I have come to the end of my presentation and you may say, all right, now you have told us what is wrong and what is bad, so now what do you have to say that is positive? What is a healthy, realistic attitude toward death? I will start by saying: the capacity on the one hand to face death, but also to be able to push it away, to not think of it. Face it when there is a reason to face it, when death is imminent; somebody's death or your own, or society's. But not to live with it as your constant companion, to be able to forget it, to repress it, to suppress it. Not to deny it or glamorize it. Death is unpleasant, it is painful, it is sad, to say the least. But, neither dying or death has to be a sheer terror. It should not and does not have to be unbearable. One should be able to die as a human being, decently. That is enough.

The realistic pain in death is due to the fact that death is inevitable, it is inescapable, it is inexorable. There is no choice about death, one must die, one has to die, eventually. How, when, and where may be altered in one way or another. But eventually, time wins out and we all have to die. However, I want to emphasize that this is one of the great bonds of suffering that man shares with *all* his brothers. It is the one place where we are all equal victims, where we are all equally tyrannized. Death is the only common enemy of man. To realize this makes a person who faces death feel a certain closeness to his fellow man, and feel a common bond of hating all forms of tyranny. It makes people who are civilized and intelligent love the opposite—freedom. Freedom is the great antithesis to death. And people who are aware of death but do not dread it or worship it, cherish freedom, they cherish their options.

I want to mention a side issue. People who recognize death for what it is hate capital punishment. If you are familiar with Albert Camus, and I would recommend you read him, you know there was a man who loved liberty and freedom and hated death. I want to quote what he said about capital punishment:

> Blood thirsty laws, it has been said, make blood thirsty customs. But any society eventually reaches a state of ignonomy, in which despite every disorder the customs never manage to be as blood thirsty as the laws. Those executed during the occupation led to those executed at the time of liberation, whose friends now dream of revenge. Elsewhere, states laden with too many crimes are getting ready to drown their guilt in even greater massacres. One kills for a nation, or a class that has been granted the divine status. One kills for a future society that has likewise been given divine status.

In another place, he says:

> If public opinion and its representatives cannot give up the law of laziness which simply eliminates what it cannot reform, let us at least while hoping for a new truth, not make of it the solemn slaughterhouse that befouls our society. A death penalty as it is now applied, and however rarely it may be, is a revolting butchery and outrage inflicted on the person and body of man.

I quote this because it is inconceivable to me how a person can think about death and face its inevitability and still believe in capital punishment.

People fear death because death is really truly the end of life, the termination. There are those who hate to give up life because life is joyful and they hate, therefore, to die. Life offers hope, and it is sad to die, even when you are disappointed, as long as you have some hope. Only the hopeless want to die, and, interestingly enough, they do. You know they are the only unexplained deaths in medicine today. Hopelessness can cause death. Apathetic children who are deprived of love for prolonged periods in early childhood, die. Experiments with mice show the same thing. But, all the rest of us want to live. The sick want to live, even the old. I spoke to an old lady I know, a friend, who said, "Don't believe it when they tell you that when you get to be seventy-five you don't care about living. We pretend it. We want to live every day, and another, and another, just as much as you."

I have only a few more points to make. One: There are things even worse than death. If you can really believe that, it is a consolation, small, but it is a consolation. I believe torture, slavery, and tyranny, are worse than death.

Second, one can die more easily for a cause than under any other circumstances. I think there are times when a healthy adult human being is unafraid of death. When he is full of righteous anger and hate, but righteous anger and hate without guilt, he will be unafraid to die. If you love justice, and you must be a justice lover to hate without guilt, and you see a little child being mistreated, I am sure you could attack the biggest bully and monster without any fear of dying and without any thought as to the consequences. But for that you have to care about people, you must be involved, it must matter to you.

Another point, if you want to face death without panic, you must have respect for yourself. You have to retain the sense of who you are even in sickness, even in pain. It is not loving yourself, it is not narcissism; it is not grandiosity, it is accepting who you are, and not giving it up, because you are in pain, or frightened. Not changing your name or your religion, your beliefs, your values, because you are scared. The atom scientists who become religious at the last moment of life because of their guilt for Hiroshima—I must say though, I can understand them, I do pity them. One has to respect one's past and face death in one's own way. Freud, after twenty years of cancer and some twenty-five operations, finally resigned himself that he was going to die and wanted to die. He was eighty-three years old. He did it with dignity, quietly and resignedly. That was his way. He was a great man and an old man.

Others can do it in other ways. Dylan Thomas, the poet, died at thirty-nine, and I will quote a passage from a poem of his: "Do not go gentle into that good night; rage, rage, against the dying of the light." He died an alcoholic. I cannot say raging was wrong for him, I have a feeling raging was more honest, it suited him, he was an angry man, many of us are.

There is only one kind of immortality that I believe in and that is to be remembered as a person who mattered and that people who matter to you remember you. But that kind of immortality is only for those people who care about others, not only themselves. For that you must be committed and, above all, you must be involved not only with your own circle of friends, but with the next generation, the children, the pupils, the students, the young. I think if one does that, one has achieved some form of immortality. It is only a small consolation, but it is realistic.

I want to conclude by saying I fully believe that life and living is to be enjoyed to the fullest, and death and dying is only to be endured. That's all—but that we should be able to do. I am sorry that I have no cheerful answers, my answers are hard. But to paraphrase something Freud once said, what one cannot reach by flying, we must reach by limping. Thank you.

# 6 Varieties of Love (1961)

*This lecture deals with many different aspects of the alienation of feelings. In "Varieties of Love," Romi feels that the emotion of love is neglected and not respected in American society. With particular relevance for the materialistic 1980s and 1990s, Greenson described how love is far less important to most people and especially to our youth than success or security or popularity. In this lecture, he made the important distinction between the passive wish to be loved and the active capacity to love another. This lecture is a tour-de-force in that Greenson, ever the modern developmentalist, traces the very origins of the capacity to love through the entire life cycle. In doing so, he anticipated in 1961 the discussions of narcissism, object relations, and the problems of establishing and maintaining intimacy that occupy center stage in psychoanalysis today.*

Ladies and Gentlemen, my subject is the varieties of love. Now, I do not know what you expected when you heard that title,

---

Presented as a broadcast on KPFA-FM radio station 94.1, Berkeley, on October 5 and 27, 1961.

but I would like to begin by disenchanting you if you hoped to find here some kind of do-it-yourself kit on the approach to love. This is not entirely a humorous remark because some people, supposedly intelligent, and even scientifically trained, and even so-called analysts, have stated that love is an art that can be taught. I disagree. You've come to the wrong place if that is what you expected. No, my point of view about the subject of love is quite different. One cannot teach people how to love. One can help those who are disturbed in their capacity for love by removing the obstacles which keep them from loving. The inability to love, restrictions in love, inhibitions of love, all of these are a sickness and require treatment to a greater or lesser degree.

The subject of love is an enormous one, complicated, complex, difficult, because we mean so many different things when we talk about love. Love, as you know, according to the poets, the writers, and even the philosophers, romantic love is one of the most powerful of human emotions, and one of the most normal. It is the source in fact of greatness, of creativity; it is a source in fact of life. And yet this love, which is so ennobling and enriching, when frustrated can lead to terrible hatred and destruction. Love on the other hand, if you observe scientifically, psychologically, is also a passion, a lust, and at the same time, love is also tenderness, gentleness, concern, affection. Love is an appetite, a craving, a hunger, a greed, basic, animal-like, and yet it is the source of altruism, compassion, friendship. Love brings great joy and pleasure and also the greatest tragedies concern love. All of this is true.

But it is even more complicated than this because when we talk of love, we can talk about it in terms of man's and woman's love for one another, romantic, passionate, powerful, or we can talk about motherly love, fatherly love, the love for a child, or platonic love; or, for some people, love means the love of God, and to others yet, the love of truth. And all these are varieties of love. All that I have said indicates, I hope, to you how enormous and how complicated our subject is, and also I hope it has indicated to you how terribly important. Yes, love is an appetite, an instinct, a hunger, but love can be changed and transformed. Yes, love can be irrational, overwhelming, but love can be tamed and civilized. Yes, love is childish, infantile, narcissistic, but love can grow and mature. Love is many things to many people and different things to many people, and I would like to make some order in this huge panorama that I have sketched, and make some order in your thinking about love from the point of view of a psychoanalyst. My approach to this subject stems essentially from the work of Sigmund Freud, and some of his followers; to mention a few, Karl Abraham, Otto Fenichel, Eric Erikson, and also there is a touch of Greenson in all of this which I cannot avoid.

Now, I have chosen this subject for tonight's talk, love, the varieties of love, because in my opinion the emotion of love is neglected and disrespected in our society, and in our country. It is far less important to most people, and particularly to our youth, than success, or security, or popularity. If you ask people, "What do you want out of life?" the answer you will get is, "I want security, I want success, fame, money. I want lots of friends." Whatever they say, it all boils down to something which is not love. It is *being* loved, which is very different, enormously different. The wish to be loved, I will talk about this later. I speak about the subject because love is confused, in many people's minds, with sexual satisfaction and they equate enjoying somebody sexually, having a pleasant time physically, with love. Or, they confuse it with peacefulness. "I live with her and she doesn't bother me and I don't bother her and we love each other." And this is not love. It is a question if this is living! No, love and the capacity to love, is relatively rare in our society. I think if you look around you, you will see how rare it is to find a married couple who love each other, and enjoy each other. How rare it is. How much more we find the many divorces and the separations, and the alienations, and the running away from people, from places, from things. Television is so popular because it keeps you from loving or hating anybody. Unfortunately in our society, to talk about love or to believe in love is either considered corny or weak or perhaps subversive. Sounds like a foreign idea—love. Or, if not that, at least perverse. There must be something sick about this. Yeah. And so, I would like to talk about it, to try to educate you differently about this subject.

According to the tried and true formula of the psychoanalytic point of view, we try to understand any complex phenomenon in our society, or in a person, by asking where does it begin, what is its origin? In my opinion, the high point, the epitome of love, is the capacity of a man and woman to love each other, emotionally, spiritually, intellectually, sexually. This is the high point, but there are other kinds and varieties and forms of love. Where does all of this begin? If we understand its origins and its maturational development, we can perhaps get a good insight into some of the problems concerning love.

So, bear with me if I start with the newborn baby and ask the question, "Does the newborn baby love?" and the answer is "No." No, babies are not born with the ability to love. Babies try to breathe and to eat. They have no concern for anything except survival for the first days, weeks, and months of life. But they are born with hunger, and hunger drives them toward somebody, toward something outside themselves, and the forerunner, the antecedent of love, is hunger. The child is hungry, and his hunger is painful, and he craves and needs something from the outside world to fill this terrible miserable emptiness inside him. What he needs is milk, and he needs it to be given to him, and if this is done, this miserable, cold infant is transported from gloom and despair and pain and anguish into a blissful state of satisfaction. And when he feels this he sleeps. This peculiar polarity, pain, craving, longing, some kind of satisfaction and oblivion, peaceful oblivion, is not love. It is a search for satisfaction, it is an attempt to satisfy needs, it is an attempt to get rid of terrible pain, it is the attempt to find certain wonderful sensations that lead to a peaceful oblivion. This is not love.

This search for oblivion, I want to point out to you, exists in grown-up people too, who do not want to live, but they want to black out. The alcoholic who gets stuporously drunk, the addict, the LSD people now running around for all kinds of extravagant sensations, are stuck back there, looking for sensations, and this has nothing to do with love, although it is the forerunner. It has nothing to do with love because the character, the individuality of the person giving the food is unimportant. They want the food, the milk, the liquor, the dope, but who brings it is unimportant. And you cannot call anything love until the character of the donor, the individuality of the person, is the important thing. If that doesn't matter, you are talking about something besides love.

But, let me go on. The infant is interested in getting something. He is passive about it, he is helpless about it. Whether he gets it or not is the all important factor, but when he gets it he loses all interest in the outside world. Now, interestingly enough, this is true for the first few months of life and then it is not true any more. Just giving an infant milk does not suffice to keep a child alive. They have found in studying children brought up in orphanages, who were neglected by their mothers, or deserted by their mothers, these children who were given a good diet of vitamins and food and milk and cleanliness, these children became apathetic and depressed, and they died. And they could not find a good medical diagnosis for it. But, they died. They died [at a rate] four times as high as children brought up under other circumstances. And so they decided to bring in, hire women, who would, in addition to seeing that the children got the food, hold the children on their laps and cuddle them and rock them for twenty minutes a day, twice a day; and the children stopped dying.

This is not a fairy tale. This is a scientific fact. Already in the first six months of life, getting rid of hunger for food is not enough. Children need tender, loving care, touch, warmth, cuddling. They need a person, not an apparatus, if they are going to survive. Nevertheless, I think you will see here that the person who gives it is not important, it is only important that they get it. So this is still not love, it is a forerunner. It begins to have some resemblance, but it is still not love. Some person who has warmth, that is what they need. What is important, however, at this time, is that if a child is given milk and some tender loving care with any degree of reliability and regularity, it can develop one of the most important ingredients to what will later become love, namely trust. In the first year or year-and-a-half of life, what a psychologically healthy child can develop is the capacity to trust, to depend that something will come from the outside world.

That is an enormous accomplishment because many, many people do not achieve it, and live their lives full of mistrust, full of readiness to expect evil and hurt and disappointment. This is the first failure of life, mistrust, and the first success, the capacity to trust, to expect something good. Those people who are stuck at this early stage of development, and there are many who are, only are interested in, "What can I get out of you?

What's in it for me?" Their conception of love is only getting, gimme, gimme, gimme, gimme, momma, in some form or another. They have still no idea of giving, only getting. And, as I said before, I think you know people like this. We would not call them our best friends, but other people's friends, who still are oriented to "What can I get," and "I only wanna get, and then I might give, but first I wanna get. And once I get, then I can turn over and go to sleep. Or watch television. Or something." As I said, this is the early phase of love; it is certainly very far removed from love and a long way off from what we are considering today, some of the more mature aspects of love.

Let me go on to a second phase of love, or the next phase of development, and what it contributes to what becomes love. Here I am talking of that time of life, usually somewhere around one-and-a-half to three years of age, where the child learns to master walking, it has mobility, it can escape, it can go away from things. Second, the mastery of speech, it can communicate, not just emotions but thoughts and ideas. And, third, it has control over its bodily sphinctus. It is toilet trained, it can be clean or it can be dirty, it has some choice. This is also an extremely important development because you have the first independence, the first possibility to rebel or submit. Here you have the first possessions. Here the child is able to distinguish what is "I," what is "me," what is "mine," and what is "you," or "yours." He distinguishes me from you, and what is mine and what is yours. Possessions mean something to him. Here is the first mastery, control of walking, control of talking, control over toilet functions. Here you have either the first sense of accomplishment, or the first sense of failure; the first sense of control, or the first sense of doubt and shame. Here you also get the first ambivalence. Love and hate, positive and negative, kinds of feelings toward the same person. There is a good mommy and a bad mommy, but it is still mommy. And they learn to feel, both love and anger and resentment and affection and hostility and friendliness to the same person. If all of this succeeds at this particular time, the child will develop a sense of pride, a sense of control, a sense of autonomy, mastery; and if it fails he will become a doubter and one full of shame.

People who grow up and are still fixated to this way of feeling and reacting are people who are afraid to fall in love because any kind of love is to them a danger. It is a loss of control, and loss of control means making a mess. They think any kind of strong emotion which you could lose control of is shameful, dirty. They confuse sexual matters with toilet matters. They are all the same. They confuse loving someone and becoming a slave to someone, or loving someone and becoming a tyrant, a possessor of somebody. Very often they are collectors of people. They think they love, but they really possess somebody. And then they say, "Look what I got. How d'ya like what I *got*?" And they call it love. They love to show off their possession of their wife or their husband, to strangers or at parties, but at home they are bored, because all these people are to them are objects of value, collector's items.

I go on to a third phase, age three to seven roughly, and this I think is well known to many of you. We call it the oedipal phase of development. This is the time of life when the boy or the girl, who is healthy, develops the capacity to feel not only love and tenderness and affection, but also has sexual feelings for those closest to him: for the family. Naturally, who else should they feel it for? The outsider? This combination of, on the one hand, feeling love and sexual feelings to one parent, and to feel at the same time jealousy and rivalry and hostility to the other parent, this combination of events we call the Oedipus complex. It is crucial in the emotional development of the child. It is the source of more difficulties than any other single goings on in bringing up a child. However, it does not have to be traumatic, it does not have to be a failure. This combination of love and sex to a parent of the opposite sex primarily, and hostile jealousy, death wishes, hatred, rivalry to the parent of the same sex, brings with it great guilt, because children also love their fathers and mothers. They want them and need them. It isn't so simple that they are just carried away by passion and that is all. There is a lot of conflict and a lot of guilt. I stress all of this because this is the first time in a child's development where not only certain affectionate, tender needs are involved, but also the genital organs. This is part of how they love, and this causes a great deal of difficulty.

I want to say here that the struggle with this triangular situation is of greatest importance to whether or not a child is going to develop the capacity to have romantic feelings of love, and sexual feelings toward the same person. Whether or not they are successful in this phase of development will determine what kind of a conscience they will develop, a reasonably healthy conscience, or a tyrannical, severe conscience that will torment them. Will they develop ideals and standards and goals of importance, or will they be delinquents and psychopaths, derelicts? If this phase is successful, the child gives up its sexual feelings, because it is unable to handle them, it is too young. They are repressed, or deflected, and go into other channels. The child retains its affection toward the parent of the opposite sex, its tenderness, its caring; its rivalry still exists but it is now a friendlier rivalry, with the wish to become like the father. At this time of life, boys become boyish, girls become girlish, there is a definite difference in them, which might not have been discernible in their behavior before. Now you see a certain manliness about the boy in his imitation of the father, and a certain femininity in the girl, as she imitates her mother in certain ways; that is, if the situation is worked out in a healthy way, without tyrannical suppression or neglectful indulgence—either of which would be wrong.

If this phase of development is successful, the child develops the capacity for initiative, to risk, to dare loving, to take a chance and love somebody. If it fails, the child will become guilt-ridden, it will not be able to love along with sexual feelings, it will tend to become withdrawn from all kinds of intimacies, it will become timid, it will become afraid of people. Adults who grow up and who have never successfully gone through this phase of development, who are fixated on this level, can be recognized by certain characteristics. They tend to always get involved in triangular affairs, men who never can love a free woman, only a married woman, or the best friend of their good friend, or the sweetheart of their good friend. Always triangles, falling in love with somebody who belongs to somebody else.

A typical sign of childhood oedipal stage of development is seen in people who can only fall in love with someone old enough to be their fathers or mothers. Women who can only love a man 25 to 30 years older. Also a sign of oedipal fixation are people for whom love is possible but love without genital organ involvement. Or, they only love that person because of his genitals. Curious combinations of things. You know there are some women who love a man, not because of what he is, but because he represents to them somehow an idealized genital. This might sound strange to you but so does sometimes a man love a woman just because he wants to show her off. Look what I got. And it is, to him, an idealized part of the sexual apparatus of his own body. Curious. And all of these confusions about love and sex and genitals come from difficulties in this particular phase.

I want to go on. Latency, ages 7 to 12, is very complicated because at this time we get the development of ideals, values, the rights and wrongs, what is important in life. At this time the child who is healthy, and who has gone through what I have described more or less successfully, now sets up in himself something which is wonderful, something which is bigger than himself, *a conscience*. What happens to this conscience plays a very important role in people's lives. In some it becomes a tyrant, drives them unmercifully, cruel, mean, sadistic, instinctualized. In others, it becomes something so awe inspiring that it is transferred outside and now God is made to be the bearer of the ideals. Come look to God, this mighty omnipotent omniscient creature above, and feel low and craven compared to Him. Such, too, is a distortion in the development of the conscience. In others what is valued is not anything omnipotent or omniscient but rather the search for law and order and truth, which it is felt man can attain, and these become the ideals that are striven for. All of these are developments of the latency period, roughly ages 7 to 12.

And then we come to adolescence, which as you know is an enormously important phase of development in all relationships, particularly for the capacity to love. During latency there was little sexuality and instinctual life, and now, in adolescence, which begins with puberty, comes the eruption of the endocrinological system. All the instincts come once again violently to the fore. With all the instinctual activity of adolescence comes the capacity to love, the capacity to feel someone else is more important than you, someone else's happiness and pleasure and joy and welfare are more important than yours. You would sacrifice yourself and your comfort for them. And when that happens you start to get what is called, and what deserves the name of, love. But you know, in adolescence it is not so simple, because love happens suddenly, inexplicably, often, irrationally, there are infatuations, one falls in love and one falls out of love; and when one falls in love, love very often becomes related to identification. One loves somebody and one becomes like them, one imitates, unconsciously, the other person that one loves. And so it is hard to tell, do you love him or are you becoming like him? Very complicated. In adolescence there is this great conflict between the wish to get close and intimate and the terrible fear of it, and the wish to avoid it and become isolated and withdrawn. There is great difficulty in adolescence to blend the affectionate, romantic, tender part of love with the primitive sexual part of it. And the tendency is to split it off: with some, one is affectionate and romantic, and with others one is sexual, and which it is depends on the community or the family or on what happens to be the vogue at that time. Now, when I said this recently I was corrected by some adolescents, my children, who said, "You're very old-fashioned. This is not true any more. In your day" (meaning, you know, a hundred years ago) "this might have been true, but today adolescents are able to fuse both sex and romantic, tender feelings." Well, you are never at an advantage in arguing with your own children, so I didn't debate the point, but I thought to myself, they think this is what they are doing, but I don't know whether it is true. I still am not sure. I don't think they achieve it, I think they may try. But our whole society, all our conventions, make it very hard, because as much lip-service as we give to progressive attitudes about freeing our children from all kinds of old-fashioned conventions, it is one thing to really free them, and another to just talk about it. At any rate, I want to bring out that if it is successful, at this time of life, the child will develop the ability to become intimate with the person they love. Now this is a very important point because failure means to remain isolated, remain alone. Many people can be intimate only with strangers. It is curious. You meet someone on a bus and you can tell him the story of your life. You never see him again. The taxi driver, you can ask all kinds of questions, but your wife, well, there's nothing to talk about. Let's watch television. It's very curious, this kind of isolation. These are people who are fixated where they cannot be intimate with those they love or they have difficulty in being sexual with somebody they are intimate with. Intimacy interferes with sexuality. They can be compassionate about a stranger. And you know this is a sad commentary, how many people can go off to a convention in a strange city, get slightly drunk, have all kinds of sexual goings-on with total strangers that they never remember, can't even recognize. And yet with their own husbands and wives are ill-at-ease, awkward, and self-conscious. How sad. How frequent. You see it so many times when people cannot express love and affection, or sex or passion to one another, but they can go and watch a television program together and both get very sentimental about the picture, but not about each other. Oh yes, oh yes, you don't like to hear it. Yes, many people can cry buckets full of sincere tears about Gregory Peck but they cannot feel these kinds of simple emotions for people closer to them, with whom they live. I didn't mean to pick on Gregory Peck.

At this stage of development you will see promiscuity and promiscuity always means inability to love. Men who go from one woman to another or women who go from one man to another, are not able to love. They have an incapacity to love. The same goes for the many infatuations and the search for glamour with all its deceit and deceptions. All of this means, I cannot love. I cannot love a real human being. Real human beings, you know, are not pretty all the time. None of us are, none of us, even the most glamorous movie queen, and including Gregory Peck. Yet, it is possible to love somebody, if one has the capacity to love, and glamour will not make it so. It will only deceive you.

Let me sum up so far what I've said.

The capacity to love reaches its height, I think, when a man can love romantically, spiritually, emotionally, sexually, a woman, or vice versa. And this depends on their being able to feel love, passion, and affection for one person, and this person should be of the opposite sex. It is important because this—(laughter): I will come back to this point, because it is important. This means also that they can be intimate and yet retain their own identity, their own independence. To be intimate does not mean to give up one's uniqueness, one's individuality. They can be intimate and attain a kind of mutuality, but to do this they must have the capacity to trust one another, the capacity to expose themselves to one another, the courage to dare to do this, to try to do this, and have respect for one another. All of this is necessary to be able to love the way I have described it.

But, ladies and gentlemen, all of this is only the core, the central part of my speech to you tonight. I want to talk about a few more things which are very important in understanding the varieties of love. You will interrupt me when you get bored, and I will stop. Well, on what does this capacity to love depend? How do you achieve it? Of course you know the way we achieve it is we bring up children properly. That's again such a formula—how do you bring up children properly? Well, of course, you must love them and care for them and have this capacity I'm talking about, namely to make their welfare more important than yours, and not to make them your possession or your slaves, or mistreat them, sadistically, or use them, for your own gain or your own pride. But so many of us have learned this too late and we have difficulties in our loving, with all our good intentions. So what do we do? Those of us can only either try to get some help, or to get some education or both. Tonight we are dealing with education. I want to point out a few things which are misconceptions or differences of opinion about some aspects of love. I stress these things because they are very important to understand. Loving a child is not enough. A mother may love, and this love can be harmful, because it is possessive, or too sexual; or too cold, whatever. One also ought to have some intelligence. This helps in bringing up a child. I am sorry to be so old-fashioned about it; well, I am always tending toward the unpopular point of view, so let me try to make a few points that one ought to know about loving.

I want to talk about, "Who does one love?" Let's talk about self-love, and let's get something very clear about this. I've heard it said that the basis of love, or loving, is to have self-love. First you must love yourself and then you can love somebody else. Now this, to my mind, is not only wrong, it is dangerous and leads to misunderstanding. It is a lot of glib words put together, which are not true. Let's be very clear about self-love and loving somebody else. They are enemies of each other. The enemy of loving somebody is self-love, is narcissism. The enemy of narcissism is loving somebody else. The person who is absorbed and concerned for himself has little left over for anybody else, except "What can he gimme?" and this is not love. I want to be awfully clear about this. Yes, I think what is meant is that to have the capacity to love one must have some self-respect, but then it should be stated as such, not self-love. That makes a mockery of love.

It has been said by many, "Brotherly love is the basis of all love." I'm sorry, I disagree. I believe too that it is wonderful if one has brotherly love; I'm in favor of it. But, let's not deceive ourselves; this is very hard to achieve. I know it is said in the Bible, "Love thy neighbor," but it is hard. It is even harder when they say, "Love thine enemy." If you have trouble with your neighbors, what can you do with your enemies? And I do not mean to be facetious about it, but I think mankind has enough of a burden to be decent, to be considerate, to be tolerant; let's not call these things love. Let's call them what they are. Let's be clear about this. Not everybody deserves to be loved. I don't believe in it. I do not think being born gives you the right to be loved, I do not think Mr. Eichmann should be loved. Pity, maybe? I don't know, I don't even know that. But that's not love. Please. Freud was a hard-headed man, but he had a soft heart. He thought about these problems long and hard, and he felt, and I think I quote him or if not quote him, I give you the essence of what he meant when he said, "Not everyone is worthy of our love." No. Mankind has to make progress, and people must learn to curb their aggressions, their suspicions, their hatreds, their hostilities. They must learn to have concern for each other and try to understand each other. But this should not be called or equated with loving. I think compassion is a wonderful attribute and certainly you can trace it if you try long and hard, back to love. It's a long, long way away from it, and I think one ought to be clear when one talks about these things, not to make things confusing and perplexing, particularly for the young. I believe in tolerance. I believe in concern and consideration and fairness and decency and all of these things. But I think they should be separated from what we talk about when we talk about love.

Now let us talk about mature love. It is discriminating. It is picky. It is finicky. The ability to love anybody and everybody is not love. It may come from loneliness, or fatigue, it may be intoxication, it may be childishness. Mature love discriminates, mature love is exclusive. The mature person wants few people to really love, he insists on them, demands them. They are not equal, they're not interchangeable. A man who can't make up his mind whether he loves this girl or that girl loves neither, believe me. You cannot love two people that way. You love neither. Something else is involved, this is a confusion, it is not love. You may be undecided if you love at all, true. But this kind of business, "I don't know who I love," is infantile, immature, undeveloped, only a forerunner of love. Why do I say this? Because mature love depends on the uniqueness of the person who is loved. One loves only people that one knows and knows well. To truly love a person one has to know them, know them not only intellectually and verbally, know them not only now, but know them as of the past and of yesterday and years ago. All this is part of loving and knowing. Not only to understand intellectually and emotionally, but empathetically, to feel for the other person. This is mature love. You know, this depends to a great extent on certain similarities, on certain compatibilities, and part of mature love depends on certain similarities between people. But if there are mainly similarities, the greater danger is that this will not remain love, but become some kind of companionship, some kind of pleasant proximity, togetherness. Not love, because for love there must also be differences, differences between people. You laughed before when I said, "Yes, to love a person of the opposite sex," but that is not the only difference that is important. Differences of other kinds must be present for it to be a mature and full love, because differences make for excitement, differences make for growth, and differences always retain a certain aura of wonder in the relationship, so that people can live together for many, many years, and the differences make you look again and again and think, "My, interesting, that person I live with." I know, I see many of you shake your heads against me as I talk. All right, you don't have to agree with me, and perhaps much of what I say is unpleasant to you, but I feel it is my duty to say what I think. I would like to take a few more minutes, please, to make some other points about love.

I want to talk about certain transformations of loving. Number one, let's talk about falling in love. Falling in love is a very special aspect of love. It's the acute, intoxicating phase of love, I don't know what else to call it because certainly it is irrational, it is uncontrollable; you can be wonderfully, deliriously happy, or devastatingly miserable in this state. It is always a transference reaction. By that I mean, a person who suddenly falls in love will have found in the object of his love somebody from the past. What he fell in love with so suddenly, and why he could fall in love, was that this person triggered off memories and feelings from somebody in the past, and, therefore, there is always a physical element of some kind in falling in love. This is not the forerunner necessarily of great loves because there are many people who can fall in love and can never *stand* in love. The so-called love disappears and something else takes its place. But sometimes falling in love can be the first stage of what leads then to a steady, reliable standing in love.

Another point. There is a difference of considerable quality, of great significance between actively loving and passively loving. I want to distinguish between people who love actively and people who want someone to love them. This is how love begins: to wish to be loved, and this goes on to the wish to be loved by people, the wish to be lovable, the wish to be popular—it is the present day, terrible fad. The wish to be popular is more important than the desire for intelligence, more important than anything else. A sickness. It is by all means an immature form of love. Yes, all of you who raise your kids to be popular, I tell you this is immature, it does them little good, because the thing to achieve is active love, the capacity to love somebody else, much more important. To dare, to risk, to take a chance, to be vulnerable to somebody else, this is what is important. This takes courage, this takes a certain kind of security, but this takes above all a willingness to expose oneself. However, nobody can actively love a 100 percent; everybody has some part of himself that wants to be loved, that needs to be loved. Nobody's a 100 percent mature, active loving person. We also want to be loved, and we need it, too. It is a question of preponderances, and that is why I stress it. In fact I want to say that there are some people, men for example, who cannot bear to be loved, and when the wife shows affection or tenderness, push her away and say, "No, no, bring on the dessert"; what are they? This inability to tolerate someone's loving is also a weakness, an immaturity. You cannot talk about love without talking about hate. No one who understands love can omit hate from the discussion, because these two are close relatives, and like relatives they do not get along well. But, they are always there together, and this must be remembered. I want to say this: a person who cannot hate, cannot love. All people who can love can also hate. They both represent different peaks of relationships, it is human, being oriented to love, and to hate. More important, never in your life are you more vulnerable, more exposed, more tender, more defenseless, than when you love. And when you are in such a position, how easy it is to be hurt. And when one is hurt, one hates and one gets angry. Now this is natural. Therefore, it is no wonder that one tends so often to hate those we love, but I hope, temporarily and partially. Then one gets over the hate and the anger; and, even when one hates, one has not completely obliterated the good qualities, vague as they may be in the distance, of that person who you are now hating, but once you loved.

# 7 Emotional Involvement—Genuine and Counterfeit (1961)

*Given in the same year as the preceding lecture, "Varieties of Love," these two lectures were felt by Hildi Greenson to be particularly relevant to the young people in the audience. She relates how one young woman exclaimed, "I could not have gone off to college without a copy of 'Emotional Involvement' tucked in among my books."*

*With "Emotional Involvement," Greenson achieved new heights in his ability to reach an audience with poignant descriptions of grief and obstacles to love and meaningful involvement. Here he dealt with the theme of true emotional involvement versus pseudo or false emotional involvement, pointing out the ways in which many people confuse physical closeness with emotional closeness. Such people do not realize that physical togetherness is a wonderful addition to emotional, intellectual, ideational, and verbal relatedness, but that physical involvement cannot replace emotional closeness. "They touch each other, but they do not really touch each other emotionally." Other examples of emotional impoverishment include those who conceive of relationships in terms of things, objects, and possession. Pseudo-involvement, really noninvolvement, is present in those who hunger for multiple relationships, who are in actuality simply demanding to be fed in some way.*

*Greenson defined what he meant by true emotional involvement as being able "to care when it hurts you, when it bothers you; to subordinate your own needs and to sacrifice your own pleasure for the care of someone who means something to you . . . the greatest intimacy comes from the sharing of fantasies and imagination with another human being." True sharing requires a "willingness to be hurt" and to have a relationship endure even if you are hurt. In addition to giving, there must be a willingness to take. In "give and take" there is also "the willingness to give others the pleasure of giving to you." All real emotional involvement ultimately brings on the capacity to risk in relationships.*

*He described two groups of people, the involved and the uninvolved. "In one group, the involved ones, if they feel loved, they feel secure. In the other group, they first have to feel secure and then they are able to love with what is left over." The uninvolved say unconsciously, "I want to be safe—I want a fallout shelter—the hell with . . . I mean, you know, the rest of you take care of yourselves."*

*Finally, the developmentalist in him returned yet again; the issue of emotional involvement poses a tremendously important child-rearing question. He asked, "How do you bring up children then? What's the emphasis, safety or love? Do you want your child to be related to the world and to suffer the blows of fate, whatever they may be and be able to love; or do you want them to be safe?"*

I enjoy having the opportunity to talk to people who are interested in psychoanalysis other than my patients who are forced to listen, or my pupils who have no choice.

My subject tonight is a rather complicated one. The title, as you may know, is "Emotional Involvement—Genuine and Counterfeit." Actually, my subject will be to describe for you disguised emotional *un*involvement. That is what I mean by counterfeit emotional involvement; and by genuine emotional involvement I mean both healthy *and* neurotic involvement. And even that does not tell you very much, so let me try, rather than define my terms, to illustrate what I mean by giving you a brief picture of people I

---

Presented in October 1962 at El Rodeo School, Beverly Hills, CA under auspices of the School for Nursery Years. Also broadcast over listener-sponsored Pacifica radio stations.

have seen in recent times who portray one form or another of this particular kind of problem. What do I mean by emotional involvement or emotional uninvolvement? I will begin by describing to you a group of men I have heard about, usually from women—in fact, almost always from women—who will tell me that they are spending time with a man who seems pleasant, entertaining, polite, courteous, considerate; who will take them to a good place to eat and some entertainment, and then would expect some kind of sexual satisfaction. And what puzzles these women when they describe these men is that these men don't talk, they won't talk, about anything except trivia or gossip or some current event which is removed and remote and distant. And when they make any attempt to ask them about themselves, they are met with a rebuff. These men seem consciously to be saying, "I don't want to get involved. I'll walk with you, I'll talk with you, I'll eat with you, I'll go to the theater with you, I'll sleep with you, but I don't want to be involved." And they give the impression, and actually say, "Look, I've been hurt, and women are dangerous. Who needs it?" But they want everything else. They expect everything else. In fact, they demand everything else. And if you break off with them, they do not understand. They are not terribly hurt because they have invested nothing. They are only nonplussed, surprised, resentful. Their attitude seems to be: no strings attached, no strings and no attachment, nothing. They are willing to give everything of themselves that is impersonal, but nothing which is personal. Now I have heard this story so many times that I am sure these kind of men exist, although I can assure you they never come to me for any help. Why should they? They seem to have found a way of existing without being hurt, without being frustrated, and without being miserable. And they think they are living! These people that I am describing, this group of men, are consciously uninvolved. This uninvolvement suits them; it is egosyntonic. They have proven it.

I think I have heard similar stories occasionally about women, but much more rarely, and always obviously defensively. Women who are afraid. These men I describe are no longer even afraid or, let me say more correctly, they are no longer aware that they are afraid to be involved. They have found a mode of living: uninvolved, invulnerable, and untouched.

Let me contrast this kind of man with another: A man who comes to me for help because he is unable to remain and maintain an emotional involvement with a woman for a period of time, or even with a man for that matter. And when he talks to me about it he talks with great feeling; he is upset, he is disturbed, he is bothered, he is lonely, he is miserable. He also seems to be complaining of uninvolvement, of an inability to maintain any kind of a human relationship that will deepen and broaden and be meaningful to him. But what a difference! It bothers him, he suffers from it, he considers it ego alien. He is conscious of his uninvolvement. He is not involved with human beings on a conscious level. In this particular instance that I am thinking about, I had talked to this man about how he lived and he talked about his terrible loneliness. Only when he described to me in great detail *how* he lived, was I able to discover what seemed to be the basis for his problem. This particular young man was intelligent and sensitive and perceptive. He worked, and he came to this town to get away from his family who lived in another city. He described to me how, after the analytic hour and after his work in the office, he went home and spent time all alone, day after day, and night after night, and week after week, and month after month. I one day asked him to tell me more about what was happening, at night, for example, when he thought he could not sleep. He told me about the apartment he lived in: he had money, and so he had a bedroom with two single beds, and it was well furnished, and he had some nice paintings and he collected books. But one day he told me that he awoke in the middle of the night and had to go to the bathroom to urinate, and so, he said, he got up and put on his bathrobe and went to the bathroom. And I suddenly realized something: why did he put on his bathrobe? I realized he was not living alone and that in that other single bed in his room, somebody was living. I said, consciously he thought he was living alone, but unconsciously he wasn't. He was living with someone, someone who made him put on a bathrobe. And he said, "My God, my mother!" and so here is another example of a problem with emotional involvement, except of another sort. Here is a man who is unable to be involved, but unconsciously, he *is* involved. In fact, it is the unconscious involvement, the unconscious fixation, the unconscious or preconscious fantasy life of this man that keeps him from becoming involved elsewhere.

Let me give you another example of some of these problems. A woman calls me up, a forty-year-old woman, because she wants marital counseliing. And I was rather leery about this because people come with the most fantastic expectations of marital counseling. But I heard she was referred to me by someone whom I knew who knew about my work, so I agreed to see this lady about her marital counseling problem, which was as follows: Very matter of factly she told me that she had been married for some sixteen years and she had a wonderful marriage; in fact, it was a perfect marriage—she and her husband got along like "clockwork." Everything went smoothly, there were no quarrels, there were no problems, there were no difficulties, there were no conflicts. It went smoothly and, she again insisted, "like clockwork." And then suddenly, a week ago, her husband said, "I want a divorce." (Laughter) It is not a funny story. It is rather pathetic because she was so startled by it, and when I tried to determine how she could be so surprised, didn't she have any indications? She said, "No, we had a perfect marriage." And, once again, "like clockwork everything went." I proceeded to explore the marriage, what happened in this kind of marriage, how did they live together, what did they do? "Well," she said, "I took care of the house, and I cooked and cleaned, and I took care of the children and he went to the office and he came home, and I served dinner and I washed the dishes and he dried the dishes, and then we watched television, and then we went to bed." And I said, well, but there must be other things that happen. And she said, "Oh, yes, yes, and once a month we see his relatives and once a month we see my relatives, and . . ." I said, but there must still be other things that happen? "Yes," she said, "on Saturday night we go to the movies and once a month we entertain people." I couldn't believe this and I said, but there must be other things. And she said, "Yes, we are always together, we are inseparable. He travels sometimes and I always go with him, he would never be without me." And I tried to find out what else there was in this relationship; what else did they do besides "being together." Oh, she then thought, aha, you are a Freudian. "Yes, we even have sex together, although the last two years we haven't had any." And I said, well, why? And she said, "Well, I didn't ask. I didn't want to intrude."

I think this gives you a rather stark picture of what looks to be like a marriage and an emotional involvement, yet it is all fraudulent, it is all superficial, it is all phoney. All of this facade is only a screen for people who confuse spending time together with being related, with relatedness. It was shocking to me to see how little this woman knew about her husband; how little she was really concerned about her husband. She wanted to maintain this "clockwork" relationship; this mechanical, smooth-running, conflict-free relationship. This she considered relatedness. And she, like so many people (and one of my pet hates), stresses togetherness, confuses togetherness with a relationship. "We were inseparable," as though this means how we loved each other; instead of meaning: we were afraid to leave each other alone or, I always needed someone to watch me, or, I needed a baby-sitter, or something; who confuse the fact that physical togetherness is a wonderful addition to emotional, intellectual, ideational, verbal relatedness—but who instead replace emotional closeness with physical closeness. It is a substitute. They confuse physical contact with an emotional contact. They touch each other, but they do not really touch each other emotionally. So, she is again an example of counterfeit, fraudulent emotional involvement which really camouflages an uninvolvement. Incidentally, I told this lady that I thought I would like to see her husband and she was very hesitant about telling her husband, but thought, well, maybe now that she had talked to me, she would change. Well, I said, I do not know if you can change. She said, "I will change." My heart sank and I said, well, fine. She said, "Well, I paid attention to you and what you asked me. I know, I know I am going to change," and she left. I am sure you know that something is going to change, but how or whether it will be with any kind of greater capacity for relatedness, I would certainly doubt.

Let me contrast this with another lady I saw some months ago. This woman was forty-five years old and told me that she had been referred to me by many of her friends who were very worried about her. They were worried about her because for the last many months, four or five months, she cried all the time. She cried, she was sad, she was woebegone, she was miserable. And every time she spent time with her friends, she would burst into tears and would cry. And when they tried to tell her to come out and have some fun, she did not want to. Or when they were surprised that she was not interested in meeting some men, they were alarmed and anxious. They told her, "Look you ought to go see a psychoanalyst." And they persuaded her to come to see me, although she said, "I didn't feel I should see you." I asked her, well, tell me, why do you cry? And she said, "Well, I have had two terrible experiences in the last half a year. I had an only child, an eighteen-year old daughter, who was beautiful and intelligent, and who was going to college, and she suddenly contracted polio and died within three months. And while my husband and I were grieving about the loss of our only daughter and beautiful child, my husband had a heart attack and died. I had suddenly lost my whole immediate family. So I moved to Los Angeles because I have a sister here, my only living relative. And when I came to my sister I noticed she was cold and strange and distant to me. And when I tried to find out what was the matter she said, 'Look, I can't see you too often because my husband is jealous of it; he doesn't want me to.' So," she said, "I cried, and I keep on crying, and when people talk to me and I talk about my husband or my daughter, I cry." And I must say, I listened to her and I thought: yes, of course she cries. What else should she do? This is a normal, healthy reaction to the loss of people who are dear to you. This is a healthy woman. This is a healthy involvement. Of course she should cry. It's only been five or six months. Lucky woman that she can cry. And I said to her, "You don't need to go to an analyst; you only need to find some people who will let you cry." Which wasn't as easy as you may think. But I ought to tell you I wondered what kind of friends she had. They worried me, these people who wouldn't let her cry. And I submit this lady as an example of a healthy emotional involvement as contrasted to every one of the other cases that I have talked about. She was fortunate.

All right. These are people who have some kind of problem with emotional involvement. But now I would like not just to look at individuals, but to look more at society and see what you can notice and observe in people and groups of people who also seem to manifest a disturbance in their capacity to become related in a meaningful way to others.

I was struck when I decided to talk on this subject by a current expression in our present-day slang which has to do with the word *cool*. The word *cool* has become an expression indicating that something is good. "How did you like it?" "Oh, it was cool." "How was the concert?" "Cool." "How was the . . . ?" "Cool." Cool means good, great. And this bothered me since I always thought of it as exactly the opposite. When something was good, it was hot, or at least warm! And I grew up with the understanding that when something wasn't very good, we said, "It isn't so hot." Now, the whole thing has become twisted around, and it is "cool," and to "play it cool" is the epitome of doing something well and skillfully. It seemed to me an indication of the times, this detachment, this aloofness: play it cool. And as I began to think about problems of involvement or uninvolvement, I began to see a big variety of kinds of people, only some of whom I will mention because it would take me too long to describe them all, but they all belong in this category of people who have difficulty in their capacity to relate themselves emotionally and meaningfully in any kind of an intimate way with other people.

For example, I want to take as the first group those people who can get involved only with things, inanimate objects, or with certain kinds of concepts, or who are, let us say, particularly interested and concerned only with possessions. I am appalled, absolutely appalled, the older I get and the more people I see, I find the most important thing in some of their lives is what they possess, what they own. I see it not only in people who want to be wealthy and want to amass great amounts of money, but people in general who feel never satisfied with any amount of money that they have. They want more and more and more. But not only in this way, but in the homes that they possess, they must be bigger and bigger. Or the paintings they collect, they must be more expensive, more expensive and more and more. In general there is this tremendous emphasis on more and bigger. There is this confusion that the more you have and the bigger you have, that this is equivalent to better. These people are driven by it and will exploit everybody in order to get some material advantage. People are "contacts" of whom you take advantage; they are good to know because they are "deductible" or they will bring you some kind of business. People, to them, are "opportunities" to accumulate something; if they spend time with you, they want to get something from you—some advantage, either in terms of status, or material gains, or popularity—to add more anonymous people they can call their friends (i.e., strangers who follow them about).

I am absolutely flabbergasted by this kind of drivenness for more and bigger and more and bigger, until I begin to realize that with all their wealth in terms of material things, they are poverty-stricken people. They feel, whether they know it or not, and many times they don't know it, but I assure you it is there, they feel on the verge of poverty. But this poverty is emotional poverty. What they misinterpret is their fear of being poor, of losing their millions, or thousands, or hundreds of thousands—not because they have financial insecurity but because they feel, but cannot properly interpret, that this concern about money is really a concern about emotional impoverishment. That is what they suffer from. And they displace it onto things and objects and possessions.

Many of these people are very guilty and try to pay off by making all kinds of contributions or doing all kinds of charitable activities, which is fine. I am all in favor of people doing charity even for bad reasons, but they never feel that they get rid of their guilt anyway, because their guilt comes from unconscious sources and has other origins.

This whole group of "thing" lovers who can only become involved with inanimate objects are related to people who find that cleanliness, for example, is more important than an emotional relationship. You can be having this most impassioned discussion with a friend, and this housekeeper-lady says, "Pardon me," comes in between the two of you, moves you away to clean up the ashtray, because there are some ashes there. It is a small thing but it is absolutely shocking. Those ashes are more important than all the things that have been going on with this active debate or discussion or whatever. You can imagine what happens with such a lady when you try to make love to her! This belongs in the same category: there is an involvement, but with the wrong things, for the wrong reasons, and the wrong motives—completely distorted and neurotic.

Let me describe another group. Again, a strange kind of thing that looks like involvement. I want to describe a group of people who are at best called frantic—chronically intense people who are always entranced and chronically enthusiastic. Something has to be the greatest or the worst or the best, but it is always a superlative, never less than a superlative. And if something isn't very good, then it's at least the worst! I am sure you have met such people. It is hard to get away from them because there is something contagious about them and they can be very charming, for an evening!

Incidentally, please don't think I am only describing other people, part of the time I think I am describing myself. And I am sure all of us who listen and all of you who listen will find qualities of one or another belong to one or another of us. I don't mean to make an attack, and I deliberately exaggerate in order to make my points clearly. So, let me go back.

These frantic ones, these chronically intense enthusiasts, are very interesting in how they operate. First of all, it seems, they are very quick to relate to you. If you ever go to a party in their house—and they are great partygivers and partygoers—the minute you walk into such a gathering you are instantly called by your first name and you are introduced to everybody by their first name. Right away it's there: instant warmth! And to really make sure it is instant warmth, they give you some alcohol and stir you around in the group; and now everybody is dissolved in this kind of an amorphous glow that looks like a relationship—except that you cannot remember who these people are and what you are doing with them. Sound familiar? They won't ever serve you dinner for two hours, until you are so plastered that by this time even the food tastes good and the people begin to look familiar, and when you wake up from such an evening you wonder: what really happened? Now, are these people really involved? Not in the sense I mean. This is again a pseudoinvolvement, a search for involvement, a frantic wish to become involved, but they cannot really do it because it is indiscriminate; it is almost impersonal. And it goes on and on, and it never stops. These people can never be quiet, and they confuse noisiness with joyfulness. If you make lots of noise, then everybody's been having a great time. If you ever stop for a moment and are thoughtful, they say, "What's the matter? What's wrong?" And you say, "I'm thinking." And they say, "Oh, don't tell me that," which means you are not interested because they demand your constant attention to them in this very, very superficial way. These are people who, above all, have this terrible need to be popular. They have an inability to discriminate between friends, acquaintances, strangers, and enemies. If you're there, you're my friend; in fact, you're my dearest friend and I call you "honey" and "darling." This is typical. They call everybody and anybody "darling" and "honey." This goes for the husband, the children, even the people they despise.

You can see that, underneath, what looks like relatedness can't be, or it wouldn't be this indiscriminate and it wouldn't be this quick. They lack the ability to be related but have this hunger for relationships, which demand that you feed them in some way.

Let me describe another group of people whom I would call the sleepwalkers, the quiet ones. Just the opposite from these noisy, loud, frantic, instant-warmth people. Ah! the peace of mind people, the peace of mindlessness people, where everything has to be peaceful at any price, even at the price of living. Their whole attitude of being with people or relating to people has to do with "killing time"—finishing one day after another, in going from one day to another. What looks like tranquility is really a kind of apathetic boredom. They are also "togetherness" people who confuse physical proximity with any kind of a relationship, and spend a great deal of time watching television, eating, drinking, together with someone; and also usually accompanied by some tranquilizer: Miltown, thorazine, etc. These people are actually *un*dead. If you look at how they live you will see they are only *un*dead. This blandness hides a terrible inertia; they lack fantasy and imagination. These people, incidentally, I have described them before, they do a lot of things together and it's interesting they can *feel*, but not for each other directly, in a one-to-one relationship, and never alone. But if you put on the television set they will sit and watch it together and cry about the person on the television. They can cry about a movie, about a TV show, they can become excited by a movie, and a TV show and very often they can even become sexually aroused, not from each other but by the TV show. In this curious kind of peculiar uninvolvement only indirectly do they dare to let themselves feel. They need the safety of television or the Miltown, which I feel are pretty much the same thing. I do. I do not want to run down all television shows. There are some which really stimulate you and really entertain you. But, the vast majority just distract you and I think they are a kind of Miltown taken in with the eyes instead of by mouth.

I want to take up a last group, and those are the pseudosexual people. It has become popular in our society for people to behave much freer sexually than they used to. And now you find a very interesting group of people who apparently are very prone to having sexual relations, but they have sex without passion and also without guilt. It is an amazing thing, they can be unfaithful and readily admit it and apparently without any remorse, any regrets, or any guilt. And also if you listen to their sexual adventures, which they are quite willing to tell you, you will find they are so boring, which is remarkable. It used to be that sexual stories or adventures were exciting; not with this particular group of people. They, again, are boring because they are indiscriminate. This is not a person falling in love with another person and trying to woo or court, conquer or seduce them. No, it is only another conquest in a series of conquests. Another step in some kind of ladder that leads nowhere, some kind of a collector who adds certain trophies or people to his collection. You have the impression when you listen to these people that they are a kind of orgasm collector, and that this is what they are after and nothing more. People happen to be there, but by and large they are replaceable and changeable. These pseudosexual people seem to be interested in orgasms only and not in people. I may exaggerate slightly, but only slightly. But it is a degradation of the whole meaning of sexuality and of passion. These people are not passionate; they don't love; they don't become infatuated. They just feel some bodily needs and try to find some kind of person to satisfy them with. The interpersonal, human part of the relationship is no more than a gadgetlike replaceable thing. If this person doesn't fill that purpose and it's worn out (like you change a car every few years) so you change the person every few years and this is how they live.

Now, all these examples have to do with my subject of emotional involvement or uninvolvement. And when you look at this now a little more intently, which I now propose to do after these many examples, what am I really describing? What is involvement? What is this emotional involvement? It has to do with the care or concern or regard or interest in human beings. It has to do with relatedness to people. Obviously, care, concern is derived from love in its broadest sense, in its perhaps most sublimated sense, if you will. Because caring and being concerned have to do with the nonsexual, nonromantic part of a relationship. You can care for someone you love; that's marvelous. You could also care for someone in whom you are not interested, sexually or romantically, and that is also marvelous. It is another order of relationship. And this is what involvement refers to. It means you recognize that every human being is a unique individual and that you can discriminate and distinguish between them, and they are not interchangeable. There's a difference between sweetheart and friend and acquaintances or enemies. They are not all the same and you do not behave the same way to them. You don't call your wife "honey" and your enemy "honey." There is a difference. And you do not expose yourself or talk in the same way to your enemy as you talk to your wife, or your dear friend, or a casual acquaintance. It is the most flabbergasting thing to see people who have the ability, if you want to call it that, to talk to the milkman or the taxi driver who is driving them, and tell them intimate things about their life without awareness that this is bizarre or strange or peculiar.

Any time you go for a ride in a train or on a plane, aren't you amazed by people who sit down next to you and pour out so much about themselves? I say that because they don't know I'm a psychoanalyst; I'm just sitting there. I'm amazed how ready some people are to tell intimate things about themselves without any awareness, without any sense of discrimination, without any feeling for the mutuality or the lack of mutuality in the relationship. And that's another characteristic of relatedness or involvement: it is a two-way relationship; there must be an important aspect of mutuality and reciprocity in it. You cannot relate to someone who is indifferent to you. That's another problem. There must be a back and forth; and there is in all these involvements, always giving and taking. If it is only one, there is something wrong, something missing.

What is this giving? If you look at it you will see it is, in the broadest sense, to give interest, attention, to notice, to care, to have it matter to you. This is what you give, and this you can do on all levels of intensity—to your dearest friends or to a stranger. Aren't you amazed how many times people don't care? Ever watch an accident on a street and see how people avoid stopping or helping? *They* don't care. But, if you do care, it pains you. You sympathize, you empathize, you identify. You are not cold and you are not bland. I don't mean that you're constantly frantic or constantly intense. But you're not always bland. And, above all, you discriminate, you do not give the same quality or quantity of feeling to everybody, it matters who they are, not in terms of snobbishness as to who they are, but in terms of what they mean to you and also what you can do for them. This kind of caring brings with it the capacity that you will be concerned for someone else even when it makes you uncomfortable. (I mention it because so many people are ready to be helpful when it is convenient, but are so unready to be helpful when it is uncomfortable or inconvenient or painful.) So I mention precisely that: to care when it hurts you, when it bothers you; to subordinate your own needs and to sacrifice your own pleasure for the care of someone who means something to you. That means, yes, when you're on vacation or a Saturday night, too, to be concerned. This giving has another meaning, too, and it means a sharing of experience, the willingness to have another person participate with you in what's happening, both painful and pleasurable. Not only telling the good things, but also the bad things. And the willingness to hear the bad news and the grief, but also the willingness to share the joys, of course. Again, this has to do with personal communication; it is intimate in the sense that you are dealing here not only with events but what did you feel? Above all, what did you imagine? What did you fantasize? And the greatest intimacy comes from the sharing of fantasies and imagination with another human being. Of course, this is terribly revealing: this makes you terribly vulnerable, for these are the parts of you that are most precious and you hate to show, unless you feel it is a risk worth taking, because you can be so hurt. Nothing can hurt more than exposing a fantasy, something you imagined, to another human being and have him ridicule it or misunderstand it, or be indifferent.

This sharing has also to do with a willingness to be hurt and to have a relationship endure even if you are hurt. Emotional involvement means that someone is a friend even though he was nasty to you or mean or cruel or angry or thoughtless; and yet you can remember when he wasn't, or other qualities, and you are not willing to discard the whole relationship because of it. You are willing to endure pain for someone who matters to you. This, I think, is a very important ingredient of emotional involvement. Sure, it means a willingness to understand; but it also means a willingness to be misunderstood at times. It is based, as you can see, on some kind of trust for this other human being. And you will immediately say to me, and I immediately think of it: well, trust! You go around trusting and you're going to get hurt. These are the suckers. And it is true. The biggest trusters in the world are the biggest suckers in the world. They're the gullible ones, they're the credulous ones. But let me tell you, by and large they are far more happy than the cynical ones and the suspicious ones. Do you know any suckers? Think about it. They've usually had a lot of good experiences. I'll get into that later.

The other part of this involvement has to do with being willing to take. And I say it in a peculiar way: being willing to take. But I want it emphasized that there are some people who are quite ready to give but have great difficulty in taking, which limits the involvement and limits the mutuality and is a problem. It has to have both in it. And there must be this willingness to give others the pleasure of giving to you. You see what these takers don't realize is, they're not being noble; they're not being abstinent. They are depriving you of the possibility of giving.

There are friendships and all kinds of human relationships in which people when they are in trouble won't tell you their trouble, and you resent it and say: Why? Why didn't you tell me? Why didn't you share this with me? Well, they thought they wouldn't burden you! In a sense they are depriving you of the possibility of being a good friend.

All of this involvement as I describe it to you hinges on the willingness to risk. This is the key point. The emotionally involved people are willing to risk being hurt; they are willing to risk painful emotion; they are not playing it "cool." It matters to them, and if it matters, that means there can be difficulties, conflict, disappointment, misunderstandings, betrayals, death, infidelity. All of this can happen when you care. And so to be involved you must be willing to bear jealousy, envy, anger, resentment, mourning, and grief. Yes, if you really care you must be willing to experience these emotions because these involvements are not placid or necessarily calm, and there are ups and downs, and there are bound to be painful interludes in any kind of relationship that matters. I've never heard of a good relationship that did not have some pain in it. If it was painless, it was not a very good relationship. People say: we had a marvelous marriage; we never quarreled. Frightening! Yes! With friends, they'd say: we had a marvelous relationship, we never had a harsh word between us. Well, no harsh words, no friendship. Now, all of this risking and being involved means that you are willing to expose yourself and be hurt, because you have something to hold on to; and what you have to hold on to is the memory of what this relationship was, in addition to what's happening now at the present moment of pain.

Now I want to get to a more microscopic look at this problem of relatedness and look at the origin of this analytically. Let me preface this by saying to you that I came to decide upon talking on this subject first because I saw so much of it in my practice—this emotional uninvolvement—and second because I was once asked on a panel discussion on phobias to give an introductory speech on phobias in my practice. And when I tried to do so I asked myself: well, how were the patients I saw with phobias different from all the other patients I saw? And I was startled to realize that I could not really make them very different. Some of my phobia patients were hysterical, some were depressed, some were paranoic, some were compulsive-obsessive, some were schizoid. I could not find that the diagnosis "phobia" told me anything meaningful about these people. And I realized that all the diagnostic criteria were insufficient to describe what I was after. Sure there were similarities, but if I had to group them I would never group them as phobic, hysteric, or obsessive. And I thought of Freud's classification of the neuroses, of transference neurosis (i.e., people who have the capacity of developing a transference reaction to the analyst). The neurosis, the classical neurosis and the narcissistic neurosis, where people could not develop a transference, they were too self-concerned, too narcissistic, usually Freud meant they were the psychoses, the schizophrenias, and so on. That seemed closer to the point. And when I began to look at the people—not only my patients, but at people I knew—I realized I could divide them into two big groups. And what were these two groups? I realized it had to do with this problem of involvement. I could describe people who were involved essentially with other people, and their problems came from the miserableness of their involvement; and then I could describe a whole other group of people who were different, whose main interest was not involvement with people but who searched for security and safety. And when I looked at this real hard, and I am oversimplifying, I am exaggerating the differences, I realized it seemed to me that people are either struggling to find love or to find safety, and that these two things are separate, different, and opposed to each other. That may seem strange, but this is what I found. Either one or the other. If you want love, you have to risk. If you want safety, well, fine, to hell with people, I want the safety. And, incidentally, I do not mean to belittle people who are so anxiety-ridden. No. Once they feel safe with what emotion they have left over, they are able to love, they are willing to love. But only with what's left over. Their main focus is on the safety as opposed to the others whose main focus is on "I need people to be loved and to love." And, if you look at this real hard, as I think I have (incidentally, these are speculations of my own; I don't want you to accept these as facts or as proven or that anyone else would agree with me), I began to see other differences in how I would describe these two groups of people: the involved and the uninvolved. The involved are involved with people and are searching for love. The uninvolved are uninvolved with people primarily; they may be involved with things but they are searching for security, for safety. In one group, the involved ones, if they feel loved, they feel secure. In the other group, they first have to feel secure and then they are only able to love with what is left over.

The involved ones are afraid of rejection. This terrifies them, to be rejected, because then they will be forlorn and miserable and depressed; and they are terrified of unfaithfulness and infidelity, and they can be miserable and they can be angry. Whereas the uninvolved, the safety-oriented people, are not afraid of rejection, but are afraid of destruction, of self-annihilation. It is a cumbersome term; it would take me too far afield to describe it in any more detail. What they want to preserve is their own integrity;

whereas the depressed ones—and I am talking about the involved ones—they have integrity as long as they have someone they care about. The involved ones are ready to empathize and sympathize; while the security-seekers are those who are the loners, who play it alone, play it from the outside—they are often self-contained, self-centered. Again, I am exaggerating these differences to make my point. We are all mixtures of this, so I reassure everybody, including myself!

The involved ones, since they are riskers, are apt to be more liberal in every kind of way, including politically. They are willing to take a chance. Whereas the insecure ones, the ones who need so much safety, are much more conservative. The involved ones are apt to be gullible, the suckers. The uninvolved, the safety-oriented, are suspicious, cautious, cynical. The involved ones seem to be close or live never too far from where they can be touched and become sad, even the healthy ones can feel depressed easily. And the uninvolved ones are very prone to become mistrustful and suspicious.

How does one understand this? What is the difference? How do you understand this? You see the problem is the following: the basic or first emotion that the human infant has to cope with, the first affect, is anxiety, fear. The first emotional reaction of the newborn is panic, and in the first days he lives very close to panic and every pain is panic-producing, or can be. The feeling of being overwhelmed and of losing your identity or your integrity, losing your ego functions, it is a terrible feeling. But slowly the child learns by increasing his thinking capacities, memory, judgment, anticipation; slowly the child learns that you don't have to always get overwhelmed, you can use a little bit of anxiety as a signal to warn you of bigger anxieties. It's a tremendous step when you master anxiety, and can feel a little scared, but not panicky; when you can feel "oh-oh, something might happen" before it happens and you are overwhelmed. When you have mastered anxiety to this point, then you have the capacity to love somebody. And, if you care about somebody, if you are aware of somebody who brings you pleasure and joy (and I'm talking now about very young babies), then you can master the anxiety, even when these people hurt you or are absent, you still can remember them. Now the capacity to feel sad is based on the capacity to remember somebody who is absent, yet they are in your memory, and even though she deserts you (let's talk about a mother and baby) and is not present, instead of going into a panic this baby can remember: there was a good mother who used to come and feed me, and I am miserable and depressed and sad. Now, I think it is a tremendous accomplishment when the baby, instead of getting panic-stricken when the mother is not there, gets depressed and sad. And what I am talking about is the accomplishment of this particular feat: the ability in times of stress to feel, as I say, depression or sadness rather than panic. And this is all based on having mastered anxiety. I think it is a step in maturity. You can see this when you work with patients or observe people, when anxious people begin to improve, one of the signs of improvement is that they get depressed. Incidentally, people are far more treatable when they are depressed, than when they are in any other state. Of course, you know, happy people are untreatable.

So, the analytical point of this whole story has to do with the fact that there is a piece of progress involved in mastering anxiety and going from panic and anxiety as a signal to depression and sadness. The ability to remember somebody who hurts you, about whom you are ambivalent, and still to remember them, to long for them and to allow yourself to feel this longing, this makes it possible to cry. People never cry when they are frightened, only after they are frightened. As you know, anybody who has been terribly scared will not cry until they see a protective figure; and when you come and say, "don't worry, I'm here," now they can cry. It is very interesting. Children who can be scared to death, panicked and white and pale, won't cry until they see mother; and when they see mother, boo-hoo! And it is quite an accomplishment in an analysis when a patient dares to cry. That means, at least at the moment, they don't dread or fear you.

This capacity, even though you are ambivalent, to remember and to long for the good person is a higher state of development. I think essentially it means that the sad person is able to hold on to people even though he is frustrated and miserable, and I think it is based on their ability to handle their anxiety without becoming panic-stricken. These people essentially become people-oriented, and I think you can divide people into all kinds of categories based on this: Are they essentially anxiety-ridden people? Or are they essentially depressed people? The difference has to do with what is in the center: people or safety. Of course, this is oversimplified, but the essential thing is that the anxiety-ridden people are safety-oriented, and not love-oriented. That the sadder, depressed people want to be lovable; that's their aim: love me. This too can be pathological, please—very. Nevertheless, it concerns relationships to people, whereas in the uninvolved, lovability is not the point at all. "I want to be safe—I want a fall-out shelter—the hell with . . . I mean, you know, the rest of you take care of yourselves. . . ." Yes, yes, in neurotic people this wish to be lovable is, of course, accompanied by this terrible feeling of constantly being rejected and feeling unloved. Whereas the neurotic-anxiety people are suspicious, mistrustful, the psychotic-depressive people feel abandoned, totally abandoned and the psychotic-anxiety people feel persecuted. There is a difference, I hope it is clear.

Now you can see this difference all along the line, not only in relationship to single people or people you know, but to the world, to the concern for humanity. (This is my last point.) That the involved people are not only involved with their families, their friends, but also with mankind, with humanity; it matters, they pay attention. They have a sense of responsibility to the rest of the world. They have a kind of concern, if not a guilt, to what happens in the rest of the world, and they want to do something to help. I want to contrast them with the others who look at the rest of the world as dangerous: watch out, they are out to get you; we've got to be prepared and strong. Look, I'm no hero, but I can't believe that the rest of the world is out to get me—or us. The related people cannot forget the relatedness, even when it has to do with the Negroes in the South, or in Africa, or wherever you will; whereas the others are always willing to forget: "But they're dangerous, they're dangerous; be careful, be careful." They want to play it safe; they play it "cool."

Of course it poses a tremendous question: how do you bring up children, then? What is the emphasis, safety or love? Do you want your child to be related to the world and to suffer the blows of fate, whatever they may be; or do you want them to be safe? And I think this is a basic question; I don't think we always have to ask it consciously. But, whether you ask it or not, it's always there: What do you want? And I make a plea that we should bring up our children with a capacity to love and to be involved, and that any other survival which does not have emotional involvement is not worth anything.

# 8 Why Men Like War (1963)

*At the time this lecture was given, the Vietnam War had barely begun to occupy the thoughts of the American people. Greenson early saw the evil represented by that war and the danger it posed for the youth of our country. In 1964 he was one of the framers of the document "Individuals Against the Crime of Silence," a powerful declaration of dissent which was recorded with the Secretary General of the United Nations. In speaking out, Greenson wanted to come to grips with the general apathy about the horrors of war. He wanted to expose the hypocrisy that in fact men do like war. He said, "I think too many of us readily accept the notion that we hate war. Men hate war consciously; unconsciously men also like war . . . the illusion of man's original goodness or man's innate nobility is a dangerous myth based either on self-deception or ignorance or both."*

*He outlined the gratifications involved:*

1. *War is an opportunity for the discharge of man's destructive impulses without responsibility and guilt.*
2. *War puts an end to uncertainties. One side is good, the other is bad.*

3. *War returns us to the marvelous dependency of childhood in that "The Commander" takes care of all.*
4. *During war the individual becomes a member of a crowd and he has a feeling of belonging.*
5. *War not only provides an opportunity for glory and glamour, it also gives man an opportunity for unconscious suicide. War may expiate unconscious guilt.*

*Greenson related power, fear, and aggression in an original way: "It is striking to see how the craving for power brings with it the fear of power of the opposing force. The more powerful the nation, the more readily it is apt to feel in danger from attack from a powerful enemy. . . . The greater one's aggressive striving is for attaining power, the more likely one is apt to expect a retaliation from some hostile force." He closed the lecture with a plea, most relevant to the growing danger in Vietnam, that "civilized people ought to have a greater loyalty to mankind than to any nationalism."*

I have deliberately chosen the subject, "Why Men Like War," even though I realized it was a morbid topic. I could have just spoken about war from a psychoanalytic point of view, but I felt it was important to come to grips with an essential aspect of the problem, namely the general apathy that exists in people when it comes to combatting war. I have emphasized in my title that men do like war because I want to expose the hypocrisy that exists concerning man's attitude about war. It is this hypocrisy which is responsible for the apathy. I think too many of us readily accept the notion that we hate war. Unfortunately this is only at best a half-truth. It is characteristic for the human being to believe that we are unique creatures among the animals and that we were born with an innate nobility and goodness that sets us apart from all other animals. This is a myth, an illusion, and a lie. It tends to make us feel smug and superior and we become bored, cold, and untouched when we think about the possibility of war. No, men hate war consciously; granted. But I will try to demonstrate to you that unconsciously all of us like war and because it is

---

Condensed from two lectures presented for the School for Nursery Years, Los Angeles, taped and broadcast by Radio Station KPFK, November 19 and 20, 1963.

unconscious, it is all the more dangerous. It is true that this seems to be a contradiction, but it is characteristic for the human mind to be full of contradictions and conflicts between what goes on consciously and unconsciously. We will never solve the problem of preventing war if we all start out with this namby-pamby attitude that men hate war and love peace. It is my contention that we have never solved the problem of war for any period of time because we are full of conflicts and contradictions about war. We will never get anywhere with our negotiations and deliberations about achieving an enduring peace if we do not keep ourselves alert and vigilant to the fact that there is a part in every one of us that likes war. Some of the facts of human psychic life are ugly but they have to be faced. Man's love of war is one of these ugly facts. The illusion of man's original goodness or man's innate nobility is a dangerous myth based either on self-deception or ignorance, or both.

I am a psychoanalyst and am therefore limited in what I have to contribute to this problem. For a more thorough study of the subject, one ought to be trained in history, sociology, anthropology, political science. It has been necessary for me to look to others who could help with some aspects of this topic and I want, therefore, to thank Almira Struthers, William Sater, Gerald Aronson, Walter Millis, and James Reed for their book, *The Abolition of War*; these, among others, have been helpful to me.

Despite my limitations I feel that the possibility of war makes it imperative for everyone who has something to contribute on this subject to speak out. I feel this responsibility very keenly because so many people are working in different fields concerning the making of war, are working on missiles, radar, deterrents, fall-out shelters, etc., and so few seem to be actively working on peace. Furthermore, those who work on war are so revered in our society, whereas those who work on peace are relatively neglected or looked on with suspicion. Isn't it striking how any group of people who advocate attacking Cuba, for example, are immediately considered to be upright American citizens, whereas anyone advocating disarmament evokes the suspicion of being influenced by the communists. Compare the coverage in the press that Linus Pauling received when he was awarded the Nobel Peace Prize, and the enormous coverage in the press that Madame Nhu received. Psychoanalysts have always had an affinity for bringing up unpopular subjects, and the notion of man's liking war is certainly a good example of this. However, Freud concerned himself with this problem in 1915 when he published a paper called "Thoughts for the Times on War and Death," which exposed a good deal of the fundamental psychology of war. In 1932 he exchanged some letters with Albert Einstein which were published under the title of *Why War*? Since then several other analysts have written on the subject, and I want to mention the names of Glover, Walsh, Ostow, Marmor, as having made contributions.

I want to begin by giving the evidence that is available, which indicates man does like war, and that this is not just a theory of mine. Then I would like to address the question of, what is there in man that predisposes him to like war. Is this an essential aspect of human nature? Following this I would like to discuss the subject of, what is there about the institution of war that is so appealing, so attractive to all of mankind? Finally, I would like to make some suggestions about how one can change man's attitude about war and make it possible for man to endure peace.

The most obvious material that I have at my disposal to demonstrate to you that man does like war is the evidence from history. In fact, the study of history can be regarded as essentially a study of war. What led to a particular war, what happened in that war, how did one war lead to the next war, etc. Perhaps I am exaggerating, but only a little. If you look at history from the time man left any kind of records behind him that were readable, you will see descriptions of war, weapons, battles from Egyptian times to Babylonian times to the Greeks, etc. The conquests of Alexander the Great are well known, the history of Rome and the Roman wars, the Crusades of the Middle Ages, the Thirty Years War between the Catholics and the Protestants, are good examples. Incidentally, in the Thirty Years War it has been discovered that the prisoners were eaten by their captors, but I understand that is not unique. If you just look from the 1800s to the present, and go over the list of international wars, I think it is impressive. Let me quickly itemize the international wars only: The Napoleonic Wars, the War of 1812, the Crimean War, the Franco-Prussian War, the Anglo-Boer War, the Russo-Turkish War, the Russo-Japanese War, the Spanish-American War, the Balkan Wars,

World War I, World War II, the Korean War. Thirteen different international wars! I have not mentioned any revolutions, any civil wars, local wars, border wars, or brush wars. I think this is rather impressive. In the last 150 years there have been thirteen major international wars. This is tantamount to saying that every generation has had to go through its international war. I read in last Sunday's *Los Angeles Times* that Eric Sevareid said that the peace cycle seems to be coming to an end. It lasts about fifteen years and it is about up. Watch war talk start to mount and war activity start to mount.

But, let me go beyond history. Let me take you to the writings of distinguished men, philosophers, authors, statesmen. Let me read to you a few brief excerpts concerning their feelings about war. Montaigne, the great French essayist: "We suffer the ills of a long peace. Luxury is more pernicious than war." The philosopher Kant:

> A long peace favors the predominance of a mere commercial spirit and with it a debasing self-interest, cowardice and effeminacy and tends to degrade the character of the nation. Provided it is conducted with order and a sacred respect for the rights of civilians, war itself has something sublime about it and gives nations that carry it on in such a manner a stamp of mind only the more sublime the more numerous the dangers to which they are exposed and which they are able to meet with fortitude.

Hegel: "Not only is war not to be regarded as an absolute evil, but it is a necessary corrective for the corrosive influence of peace." And if you think I am picking on the Germans, which I am not, I will quote from Winston Churchill, a man whom I greatly admire, but this is what he had to say when he was a young man about war:

> War which used to be cruel and magnificent has now become cruel and squalid. In fact, it has become completely spoiled. It is all the fault of democracy and science. From the moment either of these meddlers was allowed to take part in actual fighting, the doom of war was sealed. From the moment democracy was admitted to, or rather forced itself upon the battlefield, war ceased to be a gentleman's game. To hell with it.

Here we have quotations from a few men, distinguished men, who demonstrate, I believe convincingly, that they like war, even consciously like war. I would like to turn to Freud and read a couple of sentences from a paper of his, "Civilization and Its Discontents," which is pertinent.

> Men are creatures which are full of aggressiveness which only awaits for some provocation. Anyone who calls to mind the atrocities committed during the invasions of the Huns or the Mongols under Genghis Khan and Tamerlane, or the capture of Jerusalem by the pious Crusaders, will bow humbly before the truth of this view. In abolishing private property the Communists have made a psychological error. Private property offers the human being's love of aggression one of its instruments and motives for aggression. Aggression was not created by private property; it reigns already in the nursery, even before property. What will the Soviets do after they have wiped out the Bourgeoisie?

I could give you many other quotations. I have not mentioned such well-known people who loved war as Kipling, Theodore Roosevelt, Camus and others.

I would now like to turn to other evidence which indicates man's love of war. Do you know what are the most popular books, the best-sellers of all time? Books about war. Napoleon and the Napoleonic wars far outsells everything outside of the Bible, and the Bible is often donated free of charge. The American Civil War is by far the best-selling book topic we have ever had. Perhaps in the near future the books on World War II will give it some competition.

What movies do you think are the most popular? War movies, of course. They were even popular during World War II. You could not get into a war movie on an Army post! I admit for a few years after the war they lost their popularity, but notice that today they are coming back. But, as impressive as the popularity of war books and war movies is, there is one even more impressive piece of evidence. The most popular toys in any child's nursery in our Western culture are war toys. Look at any nursery school, any child's bedroom, at any place where children play, and you will see soldiers, guns, cannons, and by now rockets, missiles, etc. The most popular games are some form of war. The soldiers may no longer be made of tin, but are now made of plastic; this makes the soldiers cheaper, like peoples' lives. The only country I have ever heard of which does not have war toys is the Soviet Union, and they had to be forbidden by law. So I think it is clear that not only do men like war, but children like war. In fact that may well be where this whole business starts.

Incidentally, when I say that men like war I do not mean to be leaving out the women, because I am convinced that if women did not like war, we would have no war. I am only using the term *man* as men are wont to do, namely to include women.

My next point is: What is there in man's nature that predisposes him to liking war? The answer is, man's instinctual endowment. Now from the psychoanalytic point of view I think you are familiar with the idea that all men are born with two sets of instincts; libidinal or sexual on the one hand and destructive and aggressive instincts on the other. The libidinal instincts eventually lead to love and the destructive impulses to hate. For this discussion I will skip over the sexual instincts and emphasize the aggressive and destructive impulses in man.

If you dare to open your eyes and observe the newborn child, watch him as he grows, you can see aggressive, destructive impulses from the time he is born. The moment he feels pain, cold, or hunger, he reacts with obvious rage. The muscles of his entire body are contorted, contracted, his face is distorted, his fists are clenched, his body is stiff, he is crying, the color of his face is red, if not purple, and then white. This is present from the time he is born. For the sake of completeness I should mention that aggressiveness is necessary in the human infant to overcome the choking of suffocation as he is being born. That very first struggle to get his first breath requires some capacity for aggressiveness. But if you continue to observe the growing child, you can see his biting pleasure, his pleasure in inflicting pain on others, the capacity for stubbornness, defiance, and spite already by the time he is two-and-a-half years old. It is not long before you can see envy, greed, hatred, and other evidences of what we call rugged individualism.

I do not mean to minimize these manifestations because the aggression involved can be quite enormous. For example, I have seen children who refuse to move their bowels for two weeks, terrifying their parents, and all of this was nothing more than spite and defiance and could be cured by psychological means. I can go on and point out the death wishes that occur with the oedipal phase, the gang warfare of latency, the delinquency of adolescents, etc. I do not mean to overlook the screaming girls who enjoy all of this and provoke all this and admire it. The reckless driving, the beatnicks, and the promiscuity are also evidence of rebellion and hatred for the rules of society and convention.

Freud eventually developed a special theory about an instinct of destruction which he called the death instinct. He believed that in man there is an instinct at work which goes at least halfway to meet the efforts of the warmongers. I remember some thirty-five years ago, I used to believe that war was caused by warmongers. How innocent, how naive, how wonderfully simple it was to believe that then. It is true that the warmongers do their part, but we the peace lovers, we always manage to find reasons to go to war, we always fight the wars, we do not seem to learn from past experiences, and so it may well be that we are war lovers, if not warmongers. Freud once pointed out that he was very impressed by the psychological significance of the Ten Commandments. Of all the commandments, the one that man seems to make his own personally, the one which dominates his conscience is "Thou Shalt Not Kill." Such a powerful prohibition can only be necessary if it needs to be directed against an equally powerful impulse. After all, what no human soul desires stands in no need of prohibition. In connection with this, Freud discussed the psychological meaning of the death of Jesus Christ. Jesus Christ died in order to redeem man for his original sin. But why, asked Freud, was Jesus obliged to sacrifice his life? This can only be explained by the law of tallion, the law which says that like can only be paid for by like; an eye for an eye, and a tooth for a tooth. Therefore, if this reasoning is correct, the original sin which Jesus had to expiate must have been murder. Nothing else would have called for the sacrifice of his life. But, this is a digression and I want to return to a brief discussion about man's destructive instincts.

Freud's concept was that man did not just have an aggressive drive, man had a death instinct, a drive which impelled him to seek his own death. This is a rather complicated idea, based on the notion that man, like all other living substances, is driven to return to the peace which it once knew when it was inanimate. Freud felt that man has two basic sets of instincts: Eros, or the life instinct, which is manifested mainly by sexuality. This leads people to join with people, to form bigger and bigger units with people. The other group of instincts is internally directed, its aim is to destroy oneself. He pointed out that certain animals, certain birds, certain fish seek death, and further, how closely sexual gratification is tied up with death; salmon have to spawn in a certain place and then die.

At any rate, this concept of a death instinct was accepted by few analysts. Most analysts believe there are aggressive instincts and like the sexual instincts, the *aggressive* instincts have their source inside the human being, but the gratification of the instincts occurs with the help of some external agency. Whereas the death instinct implied that man is driven to die unless he can direct his destructiveness outside of him, meaning if you wanted to take it to its extreme position, that to preserve his own life man had to kill. The theory of aggression states that the aggressive instincts are originally directed externally and we manage to cope with them, to tame them, to civilize them, by internalizing them.

This is a very interesting theoretical position if you compare sex and aggression. It is as though originally sexuality or the love object was focused internally, that the first love object was the self: narcissism. In order to mature one had to learn to love outside oneself. As contrasted to destructiveness or aggression, which is first directed outside yourself and in order to mature, you have to internalize it. This is an interesting juxtaposition. Freud never quite said that exactly, but he hinted in this direction in some letters he wrote to Marie Bonaparte, his pupil.

There are, however, analysts who do not believe there is an aggressive instinct and think that man is born without aggression. You know, they belong to those people who believe in man's unique goodness. Man is born good, not like the animals, and the only unfortunate thing is that pain and frustration is imposed on him, and that is how he happens to become aggressive. Well, I think that is incorrect. I think that is wrong because my own clinical experience with patients, and not only with patients, with people, indicates to me that aggression is so deep-seated and so fixed and so ancient, and so out of proportion to what has happened to a person so often, that I cannot explain man's aggressiveness by his adversity. I have to look for some other reasons. I think there is also this danger of idealizing man and trying to belittle man's destructiveness.

You know, it is very striking how long it took Freud to come to the idea that there was an aggressive instinct anyway. It was only in 1920 that he first began to consider it, although the evidence was there. But we do not like to face this. We would much rather talk about other matters, even sex. There is a striking contrast between how reluctant people are in facing their own destructiveness and how ready and eager they are to watch destructiveness, brutality, and violence in others. The most popular television programs and books concern murder, violence, and crime. However, as one watches or reads one is vicariously participating; only one tends to forget that one temporarily enjoyed the role of criminal, fighter, etc.

At this point I would like to turn to other evidence concerning man's natural destructiveness. I am referring here to a book written in 1962, called *African Genesis* by Robert Ardrey, which deals with some anthropological and paleontological findings made in South Africa. Ardrey quotes in particular the work of a man named Raymond Dart, who found fossils going back thousands of years, and he found them in striking locations and in significant selections. For example, he found many humerus bones and nearby, fractured skulls. It was striking that the skull fracture fitted in with the form of the knobby end of the humerus bone. This seemed to indicate that there was some animal which used the humerus as weapons for killing.

This and other similar evidence seemed to point out that primitive man was not just a user of tools but a user of weapons. Man must have been a predator in order to sustain himself. That is perhaps the reason that his canine teeth were reduced in size compared to other animals. The only carnivorous animal with small canine teeth is man. Every distinctive human physical characteristic can be understood as features which make man a better killer. The flat face without a snout makes for stereoscopic vision; the hand with a thumb which is not used for locomotion but is free from all the needs of locomotion can be used for weapons. The flat feet for standing, the relatively large buttocks of human beings, compared to other animals, for running, pursuing, hunting; and even the large brain, for planning how to kill. And this is the reason they say man was able to survive. This ability to survive, however, brought with it certain disadvantages.

Apparently man's large cortex freed him from the innate heritage of other animals. Man is born with fewer instincts than any other animal. On the other hand, man has an enormous capacity to learn. Perhaps this is due to the fact that man spends proportionately less of his lifetime within the womb of his mother than any other animal. At any rate, man has lost the instinct of self-preservation. He has to learn it. In man, self-preservation is an ego function and not a function of the instincts. Man is the only creature who regularly kills his own species. He has lost the instinct that seems to be present in other animals for preserving one's own species. Other animals attack other species for food, or they may attack a single member of their own species for sexual reasons, but the only animal who will hunt down and plan and organize the killing of his own species is man. All of this data seems to confirm the innate aggression and destructiveness of man.

To continue our discussion of what predisposes man to war, I would now like to turn to a study of social institutions and their influence upon man. Man is not only an instinctual animal but a social animal and his social institutions influence his instincts. You know we psychoanalysts have always believed that there is a basic and irrevocable antagonism between the instinctual drives and the restrictions of civilization. Now social institutions are on the one hand made by man, but once they are made they influence man and this becomes a two-way relationship. To be sociable, man had to learn to tame, control, polish, restrict, sublimate, internalize, repress, displace, project, his instincts. Societies vary in how and in what way they permit instinctual satisfaction and what instinctual renunciations they demand. Think for a moment about our social attitudes toward aggression. For example, there is the biblical commandment, "Thou Shalt Not Kill." Yet aggression is committed and encouraged in regard to money matters, to make a killing in the stock market, for example. To drive a hard bargain is virtuous. In all kinds of games and sports we encourage aggression. In fact the most popular and beloved are the most violent: football and boxing. Hunting is admirable; it is even aristocratic to ride on a horse and kill a little fox. It is not only permitted but encouraged. Not just killing animals or game fish but birds, doves, etc. It is interesting to see how our society manages this. It is considered sport for a man with a high-powered rifle to kill a little bird, for example, although I am sure everyone would agree that the bird has no sporting chance. It is amazing how hypocritical society can be and I mean not only our society but societies in general.

We can see this in how societies give us special permission to break laws upon occasion. We usually call these times holidays. Perhaps one of the best known is the office Christmas party when it is permitted to get drunk, promiscuous, and aggressive with your employees or employer. Let me quote Freud again from his 1915 paper:

> The State has forbidden to the individual the practice of wrongdoing, not because it desires to abolish it, but because it desires to monopolize it. A belligerent state permits itself every such misdeed, every such act of violence as would disgrace the individual. The State exacts the utmost degree of obedience and sacrifice from its citizens, but at the same time it treats them like children by an excess of secrecy and a censorship upon news and expressions of opinion. The State exhibits a double standard of morality; externally it can do what it wishes, but internally it poses as the guardian of moral standards.

And just think for a moment about all this hypocrisy about "Thou shalt not kill." We have the death penalty in our State of California and this is considered to be a just and honorable law; the state may kill in cold blood. I think it is the same kind of hypocrisy. This double standard of demanding instinctual renunciation and virtue from man and then permitting the state to make exceptions complicates man's attitudes about aggression, violence, and war. Society tries to get man to subdue his instincts most of the time, but we know that instincts are imperishable.

They develop and they mature, but even when they do, the original primitive impulses live on in the unconscious and can be remobilized under certain conditions. Look at the Eichmann case. How was it possible for millions of Germans to passively permit the murder of six million Jews? But, one could also say, how was it possible for millions of Israelis to permit the murder of Eichmann to take place? It seems that if man's aggressive drives are repressed it will lead to some form of psychoneurosis. If they are expressed without sublimation they will lead to delinquency, prejudice, crime, or war readiness. Apparently psychoanalytic findings, anthropological findings, and sociological findings seem to indicate that man is instinctually endowed with a powerful aggressive instinct which leaves him predisposed to violence, brutality, and murder.

I would now like to turn to another basic question, in trying to understand why men like war, namely the question, what is there in war that makes it so particularly appealing to man? What makes war so attractive? At first it must have seemed a startling question but after this discussion I am sure it is not. Nonetheless, it is worth spelling out. Why is war attractive to man?

1. War is an opportunity for the discharge of man's destructive impulses *without responsibility and guilt*. Not only that, with virtue. Think of it. In war it is possible to be as absolutely destructive as you can be; there is no responsibility, no guilt, and you can be a hero. I recall talking to a gunner during the war who had been a gangster in civilian life. I asked him how he happened to get into the Air Force and he told me that he had been arrested for hijacking and when his case came to trial the judge offered him the possibility of enlisting in the Army or going to jail, and so he rather impulsively picked the Army. I asked him how he found it. He answered, "Great, great! First of all, you get all the ammunition free! Not only that, you can even go out killing on Sunday. In our hijacking business we never worked on Sunday; we had our scruples!"

2. War puts an end to uncertainties. Everything in wartime is either good or evil. There are no doubts, no vaguenesses. People are either your enemies or your allies. Think of how propaganda reinforces this by preparing you for war and making you warlike. Once the war is declared, how relieved people are not to have to

struggle, to debate with themselves about what could or should we do. Do you remember the time of Pearl Harbor, and the sense of relief that swept over most of us? It was so hard to know what was right to do. There was Hitler, that monster, and there was poor Czechoslovakia, and France. But to intervene meant war and we were in conflict. What was there to do? And when the Japanese attacked at Pearl Harbor, at least there was no more doubt, there was no more uncertainty. We knew what to do. And this is one of the attractions of war. War reduces everything to its simplest; it is the enemy of complexity.

3. Furthermore, there is a return to that marvelous dependency of childhood. Do you realize that the term *infantry* comes from infant? That is why we have an infantry. You have a commander, you obey all his orders, and you believe in him and all you have to worry about is when you get your next leave, while he takes care of everything, your clothing, your lodging, how to dress, how not to dress, etc. Talk about infancy in the infantry, or the Air Force. War makes possible the return to the state of being taken care of as in childhood. There is no time in war except the present. The past is just for telling stories and the future can wait.

War appeals in other ways as well. War is attractive because it offers the possibility for the individual to become a member of a crowd, of a mob. If you realize, and I don't suppose you do, how many people in this world are lonely creatures who don't belong anywhere. They go through the motions of living. They do not enjoy their freedom, their uniqueness, or their individuality. They just feel alone and lonely. War ends it. You belong. You are a member of a crowd or a mob, and I refer again to Freud on this subject: When people stop being individuals and join a crowd, they become bound together and they regress. They become infantile, impulsive, irritable, changeable, credulous, and barbaric.

If you think I am exaggerating, I remind you of what happens to a lynch mob or to any mob at a sporting event. The word for Jew hater in German is *Judenfresser*, eater of Jews, or in English *Jew baiter*, which has a similar tearing to pieces connotation and indicates the primitive mob spirit. People in crowds believe in magic, believe in illusions. The leader becomes their ideal and replaces their ego ideal. His values become their values. That is what Hitler was able to do. Bound together by the bond of identification, we are all equals and the leader does not love any one any more than any of the others; and with this return to childhood comes the return to all kinds of childhood thinking. The minute you regress and go backwards in time you become a child, you start to believe in magic, and then man begins to believe again in immortality. You know this is how heroism comes about. Man denies the fact that he will die. Or, if he will die, then he says, it is only my body which will die; my soul goes on forever. You know that religions have capitalized on this notion. But so does the Army. It is an interesting fact that even in our present-day missile age there seems to be some attempt made to connect religion and missilry. Isn't it striking that all of our missiles are given the names of Gods: Thor, Atlas, Zeus, Hercules? Isn't this playing on the notion that God is on our side, a notion that men of religion have always insisted about their particular religion and about their particular nationality.

Let me return to the point that in a regressed state man believes in his immortality and in the denial of death and this is fostered by the Army and by religion. I think we also have to recognize that war also appeals to man because it not only gives him an opportunity for glory and for glamour, but it gives him an opportunity for unconscious suicide. There are so many people so burdened with unconscious guilt that they are driven to armies and wars because they unconsciously want to die. They want to be killed.

There seems to be a special affinity between war and nationalism, which is partly related to the kind of regression we have just described that occurs in crowd psychology. There is no doubt that people tend to become more warlike and do become involved in wars, the more nationalistic they are. Every political party which is strongly nationalistic in this country has always been a party more inclined to war. Look at what has happened in Africa the moment new nations were created. Patriotism seems to promote a warlike drive. George Bernard Shaw says this very brilliantly in *Don Juan in Hell*, that it was man's patriotism above all which is his most dangerous weapon. To understand the relationship between patriotism, nationalism, and war is not very easy. From one point of view it can be approached in studying animals. I am referring here to territoriality—the animal's instinctive reaction to defend his territory. It can be very clearly seen in dogs, for example. Your dog may be the skinniest, puniest little dog, but, if any other dog comes around your house, he barks his head off. And when he urinates he always urinates around the boundaries, never, or almost never, inside the territory. He puts up his leg as if to say, "This is my territory . . . keep out!" When he goes onto some other dog's territory, he is a meek dog; but let some other dog come on his territory and he becomes a lion!

The point is, this is what does happen in all kinds of animals and fish in defense of their territory. And it is a question whether there is not something like that in man. When they talk about war they ask, "Under what conditions would you go to war?" Most people would say, "Well, of course, if they would invade my country." And people are horrified if you were to say, "So what?" "What do you *mean*, 'So what?' " There is almost an instinctual attitude about defending one's country. Then you also begin to see how one's country becomes a symbol for one's home. Invade my country, you invade my home. Now, even homeless people who never had a home, never owned a piece of ground, feel that way about their country. Invade my country, you invade my home. And I will fight to protect my home. Then you can begin to see how one's country really means one's family. Country means countrymen and country means the fatherland or the motherland and we are all brothers and sisters who have to defend our fathers or mothers, our younger brothers and sisters. This whole question of nationalism becomes tied up with the instinctual elements involved in the family, the homeland, and eventually mother earth.

Related to the problem of nationalism is the problem of power. The driving force in nationalism is the desire for power. Power may roughly be defined as the ability to impose your will upon somebody else. Power is the ability to force someone to submit to your wishes. Leaders in general seek power, and once having had power are most reluctant to relinquish it. The essential element in power is that is gives the powerful one the ability to enforce his wishes.

I deliberately chose the term *enforce* because I want to indicate that it is derived from aggression. Power is always tied up with force, strength, and violence. In every nation there are leaders, and leaders seek power. These leaders may be politicians, industrialists, or anyone at the head of a strong and important group. These leaders then have followers, and they influence one another in a regressive, infantile way. The leader becomes the father, or the Führer, and the followers become his children, or his soldiers or slaves. The leader searches for power, conquest, glory, and he promises his followers great rewards, freedom from guilt, etc. If you study what has happened throughout history, you will always find the powerful leader and his submissive followers organizing themselves in ways to acquire more power, be it territory, money, or glory. You can see it in Hitler who claimed to need Lebensraum, or Napoleon. You can see it when the Soviet Union takes over the satellite countries but claims this is for defensive purposes. And we seem to be doing something similar in Latin America or in Vietnam. It may well be true that there is some defensive purpose in what we are doing, but let us not be blind to the enormous need for power that is going on at the same time.

It is striking to see how the craving for power brings with it the fear of power of the opposing force. The more powerful the nation, the more readily it is apt to feel in danger from attack from a powerful enemy. Let me speak in psychoanalytic terms: the greater one's aggressive striving is for attaining power, the more likely one is apt to expect a retaliation from some hostile force. I do not mean to imply that this is the whole story in understanding the struggle for power going on in the world today, but it has to be taken into account in understanding the reactions of men and leaders of men in particular. There seems to be a cycle of aggressive instinct, projection, and fear of the enemy's retaliatory power, which then justifies our aggressive behavior. This leads us then to search for more weapons, more stockpiles of missiles, and more armies which then justifies the Soviet Union in doing the same, which then justifies us for increasing our stockpiles, our allies, etc.

I think you will agree that this has a distinctly paranoid quality to it. Now I know there may be realistic reasons for all of this, but I also submit to you that this is terribly infantile. This reliance on force in civilized people does not seem to be in accord with what we would expect from the so-called "leaders of civilization" today. But we have gotten ourselves involved in an arms race, a missile race, a space race, and a thermonuclear weapons race. We say *we* have a bigger power now; no, *you* have a bigger power now. If *you* are going to test, *we* are going to test. If this does not sound childish, I do not know what does. And, please, I do not want to discount the danger, but I do maintain that it is very dangerous to be so childish.

Now let me continue with this study of power and extend it a bit, and talk for a moment or so about the relationship between right and might. Power has to do with force, with aggression, etc. But what about right? What is the meaning of "to be in the right"? Now I am quoting Freud again on "Why War."

If you study what is the concept of right, it is surprising to find that right and might are not really as antithetical as you might imagine. Whereas "might" refers to the power of an individual or an elite group, "right" is the might of the community. When right prevails, it means that most of the individuals consider this to be in accordance with their wishes or desires or ideals. In a very curious way, and again I know I am straining a bit to make my point, but it is important to see the connection, it seems that right is nothing less than the extension of violence and force, but divided over a greater number of people. The more you distribute force, might, power, strength, the more you get to law. Law is nothing more than the assertion of the community about what it considers that it will maintain and uphold, and what it will punish if you violate it. If you look at it from this point of view, you can see that right is might distributed over a greater number of people. This leads eventually to what we consider justice. But it does point out to you that what starts out to be aggression can end up in something relatively nonaggressive. Like the transition from might to right, from force to justice.

Up until now I have been trying to show how a psychoanalyst would attempt to explain why men like war. I would now like to at least sketch for you briefly certain additional factors which are responsible for our current conscious attitude about war. In other words, I would like to consider how it is possible that civilized people can still respect the institution of war apart from the instinctual aggressive factors that I have thus far described.

Partly we have become saturated by such terms of terror like kill and overkill, megatons, megadeaths, tolerable death rates in millions, so that the whole conception of living in an age of balance of terror has lost its meaning. Terms which should incite terror leave us untouched. Millis and Reed point this out very clearly in their excellent book. I would like to remind you how horrified we were by the revolt in Hungary and the brutality that it met. I would also like to point out how far less touched we were by the barbarism in Algiers. Now true, in one instance it was the Soviet Union; in the other instance it was France. But, nevertheless, both dealt with man's inhumanity to man. We are getting bored with it.

I would like to point out to you how few people ever mention the horrible flood which occurred in Italy recently. It occurred in the town of Langaroni (I, myself, had forgotten the name of the town and had to find it out so I could tell it to you) and there were 1600 dead bodies found. The flood, the devastation of which was the equal of the destruction of Pompeii, is forgotten. Who was horrified after the first five minutes of the broadcast? We are bored and untouched. We ought to be civilized enough to have a decent amount of anxiety about war and brutality.

We have more than an ordinary stake in a warless world. At least I think so. We were responsible for the only atomic bomb explosion that was ever perpetrated upon human beings. We did it. I say we because the majority of us at that time were not opposed to it or did not protest it, or would not have if we had had the possibility. So to some extent it is our guilt. I do not want to get maudlin about it, but I don't want to let any of us forget that we, the American liberated people, we, the greatest democracy in the world, that we were responsible for the death of over 100,000 people in Hiroshima, more than half of whom were women and children. And I do not think it is neurotic to feel a certain sense of guilt and responsibility for this. I think it is not only right but our duty to think about war and what we can do to make it impossible.

War has changed in many ways since the days when one could look upon it as an opportunity for glory and heroism. Ever since we have had armies of the people and not just professional soldiers the whole character of war has changed. More than that, ever since the American Civil War, all thoughtful students about war realize that war is nothing more than economic and social suicide. The Civil War was the beginning of siege warfare which devastated human life and property beyond nature's limit to control. The repeating rifle and the machinegun made war suicide for the soldier. In 1897 Ivan Bloch, a Polish banker, wrote a seven-volume analysis of wars in which he demonstrated that any international war with modern weapons would only lead to military and economic suicide. World War I proved this. By 1916 the military aspects of World War I were over; what was left was only the struggle for power. It is amazing how little of this knowledge has filtered down to the average man and how readily this can be forgotten by the politicians and others who seek national power.

War is no longer and has not for a long time been a means of solving any international dispute. Wars have never and I want to stress *never* led to any reliable or lasting peace. It is a myth what you may read about Pax Britannica. You cannot enforce peace by military power, and it is never a useful instrument. Hitler used the Treaty of Versailles, the peace treaty of Versailles mind you, as a pretext for gaining power. World War II proved that the system of international wars was impossible. Unfortunately the discovery of the atom bomb reawakened in man, particularly in some of the leaders of men, the hope that once again it would be possible for a single power to attain overwhelming superiority and once again the mad dash for military weapons was on.

I would like now to turn to a discussion of deterrence as an international posture. Again I want to stress that I shall discuss this from a psychoanalytic point of view which is limited but may not be dismissed or disregarded. Deterrence means that we have based our security on the fact that we have huge piles of deadly weapons within our country and scattered all over the world which we can use against any enemy who will have first attacked us. I believe this is a very dangerous policy on psychological grounds.

First of all, the greater amount of thermonuclear weapons available to greater numbers of people increases the likelihood of accidents. That point is obvious. Second, how can any group of experts or any single expert determine when a pile of dangerous weapons will be a deterrent or when it will be a provocation? Let us admit that it is far easier to predict in a given individual what will provoke him or what will deter him than it is to predict about a group. Let us agree that it is easier to predict about an individual we know than it is to predict about an individual who is foreign to us, but let us also agree that even the best of us who specialize in the field of psychology have a very difficult time in predicting the behavior of a single individual unless we have studied him for years in great detail. The best of us cannot predict under those ideal conditions when a certain activity will be a deterrence or when it might become a provocation. I cannot understand, therefore, how we can be so smug as to believe that there are experts who can believe that they know what will serve as a deterrent for the Soviet Union.

That nation is thousands of miles away from us; we hardly know them, and they hardly know us. I think banking on such a position of deterrence is foolhardy. It becomes even more obvious that this is reckless thinking and irresponsible thinking if you realize that there is a widespread belief that the Russians are out to destroy us because they feel we will destroy them the first chance we get. Just as we find every excuse to uncover and expose communist spies who are plotting to overthrow our Government, and they find American spies or counterrevolutionaries who are doing the same.

I think we ought to face the fact that they seem to be paranoid about us and we are paranoid about them. Let us go back to the question of deterrence. It is difficult enough to predict what a foreign country will do if we build up a huge pile of thermonuclear weapons. Will it deter him or provoke him? Think how much more difficult it is to predict what a parnoid foreign country might do in response to another paranoid country. Will the many guns quiet him? If you threaten belligerence, will this calm him or frighten him, or will he become pugnacious?

I think the advocates of deterrence are being presumptuous if they claim to have the answer to this. I think this is a most poorly thought out idea. That this can preserve peace momentarily, yes; but turn your back for a moment on a paranoid, belligerent, disturbed, emotionally distraught person—will deterrence really quiet him down? No. You know, I don't understand. Are we such good predictors anyway? *Who* are such good predictors? We psychoanalysts certainly don't make such predictions. We have enough trouble predicting what is going to happen tomorrow with our next patient, let alone with a foreign power we hardly know, and the rulers in that foreign power. Who are making these predictions? The same people who made the predictions in World War II that the Soviets would collapse within a few weeks after the Germans marched in? Or the people who predicted our strategic bombing of Germany in 1945 would destroy the Nazis? Experts predicted this. And they were terribly wrong. I do not know who is predicting this and I don't want you to believe what they are predicting. I am not preaching against deterrence, but I ask you to please be skeptical. It is dangerous.

Before I leave the subject of deterrence I want to bring up something pertinent which can be observed in animals, dealing with the question of provocation and deterrence. Konrad Lorenz, the animal psychologist and ethologist, wrote in his book *King Solomon's Ring* on what happened with two wolves, an old one and a young one that began a terrible fight to the death. These two wolves fought each other fiercely. Finally one (I think it was the older) had the younger one down and at his mercy and he had his jaws and his teeth poised for the kill. Then the one who was the underwolf turned his jugular vein toward the wolf on top. And the wolf on top stopped. The battle was over. You watch dogs in a fight and when two dogs fight to the bitter end, when one dog has the other at his mercy, at that moment the underdog will turn his most vulnerable spot to the aggressor and the aggressor will stop fighting. As long as the underdog remains humble.

I think one ought to remember this. I never knew this about wolves but when I was trying to treat disturbed, pugnacious, and belligerent patients, I remember it seemed the smartest thing I could do, to turn my back and let him hit me. But, I was never hit from the back, I should add. I did not know that there was some old truth in this business about showing your vulnerability.

Let me go on now to my final points. I realize I have talked long but I wanted to come to some kind of conclusions about what we can do about the fact that men like war. How can we change men? First of all, let us face it, we cannot change the fact that man is aggressive and destructive and that he needs plenty of outlets for his destructiveness. We are not going to eradicate these destructive impulses. Let us grant that and say okay, that is not what we are going to do. What we can try to do is change the *way* in which he expresses his destructiveness. Change, perhaps, even the social institutions which we have begun to accept as inevitable. And I mean, first of all war has to become obsolete. War has to become not only eradicated but impossible, abolished. War has to become *stupid* because that is what it is.

What I mean is, one ought to develop an ego-alien attitude about war. Stop glorifying it. Stop making it inevitable or even pathological. It is too dignified. It is mainly useless, obsolete, stupid, wasteful. I think one has to develop a different attitude about it and not be awed by the idea that it is inevitable that we have some sort of international war. Nonsense! We must change. You say, well, is that possible? Of course it is possible. Other things have changed. Lots of other social institutions that were considered inevitable have changed. Slavery, for example, is no longer considered inevitable. The divine right of kings. Human sacrifice. They were all considered inevitable. Part of human nature. Nonsense! Segregation, I may also add, will disappear. So can our attitude toward war. The institutions of war change. I think it is important not to feel helpless and hopeless about changing it.

*How* we are going to do it is much harder to talk about and far beyond me, but there are a few things I could say. I think we have to recognize that we have a bigger loyalty than nationalism. I love being an American. I love to live the way I live. I love democracy. But, I am sorry, I believe it is a real handicap in terms of preventing war, to be more loyal to America than to mankind. I think we have to become more and more conscious that we are part of man, mankind. We have to be human rather than primarily Californian, or white, or American, or anything like that.

Again, this is nothing new but it is important that people take this seriously. But you see, I know if I say this there will always be Birchers who will say, "Well, this man is a communist, he sounds like one." I will tell you something. I find communists no different than Birchers. I find them both a menace and both distasteful to me. But I do not want to have them killed, just ignored. It takes courage to stand up against patriotism and recognize the regressive, destructive pull of patriotism and nationalism. I see how they attacked Hutchins recently and the Center for Democratic Studies. Same grounds. Nonsense! We civilized people ought to have a greater loyalty to mankind than to any nationalism.

Now my next point is that we have to learn to *try* to have more trust in man. I think the idea of getting rid of war with deterrents and arms is terribly weak; it is terribly hackneyed. And we are so loaded with mistrust and suspicion which poses as vigilance or intelligence or smartness or courage or masculinity. And I say to you, one of the most masculine things we could do, one of the most courageous things we could do, one of the smartest things we could do is to be more trustful, more vulnerable. I mean, to dare to take the risk to trust other nations, even those who differ from us. Again, I don't know if this makes any sense to you. But I tell you, this frightened, paranoid, belligerent attitude we have toward those who are different will get us nowhere. And we have had enough time now to see that with all our differences with the Soviet Union and with all their differences with us, Berlin is still standing, even with the wall, it is still there. Cuba is still there. We have not been attacked by the missiles there, or by the Russians, I could point out to you all kinds of things which say maybe the Soviets are changing and perhaps we are also changing. I suspect there is slowly a change in our administration's attitude of trying now to accentuate the more positive and less of the old belligerent, paranoid, threatening attitudes that we have depended on up to now.

I think it is necessary for us to realize that if people were fed they would not want war. We have the possibility for enough food to feed a great many more people than we do. We have enough medicine to treat a heck of a lot more sick people in the world. And people who are fed and healthy do not want war. War and armaments are not necessary for economic purposes. This has been told me by people who are supposed to be experts in this field. As long as we don't have to be the *supreme* and *only* power. As long as we don't *have* to be loved by everybody. If we will try to bend our efforts toward peace and toward being a member of mankind, I think we have a real good chance of making it possible for war to become abolished. I think we have to be willing to share our power.

I want to go back to one of my last points; this is my last sentence. We must be willing to give up some of our power. We must be willing even, I would say, to give up some of our standard of living, to share it with the rest of the world. In the greater distribution of wealth, in the greater distribution of power, there is a much greater chance that right will replace might and war will be abolished. It would be wonderful if our Peace Corps could become a Peace Army and go all over the world. It would be a great step forward. We could become patriotic about mankind and nationalistic about our universe. My great fear is that if we don't become better human beings, there will be no human race.

# 9 Laughter and Tears (1963)

*This lecture was given to the Mental Health Association of Fresno, California, where Greenson was introduced by the governor's son, Jerry Brown. With the subject of humor Greenson was at his performing best. There were many opportunities for laughter, and Greenson and the audience thoroughly enjoyed themselves. He took as his topic the psychoanalytic view toward laughter and tears. One of his first important points was that the capacity to laugh and the capacity to cry are distinctly human. No other animal has these capacities. Greenson analyzes how any joke or funny situation deals with painful stimulation or forbidden instinctual impulses, "but pain has been transformed into some pleasure, the danger has been transformed into some kind of joy, or some kind of reassurance—a transformation takes place to make it laughable; the forbidden has become permissible; the painful has become pleasurable, and this is what provokes laughter." Romi summed up his thoughts on laughter and tears with this advice for his audience: Crying and laughing are two basic, inborn emotions and ways of expressing emotion that are terribly precious for good health and for happiness and for a rich life. They have to be protected and they have to be respected. If we retain the capacity for laughter and tears it is better for us. We have a chance then to remain civilized human beings.*

My subject has to do with laughter and tears, the psychoanalytic point of view and approach to laughter and tears. I want to prepare you for the fact that I do not think that this is going to be anything funny, I have very few jokes. A few old ones I tried to remember just to illustrate a point. If anything is amusing or entertaining it is purely by accident, it is not my intention.

My intention, actually, is to explore with you a very interesting and important aspect of human behavior. Do you realize the capacity to laugh and the capacity to cry is distinctly human? No other animal has this capacity. We are the only animal who can laugh and we are the only animal who can cry. Too bad many of us have lost it, it is a relatively healthy person who has retained the ability for laughter and for tears. In fact, it is an indication of mental health.

Through the course of our development various factors in our society have discouraged us from laughing or crying and there is a great deal of conflict in people about laughter and also about tears. It is not considered very well bred to laugh too heartily, nor is it particularly considered an indication of high character to weep too readily. Yet we also know that the absence of tears, when they are expected, or the absence of laughter, when expected, indicates something is wrong. This person must be in some kind of unconscious mental conflict. Or, when you find people laughing when they should be crying, or crying when they should be laughing, your reaction is that this is weird. And you wonder what is wrong. If you ever saw a depressed person walking down the street, bent over, bowed, slowly walking and if he has a smile on his face he looks sort of crazy. And he is. One of the most menacing figures that you could imagine would be just such a figure, slouched, bent, slow, head bowed, with a smile on his face.

So, there is something here that deserves our attention. What is all this about? I propose to begin by talking about laughter, and what can an analyst tell you that would be interesting about laughter?

---

Sacramento Mental Health Association, 1963 to 1964.

Many of these points, I think, are well known, but they ought to be collected and put together because it is worthwhile studying since there is so much we still do not know. I would like to begin with a few general characteristics of laughter to make you aware of them. Certainly you will agree that laughter is an involuntary emotional discharge except when you pretend to laugh, or fake a laugh. Laughter, hearty laughter, is a real involuntary (i.e., uncontrolled) emotional discharge. If you examine what it consists of, you will see that it is a rather explosive discharge of emotion, spasmotic, and has to do with expiration of breathing. It is done with the face, the mouth, the eyes, as well as the larynx, the chest and the abdomen. A good deal of the body is involved in laughter. It is a joyous expression of emotion, it is not just a satisfying discharge like other discharges might be, but it is a joyous one, and there is something playful about laughter. It is transient, that is, you can laugh and then stop and it can be repeated. This is not true of all emotional involuntary discharges. Some of them can happen once and then stop, but laughter can be repeated.

It is also a discharge which is socially permissible. It is permitted for you to laugh in a group in contrast to other examples of discharge phenomena which are not permissible in a group. I mention here involuntary discharges of the excretory or sexual organs, which are all right when you are in private but you ordinarily do not do it socially.

Another interesting thing is that laughter is contagious. When one person, or two people start laughing, and if you are not really fed up with the whole thing, you will laugh too. You see this one laugh, so the next one laughs and God knows why the two of them are laughing. But, nevertheless, it spreads, and if given the signal, and given permission, you join into it too. There is this curious contagiousness about laughter.

There are also different kinds of laughter. One could go from the most mild forerunner of laughter, which is a smile where all you do is something with your mouth, to quiet laughter, loud hearty laughter, the belly laugh and the boff. In Hollywood I know people who call certain kinds of laughter the boff. There is malicious laughter, sadistic laughter, there is also sad laughter. Very peculiar, all the things that can be expressed in laughter. It is not so simple when you realize what triggers the laughter varies enormously. It is very different what will make a little child laugh and what will make a grown-up laugh, and what will make an older person laugh. It is different in different societies, what is considered funny, and it is different according to your own mood, as to what is laughable and what is not. Imagine the difference after you have had a couple of drinks, and more than a couple of drinks, well, then it doesn't matter much what is considered funny, you just laugh.

A curious enigmatic thing is that if you laugh hard enough you begin to cry. And this is certainly true with women in our society, the closeness between laughter and tears. You laugh long enough and hard enough—tears. There is a lot worth looking at here; what is all of this about?

I would now like to start by taking a few examples and see what evokes laughter. In other words, let me try to make up, out of really raw elements, something laughable. I will not start with a joke. I will start with an ordinary situation in order to try to indicate what the raw ingredients are, the elements that make up a laugh-evoking situation. I will take something very primitive.

Let's say we watch a man walking on the snow and ice and he falls down. Simple, not an every day situation in Sacramento nor in Beverly Hills, but let's say I watch a man walking and he falls down. What would make us laugh if we saw this? If this man were a poor man, or a skinny man, or an old man, or a weak man, we would not laugh. Let's imagine a man walking on the snow and ice, and he is a big, fat, pompous stuffed shirt man and he is strutting on the ice and he falls down. Admit it, it's funny. And if I were to tell you that this man is the principal of a grammar school, delightful! Or he is the chief revenue collector of the state, great! Isn't it striking what it is that makes this man falling down, laughable? In my house, if it is me, it is laughable. If I fall down ten stairs, my children are hysterical with laughter. I would add my wife too, but she is sitting in the audience.

When anybody else falls down there is concern, or if anybody else does something clumsy there is anxiety. In my house, the father, if something happens to the father, it is delightful, it is delicious. And I realize that this seems to be a typical American characteristic. If you want to watch something funny on television, you watch a father-figure who is clumsy, inept, doing all things wrong and you laugh hilariously. If the wife does anything wrong or inept, that is sad. Some kind of discrimination against fathers, but I don't want to go into that. It is a peculiar thing, if you build up a figure of strength and power and you deflate it, that's funny. But that is only one kind of a laugh-evoking situation, but I could describe to you another.

How many of you are old enough to have seen, let us say, Charlie Chaplin in *The Goldrush*? Those of you who have seen it will know what I refer to, for those of you who haven't I will describe it. There is a scene where Charlie Chaplin, starving, freezing, is sitting in his little shack up in the Klondike, or wherever it is. He has boiled one of his shoes for dinner. With his fork he is testing if it is done enough, and apparently well done, he takes the shoe out of the water and puts it on his plate, to eat the shoe. He takes his fork and very carefully takes the shoelace and winds it around the fork, like spaghetti. With his pinky finger curled and with immaculate manners, he tastes the shoelace to see if it is done properly. He nods to signify that it is quite good. Then there is the nail of the shoe. He takes the nail of the shoe and quite apologetically picks it up with his naked fingers, and as though it were a chicken bone, he bites off the meat, i.e., the leather from the shoe nail. It is terribly funny. But this is not a big, powerful, pompous man, and yet you laugh, or at least you smile because what he has done is to show you how this poor little guy (Charlie Chaplin), this woebegone creature, prevails despite horrible adversity. There he sits with his knife and fork and meticulously eats the shoelace, and the nail from his shoe, it is his triumph.

Let us see how different yet another situation will be. Again I like to take simple examples, let us take a little child. What do you do if you want to make a little child laugh? Oh, many things, let us say you play peek-a-boo. You hide your face behind your hands and then you suddenly bring your hands apart and say, peek-a-boo. (You don't say it that way, you say it, you know how you say it to a little child: "Peek-a-boo," and the child laughs.) What's funny? In some way, by hiding your face, and then suddenly revealing it, you did something that made this child laugh. We have to come back to analyze that.

Let me take another situation and now let's take a story, a joke. This is a very old joke, I haven't—why should I explain—I don't remember too many jokes, but this one I remember and I don't want to explain why I remember it. Now, let us see what is funny about this joke, remember you are supposed to laugh at the end, don't disappoint me.

There is a painter, an artist, who paints a nude model. He works in his own home in the attic and every day this beautiful girl, I must add, comes to this middle-aged painter's home and she goes upstairs with him into the attic and she gets undressed and stands naked in front of him and he paints her. But one morning she comes to his home and they go up into the attic, but instead of getting undressed, they start to talk. She is telling him something about the hardships of everyday life, and her background, and what made her an artist's model, and why she didn't get married, and they sit on the bed and talk. Suddenly he hears some noise and he says to her: "Quick, my wife is coming, get undressed."

I notice most of the men are laughing. Something is funny. What is it? Let me tell you another kind of story that will make you laugh. I think nothing can kill laughter more than telling people you are going to make them laugh. Nevertheless, here is another kind of situation. It is a personal one, an anecdote, a piece out of my past.

During the war I served for four years in the Air Force as a psychiatrist, and early in the war I was stationed on a new post, an airfield in Arizona. I don't want to go into it, Barry Goldwater was stationed there. (Laughter) That's not the joke—(laughter) sorry, I withdraw the comment. Nothing was ready at this Air Force base. They rushed us in and we had about twelve doctors and three thermometers and about 200 patients. Anyway, slowly, they built up this station hospital, and eventually my psychiatric ward was finished, they said.

In those days they were very careful how they built the psychiatric wards. I don't know how familiar any of you are with such installations and you don't have to tell me, but nevertheless, the toilets were made in such a way that there were no toilet seats, you sat on the tiles. This was so the patients would not hurt themselves or you with the toilet seat. (Laughter) That is still not the funny part of the story. The funny part is that one day my wardman came to me and said, "Captain Greenson, something is wrong with the toilets." We had so many things going wrong, it was a terrible thing. We always had to call the Colonel and say something is going wrong with this or that. He hated psychiatry anyway and psychiatrists even more than psychiatry. I said, "What's wrong?" and he said, "It's a funny thing but the patients are complaining that the toilets are flushing hot water." (Laughter) I didn't think that was funny, I couldn't believe it—he had lost his mind. I went and tested it out and by God, when you flushed the toilets, it was hot! You ran the showers, they were cold. So, I get to the phone and I call up the Colonel, the head of the hospital. I say, "Colonel McDonough, this is Greenson." He says, "Okay, what's wrong?" I replied, "Well, we have a little something wrong here. The toilets are flushing hot, the showers are running cold." He says, "Greenson, don't talk to me!" and he hung up the phone. So I call him back and he says, "Listen, I have enough trouble and now you are making it up." Well, I tried to persuade him to come and test it out but he says, "I wouldn't go into your ward period." So, I got the Executive Officer to come who was a southerner and didn't like me either. I said, "Please test it with your fingers or with your hand." This did not seem very funny to him at all, nor to me. I was miserable. Yet there is something funny isn't there? I want to add that we had the toilets straightened out eventually.

Look how different all these stories are. Peek-a-boo to a baby, the artist's model, the man falling down, and Charlie Chaplin eating the shoelace with a fork. All of this is funny. And I would say let's look at this as raw material and let's analyze what do these situations have in common that make for laughter, and you will see all of them have to do with one of the following:

Either I have described painful situations which were scary or sad; or I have described situations which seemed to be dealing with forbidden instincts. Every one of these situations can be explained on this basis. Look, a man falls down, big fat father falls down, obviously, hostile destructive impulses toward father have surfaced.

The artist with the naked woman. That story does not make you think about the painting, you are thinking of the sexual possibilities. To the baby with whom you are playing peek-a-boo, you are saying, "I am not here" and that is scary for a baby. Charlie Chaplin is pathetic, that is sad. He is starving and freezing in the Klondike. The toilets running hot, I think is sad. (Laughter) Okay, painful for me and the patients. Sad.

Every one of these situations deals either with painful stimulation or forbidden instinctual impulses. And yet, in every one of these situations the pain has been transformed into some pleasure, the danger has been transformed into some kind of joy, or some kind of reassurance. All the artist said was to get undressed in order to work; see, it was not sexual after all. Charlie Chaplin was not dying, he was conquering his misery. The child did not lose you behind the peek-a-boo, you were still there. And the toilet situation, well you think, thank God it was him and not me, so it is a pleasure anyway and nothing horrible happened to him. In every one of these situations a transformation has taken place to make it laughable. The forbidden has become permissible; the painful has become pleasurable, and this is what produces laughter. The essential dynamics of making people laugh is to create a situation which is full of tension, either tension due to a forbidden instinct or due to some kind of painful condition.

When you have built sufficient tension by making illusions, by concealing, by disguising and you take a little time to describe the situation, to build it up, like forepleasure, then, when the expectation is there, at the last moment you make a telling, sharp point and suddenly all the anxiety and fear that was building up (My God, this is awful!) becomes unnecessary. It is not unpleasant after all, it has become a funny situation, the tension is broken, resulting in a discharge and release and laughter. That is the technique for making people laugh.

It is the suddenness, the unexpectedness, the surprisingness of this punchline that transforms the pain into pleasure; the forbidden into the permissible, and gives you the chance to discharge the tension you have been building up.

The more surprising it is, the better it is built up, the more you will laugh. If it takes too long in the building up, you are not going to laugh, you are going to get annoyed and say, all right, come to the point. If it is too quick, you have not built up enough tension, and you are not going to get enough of a laugh.

It is a very curious structure, a good joke makes all your worries, all your defenses unnecessary. A bad joke embarrasses you and embarrasses the person who made it, because then all the forbidden instincts are still intact. Instead of laughter you feel embarrassed for the person who is telling the joke, you feel ashamed or you feel guilty for him. You look at him and you think, my God, what is going on in his mind? Very prudish people feel that anyway, even if you tell a good joke. To prudes, chronic prudes, you can tell the funniest joke and they sit there thinking, what is going on in him?

But ordinary people will laugh, though they may think the next day, what made him tell that joke? If you tell a bad joke it is terribly embarrassing. You feel exposed, revealed, ashamed, and guilty. You have been caught, if I may use a vulgar expression, with your pants down, and it is not just a vulgar expression, it is to the point.

You know, there is a very interesting similarity between building a good joke and the building of a dream. In a successful dream, all the forbidden and painful impulses are covered over. They have a rather pleasant quality in a happy dream. But in a nightmare all the bad impulses stand exposed. There you were, killing your dear mother, that is like telling a bad joke. Although that example might be rather harsh, it is appropriate and that is what happens in a nightmare. The dream did not succeed in transforming, disguising, the forbidden instincts, which is necessary in order to have a good dream or a good joke.

Let me say a little about people who make you laugh, the laughmakers, the jokesters. There are several different kinds of joke tellers. There are those kind of witty people whose jokes have a sadistic quality, and they are famous for their sharp tongues. You know, they make cracks and if you did not like them you would say they are nasty. But since it is not directed at you, but, let's say, Barry Goldwater, you laugh. Mort Sahl would be a good example of this kind of sharp, sadistic tongue, which you will find very funny if you agree with him, but not at all funny if you don't.

Then there is the kind of joke maker who makes you laugh at him, who says, look at me, I'm not much, I am here on false pretenses, an imposter, a fraud, and somewhat impotent, that is the jester, the guy whose shortcomings you know and you cannot wait to see them exposed. Jack Benny made a career out of this. How you laugh at his stingyness, his always being thirty-nine. He is not an imposing figure, he is a kind of "Please laugh at me" comic. Jackie Gleason also says, laugh at me, big, fat Jackie Gleason; but underneath it all, "we know" he is a scared and insecure guy, who makes you laugh at him. The clown is a little different. I think of Charlie Chaplin as the clown. He is a really pathetic figure but you laugh because somehow he has the capacity to triumph over his adversity. And then there is the humorist who is still different from all of them, who laughs at himself *with* you. He tells you about himself but he has a distance to himself and he says, "Look at me. This is what I did. Or, look at us, our society, this is what we do." And now you both laugh and he is the one who demonstrates how we can laugh at ourselves.

It is so different whether you laugh with these joke makers or at them. The comic, the jester, make you laugh at them, while the humorist, the wit, let you laugh with them. You don't laugh at Mort Sahl, you laugh with him. Interesting too is the question of what role the audience plays.

The joke tellers, comics, humorists, all need an audience; without an audience they are miserable. This is a very important point. They all need an audience who will laugh. This will prove, will confirm, see, what I did was permissible. It wasn't gauche, it wasn't primitive, it wasn't instinctual, it wasn't aggressive, it wasn't sexual; it was only funny. People who need an audience want the audience to be a witness: I didn't say anything offensive, or harsh or bad or hostile. I was just being amusing.

If you ask yourselves what kind of people are humorists and comics, you can see that usually very good-looking people, and sexually attractive people are not terribly funny. Plain people, homely people, sexually not very attractive people, they are funny. The great comics so often come from minority groups, the Irish, the Jews, the Armenians. It is very striking. What does that mean? What does that indicate?

You see, there is a certain connection between laughing and making people laugh, and trying to overcome other emotions that you are trying to hide. The man who always wants to make you laugh, the man who is ready to be the life of the party, the jokester (incidentally, that can be any one of us; we all have these tendencies) these are people who underneath are full of depression. They want to laugh and make you laugh because they are relatively close to tears. Any good humorist, any good clown, is a sad person. He makes you laugh and he loves to laugh himself in order to stay away from a depression. He is usually a member of a minority group, or feels himself otherwise mistreated, is full of aggression and hostility and destructiveness, which he denies by making you laugh about it all. Those laugh producers are struggling with their aggressiveness, their depressiveness, and their exhibitionism. Don't forget this exhibitionism. They are always the center and saying, look at me, look at me, because they feel they are homely, they are the unattractive ones.

Among women you will rarely see a beautiful comedienne. Did you ever see Elizabeth Taylor being funny? Maybe with Richard Burton, but otherwise she is not funny. She does not have to be funny. Homely women, or plain women, or, yes, sometimes even a pretty one who isn't so sure she is good looking, these are the people who go out and get a particular joy in making you laugh. Incidentally, interesting to think about the aggressive language used to describe how funny a man was. Oh, he killed them, they were rolling in the aisles. You can hear all the aggression that comes out in those expressions. However, the laugh maker is a guy who is willing to be the scapegoat, or the tease, the provocateur.

You know teasing is very closely related to humor, and there are always masochistic people ready to provoke someone, ready to be teased. They hope to stop the teasing before it becomes painful, and they hope the attack will be playful; but, they are always provoking aggressive behavior. I have already mentioned exhibitionistic, aggressive, depressed, and now also masochistic elements which gives you a rough idea about the psychology of the people who make you laugh. Of course, the very fact that if you laugh long enough you get close to tears indicates that this relationship is a very intimate one.

Tears. What I want to say about tears is what I have already said about laughter, namely, we are the only animal who cries. We are not the only animal who has tears. Crocodiles have tears, but they don't cry. There is a difference. We are the only animal who, under emotional conditions, has tears, and weeping has to do with sadness. We are all born with that capacity, it starts in childhood at about six weeks of age. For the first six weeks, children cry but are dry eyed. From six weeks on, all children cry with tears. And then we knock it out of them, yes, I will say it bluntly. We teach them that you are not supposed to cry. It is not grown-up to cry, it is not manly to cry, it is not ladylike to cry. And why do we do that? Because it is painful for us who have to hear it.

By doing so we deprive our children of a very important safety valve. Healthy people can cry and it is a pity, a real pity that people have lost the capacity to cry tears with sadness.

Let me say a little about the physiology of crying. You know we are always producing tears, whether we cry or not. Usually they run from our tear ducts into the nasal lachrymal ducts. But what makes them overflow?

Well, it has to do with sadness or with an eye irritation. You can get tearing from an eye irritation and it has nothing to do with sadness. Get a chemical irritation or a foreign body into your eyes and your eyes will tear. That is not crying. Crying is the combination of sadness and the tear production. Incidentally, fish are the creatures with no lachrymal ducts at all because the water washes their eyes. And, they apparently don't get sad. I have never talked to a fish so I cannot verify this.

To go on about weeping. Again, it is curious, the same parts of the body that are used for laughing are used for crying: the face, eyes, mouth, larynx, chest. In children, crying is a very important signal device. Children use crying as an alarm to give a signal to the parent: I'm in trouble, help! It's a preverbal, vocal expression—vocal, but not verbal. It is made with the larynx, made with a sound but not a word. In adults it has still other connections to sadness and to pain. By and large the most essential cause for weeping is the loss of somebody you love. Other emotions can produce tears. You can have tears in anger, tears of rage, all kinds of tears, but that is not really weeping. Sadness and the loss of someone you love will produce that.

Tears also evoke sympathy, and there are people who can turn them on. I hate to say this, but women are great at it. To men this trait is lost because in our society people feel it is immature, or it is feminine, men are not supposed to cry.

There are many social differences when it comes to crying. In New England you try not to cry, in Italy you've got to cry. How different that is in different parts of our culture, whether it is permitted to cry or not. I was struck by how many people cried when Kennedy was assassinated. It was a horrible experience, but it was in a way moving and reassuring to me to see how many people could cry. All kinds of people. Even people who did not particularly like him. I was also struck by Mrs. Kennedy's not crying, though she must have grieved. As the wife of the former President she probably considered it her duty not to be crying. I was touched that so many people cried over Kennedy's death. It made me think: maybe the country is getting somewhere.

To go back to the developmental history about crying tears. Usually boys cry more than girls in the first year of life. The subject has been studied and boys cry more than girls, but usually at the end of the first year it changes and girls cry more than boys.

Another interesting piece of experimental evidence about crying is the terrifically close connection between crying and urinating. I don't know if you ever thought of this, but both have to do with getting rid of water. There is an interesting correlation; studies have been made by measuring crying and urinating in children and they found that the ones who cry more, urinate less. You know, one could say people can become incontinent with their crying, they cry over everything. In children's language, very often a child will call crying urinating or making water with the eyes.

Sphincter control is the first morality that children learn, the first concept of good or bad is, are you wet or are you dry? You are good if you are dry and you are bad if you are wet. And for many people it remains that way for the rest of their lives.

It is important to realize that when you are crying, you are very vulnerable. One of the basic reasons one fights against crying is that it makes one feel terribly vulnerable. Your eyes are closed, your vision is blurred, usually your mouth is open, and, therefore, I think one does not cry when one is terribly afraid. It is very striking that if a kid hurts himself real badly, he won't cry until he sees his mother, then he will cry. Even a grown-up will go through a harrowing experience, frightened to death, but will not cry until, let's say the husband or the wife comes, then come the tears. You can only dare cry when you feel protected.

The most common kind of crying among adults is when you

feel sorry for yourself, "poor me." There you see yourself a little, fragile, pure creature surrounded by the monstrous world, and it breaks your heart. There is no greater tear jerker than any movie where there is a big bad one and a nice little one who gets hurt. Oh, how you cry for that little one who is, you, you, and you! There you see yourself the epitome of virtue, the misunderstood waif, alone. Such movies are always calculated to make you cry. That is quite typical because you identify with the little one. However, you are not really aware that you are crying for and about yourself. At the movies it is much easier to cry about some stranger's death. Somebody else's father dies in a movie and you cry; with your own it is harder. Or, some poor wife has a misfortune and you shed tears, with your own wife you may think how the insurance will handle the damages. I don't mean to be cynical, but a lot of us have lost this capacity to cry over people who are close. The same with going to a movie where you see a romance on the screen, then you can hold your wife's hand. But with nobody there, no television, do you hold her hand? That's another lecture for another time.

I want to stop with only a couple of words about certain equivalents of crying which are very important somatically. There are psychosomatic equivalents to crying. Asthma is a form of crying, repressed crying. Kids with asthma, even grown-ups with asthma, are crying. Do you know that many people suffer from a pain in the throat? That is repressed crying. Sometime when you are trying not to cry, your throat will ache. You wonder why. Because you were trying not to cry. Certain skin lesions where the skin weeps is repressed crying. In order not to cry externally, you displace it and cry internally.

Crying and laughing are two basic, inborn emotions and ways of expressing emotions that are terribly precious for good health and for happiness and for a rich life. They have to be protected and they have to be respected. If we retain the capacity both for laughter and tears it is better for us. We have a chance then to remain civilized human beings.

# 10 Masculinity and Femininity Reconsidered (1965)

*Hildi Greenson notes that concepts involving changing gender roles provided the theme for the next two lectures. Similar emerging attitudes were dealt with in Greenson's scientific writing at the time. "The Enigma of Modern Woman" was the title of the Freud Lecture he gave in Philadelphia, and to the convention of the American Medical Association in Las Vegas he spoke on "Sexual Apathy in the Male."*

*Greenson began by saying that he was turning his attention to these topics because he had become increasingly impressed by the misconceptions, confusions, and disagreements that exist about sex, sexual practices, and masculinity and femininity. Further, he observed that frigidity in women seemed to be decreasing while frigidity in men was greatly increasing. Behind many of the difficulties regarding the above issues is the perpetual "battle of the sexes," which Greenson saw as "the unconscious tendency to prove one sex superior to another." He felt that there is so much unconscious fear and hatred of the opposite sex that it greatly influences not only the feelings individual men and women have for one another, but also distorts "scientific" findings and conclusions about the relations between the sexes.*

*Going deeper into the problem, he highlighted a well-known dynamic—men's secret envy of women. He described how "underneath man's conscious contempt of woman lies a great unconscious envy . . . and it is this envy which is at the bottom of much of his hatred and fear of women. Related to this fear of women is to a great extent his fear of retaliation for his hostile impulses toward women."*

I have selected this subject for discussion because I have become increasingly impressed by the misconceptions, confusions, and disagreements which exist about sex, sexual practices, and masculinity and femininity. This is not only true of the society at large but also among educated people, amongst physicians, psychiatrists, and psychoanalysts. At the same time it is striking how many changes seem to be going on in our society on these matters. Furthermore, my clinical observations have persuaded me to change some of my own theoretical thinking on the subject.

My plan is to describe the changes in masculine and feminine behavior which I have observed clinically and also in people at large. Then I propose to explore some of the powerful resistances which interfere with our increasing knowledge about this subject. Finally, I will indicate a more systematic approach which might help clarify some of the issues.

## Clinical Observations

Before World War II most of my women patients suffered from frigidity, but this was not a major complaint. They usually came for other reasons and their sexual frigidity was an ego syntonic piece of behavior. Today I rarely see a woman patient who accepts her frigidity. In fact, most of them demand orgasms and feel they are cheated by their sexual partners if they do not obtain them readily. Previously, women patients seemed relatively inhibited about sexual activity with the mouth, and today

---

Presented at the Southern California Psychiatric Society, September 13, 1965. An expanded version of this lecture is included in a collection of papers on *Sexual Problems*, C. W. Wahl, editor. New York: The Free Press.

they seem to accept it as a preparation for coitus or even as a substitute.

Before World War II, most of my men patients complained that their wives were reluctant sexual partners. Today it is the women who complain that their husbands do not seem to be eager for sexual relations. Whereas frigidity in women seems to be decreasing, frigidity in men is increasing enormously. I was struck at a recent panel discussion on sexual problems that many experts did not consider the term *frigidity* a suitable one. They also objected to my use of the term *frigidity* in men. This is another indication, in my mind, of the prejudice which exists in matters of gender. Frigidity means coldness and lack of passion. It can occur in men as well as in women. I contend it is increasing in men. It is related to but also separate from problems of orgasm.

My work in the Gender Identity Research Clinic at the UCLA School of Medicine deals with the psychiatric examination and treatment of patients who are seeking a surgical change in their anatomical gender. My previous psychoanalytic training and experience had led me to expect that because of the prevalence of penis envy in women, more women would come to this clinic than men. I have been very impressed by the fact that more than two-thirds of the patients who seek a surgical alteration of their gender are men seeking to become women.

Theoretically we know that envy begins at the oral phase and goes through all the main phases of libidinal and aggressive development. There is no doubt that in our society penis envy in women is very important. (For the classical psychoanalytic point of view on this subject, the reader is referred to the works of Freud, 1905, 1933; Helene Deutsch, 1944, 1945; and Marie Bonaparte, 1953.) But other clinical data suggests that intractable penis envy in women goes back to the early oral and anal fixations.

We know that anatomy and physiology, parental attitudes, and some biological force play a role in determining one's sense of gender—one's gender identity. All these factors are important and all of them may have a different importance in the individual. For example, Stoller recently described two boys who were born without penises and yet were very phallic in their behavior. In an earlier paper he described an adolescent child who had the external genitals of a girl and was treated like a girl, but who behaved as a boy. At puberty it was discovered that this child truly was a boy. Her reactions to this knowledge were a rather unemotional "I am not surprised." The only marked change in her psychological behavior in the subsequent years was that he became an A student in math, whereas he had been close to flunking as a girl.

It is not true that girls and boys are identical in behavior until the phallic or oedipal phase. For example, girls do much more playing with dolls than do boys, and boys are more prone to be "blanket lovers." This is an indication of a greater tendency to fetishism in boys. Boys who play with dolls are more apt to become transvestites.

Deep analysis of fetishism and transvestitism in men, as well as deep analysis of neurotics, indicates that there exists in men a deep wish to be a woman. This is not just a wish for castration or a defense against castration anxiety; it is an indication of a special problem in individuation. In early development it becomes necessary to differentiate oneself from the mother. In individuals who fail or who do this only imperfectly there is apt to remain a need to become a woman. Both boys and girls go through a normal phase of envying mother. The girl has a special problem in changing her love object from mother to father. The boy has a special problem in changing the object of his identification from mother to father. This has important implications for the development of masculine or feminine traits.

## Observations of People at Large

In recent years women have become more assertive and outspoken. Since they have acquired more social freedoms, they have taken over many of the prerogatives previously reserved for men. They are able to smoke and drink in public, to work, choose a husband, divorce, own property, and vote. In addition, modern methods of contraception have freed woman from her constant fear of pregnancy. In general, women have become more active, daring, and even rebellious.

On the other hand, men have become more passive, security minded, and conforming. Young men start out their working careers thinking of retirement rather than of becoming boss.

Ambition, drive, outspokenness, and rebellion are considered old-fashioned masculine traits.

There is also a marked blurring of the differences in the appearance. Women wear short hair, slacks, flat shoes, boots, men's shirts, and the briefest of bathing suits. Men wear long hair, shoes with high heels, tight trousers revealing both abdomen and buttocks, pink or yellow shirts with ruffles, use cologne, deodorants, and wear silk underwear.

The major reason for these changes is the change in the economic status of men and women. Woman's greater economic independence has made her feel she has the right to demand what was previously considered men's privileges. In societies where a woman is still the property of a man, she still tends to be passive, timid, and envious. On the other hand, men have become economically and psychologically more insecure. The rise of big business, big government, the technological and scientific complexity, the advent of the H-bomb, have tended to make men feel more helpless over their fate.

## Resistances to Studying the Problem

Masculinity and femininity are not absolutes, they are not opposites. Everybody has some admixture of physical, emotional, and intellectual traits of the opposite sex. Each society has different and artificial standards of what it considers to be male and female attributes. What we observe in a given human being is only the dominant and superficial masculinity or femininity. In the unconscious mind we are all bisexual in varying degrees.

Male and female traits are constellations and combinations of single elements. They can be broken down into instinctual, defensive, and adaptational components which are not the sole possession of either gender, but belong to mankind as a whole.

Another source of resistance is the battle of the sexes, the unconscious tendency to prove one sex superior to another. Despite a conscious attitude of scientific detachment, there is so much unconscious fear and hatred of the opposite sex that it seems to influence and distort one's findings and conclusions. I believe this is even true for psychiatrists and psychoanalysts and explains, at least in part, the lack of progress we have made in studying this problem.

In America and similar societies we all recognize women's hostility to men. The woman as a castrator is a stereotype—as is the woman who wears the pants in the family, who is in the driver's seat. These are all rather obvious manifestations of penis envy or envy of man's favored position in our culture. This knowledge is very widespread and is accepted and propagated both by women and men. It is also generally accepted that men bear a good deal of hostility to women. This can be seen in man's fear of prolonged intimacy with a woman, his greater fear of marriage, and his idealization of bachelorhood, stag parties, etc.

What is less well known and is still the subject of great debate in psychoanalytic circles is man's envy of woman. Underneath man's conscious contempt of woman lies a great unconscious envy. And it is envy which is at the bottom of much of his hatred and fear. The clinical evidence on which this is based comes from a variety of sources.

In men the envy of the mother is harder to uncover in our society since it is covered over by many facades, especially contempt. If one attempts to pin down what does man envy most in women, it turns out to change as the boy develops into maturity. From infantile breast envy it goes on to the envy of woman's ability to create life, to bear and deliver a baby. Men's creativity in art, literature, and science is his attempt to sublimate the urge to create something living and alive. It is striking to note that the most creative women are those who have no babies or those beyond the child-bearing years. The Bible story of the first woman being created from Adam's rib sounds like the revengeful fantasy of an envious man.

Man's hostility to woman is not only expressed in envy, it is also expressed in his possessiveness. Woman is man's greatest property, a sexual object for him exclusively and a privately owned labor force who works without pay. Men try to cope with their ambivalence to women by idealizing them as the pure and holy virgin mother. Religion has institutionalized what every boy does unconsciously in his family. Father may be sexual but mother is pure, a virgin at heart. This attempt is only partly successful because we also find that alongside of this picture woman is fantasied to be the evil and sinister sexual temptress. It is striking that fate and luck are considered female, which would hint at the idea of female gods who are even more powerful and capricious than male gods. Man's fear of woman is to a great extent his fear of retaliation for his hostile impulses toward her.

## Masculinity and Femininity

The foregoing has indicated that male and female are relative terms which vary in different societies. Yet I believe that it is feasible to pick out certain traits which are largely universal and stable indicators of one particular gender. Those characteristics are the primary gender traits and are intimately derived from the anatomical and physiological differences between the genders. All the other traits of gender are far more liable to change and variation. Thus impulses, attitudes, and character traits which are closely linked to the sexual act and to childbearing and child rearing are apt to be the most distinctive for a particular gender. I shall briefly outline some of the main points.

In the sexual act the male has to be intrusive and active. He must insert his penis into a strange cavity, the vagina, which means that he must be able to face a danger, actively take a risk, and maintain an erection while he is undergoing this test. To achieve a full orgasm he has to make thrusting, forceful movements with his erect penis in the vagina. Thus intrusiveness, assertiveness, risk taking, initiative, and sadism would be traits directly linked to the masculine role in coitus.

The female role in intercourse is to allow the penis to enter, to be accepting. She should be active but never to the point of dislodging the penis. The woman must endure, submit, and enjoy the forceful thrusting movements of the erect penis against the walls of the vagina. She must wait for the penis to become erect and enter before she can allow her activity full sway. Thus, receptivity, patience, submissiveness, and masochism are feminine traits directly linked to the female role in coitus.

Procreation requires of the woman the ability to carry a baby within her for nine months. This means she needs the capacity to be patient and to allow this growing creature within her the time and space to mature. The accepting anticipation of the pain of labor and childbirth also depend on her masochistic traits, her willingness to endure bodily pain. But she has already learned this from the pain of menstruation and defloration. The special intimate and time-consuming care of the infant, particularly in the early days and months, is made possible by her capacity for nonverbal, empathic communication with the infant. Her consistent, reliable, overriding concern for its welfare means that she must be able to subjugate her personal wishes in favor of the infant's. As she handles the infant and learns its rhythms, its schedules, the meaning of its cries, a very close-knit unit is established. She becomes the baby's auxiliary ego, its protective shield, its mediator with the outside world. Childbearing and child rearing enhances woman's empathy, patience, masochism, emotional involvement with human beings, cooperativeness, and group mindedness.

The fact that child rearing in most societies is done by the mother plays an important role in determining certain characteristics of males and females. Since the early relationship of infant and mother is based on forerunners and varieties of identification and imitation, the girl has a simpler time in assuming feminine attitudes and a feminine identity. She can be assured of becoming feminine by taking over the manner and means the mother employs in bringing up the child. The little girl soon learns that she is expected to become like the mother, but this is facilitated and built into the situation by the child's natural tendency to identify with the child-rearing person. This hypothesis seems to be confirmed by my clinical findings which indicate that women, despite their greater difficulty in achieving orgasm, are more certain of their gender identity, their sense of belonging to a specific sex than men are.

The male infant raised by a mother faces a special problem in how he may use identification. If he wants to establish a male gender identity, he must differentiate himself from the mother in certain important ways. He has to find another object for identification, a male, who is far less accessible to him. In our society this is particularly true of the only boy child in a family. This selectivity of identification which begins at fifteen months is of particular importance in establishing the boy's maleness. His sexual identity does not come mainly from his anatomy. As a consequence, men are far less sure of their maleness than women of their femaleness. At the same time, man's need to differentiate himself from his main upbringer tends to make him adventuresome, rebellious, and individualistic, traits which he seems to be losing at the present time in our society.

In all societies in which the mother rears the baby, women become baby and family oriented. As a consequence, they seem to become more group minded and cooperative than men, who tend to be individualistic. In the more advanced phylogenetic species crowding produces a marked change in the gender ratio, an increase of females over males. It is noteworthy that collective nouns are universally feminine in gender. As societies become more crowded and collectivized, they tend to become more feminine in their general character.

If these last points are correct, they would indicate that as societies become more crowded and collectivized they would tend to become more feminine in their general character. It seems to hold true in this country. Industrialization, technology, and the population explosion seem to have "demasculinized" the American male. The welfare state also seems to act like a mother, taking care of the sick, the aged, and the unemployed. (This point is made without implying approval or disapproval, it is merely a statement of fact.) At the same time, there are some indications that women feel relatively emancipated in recent years and have taken on some traits we have customarily attributed to males. Gadgets have freed them from the kitchen, nursery schools have freed them from child rearing after two years, and economic opportunity has encouraged them to become independent and self-assertive.

Our ignorance and prejudice about masculinity and femininity have led to many injustices, hardships, and waste. It is our task to learn more about this and related problems. We must broaden our range as to what we consider to be male and female attributes. Further, we should permit and encourage our patients to develop their entire personality and not stultify certain valuable traits because they do not conform to old-fashioned and rigid standards of gender behavior. This will only be possible when we can recognize and overcome some of the unconscious hatred and fear that exists between the sexes. If we succeed then we will be able to enjoy the exciting differences between men and women without contempt or envy, but with gratitude.

# 11 Sex Without Passion (1966)

*In this lecture, related to the preceding "Masculinity and Femininity Reconsidered" (1965), Greenson specifically discussed the problems of married men in their forties showing a decline in their sexual desires and suffering from clinical frigidity. Often the psychoanalyst encounters wives who are sexually dissatisfied with such husbands. The symptoms reported to Greenson included the men having less emotional interest in their wives, manifested by the absence of normal intercourse, increases in masturbation and pollution dreams, and wishes to watch scenes of sexual activity in pornography or to be the passive individual in an actual menage-á-trois. In tracing these fears of emotional involvement (one of his great interests, as we saw in earlier lectures), he pointed to a reemergence in adult life of concerns relating to the oedipal complex. He described to the audience that one of the reasons middle-aged men want to get rid of their middle-aged wives and find younger women is that they cannot stand having intercourse with women old enough to be like their mothers were. Conversely, women, according to Greenson, "seem to have less aversion to Pop as a sexual guy."*

*He returned to his favorite themes of the dynamics of boredom and apathy and related them to the problem of the impairment of emotional involvement between the sexes. People block out fantasies, imagination, creativity, elasticity, and sex becomes routinized and rigid and it loses its pleasurable, creative quality. As a consequence, it is less and less of a real emotional involvement and experience between two people thus . . . sex without passion.*

*Introduction:* As first speaker of the afternoon, Dr. Greenson, from Los Angeles, will talk about problems of people after ten or twenty years of marriage.

The title of my talk is "Sex Without Passion," and I do not think you meant to change that by saying that I will talk about people after ten or twenty years of marriage. You just anticipated me. The whole afternoon is devoted to the "age of boredom." All of our speakers have a subtitle that I think is an interesting point to consider: why we should assume that people in their forties will suffer primarily, or predominantly, or so often from boredom? Wouldn't you think that people in their forties, after some twenty years of work, achievement, education and marriage, and success, would have a sense of fulfillment? Be contented people? People who would now enjoy the fruits of their labor. After their struggles they had earned it.

I am talking of people who are able to work and I am talking about educated people. Why is it we all know and accept the fact that after fifteen or twenty years of marriage, of professional work, we see, instead of fulfillment or contentment, we doctors and psychiatrists see failures. People who, despite their success, or people who *because* of their success, suffer from some sort of psychological misery in one form or another and one of its manifestations apparently is boredom. Is it because at age forty you begin to become aware that this is the end of youth? I remember until I was forty I was quite pleased when people said, "Gee, you look older than your years." At forty I stopped liking it. Curious. Does it indicate that forty may be the end of that timeless feeling of hav-

---

1966 University of California, Los Angeles, Symposium on "Age of Boredom."

ing unlimited opportunities or horizons? Or, does forty mean we are getting old, a fact we may have known intellectually but never really believed. You can no longer say, well I am young, I can still do it all. At forty-five it becomes harder and harder to believe.

Or is it because our children have become adolescents, they go through puberty, become sexual, and could even have babies? Our daughters, those pure creatures; or our sons, those manly intellectuals, they go around doing sexual things? Or is it the rebelliousness of the adolescent that is so disturbing to the man or woman in their forties? Or, could it be the fact that our offsprings have succeeded magnificently, which makes us feel like failures by comparison. Or, they may have failed miserably and demonstrated to the world what a failure we are, despite our pretensions to the contrary.

These are some of the questions I thought about in trying to understand the sexual problem of the forties. It is true, clinically speaking, that we see many patients in their forties who suffer from some variety of boredom. Sometimes it isn't a clinical entity as such, it passes for the typical, popular, American character, who spends his time between television and Miltown. But when television stops diverting him, or the Miltown stops working, we do see people who suffer from boredom in a variety of ways.

I want to direct myself to the sexual problem and the relationship to boredom in order to get to the subject I really want to stress, namely, what I mean when I talk about sex without passion.

You do find, and there have been statistical studies which demonstrate it, that married men in their forties show a decline in their sexual desires. They have less sexual appetite, they have less sexual longing, they are less passionate. I would say they suffer from frigidity. Whenever I say this, the men object. They want frigidity to be limited to women, which is a chauvinistic point of view which I refuse to accept. I think men suffer from frigidity with increasing frequency, and women suffer from it less. In the twenty-five or thirty years that I have practiced psychiatry I have noticed a remarkable change in this regard. Twenty-five years ago most of the women I saw came because their husbands insisted they seek help for their sexual problem. These women used to say, "Well, I am tired at night, or my back hurts." Or they would say,

"It is not that I don't want sex, but I don't get anything out of it." That was their attitude. Today it is no longer true, or, let's say it is far less frequently the case. Far more often in my practice (and I have talked to my colleagues and they seem to verify this) most of the men who come to see me come because their wives are sexually dissatisfied with them. The wives say their husbands don't want sex often enough, they have less desire.

The interesting thing about the married men in their forties is that they admit they have less desire for sexual relations, but if you pursue this problem of frigidity in the male you will find that they are less interested in sex particularly with their wives. It is not that they have less interest in sex in general, many of them acknowledge it, or it can be shown to them, that this lack of interest is only lack of interest with this particular woman to whom they happen to be married. They still have a good deal of interest in extramarital sexuality which they may or may not pursue. We will talk about that too. Perhaps their interest for ordinary, normal intercourse has diminished, but they are interested in certain variations or aberrations. We find, strangely enough, an increase in masturbation in men around the ages of forty-five to fifty, as well as an increase or return of pollution dreams, something that had not happened since their adolescence.

There is less interest in the ordinary variety of intercourse with the marital partner, and much more interest in all kinds of passive kinds of sexuality, like watching. These are the men who go to the Bunny Clubs, Playboy Clubs, where the girls run around with scanty uniforms with their behinds exposed and bust exposed, and after leaving lunch there, home they come and don't even look at their wives getting undressed, or they may even suggest she should go in the other room to do that. This shift from less interest in active sexuality and more interest in passive varieties of sexuality, particularly looking, is striking.

What is at the root of some of these special problems? I am talking about middle-class or upper middle-class economic groups, and I am talking about the educated and not the uneducated man in our society. The problems are very different on these various levels, so keep in mind that I am talking about people who do seek psychiatric help. I know Dr. Marmor is going to touch upon this subject when he talks about the crisis of middle years, but, nevertheless, I want to mention a few points just in outline, some I have already mentioned.

The man of forty-five or fifty can no longer kid himself that he has unlimited horizons for future opportunity for success. At forty-five he knows how close he is to making it or failing. That means in business, in his career, socially as well as sexually. At forty-five there does arise in the American male concern about his health, this has to do with the process of aging, and it has to do with many other factors. The fear of damaging one's health, which was not considered before, has now become a preoccupation. Men avoid sexuality because it is considered too strenuous, and they feel they want to save themselves; for whom, is, of course, part of the problem.

At forty-five if there should be some diminution of the erection, or in the capacity to maintain one, there does loom up in a man's mind the worry over possibly getting impotent. This fear of being found impotent might perhaps dissuade him from having intercourse, to avoid finding out about it. He may be using various rationalizations to avoid sex, or may use some kind of instrumentalities to help him with sex. I don't know how prevalent the use of various gadgets is to help along sexual practices, but I do not think it is localized to Beverly Hills or Hollywood alone. It seems to be quite frequent, at least in my practice, among some of the patients I know. Many men have a fear of promiscuity, partly out of the fear of impotence and partly in order to deny that impotence is a real consideration. They are not faithful because of a sense of morality, they remain moral because they are afraid of being a failure as a gadabout. They are true to their wives, or at least they remain unsexual or asexual because they are afraid of not being able to compete with other men anymore for a woman.

In addition, the fear of breaking up or destroying a family, keeps men from giving in to their impulses for extramarital affairs and what may look like faithfulness is really a state of inhibition. That is perhaps why these men enjoy watching sexual shows at various burlesques or girlie houses where they get vicarious pleasure in seeing other people doing sexual things while imagining it is them. This is particularly the attraction of television too, since they are afraid, as I said, of the competition and prefer being passive. As a consequence, many of these men find sex at home boring. Before I go further into why it is boring, I want to talk about women in their forties and the problems I think they have.

Many women have similar problems but I want to talk about those special, different problems for the women of today. Since women today are less frigid, have greater desire, they are more frustrated because they are not satisfied. Ever since woman gained her economic independence she not only wants and expects equal rights and equal orgasms, but she demands them. Whereas women until recently felt they had no right to expect sexual satisfaction, they now feel that equal rights means "I can get what men get." Education, and at least partly the influence of Freud, has enlightened women to a degree where they feel entitled to expect sexual satisfaction, and they want it from their husbands. Demanding it, I think is going too far. You can hope for an orgasm, but you cannot order one.

I think ever since World War II, women have become more and more independent and not only economically and politically, but socially. This has made itself felt in their sexual life and their sexual behavior. I think it is a good thing—for the women. Women demand and want and look toward sexuality more, rather than less in their forties (and that is an interesting finding that Kinsey made). Women seem to want more sex than ever before. There are many possible answers for this increase. Many women need sex and a sexual relationship to reassure themselves that they are still lovable and physically attractive people. In our society so much value is put on a woman's physical beauty and in the forties she changes, she is less beautiful, if she ever was beautiful, anyway now she is less so. Since youth and beauty are so terribly important in our society, much more important than character, brains, or anything else, a woman must feel she has lost something terribly precious when she gets older. She needs sexual intercourse to prove, "Aha, see, I am attractive, and I am still exciting to a man." Many women also feel competition from their adolescent daughters, and that proximity does not show them off to their best advantage, to put it mildly. They need a sexual relationship to convince themselves that they are lovable.

Many women find that sex is one of the few areas where it can be possible to involve a husband. Those men who are not bored, those men who are interested in sex will at least communicate sexually even if nowhere else. So, women will resort to sex in this way. Remember, a woman has one enormous advantage in the sexual act: she can perform it or let it be performed upon her without doing anything. She does not have to do anything in order to be able to give sexual satisfaction to someone. I am stretching a point, and that is perhaps not a good simile, but by just permitting it to happen she can allow a sexual relationship to take place, where a man, in order to perform sexually, must be able to have an erection. This you cannot do by conscious volition alone, in fact, conscious volition has little to do with whether or not you are going to have an erection. It is determined by unconscious factors and organic factors.

The woman has a great advantage. She is able to use sex in nonsexual ways for nonsexual purposes. You see a great deal in recent years of people who engage in sexual activity without love and without passion. They use it for one or another reason, for conquest, or reassurance, for revenge or something of that order. You know, it is an interesting point that women can play it "cool" in sex and get away with it. Many, of course, are able to be deceptive and duplicitous and pretend to get sexual pleasure. At any rate, many women complain about the boredom in their sex life at home. I would like to turn now to boredom and why sex becomes boring.

First, let me talk about boredom. What is boredom? I want to stress that boredom is one of the growing national characteristics today. I think more and more people are bored, really bored and they are more and more aware of it. Rather than something to hide, it has become a kind of a badge, a sign of being "in."

Emotional intensity is old-fashioned, square. True, if you get angry or upset or cry it is interesting, but you are out of style. There is a trend in our society toward affectlessness, which is important to recognize. A pet peeve of mine is this whole business of "cool." When I was a young man when you liked something it was called "hot stuff," now it is called "cold stuff"—cool. "Oh, isn't that great, it's cool." It may sound funny but think a moment, the height of something being wonderful, delicious, great, enjoyable, "Oh, it's cool!" I think that has to do with a general tendency, the fashion, the mode, the popular way, to become uninvolved emotionally. It is certainly characteristic of our youth, but it is also widespread among the other ages of man. Now, what is boredom, briefly.

Boredom is a state of dissatisfaction coexisting with a disinclination to action. Boredom is a state of longing and yet an inability to designate what is longed for. Some people are even unaware that they are longing for something. Boredom is a state of emptiness with a hope that the external world will somehow guess and provide that which one needs to be filled or fulfilled.

For bored people, time seems to drag. In German the word for boredom is *langeweile*, meaning long-time. I became interested in the subject of boredom some ten or thirteen years ago when I analyzed a patient, a young woman, who had made two serious suicide attempts because she was so bored it was driving her crazy. She was absolutely frantic with boredom. This young, married, beautiful, and wealthy girl found everything in life boring. She finally swallowed a bottle of sleeping pills and when she woke up she felt relieved because now she was sick, now she was miserable, and she was not bored. I worked with her for many years and that gave me a chance to understand her boredom and that gave me an idea about boredom in general and I think I understand something about it.

What you find in boredom is a person who suffers from a state of dammed up instinctual drives; but the aim of the instinct, what it is that wants to be satisfied, and satisfied with what kind of a person, the aim *and* the object are repressed. In other words, a bored person feels a state of discontent but cannot say what he does want, nor who he wants to do it with. The aim and the object of instinctual drives are repressed. Even the very nature of the impulse may be repressed, and all they feel is empty. Many such patients eat. One of the factors in obesity is that peculiar emptiness and a state similar to hunger, but it is not a hunger for food. It is misinterpreted as such, but it is really a hunger for stimuli, a hunger to be interested, to be touched and moved. If you analyze this further you will find the reason the impulse is blocked off is because the feelings and fantasies concerning these impulses and objects are too threatening. Particularly the fantasies have to be warded off.

A bored person has repressed his imagination, he does not daydream that he is aware of, nor does he fantasize. The patients I have seen where boredom was a problem, this young, married woman I mentioned who came to me as a patient, could only enjoy sex with her husband if they watched a pornographic movie. She said, "Well, then I know what I am supposed to be enjoying." But I said, "My God, you are in bed with your husband," and he was, incidentally, not only a wealthy man but even an intelligent man and sexually attractive. "Why can't you pay attention to him?" She said, "That's boring." But what it really was is, "I can't bear to think I am intimately involved with this person. It is too close. If I see it on the screen I know it is unreal, I am safely at a distance," and this distance is what she needed. As she began to improve she needed less of it. Eventually her husband stopped playing movies, which had been a nuisance, but would have to tell her dirty stories instead. She said, "Tell me about your past sex life," and he said, "I told you," and she said, "Make it up! It does not matter, just tell me."

This woman could not allow herself to feel directly, emotionally, involved, with fantasies about this man with whom she was doing something as intimate as sex, and that is what sex is, a very intimate act. To be this intimately involved with someone meant to her that he could hurt her, he could damage her, he could leave her. So she had to distance herself from him and block out her fantasies.

There are two types of boredom: agitated and apathetic boredom. The apathetic kinds are the quiet ones, who sit around longing for something and doing nothing. Incidentally, they are very apt to say, "You bore me." Let me mention something about people who are boring.

First of all, there is a tendency to deny that we are bored. We do not like to admit it. Those of us who do not want to be "hip or cool," we don't like to admit we are bored. But, when you do feel bored, the point is, someone is causing some reaction in you which you are blocking off. And you do not want to face it. The alternative would be to say to someone who is very dull, "You annoy me," or "I am not interested in you," and leave him. This is a very painful thing to do for most people. They do not ordinarily do it. Instead they get into this state where they get sort of fidgety and nudgey and they are bored rather than furious or angry or frustrated. To be annoyed is a much healthier reaction.

The agitated boredom is a state in which the fantasies are warded off as well, but distorted derivatives of the fantasies are still available. These people are always frantically doing something, but what they do is a distraction, which does not satisfy, nor gratify, only helps to kill time. Many people spend their lives just killing time. Sad but true. Their real impulses and desires are repressed and unrecognized. These people are the television addicts, the Miltowners, etc.

The sexual problem, now I am getting back to that, in the middle years of marriage is so often one of boredom because of an inability to cope with the fact that a sexual relationship is one of great intimacy and not just physical intimacy. A sexual act, to be done well, satisfyingly, capably, requires a willingness to be involved emotionally and physically with another human being. Some people used to have problems mainly with physical intimacy, that is old-fashioned now. Today we see people who get sexually involved first, and then, after they have intercourse they say, why don't we talk and get to know each other?

I may exaggerate a little bit but there is this tendency in youth, and it is certainly true in middle age, to overlook sentiments, thoughts, feelings, intellect and passion. These people are afraid of the emotional involvement and would rather face just purely physical contact. But in order to have a good sex life, it is necessary to feel with empathy what is enjoyable for the sexual partner. That is, you must be willing to let yourself imagine what your wife, whom you have known for twenty years, likes or wants today. Not what she wanted last night, or last year, or what you remember when you first met her. You must also be willing to demonstrate, to show, to reveal what you like sexually, which means exposing what kind of fantasies go on in your head. You may feel more aggressive, perhaps somewhat sadistic one day, and more passive, more masochistic another day. You may be wanting to look more, or want to use the mouth, whatever, one day more and less another. Everything to do with forepleasure is terribly intimate as it reveals the infantile desires. In foreplay, touching, looking, feeling, smelling, biting—everything like that tells about one's childhood longings, one's childishness. You must either trust somebody, or do not care about ever seeing them again, before you really dare expose yourself. People who are married ten, fifteen years, change. The young girl you married then is now a middle-aged woman. This is a blow to many people. They find they are in bed with, well, think a moment, my God, a woman who is as old as their mother was when they remember her. And this is a very disturbing notion because men still tend to idealize mother and keep her as a nonsexual creature.

One of the reasons middle-aged men want to get rid of their middle-aged wives and find younger girls is because they cannot stand having intercourse with a woman old enough to be like their mother was. Funny, women do not have such a problem about their fathers. They are quite willing to admit Pop was a sexual guy. Anyway, by the time they are forty, they are willing to admit it and they don't mind going to bed with older men. But, men have an aversion to sex with a woman who is motherly.

I want to add some thought to what I said about a good sex life. It has to be spontaneous, creative. If it has become routine or rigid, it is no good. To be spontaneous and creative takes a certain daring because it may not work out well, or it may offend or it may be embarrassing. But a good lover is somebody who takes a chance. If you play it safe you are not playing, you are investing.

There is a big difference: one is business and the other is pleasure. Some people get very mixed up about that; one of my male patients, whenever he thinks his wife wants sex, he says, "Do you mean business?" The ability to allow oneself to be creative in a sexual act means the ability to allow oneself to regress and progress in the course of the sexual play. It is not easy for a beginner in the early part of marriage to face the fact that this dear, sweet wife has all kinds of sensual longings of an infantile, primitive, as well as sophisticated nature. One should have achieved such an awareness after ten, fifteen years, but if one hasn't, if it has been avoided, or limited, or only partially acknowledged, it catches up with you in the middle years and sex becomes boring and inhibited. There is a fear of feeling what that other person is feeling, to empathize is too frightening and scary for many. They do not want to feel what their spouse is feeling, or might be wanting or longing for.

It is a sad situation since the more moral the regular life, the outside life, the more there is a need for a sex life that is creative, that is a little bit wild, to have the opportunity to be volatile someplace. This is a hard kind of elasticity and flexibility for man, and for many women, to maintain and accept. This is where it gets into all the rigidities and boredom.

I am coming toward the end of my talk and I want to say a few more words about sex without passion. It is possible for some men, even though they are sexually excited, to want to preserve their erection at all cost. It becomes an endurance contest, it is a battle against the clock. How long am I going to last? This is, of course, deadly as far as sex being at all enjoyable for the partner, unless they are a timekeeper. It becomes some kind of gymnastics, some organ manipulation done by two people lying in bed together. But it is not a tender, lustful, sensual, passionate, vulnerable making, close and intimate act that sex ought to be.

Good sex should not be just something you do for physical reasons, a gonadal exercise that you are prescribed to do like some excretory function you do regularly. (Like every week we do it.) You know there are so many people who only have intercourse when the maid is out. The maid, therefore, determines their sexual habits. Oh, I have seen this, I have seen sad examples of it. A friend of mine, when he got divorced, told me that he finally got tired of having to wait for Thursday and every other Sunday to have sex because then the maid was off. His wife was terrified the maid might hear them. How sad. Of course, there were a lot of other things wrong with that marriage, but my, they are two intelligent, college educated people.

To sum up, it is necessary to be both active and passive in order to be changeable and variable, and that is terribly hard for many people to maintain. They have to repress one or another set of impulses or drives and repressing it they blank out certain fantasies or certain imaginativeness, creativity, elasticity, and it becomes routinized and rigid and it loses its pleasurable, creative quality. As a consequence, it is less and less of a real emotional involvement and experience between two people. Sex gets boring and you find people attempting to do what is really practically impossible, which seems to be the mode more and more today, which is to have sex without passion. Ladies and gentlemen, this is the general idea that I wanted to get across to you.

# 12 The Fascination of Violence (1968)

*Returning to ideas that he started to outline in the 1960 lecture on people who hate and discussed specifically in the lecture about why men like war (1961), Greenson here refocused on man's fascination with violence. His interest was stimulated in large part by the angry vehemence of the 1960s, including the Vietnam War, the assassinations of John F. Kennedy, Malcolm X, Martin Luther King, Jr., and Robert Kennedy, and the riots in our cities. This lecture was part of his participation as both moderator and speaker at a well-attended public symposium at UCLA, "Studies in Violence." An illustrious panel of experts participated with him, including Bernard Brodie, Paul Jacobs, and Margaret Mead.*

*In this lecture, Greenson forcefully contended that the psychological key to understanding man's vulnerability to violence is based on his propensity to react to it with an admixture of dread, guilt, and loathing on the one hand and with conscious and unconscious excitement, titillation, and gratification on the other. He described how this state of affairs forms that special frame of mind we ordinarily call fascination and asserted his belief that "man is fascinated by violence, far more than he realizes. As a result he cannot understand it properly and his attempts to cope with it are remarkably inept."*

*In his description of the dynamics of man's fascination with violence, Greenson described the psychoanalytic hypothesis that man is born with an aggressive instinctual drive. By aggression, he referred to the innate urge of the child to use force in order to control, to dominate, to overcome, to master, to influence something in the outside world. Aggressiveness is necessary in order for man to establish contact with any external object, to maintain this contact, and to control objects in his environment. Greenson pointed out how the view offered by psychoanalysis had demolished two of man's favorite myths: the myth of the innocent virtue of babies and the myth of man's innate nobility and his superiority over other living creatures.*

*He maintained that we are not merely the victims of seduction by the government and industry; we are accomplices and silent perpetrators of "violent nonviolence" and violence "in good taste." Twenty years before it became the terrible problem it is today, Ralph Greenson spoke to the shame and evil of America's hungry and homeless by saying, "Aren't we all guilty, to a greater or lesser degree, of ignoring the blatant injustices of millions of hungry people in the richest country in the world?"*

*Turning once more to the developmental themes that formed the underpinning of his theoretical understanding, Greenson believed that the most important source of violence stems from the early family life of the individual. He urged us to study the social history of the criminal, the assassin, the delinquent, and predicted that we would find that all such people had suffered from excessive frustration and deprivation, that they had been neglected, humiliated, or starved in early childhood and usually also in adolescence. He stated, "The lack of any enduring loving human relationship, the absence of a reliable caring person in terms of love, concern, food, compassion and understanding makes for free floating aggression, hostility and violence. The treatment of such individuals consists essentially in supplying them with what they were deprived of, love and control, both. Children and adults of this type have to be removed from their sick environments in order to become treatable."*

*Greenson closed his presentation by urging us to face our essential fascination with violence and asserted, "Our best hope for surviving the violence that surrounds us everywhere is to dissect, study, clarify and openly discuss the origins, development and vicissitudes of violence with people of different backgrounds. . . . The combination of love, in its broadest sense, and intelligence, is man's greatest weapon against violence."*

Most people in our so-called civilized society would state with all sincerity that they hate war, abhor brutality, and dread physical violence. At the same time it is our duty as behavioral and social scientists to face the startling fact that our most popular films are full of brutality, crime, and war. The best selling books for the last fifty years concern Napoleon, the Civil War, World War II, and murder mysteries. The most beloved of all children's games involve killings and playing dead, playing cops and gangsters, or war, or cowboys and Indians, etc. During the recent assassinations, riots in our cities and universities, most people, the thoughtful and the blasé, the young and old, blacks and whites, all shared one common experience, their eyes were glued to their television sets which depicted again and again the shootings, destruction, beatings, burnings, and lootings, and they stared repeatedly at the same sensational photographs in the newspapers and magazines.

As a psychoanalyst I am impelled to investigate this apparent paradox: men supposedly hate violence and yet they seem irresistibly drawn to it. I am not going to dwell primarily on those people who are severely neurotic or perverse about violence, the fanatics or the "lunatic fringe," who derive obvious and direct pleasure from inflicting pain and destruction, I shall focus on the so-called healthy man, or to put it more precisely, the unsick or the non-patient, who deplores brutality consciously and yet in unguarded moments seems to be captivated by the appeal of violence. It is my contention that the psychological key to understanding man's vulnerability to violence is based on his propensity to react to it with an admixture of dread, guilt, and loathing on the one hand, and with conscious and unconscious excitement, titillation, and gratification on the other. This state of affairs forms that special frame of mind we ordinarily call fascination. I believe that man is fascinated by violence, far more than he realizes. As a result he cannot understand it properly and his attempts to cope with it are remarkably inept. I shall attempt to uncover some of the dynamics of the contradictory forces which make for man's fascination with violence.

Let me begin by clarifying what is contained in the concept

---

UCLA Extension Division, Chairman and Participant: "Studies in Violence," June 1–2, 1968; presented at Claremont College, February 19, 1969.

of fascination. On a purely semantic level, fascination means to be held spellbound by some irresistible charm, to be ensnared, enchanted, or entranced. It means to be in the grip of something in such a way as to be deprived of the power to think, act, or move for oneself. Fascination contains more than pure love, attraction, or appeal. Romantic love can bewitch, beauty may allure, alcohol and "pot" may beguile, but things which fascinate do more than that, they paralyze, unnerve, and incapacitate. If one analyzes a person who is fascinated by something it becomes apparent that he is in the throes of an insoluble conflict. I want to illustrate some of these points by describing a fragment from the analysis of a highly intelligent professional man, a teacher. The findings differ from the nonpatient only in being more vivid and more accessible.

The patient, Doctor X, described suddenly coming upon a terrible automobile accident in which one of the victims was lying on the street bleeding profusely. He stopped his car immediately, with the urgent intention of offering help. As he approached the prostrate form he could discern it was a white-haired old man, bleeding from the mouth and nose. He froze in his tracks. He could not go forward, nor could he leave. Other people rushed to help the injured man, my patient stood on his tiptoes to watch, but he was able neither to take his eyes off the man's face nor could he approach close enough to be of assistance. He was late for his professional appointments but he could not leave. He felt compelled to wait for the arrival of the ambulance so that he could ask the doctor how badly the man was injured, would he die or would he survive. My patient was appalled to find himself imagining telling his wife the story. He could see himself saying in a very matter of fact tone: "the man was critically injured, there was no hope, the doctor said he was surely going to die." As he thought this he felt himself quivering. He could not discern whether he was frightened or excited. Then he heard the man moan and Doctor X felt a lump in his throat, his eyes filled with tears and he almost shouted, "help him, please, somebody please help him." When the ambulance did arrive he was unable to approach. Only after the victim was taken away was Doctor X able to return to his car. Later that day, on his way home, he deliberately drove by the same spot and eagerly searched for some evidence of the accident.

The next day, after a restless night, he searched the morning newspaper avidly to see if there was any mention of the accident and was disappointed not to find anything. He reluctantly and shamefacedly admitted that he had hoped to read that the victim had died. I want to stress at this point that Doctor X was not unusually aggressive in any of his overt behavior or beliefs.

I submit this clinical vignette as an example illustrating the conflicting components in fascination. Let me briefly point out the major psychoanalytic findings. For Doctor X the accident was an exciting, dramatic, and terrifying event. He was delighted and horrified to be an eyewitness, to be "in," on such an important happening. Most of his life he was more of an observer than a participant, he was not usually "where the action is." The sight of blood stirred up his sadistic impulses, but the white hair and the moaning evoked compassion and pity. The aura of impending death mobilized old death wishes he had had toward his own father and also childhood longings to be a good, loving, and devoted son. His instinctual component urged for revenge, "let the old man die, the tyrannical old bastard." His conscience said help the poor old man, he is pathetic, he needs you. His instinctual side retorted: "this is a victory, a triumph, be glad it is not you, he is helpless, not you." His conscience warned him, if you do not help him, you will be punished, you will die. As a consequence my patient's ego was torn by the conflicts and it regressed in its functioning. His logical, reasonable mind deserted him and he lost some of his intellectual capacities. Doctor X was transported into daydreams of glory and triumph. He was immobilized, trapped, captivated, i.e., fascinated. During the restless night he dreamt of being on a raft, which was being swept out to sea. He screamed for help, but no one heard him. He awoke irritable, depressed, and puzzled. At the end of the analytic session with me, Doctor X shot me a startled glance and blurted: "My God, Greenson, your hair is white!" He shook his head, sighed deeply and left. Obviously, he had been killing off more than one tyrannical father and he felt I too did not heed his cries for help. The dream illustrated his sense of being flooded by his instincts, his reproaches to me, his father, and society for the failure to control him, as well as his need for punishment for his violent impulses.

The crucial point of this clinical example is the fact that the automobile accident provided Doctor X with an opportunity to live out some of the deeply repressed conflictual strivings from his past and current life. Riots, rebellions, and wars do the same for the average man. Let me illustrate this with examples from everyday life. I am not going to focus on the ringleaders, the anarchists, or the assassins, for they are fanatics, sick, or exceptional. I want to talk about those who are the followers, those who get sucked in unwittingly, the fascinated ones.

In the last six years, four outstanding leaders have been assassinated by guns: President John F. Kennedy, Malcolm X, Martin Luther King, and Senator Robert Kennedy—and yet we Americans are not able to pass effective gun control legislation. The popular response is to blame the legislative stalemate on lobbyists, racketeers, or sportsmen. These answers may be partially correct but they are superficial and defensive. This conclusion is forced upon me when I read that the Department of Health, Education and Welfare statistics report that 80 percent of all killings and murders in the United States are not committed by criminals but by ordinary law-abiding citizens. Since 1900, there have been 767,918 people killed by guns in the United States, twice as many as were killed in World War I, World War II, Korea, and Vietnam; 269,000 were called murder and 138,000 were so-called accidents. I say "so-called" because 360,000 were suicides, and suicide is homicide turned against the self. I am sure most of us are shocked by such facts. It seems so alien to us, and yet, we are not able to pass on effective gun control law. Dick Gregory has said, "It is harder to fill a medical prescription than to buy a gun." Perhaps Freud was right when he wrote in 1915, that governments do not wish to abolish aggression and violence they only want to monopolize it. Certainly, the persistance of capital punishment, murder in cold blood by the state, is a case in point.

Perhaps we are merely innocent victims of history, capitalism, imperialism, or totalitarianism? Perhaps we can disclaim responsibility for the thirteen major international wars in the past 150 years, and I am not counting civil wars, brush wars, border wars, police actions, etc. But how can we explain the violent student rebellions in Berkeley, San Francisco State, Columbia, Wisconsin, Paris, Mexico, and Spain? What about the riots in Watts,

Detroit, and Newark? What about the war between Nigeria and Biafra? And why the universal failure to find any workable solution that offers some realistic promise of a peaceful solution?

I propose that we turn from the more spectacular forms of violence and look at subtle violence, the cold violence, the violence in good taste, the violent nonviolence that abounds in our society. The movie stars we adore are the John Waynes, Steve McQueens, and Humphrey Bogarts. Our favorite public figures are football players, boxers, and generals. We do not lionize intellectuals or martyrs. On the day Linus Pauling received the Nobel Peace Prize, it was noted on the inside pages of the *Los Angeles Times*, while Madame Nhu was splashed over the front page.

Perhaps we should blame the news media, the motion picture moguls, or the business tycoons. They are certainly guilty of producing merchandise that appeals to man's aggressive drives. Their aim is simple—offer the consumer what he wants. And we the public fall for it. The clever industrialists and advertisers know how to titilate the public's lust for destructiveness. The most popular cars are named Cougar, Wildcat, Fury, Barracuda, Spitfire, Marauder, and Cobra. The poor Rambler is unloved. (American Motors now has a new car, the Rebel).

Let me quote an ad from General Motors for its Wildcat: "hulking under the 2+2's hood is our whacking great 4 BBL 421. Horsepower—338, torque—459 lb-ft. Blam! . . . For stab and steer men, there is a new 3-speed automatic you can lock in any gear. Turbo Hydra-Matic. . . . Just straighten right leg, wind it tight, move lever, repeat . . . make small noises in your throat. Atta boy, tiger! . . . (The 2+2) is just a friendly little . . . sabre-toothed pussycat. . . . One of these at fast idle sounds like feeding time at the zoo."

A Chrysler teenage car ad reads: "Beauty and the Beast. That's the sleek Dodge Charger with . . . a deep breathing 426 hemi growling under the hood. . . . Comes on like Genghis Khan."

The news media and the entertainment industry do the same thing. But there are other organizations who indulge in socially acceptable, polite violence. I refer here to the subtle violence of the organization man, the bureaucrats, the little "Eichmanns," the technicians, and the sane, "nice" people who work on war and instruments of destruction. All of this is very proper as long as it does not conflict with the code of conduct set up by the establishment. For example, one is encouraged to practice business under such slogans as, "success at any price," "cutthroat competition," and "making a killing." Even pharmaceutical houses manufacture and sell incompletely tested, lethal drugs, which has not led to anything but a small fine, a mere slap on the wrist.

We are not merely the victims of seduction by the government and industry, we are accomplices and silent perpetrators of violent nonviolence and violence in good taste. Aren't we all guilty, to a greater or lesser degree, of ignoring the blatant injustice of millions of hungry people in the richest country in the world? Didn't we ignore for years the degradation and mistreatment of the poor and the blacks in our ghettos, while we smuggly went about our own business, salving our consciences with an occasional check or a sporadic passionate outburst to our affluent fellow accomplices. Isn't there a touch of Eichmann in all of us; surrounded by horror, we watch it on television, and if we are upset we decide to take an extra few drinks or a sleeping pill to blot out our dreams and dull our senses? We tolerate the hypocrisy of the state and industry because we too are hypocritical in following the dictates of our ideals. We tolerate and participate in the pollution of our air, water, and forests and are willing to take some meaningful action only when we are personally injured, above all when it hurts our pocketbooks or our property.

At this point I want to explore in some depth man's love and dread of violence. The limitations of time will make this a highly condensed analysis. I shall begin with man's love and need for violence. Man is not born violent, but he is born with a predisposition to violence, which stems from an inner source, an ever-present wellspring that serves as the reservoir of violence. I am referring here to the psychoanalytic hypothesis that man is born with an aggressive instinctual drive. By aggression I refer to the innate urge in the child to use force in order to control, to dominate, to overcome, to master, to influence something in the outside world. Aggressiveness is necessary in order for man to establish contact with any external object, to maintain this contact, and to control the objects in the environment.

Aggression is the source from which violence originates. Most psychoanalysts consider aggression as one of the two major, primary motivational forces in man. This point of view is not popular, even among psychoanalysts, since it demolishes two of man's favorite myths—the myth of the innocent virtue of babies and the myth of man's innate nobility and his superiority over other living creatures. The facts are, however, that psychoanalytic investigation has revealed that the mental life of children abounds with the most hostile and destructive fantasies. Nursery rhymes and fairy tales are loaded with cruelty and brutality. The prevalence of violent fantasies is equally true for childish adults; i.e., regressed adults who are severely neurotic and psychotic.

There is further evidence for aggression being an instinctual drive. (1) We all come into the world with inborn channels for expressing rage and anger. We do not have to be taught how to express fury and we all look remarkably similar when we are enraged. (2) From birth to death various forms of aggression are present in such reactions as greed, envy, and jealousy. These tendencies can never be abolished, they are never absent for any prolonged period of time. They may be unconscious, repressed, or displaced, they may be controlled or latent, they may even be sublimated, but they are always present, like the derivatives of the sexual drive. (3) The amount of aggression in a given person may be independent of the objective circumstances. We psychiatrists see certain children in whom the amount of aggression is out of proportion to their life experiences. This is true in autistic schizophrenic children and in brain-damaged ones. One only has to visit a newborn nursery to see the enormous variation in the babies' responses to hunger and cold. Some newborns react with great outbursts of anger and rage and others are much more placid.

Violence is the exertion of force upon another person, group, nation, or upon a place, a property, or idea, against its will, so as to inflict injury, damage, or pain. A violent act may occur in behavior, but it can also be carried out in language, feeling, thought, or fantasy, it may be conscious or unconscious. Violence may take place by the omission of an act, as well as by its commission. Ignoring injustice, hunger and poverty, and degradation may be traced to unconscious violent impulses toward the minorities and the poor. Pacifism, passivity, and neutrality are often more closely related to violence than to the love of peace. Calling a piece of behavior an act of violence often becomes a subjective moral judgment, a designation of condemnation that is due to our failure to distinguish between good and bad, constructive and destructive, provoked and unprovoked, justifiable and unjustifiable violence. For example, in my opinion fighting Hitlerism was violent but not evil. Fighting in Vietnam is another matter. The riots in the ghettos were violent but I believe they alerted the dormant white majority like no other protest was able to do. I abhor the violence but I wonder whether marching in protest would have done as much, both in terms of alerting the conscientious or mobilizing the backlashers. As much as I deplore the violent demands of the militant students, I do not believe we would now be having courses in Afro-American history without them.

If we compare aggression and violence, we can see that aggression is the urge to use force without regard for the welfare of another person or thing. It is primarily self-oriented. Violence arises from aggression, but violence adds to the use of force, the intent, conscious or unconscious, to inflict pain, damage, or injury upon a person or thing.

This part of the discussion has stressed the innate and constitutional sources of aggression and violence; however, I want to emphasize now that the psychoanalytic point of view maintains that usually the quality and quantity of aggression and violence is determined decisively by the individual's life experiences. Constitution and inheritance are rarely, if ever, the crucial factor. The most important source of violence stems from the early family life of the individual.

If we explore the histories of our most violent friends or acquaintances or if we study the social history of the criminal, the assassin, the delinquent, or the fanatic, we find that all these people have suffered from excessive frustration and deprivation,they have been neglected, humiliated, or starved in early childhood and usually also in adolescence. The lack of any enduring loving human relationship, the absence of a reliable caring person in terms of love, concern, food, compassion, and understanding makes for free-floating aggression, hostility, and violence. It can be seen in the cold-blooded behavior of autistic children and schizoid adults. The treatment of such individuals consists essentially in supplying them with what they were deprived of, love and controls, both. Children and adults of this type have to be removed from their sick environment in order to become treatable.

The family or the upbringers play the major role in laying the foundation for problems concerning hostility and violence, but society, which is an extension of the familiy, also contributes significantly by its attitudes and standards concerning violence. It is important to realize that all forms of hate are far more contagious than love. Rioting sweeps many more people along in its path, and much more intensely, than do love-ins. I have already mentioned the appeal of violent movies, sports, and news items.

Now let us turn to the dread of violence. Violence is terrifying because it threatens the intactness of the self, primarily and basically the bodily self. Secondarily and later there develops a horror of being violated emotionally and intellectually. There is no self-preservative instinct in man, because man is not born with an awareness of self. However, man dreads pain and, as soon as an ego develops, he dreads all body damage since it is associated with pain. Later he cherishes his selfdom, his identity, and abhors anything which will endanger or diminish the self.

The most important factors in man's problems with violence are his conflicting impulses toward violence. He is impelled to violence upon others and he dreads it being vented upon himself. To clarify this interrelationship we have to pursue the way dread and desire lead into one another. The most extreme form of fear, or anxiety, is a state of mind we call panic. All traumatic events elicit panic reactions and the essence of panic is a feeling of being overwhelmed, of being helpless, powerless. We all dread violence unless we are caught up in a mood of committing some violence. We dread violence because we sense that violence can destroy us or render us powerless and impotent—a return to that most vulnerable frightening state of infantile helplessness.

People who find themselves in a state verging on helplessness or powerlessness may do one of two things: they may regress to despair or apathy, or under certain circumstances they may resort to violence. Here I come to the immediate and intermediate causes of violence. I have already mentioned that a history of chronic malnutrition, degradation, brutality, humiliation, frustration, and emasculation may lead to acts of violence. If this occurs in a person who senses he is being pushed to the brink of feeling helpless, an act of violence is apt to occur. Violence is not only an act of hatred and revenge against one's oppressors, but it is also a defense against falling into despair, resignation, or deadly apathy. An act of violence may give one a temporary sense of power, in fact, it may create a feeling of omnipotence, the exact opposite of helplessness. Violence is quick, and therefore enticing for those who have been forced to endure indignities for years. Violence is magical, it transforms one by suddenly changing one's identity from a feeble, dependent nobody into a sense of somebodiness, a sense of manhood. Incidentally, the gun is correctly called the "equalizer." Actually, one not only achieves a sense of equality but of superiority. Small wonder violence appeals to the oppressed, the minorities, and the disenfranchised.

There is still more to be said about its appeal. Violence is contagious and tends toward group and mob formation. All groups tend to regress; the more they are tied by emotional rather than intellectual bonds, and particularly if there is a dynamic leader, the more they are inclined toward hate reactions. The group and the leader dilute responsibility and guilt and bring a feeling of invulnerability. Furthermore, the group is an audience, a chance to exhibit one's courage and manliness by exposure to danger and death. For some violence is a means of becoming a member of a group, of belonging, and thus appeals to the alienated adolescent who needs to "be in" in order to establish an identity.

Freedom of assembly facilitates crowd and mob formation and predisposes to violence among the uprooted, the poor, and the unemployed. Mob violence produces an exhilaration due to the sudden feeling of sharing a community experience which is very gratifying to the lower classes, the ignored, and oppressed.

Violence is intense and vehement, and entices those who are searching for intensity. Empty, hollow people, people with little capacity for human relationships, are prone to use violence as a means of filling up their empty lives. For some violence is a cry for help, a cry of distress, a signal of impending danger, of suicide. We cannot afford to ignore violence or severely condemn it. The gun, that great equalizer, can be turned against the self as well as the external world.

The most explosive trigger for violence is the feeling of righteous indignation stemming from the feeling of having been mistreated, of having been unjustly humiliated and degraded. If this joins with group or mob formation, violence is almost inevitable.

Members of political parties or groups who are imbued with the absolute righteousness of their cause, the political extremists, right or left, are tempted to violence. Fanatics, political or religious, are crusaders, and history has taught us how bloody they have been. Furthermore, the revolution promises a new life, a rebirth, a complete break from the miserable past, a chance to deny the past.

Let me turn once again to those who are fascinated by violence but who, for the most part, think they only participate in it vicariously, as observers or auditors. I am talking now about the vast majority of us, not only in this country but all over the world. Most of us in an affluent society do not resort to open violence because we have enough success and status. We only fear the consequences. But let anyone or any group threaten our possessions or status, and I predict that most of us will be tempted to resort to violence. We successful ones, we who are "in," the haters of violence, will become the most violent. The greatest danger from the black militants and the student rebellion is the white backlash and the anti-intellectual backlash which I predict will be far worse than anything we have thus far experienced. The balance between the love and dread of violence is a delicate one and can easily be tipped in an opposite direction.

The fear of violence is greatest in those who repress their own violence and unconsciously project it upon people in the external world. The extreme fear, one might say, the paranoid fear of the stranger, particularly the strong one, the different one, be it in terms of color, politics, or religion, is to a great extent based on this mechanism. Blacks tend to be paranoid about whites and whites are paranoid about blacks. The same seems to be true about Americans vis-à-vis the Russians and vice versa. All of us tend to expect retaliation and retribution from those we fear and would destroy, from those we envy, and from those toward whom we feel guilty.

I turn now to the final and shortest part of this presentation: the control of violence. I do not believe violence can be abolished because it is natural to man. Margaret Mead has said she knows of no society where there is a total absence of violence. In order to deal with violence effectively we have to recognize its presence in all of us. This requires honesty and humility. We must distinguish between justifiable and unjustifiable violence, constructive and destructive violence, and defensive and offensive violence. We must teach our children such distinctions and how to cope with them. We must be vigilant with ourselves in recognizing the differences.

We may be able to control violent behavior by permitting and even encouraging certain forms and equivalents of violence, particularly about objects which are deserving of hatred. It is desirable to fight against tyranny, poverty, disease, hunger, and injustice. Here we may have the opportunity to transform physical violence into more civilized modes of action. The more we can use aggression constructively and with little physical violence, the more brutality and violence will appear stupid and despicable. We cannot do this by pretending to be above it all, that would be due either to ignorance or hypocrisy. Of all the animals on the face of this earth, man is the only one who plans the killing of his own species. Konrad Lorenz has said that man is the missing link between the animal and the human being.

To summarize: I chose the topic of fascination with violence because I believe that fascination is a particularly elusive and tricky adversary. I have the impression that we are in danger of being seduced by violence because we are not aware of how it subtly excites and titillates us despite our conscious abhorrence of it in some of its grosser forms. Unrecognized fascination with violence can stimulate our unconscious destructive impulses, blur our cognitive powers, and corrupt our judgment and morals. We shall need our best judgment and highest principles of morality if we are to maintain (or should I say achieve) our loving concern and compassion for the fortunes of the family man. I make this presentation with the belief that our best hope for surviving the violence that surrounds us everywhere is to dissect, study, clarify, and openly discuss the origins, development, and vicissitudes of violence with people of different backgrounds. My earlier emphasis on the instinctual basis of man's aggression should not obscure the fact that man also has an innate tendency to love. Man is a social creature and also a thinking one. The combination of love, in its broadest sense, and intelligence, is man's greatest weapon against violence.

To put it another way, the best hope for man is to become more human, recognizing the frailties of the human condition, including our fascination for violence.

# 13 Why People Hate Psychoanalysis (1970)

*This lecture was given in La Jolla, California for the then forming San Diego Psychoanalytic Society and Institute. Because of his great interest in the formation of the San Diego psychoanalytic community and the efforts of his dear friend Emanuel Lippett, Greenson played a generous role in its development. This lecture was the first of a number he gave in San Diego for the benefit of psychoanalysis in that area.*

*His starting point on this occasion was that one could read several times a year in widely distributed newspapers or respected magazines that psychoanalysis was dying, withering away, or dead. He stated that if one needed more proof that psychoanalysis is hated, one had only to turn to the way psychoanalysts were portrayed in motion pictures or on television. "We are almost always depicted as foolish, crazy, depraved, or criminal, and usually in some combination of all of the above."*

*Greenson discussed the hate of psychoanalysis from three perspectives: (1) why the science itself evoked such estrangement and hostility; (2) how its practitioners added to this hate; and (3) how its patients and their families might contribute to feelings of "down with psychoanalysis."*

*Both Freud's study of adult patients in the late 1890s and the later direct observation of children led to the destruction of some of man's most cherished myths. This included the innocence of children, the innate purity of the human baby, the superiority of man over animals, and everybody's supposedly happy childhood. At the basis of these cherished myths is man's wish to deny both sensual drives and aggressive, destructive urges. Greenson explained how the psychoanalytic description of the human condition, i.e., man's innate sexuality and aggressiveness as well as his inability to control the basic drives or even to consciously recognize them fully, has been a severe blow to man's "self-esteem, or his self-love, his narcissism . . . the average man hates psychoanalysis (so-called science) which brought these issues to light." He went on to say, "Psychoanalysis has made man aware of the fact that what he is conscious of is only part of his mental life, and a small part at that. As a result, he cannot trust his conscious knowledge or his own perceptions as being complete and entirely accurate. In addition, by being unknowing, he also is not able to control his feelings and behavior—he is not the master in his own house. It is not hard to imagine how such discoveries would make most men and women hate and fear the new science of psychoanalysis." As Mark Twain said about himself, the rumors about the death of psychoanalysis have been greatly exaggerated.*

## Introduction

The starting point for this presentation is the remarkable phenomenon that several times a year we can read in one or another widely read newspaper or respected magazine that psychoanalysis is dying, withering away, or dead. Every new form of psychiatric treatment, be it electroshock, or brain surgery, every new drug discovery like the phenothiazines, or tranquilizers, every new form of psychotherapy like reality or behavioral therapy, group therapy, or sensitivity therapy (with or without clothes) all lead to the conclusion that psychoanalysis is dead and we are about to embark on a new and happier era. Not only is the death proclaimed but you can hear the sounds of jubilation in the background.

---

Presented at the University of California, La Jolla, California, November 17, 1970.

If this were not sufficient evidence that psychoanalysis is hated, I ask you to turn to the way psychoanalysts are portrayed in motion pictures or on the television screen. We are almost always depicted as foolish, crazy, depraved, or criminal, and usually in some combination.

All of this may not be due to pure unadulterated hatred, because we know, or at least most of us know enough to suspect, that things or people who are repeatedly wished dead, ridiculed, insulted, and demeaned are treated so on the basis of complicated emotional reactions. No single emotion makes for such inappropriate intensity. Vehement and unchanging hatred must cover other emotional responses as well.

I want to focus on our objective, exploring why people hate psychoanalysis, but do not be surprised if we shall find other feelings toward psychoanalysis as well. I shall divide this presentation into three sections. The major one is why psychoanalysis, the science itself, evokes such estrangement and hostility. Then I shall spend a little time on how psychoanalysts, the practitioners, add to this, and finally a few words on the psychoanalyzed patient and his contribution to the feeling of "down with psychoanalysis."

## The Contribution of Psychoanalysis

Freud's study of adult patients beginning in the late 1890s and later direct observation of children, led to the destruction of some of man's most cherished myths: the innocence of children, the innate purity of the human baby, the superiority of man over animal, and everybody's past history of a happy childhood. Freud and his students discovered that children from birth onwards are driven to obtain a variety of sensual body pleasures which resemble sex in form and ultimately end up clearly recognizable as sexual, that is, in the relatively healthy child. I am referring here to the sucking and defecating pleasures of age birth to three, which matures into genital masturbation in healthy children between three and seven, and then usually temporarily disappears only to recur in puberty, again, underlined, in healthy children. This is a far cry from the virginal innocence pre-Freudian man had believed in.

With these discoveries psychoanalysis aroused the ire of most parents who refused not only to recognize the sensuality of their child, but also, and above all, wanted to keep the memory of their own infantile sexuality in a state of amnesia. This "fall from heavenly grace" was given additional import when psychoanalysis added some twenty years later, that the human child is born not only with sensual drives, but also with aggressive, destructive urges.

The human baby, said psychoanalysis, has an innate tendency to overcome all obstacles to its pleasure and to destroy all things which bring it pain or frustration. Children have little tolerance for frustration and react quickly with rage. It is only the child's physical helplessness which keeps it from acting upon its angry destructiveness, most of which occurs in fantasy life or in play in the first years of life. As the child grows and becomes physically more competent, it expresses its aggressiveness in a variety of hostile, destructive acts. This leads eventually to the rough-house play and the violence of latency and adolescence. In grown-ups the aggressive drives can, under a variety of circumstances, lead to the love of violence which makes the waging of war possible. It is worth noting that man is the only member of the animal species that plans and carries out war against members of its own kind.

These findings did not endear psychoanalysis to the man in the street. The myth of his pure and happy childhood was taken away from him and in addition, his feeling of superiority over the savage beast. Man is proud, if not vain, and these were severe blows to his self-esteem, or his self-love, his narcissism. He might accept the correctness of these findings intellectually, or partially, or he might deny them vociferously, i.e., this is only true for the poor, or the Jews, or the Blacks, but not for "our kind of people." In any case, the average man hated the so-called science which brought these issues to light.

These were not the only blows psychoanalysis dealt out to man's self-image, as a mighty and noble creature. Man has always felt himself to be supreme in his own mind. With his capacity for self-observation he could keep watch on his impulses and actions and see whether they harmonize with his wishes and ideals. If they did not, they could be suppressed, inhibited, or withdrawn. But Freud discovered that impulses which are suppressed or repressed do not disappear but return in disguised form, and are completely unknown to the individual. For example, the overly protective mother is totally unaware of her hidden anger toward her spoiled, demanding child. She does know she is constantly preoccupied with the fear that something terrible might be about to happen to him, but she has no awareness that her fearfulness of catastrophe is a distorted derivative of the healthy resentment of her son that she represses. This woman believes it is sinful to feel anything but pure love for one's child. I would like to add that pure love for anybody, is pure fantasy. Love without some admixture of hate is a sickness, a myth, or a lie, in my opinion.

Psychoanalysis has made man aware of the fact that what he is conscious of is only part of his mental life, and a small part at that. As a result, he cannot trust his conscious knowledge or his own perceptions as being complete and entirely accurate. In addition, by being unknowing, he also is not able to control his feelings or behavior—he is not the master in his own house. It is not hard to imagine how such discoveries would make most men and women hate and fear this new science of psychoanalysis. It is impressive to realize that most of these findings came to light some fifty to seventy-five years ago. But it was not just the Victorians who were upset by these discoveries, it is almost equally true today; and many people who seem to agree with the correctness of these ideas are really giving only lip service to psychoanalysis.

Up until now I have tried to show how some of the findings of psychoanalysis have estranged and angered man. To add insult to injury, the psychoanalytic method or procedure also adds to the hostility. It is not possible to go into all the varieties of ways this comes about, but let me highlight a few major points with a simple and typical example.

A forty-five-year-old, eminently successful scientist comes into psychoanalytic treatment because of a moderately severe and recurrent depression. The first few months are tough going, the patient finds free association difficult because embarrassing thoughts come continually to mind. He finds lying on the couch demeaning and my silence infuriating. However, after some six months a startling change occurs. The patient begins to see and understand connections between his current depression and the misery of his early childhood. His mother had divorced his father and was emotionally distraught, often taking out her unhappiness on her four-year-old son, my patient. Furthermore, the divorce had deprived him of a father and his hunger for a relationship to a father figure made him an excessively loving but intrusive father to his children. This hunger for a father was displaced onto me during this period of his analysis. I now became the ideal father he lost in childhood. He admired me, imitated me, became dependent on me, looked forward to the hours and hated weekends and vacations.

This may sound very idyllic as far as the course of the analysis is concerned, but it was sheer misery for his family life. His wife resented me as a rival for her husband's affection, he constantly talked of his analysis and his analyst. His teenage children were deprived of a father and pal because the patient was preoccupied and could not genuinely become involved at this time in his children's affairs. They were angry at the rejection and contemptuous of his dependency on me and his self-involvement.

This clinical example demonstrates how a fairly typical regressive transference reaction in the course of analysis can turn an entire family against psychoanalysis. It is fortunate that such changes are transient as a rule. There are occasions, however, when psychoanalysis uncovers important trends in a patient which he has spent his whole life covering up. If he then decides these new trends are valuable for his future happiness, he can disrupt his family life on this account and psychoanalysis becomes the scapegoat for breaking up the marriage. (It is rare for psychoanalysis to be given credit for benefiting a marriage, which is more often the case.)

It is worth repeating that permanent major disruptions of family life are not the rule. Transitory emotional upheavals due to the loving or hateful transference reactions to the analyst or even to members of the family are the rule. I do not know of any patient's family, husband, wife, children, or parents who have not been temporarily at odds with psychoanalysis. Husbands and wives resent the invasion of their privacy. Parents do not tolerate well the loss of their special power over their children who are in treatment. All this is understandable but it is an unfortunate fact that psychoanalytic treatment does facilitate such situations, in fact, they are a necessary and painful occurrence in all analyses of any depth.

Another regular feature of psychoanalytic treatment which evokes great hostility is in its long duration. Patients and family alike resent the three to six years most analyses require. In a day and age in which people want instant results, from instant breakfast to instant sex, there is little patience or respect for patience, or for long-term projects in general. Part of the popularity of the encounter groups, the marathon sessions, etc., is the hope for quick, emotional breakthroughs and quick changes in life-style, values, and attitudes. I do not deny that this may happen, but I wonder how enduring such changes can be and what will happen to the old personality that one has so laboriously built up during one's lifetime. To change major personality traits, means to change what one is, one's identity. Personality and identity consist of such complex and delicate balances of so many forces and counter-forces that I would be reluctant to advise any but the desperately despairing to undertake such a hazardous therapy.

This brings me to the relatively poor results of psychoanalytic therapy, another cause for hating psychoanalysis. There are several reasons for the poor therapeutic results. First of all, people who enter and remain in psychoanalytic treatment for any length of time are not trying to change a superficial symptom, even though they may have begun treatment with that idea. For example, a young woman comes for treatment because she has a phobia of being in any room where she has no immediate access to an exit. She becomes panic-stricken to the point of hysteria, loss of control, and even fainting. In a few months we discover that she also suffers from insomnia, has an inability in controlling her children, and is sexually relatively nonresponsive. As therapy progresses we discover that in all her relationships to people there hovers in the background, a dread of losing control of herself either sexually or in terms of aggression or both.

We also find out that his lady does not trust her body nor her mind; they are both potentially dangerous to herself and to others. The original phobia which brought her into treatment sinks into the background as we work with the many fears and terrors which long preceded the outbreak of her phobia. Our task now is not merely to cure the phobia, that will probably disappear and reappear many times throughout the treatment. Our goal is to help this woman become able to trust her body and mind, to make peace with the crucial people of her past who played a role in producing the basic mistrust. Our success or failure will depend on the patient's willingness to search within herself for new insights and to try new ways of thinking, feeling, and acting. It will also depend on our skill and experience as a psychoanalyst and person in giving her the correct insights in a time and manner that she can use.

Many patients and analysts expect more from psychoanalysis than it can give. Many times we have to be content with partial results. Sometimes all we can do is stave off something more terrible which had been in the making, unbeknownst to patient and therapist, when treatment was begun. At times circumstance is kind and helps produce changes which are beneficial. At other times circumstance is harsh and all we do is change neurotic misery to real misery. Even then, there is some compensation. Neurosis means tyranny of the past, the repressed, and the warded off. Real misery is miserable, but if it is real, it does imply the individual has some measure of freedom of choice and that is not to be despised.

Our poor results come in part from the enormity of our undertaking, of trying to help the patient make major changes in the way he feels and functions as a whole person. Another factor is that our theoretical knowledge has outstripped our technical skill and know-how at this point in our history. Sometimes we mistakenly treat patients who would do better with other forms of psychotherapy. Sometimes the life circumstances make psychoanalysis a poor choice of treatment. For example, a twenty-two-year-old college graduate, who has no job, no desire for one, no wish to continue further studies, who comes to a psychoanalytic treatment for one hour, five days a week, and does nothing else all day but sleep, watch TV, and read magazines is not a good candidate for classical psychoanalysis. He needs preparatory therapy and counseling before he will, if ever, become a good candidate for psychoanalysis.

By and large, psychoanalysis treats people who have serious problems and who attempt to achieve major and lasting changes in themselves. We do not believe anyone is ever completely analyzed, that is much too mechanical a concept. Analysis is an ongoing process, if it has been successful to any degree. Our good results are quiet, our bad results make headlines or great gossip.

## The Analyst's Contribution

A few words about how psychoanalysts themselves evoke hostility to psychoanalysis. Some analysts act as if they can explain all of human behavior and are quick to make interpretations in social situations based on skimpy clinical data. Some are prone to act as experts in fields in which they are not trained and make pronouncements on war, racism, riots, etc. There are some analysts who love their theories more than their patients. As a result they treat all their patients alike, which cannot produce good results. Working alone with patients for months and years on end, tends to wear away the analyst's original scientific skepticism and turns him in the direction of feeling omnipotent. These traits evoke resentment or contempt in the community, and rightly so. In one area the analyst is innocent: He works in a fascinating field, he is in demand, his patients are interesting, they come from various walks of life, they are all different, no two patients are alike, and he is well paid, if not overpaid. For this the psychoanalyst is envied, and understandably so.

## The Patient's Contribution

Finally I should mention some ways in which the psychoanalytic patient himself stirs up hatred for psychoanalysis. If the patient changes, the change is disliked by the spouse or friends—often on the basis of envy. This is particularly true when the patient gains a measure of greater self-confidence and security which gives him more freedom. Most people are so bogged down in their rut and so afraid to change, they unconsciously hate and envy the improvement of the patient who dares to undertake psychoanalytic treatment. It should be remembered that despite all the overt hostility, only a small percentage of people seeking treatment can be taken. This is another source of antagonism.

Some patients go through a phase of identification with their analyst and act and speak like junior psychoanalysts. They interpret everyone's behavior, smile mysteriously and knowingly, with an air of superiority and smugness. They can be truly obnoxious until you realize this will not last, they will lose their temporary and illusory power just as their own analyst will. It is striking how half-baked patients talk so much about analysis and the patient who is working well talks so little. Patients who break off treatment often speak harshly about psychoanalysis with more or less justification, all of which stirs up the latent hatred in the community at large.

## Conclusion

I hope I have sketched for you the many different sources of hatred for psychoanalysis. The science itself does so by the nature of its discoveries, which destroys some of man's most cherished myths, and deflates man's self-love. The procedure produces certain temporary reactions like transference and acting out in patients which antagonize the people in contact with the analysand. Then the psychoanalyst himself may have weaknesses as a human being which evoke exaggerated hostility in his surroundings. Finally, patients themselves may behave badly, by distorted notions of what a psychoanalytic patient should be, or by getting revenge against what they believe psychoanalysis did to them.

However, it is also clear that people do not only hate psychoanalysis, they also fear it because it deals with the unconscious and infantile mind full of primitive strivings and unhappy memories. In addition, there is an important element of *unconscious* envy in regard to psychoanalysis and its followers. These people dare to explore and try to cope with areas of mental and emotional life which, on the surface, seem incomprehensible and terrifying. As I said earlier, such intense hatred does serve as a screen for other emotions as well.

It is for all these reasons one can read and hear every few months in newspapers, magazines, or platforms that Freudian psychoanalysis is dead or dying. I am happy to say to the death-wishers of psychoanalysis, that wishing does not make it so. The number of psychoanalysts in this country has risen tenfold since World War II and similarly all over Europe and South America. With all its shortcomings, psychoanalysis is recognized as a serious and systematic attempt to understand and treat the neurotically disturbed human being. Every branch of social and behavioral science makes use of psychoanalytic ideas. We have a great deal still to learn, the best of us are little better than beginners, and we are still a young field. We are not competing with other forms of psychotherapy but often serve as a partial basis for other therapies. We know that psychoanalysis is possible only for a handful of people, and we hope to find means of prevention and treatment which will be helpful to the masses. As long as we know what we are doing, cooperate in the field of mental health with our own expertise, and retain our humility, we have a right to exist. So continue to hate us—but now I am afraid it will be harder for you, because you know too much!

# 14 Hate in the Happy Family (1970)

*Hildi Greenson writes that the topic of this lecture had a surprising appeal for the news media. Excerpts from the lecture and interviews with Romi were widely quoted, not only nationally, but in the French, German, and Italian press. This no doubt had to do with the fact that in all families aggression is present and must be recognized and dealt with if the family and its members are to survive emotionally.*

*Greenson described how in all so-called happy families most people tend to ignore the hatred that exists within and among them. He wished to show that only families who hate well, stay well and together. "The happy family does not consist of pure love and kindness. Hate has to be a respected member of the group. If it is not, the family is not genuinely happy." Further, hate unrecognized, in disguise, is more dangerous and damaging than when it is open and dischargeable. He explained that when hidden, "hatred leads to prejudice, fanaticism, sudden eruptions of violence, suicide, phobias, obsessions, [and] failure in work, sex, marriage, and child-rearing. This occurs because unconscious and unexpressed hatred festers, grows, and becomes regressively more primitive."*

*Mixing psychological truth and humor as only he could, Greenson enumerated the "haters in disguise" including the I-can't-kill-a-fly people, the overprotective parents, the blood-is-thicker-than-water people, the thing lovers, the poor-me people, and finally, the jinxed people. His message was that "hate must be recognized as an integral part of life and living. . . . The more you love, and this is particularly true of romantic and sexual love, the more susceptible you are to being hurt, and if you're hurt the natural response is anger and hate in some form or fashion." It has become increasingly clear in contemporary society that those families that are unable to deal with the normal hate that exists in all families, escalate or transform their feelings into more pathological forms of hate, as expressed in spouse and child abuse.*

## Introduction

I chose this topic because most people hate hate, at least consciously. Yet it attracts them. Hate is contagious. This is particularly true in groups. Gangs and mobs are prone not only to hatred, but to violence. Even at a social gathering you can stifle any conversation by saying that Mrs. Maggie Smith is a nice woman. You can convert almost total strangers into a cozy talkative group by stating that Maggie Smith is a promiscuous bitch. The transformation can be startling. It is worth noting, however, that love is private and sex too—especially passionate sex. The more mature and civilized people are, the less likely they are to be swept up by mob fever, but all of us have our limits in this regard.

In the so-called happy family most people tend to ignore the hatred that exists within themselves and among one another. I am referring now to everyday ordinary hate—not murderous outbursts of rage or the sadism of child or wife beaters. I want to talk about how people in what appears to be happy families, hate one another, what they do to hide it from themselves, each other, and their neighbors, and, finally, what one can or should try to do with hatred and hating in order to maintain or achieve a happy family life.

I hope to show that only families who hate well, stay well and

---

Presented to the Reiss-Davis Child Study Center, Women's Division, Los Angeles, April 28, 1970.

together. The happy family does not consist of pure love and kindness. Hate has to be a respected member of the group. If it is not, the family is not genuinely happy.

## Some Theoretical Remarks

As a psychoanalyst I believe all human beings are born with two basic instinctual drives: one propels us toward people because it is driven by bodily needs like hunger, body warmth, touching, etc. Such needs, if satisfied, bring gratification and pleasure which leads to loving the person or persons as instruments, conveyors of milk, and other supplies which provide the pleasurable experience. As the baby matures he develops from a cupboard lover who needs to be loved, primarily, into someone who can love actively and eventually into a person who can like, be affectionate, can care, be concerned, can become emotionally involved.

At the same time the human infant is born with an aggressive drive—an urge to overcome the obstacles to his pleasure, to destroy and get rid of those things or persons who hurt and give pain. The baby screams in fury, rages at his frustrations, destroys in his temper tantrums, and also feels annihilated and crushed when he is neglected or deprived. The child matures from aggressive, impotent rage to destructiveness, and eventually is able to be angry and hate. If he is fortunate in his development, he is able also to modulate his hatred into dislike, to compete for what he wants, to master problems, to fight for and against things, and also to have a conscience which can praise him for doing good and curse him for doing bad.

The earliest and most primitive aggression is deadly and destructive, above all to the self, in the early helpless years, and later, to others. The decisive question of whether rage will mature into hate, dislike, and mastery, hinges on whether, and to what extent, aggression will be neutralized and fused by Eros, the loving forces. This is based on having loving, satisfying experiences with and from the important people of one's life.

There is much more theory but this will have to suffice. What has to be remembered is that there are varieties of hate, just as there are varieties of love. Hate cannot be abolished, it can be buried, displaced, or ignored, but it will not disappear. It is ever present in different forms and to varying degrees in all people (all living people), of all classes, colors, sexes, with or without college degrees, with or without money, in religious people and in nonbelievers, even in professors and psychoanalysts.

Unrecognized hate, hate in disguise, is more dangerous and damaging than when it is open and dischargeable. When hidden, hatred leads to prejudice, fanaticism, sudden eruptions of violence, suicide, phobias, obsessions, failure in work, sex, marriage, and child rearing. This occurs because unconscious and unexpressed hatred festers, grows, and becomes regressively more primitive. This is true of all repressed drives. People with relatively obvious problems with their hatred eventually end up in the psychiatrist's office, in jail, in the hospital, in the morgue, or as dictators. I want to focus my talk about the more subtle haters, people we all know, people like you and me.

## Haters in Disguise

### *The "I Can't Kill a Fly" People*

At first blush they seem so gentle, fragile, and delicate, but are they really? The little wisp of a woman with the fluttery voice and trembling hands somehow manages to rule her large family with her "excruciating and incurable" headaches. She can destroy any happy event in the family by suddenly becoming stricken with a "delivish headache." She does not demand that the family give up the outing, but the way she says, "Go on, go without me, I'll be all right," with quivering voice, brimming eyes, and pursed lips, makes everyone feel it would be sheer brutality to leave her alone with the ravages of that beastly headache. Yes, she cannot kill a fly, but a killjoy she is, a killer, par excellence!

Mr. Casper Milquetoast shakes before his boss and his wife, faints at the sight of blood, and is a rigid vegetarian. He lets his wife take care of all money matters, is devoutly religious, strictly faithful to his wife, and devoted to his children. Yet, this man believes most Jews are communists and also cleverly manage to control most of the wealth in America and Europe. He sees no contradictions in his beliefs. He is also convinced Negroes are inherently oversexed, lazy, and mentally inferior, but they may well take over the United States unless "we" stop them. Mr. Milquetoast detests violence, it repels him, but he is strongly in favor of capital punishment, he prefers the more humane form, cyanide gas. He was sent to me by his physician because of insomnia of a particular kind. He could not sleep in the same bed with his wife, he feared he might accidentally roll over on her and suffocate her. When he slept in a separate room, he had a queasy feeling that an intruder might enter the room and hurt him, strangle him, to put it more precisely. This man eventually refused all psychiatric treatment, he had come only at the insistence of his internist. He found my ideas interesting but odd, "and to be completely truthful, they grate on my nerves." I must admit he did the same to me.

The various forms of hate in Mr. Milquetoast are fairly transparent to even untrained observers. His overt contempt and hidden envy for the clever, rich Jews and the sensual, powerful Negroes, his belief in the state's right to cold-blooded murder with cyanide, and his fear of suffocating his wife or being strangled—all indicate why Mr. Milquetoast trembles alone in his bed. I would love to say to these two examples of "I can't kill a fly" people: Please kill flies. If you could, perhaps you would not hurt so many human beings.

### *The Overprotective Parent*

All the types of people I describe are usually not seen in pure culture, but mostly in combination with others. The overprotective parent may also be a fly protector. After all, Mr. Milquetoast was a vegetarian, he was kind to oxen and fish. The type of person I am now referring to is the parent who is so terrified something harmful or evil might happen to his children, that he constantly reminds them of the potential catastrophies that are lurking in the world around them. Their typical advice is: Don't go out in the cold, or when it is hot; avoid drafts and keep out of dusty rooms; don't go to school or to the movies or a dance, the flu is "going around." They give lectures to their children on why the child is better off not staying overnight in a stranger's house: the parents don't belong to the Temple and one older sister is supposed to be strange in the head, she goes with all kinds of boys. The term *goes* means has sex with all kinds of boys and *kinds of* means a different religion or color. There are also warnings on the hazards of camping trips, particularly the prevalence of rattlesnakes and poison ivy. No word is said about the beauty of the mountains, the trees, or the flowers. If the child sneezes he is "getting something" and is forced to take extra vitamins, allergy pills, and usually put to bed. These poor children spend more time with their doctor than they do with their friends playing doctor. These well-intentioned, misguided parents have succeeded in making the child's outside world and his body, his inside world, predominantly a source of fear, pain and disaster. Imagine the sex life of this child twenty years later, or his self-confidence in general.

Another overprotective type has to pretend she is not prone to the human weaknesses of anger or temper. Her four-year-old child kicks her in the shin and she responds through gritted teeth and clenched jaw, voice carefully modulated: "We don't kick people, do we? We don't get angry or lose our temper do we? Say you are sorry, darling." Pause. "Say you are sorry" is now hissed with serpentine venom mixed with equal parts of saccharin. But no simple anger. No, instead this mother is doing the following to her child: (1) We don't kick means: we superior human beings do not kick, only beasts like you do. If the child is quite young he may think he was hallucinating and he only wanted to kick. (2) The words "we don't get angry, do we" are pure unadulterated hypocrisy. The mother's tone and action are clearly loaded with hatred, but cold blooded compared to the child's honest outburst. (3) "Say you are sorry" means to the child: all that matters are words, just say the right words, and then actions, behavior, and feelings can be overlooked. Conformity, lip service, and the cliché are what is important. Human relations are dehumanized.

People who cannot simply say, I hate or dislike Sam Katz, and instead say, oh, I'm not crazy about him, or the "social worker" types who talk of negative feelings or hostility, belong in this group. So do those parents who can only punish a child by adding the hypocritical phrase: "I am only doing it for your own good," or, "This hurts me more than it hurts you." All such people are very prone to psychosomatic illness, particularly of the gastrointestinal tract. They are the people who only eat what is good for them, hating every mouthful. With all the venom they swallow, no wonder the stomach and bowel is forced to express the explosive spasms of rage they dare not expose verbally or in overt behavior.

The overprotective parent does not seem to realize that the child *needs* boundaries and restraints on his impulses. He needs the parent's rewards *and* punishments to help him establish control over his drives. A parent who never says no will have either a delinquent child or a frightened one. Overly permissive parents have children who feel neglected. The child often interprets the overpermissiveness as the parents' not caring. Finally, if you always say yes, you rob your child of the delight of transgressing. Instead of being able to enjoy a little mischief he will either become bored or have to resort to causing big trouble in order to provoke a "no, no" out of you, or later out of society.

*The "Blood is Thicker Than Water" People*

This type of person is characterized by such phrases as: My family, or my father, or my mother, or my country, it does not matter what the noun is, the point is, "My blank is right or better, even if all the evidence and the whole world believes otherwise." In these people it is obvious that in them it is not only the blood which is thick. They adore, worship, and sometimes even love their parents or children and occasionally their husbands and wives. There are wife idolizers who proclaim loudly they would gladly give their life for the little woman, but often donate their love and sexual desires elsewhere, and quietly.

The family worshippers, the "my" addicts, are never comfortable with strangers or away from home. They tend to see communists or anti-Semites or Black Panthers or Birchers around every corner and under every bed, and if not today, tomorrow. If they are rich they have contempt for the poor, silently believing the poor for the most part are lazy, vulgar, and insensitive. If they are poor, they believe most of the rich are selfish, callous, and wicked. These people mistrust foreigners and foreignness of all kinds. Even if only your accent is different, you are considered an outsider and potentially dangerous.

The *my* people believe strictly in law and order, above all, in order, even if it is against the law. Order means to them nothing may change, keep things the way they are. Some of them are 150 percent Americans, at least in their opinion, and are unaware of the harm they do their country by making America and Americans seem paranoid, self-centered, and power crazy.

How have the *my* worshippers managed to build their strange, warped psychological structure? Essentially they have split off their love from their hate to an enormous degree. My family, my country is good, the rest of the world is evil and dangerous. To worship means to love blindly and these people are blind to the shortcomings of those they like or who are like them. Actually they are blind to the fact that the strangeness, the foreignness they loath and dread is inside themselves. They deny this and displace it, project it and see it so readily in the world outside. Sometimes they displace these evil forces inside their own bodies. They are then hypochondriacal if not paranoid.

The lack of time permits me to mention only briefly other kinds of Haters in Disguise.

### *The Thing Lovers*

They compulsively collect and hoard money, art and antiques, etc., which they treat with great loving care and are cruel, cold, or disinterested in people.

### *The "Poor Me" People*

No matter what happens in the world, it might be the outbreak of World War II, or the assassination of President Kennedy or Martin Luther King, their reaction is "I have a severe sinus headache, or, I haven't been able to move my bowels yet today." They often complain of being alone, nobody loves me, but they do not realize that such narcissism makes them unlovable.

*The Jinxed People*

Here I am referring to people pursued by bad luck. The kind of person who married three times but each time the husband turns out to be exactly the same type of drunken brute she married the first time. They are accident prone and sickness prone. To them, let's go to bed means sickness, not pleasure. They hate Sundays, no work means no suffering, and they need to suffer. They are guilt-ridden, self-punitive, and masochistic, i.e., get satisfaction from suffering. The bad luck which pursues them comes from their guilty and sadistic conscience which persecutes them, hates them and gives them no peace.

After all these descriptions of hate and haters, disguised or ignored, the question remains: What can we do with hating and hatred and still be happy?

## Hate and the Good Life or How to Hate and Be Happy

1. *Hate must be recognized as an integral part of life and living*. If you can feel pain you can hate. In fact, the more sensitive one is to pain, to painful emotions, like rejection, humiliation, shame, jealousy, etc., the more likely one is to react with hate. Love and hate are inextricably interwoven. You cannot love without hating. The opposite of love is not hate, it is indifference. If you love someone you are very vulnerable to their treatment of you. The more you love, and this is particularly true of romantic and sexual love, the more susceptible you are to being hurt, and if you are hurt the natural response is anger and hate in some form and fashion. If you believe that people can love, then you must also believe we all do hate. I know it is hard for parents to believe that their little children are full of rage and fury. But if you think a moment, why are all fairy tales full of evil witches and stepmothers who mistreat little children and are eventually brutally killed? Why do your children laugh when Daddy falls on his backside? That comes from their stored up resentment and hate, which does not preclude that they also love and need Daddy as well.

2. *Hate needs to be expressed*. As I stated earlier, repressing aggression keeps it alive and fixated. It will not mature, it will grow in intensity and eventually turn upon the self. The more infantile hate is, the more primitive and destructive it is. Rage is harder to handle than anger, it is harder to control, to channelize, to sublimate. If your child is to learn to discriminate among the forerunners and derivatives of hate, he must be given the opportunity to see that his hate does not really kill and also that you too can be hateful at times. You should not hypocritically approve of all forms or degrees of hatred in yourself or in your child. You should be big enough to admit it exists in both you and them. Furthermore, the child has to learn there are appropriate and inappropriate times and places for rage, hitting, fighting, screaming, obscenities, etc. If he cannot learn this at home, where will he? It is far better for a child to see his parents quarrel and make up then to see the phony peace that exists in many homes. I think it is much better to shout at a child who kicks me in the shins, or even swat him, than to make an interpretation or say, "We don't kick people in the shins, do we?" If I get inappropriately angry, I apologize, but only when I truly feel sorry. At least I hope this is true for me. Children must be given the opportunity to show their hatred or contempt for their parents without being crushed in retaliation or seeing their parents collapse. I would much rather have my child say "I hate you" than "I want to die." Hate is to be lived with.

3. *The uses of hate*. Hate is a painful emotion. But one should realize that all pain brings wakefulness, alertness and, if controllable, it leads to thinking and action. Pleasure, love, and satisfaction bring joy, contentment, and eventually sleep. Far be it for me to belittle pleasure and sleep, but the great doers, the thinkers, the creative artists, the adventurers, were all people with a goodly admixture of hate in their veins and they used it. Reflect a moment: there are problems to be *tackled*, obstacles to be *attacked*, road blocks to be *smashed*, fears to be *conquered*, new areas of thought and action to be *mastered*—in inner space as well as outer space. To learn, to work, to bear pain and fear requires determination, the urge to succeed and the willingness to fight and endure. Different forms of hatred play a role in all of these processes.

Not all types of hatred can be sublimated or tamed. But there are many harmless outlets in sports, in games, and in daydreams. I once said, "A death wish a day keeps the analyst away." Amended: a conscious death wish a day, without guilt, keeps the analyst away. This brings me to my last point: there are things worth hating, deserving nothing less than hatred, and hatred without guilt. I firmly believe that all intelligent, sensitive and concerned people ought to hate and to be willing to incur enemies. In my opinion, people without enemies are not worth very much. I have never met a person, male or female, above the age of ten, who was very popular and who had a valuable new idea or was truthful. I believe it is right and just to hate injustice and tyranny in all its forms, to hate violence and war, even though on rare occasions they may be the lesser evil. One should hate, above all, the immoral and unnecessary wars like, in my opinion, we are now involved in, in Vietnam and Cambodia. I think it is virtuous to hate poverty, starvation, disease, and ignorance. But hating is not enough. It should lead to some action, even if you, the hater, will be hated in return, the pain and retaliation must be endured. You may even have to admit to one of the greatest of all pains, the pain of having been wrong, or having misunderstood or of having failed. I can promise you little in return if you follow this prescription. But the little reward is precious. If you can hate effectively and constructively, and if you teach your family to hate well, then you will not hate yourself. You will then discover that you can love better and also that you are a part of the family of man. And you will never be alone.

# 15 The Dread and Love of Death (1971)

*A University of California, Los Angeles, extension division program titled "Violent Death" was the occasion for this lecture. Ralph Greenson joined authorities from the sociological, judicial, and medical fields to discuss the topic. He began by stating that one of the keys to understanding man's contradictory reactions and behavior toward death stems from the fact that he is fascinated by death. Among the variety of contrary feelings and impulses that make up this fascination is the experience of many that although death mobilizes dread, loathing, and hate, it may also be appealing, glorious, and irresistible. The difficulty is compounded by the fact that we have never experienced death and tend to be frightened of the unknown.*

*Giving poignant clinical examples from his practice of psychoanalysis, Greenson elaborated on Freud's observation that everybody is convinced of his own immortality in his unconscious and irrational mind, no matter how logical, reasonable, and scientific he may be on a conscious level. This welter of conflicting feelings may prevent us from dealing rationally with death, suicide, war, and violence.*

## Introduction

As a psychoanalyst contributing to a symposium on violent death, I shall try to focus my brief remarks on an exploration of the contradictory nature of man's reactions to death. Although the title of my presentation deals only with death, I am quite sure you will not be surprised to find that a good part of my discussion will touch on violence, because death and violence are so often almost inextricably interwoven.

Although most people in our so-called civilized society would state with all sincerity that they hate brutality and dread death, it is a well-known fact that our most popular films are full of war, violence, and crime, the best-selling books for the last fifty years concern war and murder mysteries and the most beloved of children's games involve killings and playing dead in various forms. During the recent assassinations and the public funerals, whenever there are riots in our cities and universities, most people, the thoughtful and the empty headed, the young and old, blacks and whites, all share one common experience, our eyes are glued to our television sets which depict again and again the shootings, killings, and destruction, and we stare repeatedly at the same sensational photographs in the newspapers and magazines.

It is my contention that one of the keys to understanding man's contradictory reactions and behavior to death stems from the fact that he is fascinated by death. To be fascinated means that one is ensnared and captivated and robbed of one's good judgment because one is flooded by a variety of contrary feelings and impulses which cannot be dis-entangled or integrated because some of these reactions are conscious and others unconscious. Death mobilizes dread, loathing, and hate but it may also be appealing, glorious, and irresistible.

There is a further complication in man's reaction to death. Most of us dread the idea of our own death consciously, and although we know intellectually that death is a natural, undeniable, and unavoidable outcome of life, most of us behave in reality, however, as if it were otherwise. Freud wrote in 1915: "It is

---

Presented at a panel "Views of Violent Death" at the UCLA Extension, October 23 and 24, 1971.

indeed impossible to imagine our own death; and whenever we attempt to do so we can perceive that we are in fact still present as spectators. Hence the psychoanalytic school could venture the assertion that at bottom *no one believes in his own death*, or, to put the same thing in another way, *in the unconscious, everyone of us is convinced of his own immortality*."

Man eventually is forced to face the painful knowledge that he too will someday die when he observes at first hand the death of people close to him: like his wife, his child, or his friend. His emotional inability to accept this fate for himself impels him to devise a compromise: the body may perish but the spirit, the soul, or the demon lives on. This forms the basis for assuming other forms of existence and a continuing of life after death. Different religions have seized upon these primitive beliefs to promise eternal life or reincarnation if one adheres to their particular brand of dogmas and rituals.

Man dreads his own death and the death of those he loves, yet he is able to kill others in fits of anger, and also in cold blood, for material gain or at the order of his government. Freud stated rather cynically, but correctly, that the state is not against killing, it only wants to monopolize the right to kill, in war and in capital punishment. To conclude these introductory remarks, I must add that man is also able to kill himself, an act which is far more widespread and frequent than we ever dreamed of. The work of Schneidman, Farberow, Litman, Feifel, and Tabachnick, among others, have made this depressingly clear in their work in suicide prevention centers. Now I shall try to explain some of the paradoxes of man's apparent dread of death and also his affinity to suicide and other self-destructive acts. I shall use clinical material, which may be more depressing but is more convincing and less boring than theory.

## The Dread of Death

A mature and intelligent man of my acquaintance joins a small group of us at supper and explains his lateness by stating he had been detained by his attorney's office where he had just signed a new will. He turned to his wife and in absolute seriousness said: "I realize I forgot one important stipulation in the will. I don't want to have any formal religious service of any kind." He pointed his finger at his wife almost threateningly and added: "If you forget this, I will be furious with you and I shall never forgive you!" After a brief pause all of us burst into laughter, eventually my friend as well. We realized that *emotionally* he could not accept the fact that dead means dead and when he will be dead, he, like the rest of us, will not be capable of anger or any other emotion. He had temporarily denied the real meaning of death.

A man comes for urgent psychiatric treatment because he is so frightened of having a fatal coronary attack that he has made several serious suicide attempts. He has no physical signs of heart disease and the man is not psychotic. It becomes apparent to me that he is far less afraid of death if he can choose the method and time. He could not bear the thought of his utter helplessness and the agonizing pain if he sustained a heart attack. It was far easier for him to swallow fifty sleeping pills and to prepare himself for death by falling into a deadly sleep. In this situation he felt at least he had some control and furthermore, the dying was not painful. He had studied coronary disease carefully, as well as suicide by sleeping pills, and was aware that the pain in a heart attack could be excruciating and devastating and that death by sleeping pills was painless.

Several clinical findings became clear to me in working with him. First of all, the patient was confusing dying with death, a very widespread confusion in people's minds. So often people dread the agony of dying, the physical pain, the sense of wasting away, becoming mentally incompetent, the general feeling of losing one's identity, of feeling dehumanized, that often occurs in drawn out states of dying. They dread dying far more than death. Yet they think of it as their fear of death.

There are less severe forms of this type of reaction. There are people who think they are on the verge of death when they have any unexpected pain or physical dysfunction. They call the doctor in panic, they "know they are dying." Such people live with death like an ever present nearby enemy, ready to spring upon him at a moment's notice.

In my patient there was also the terror of being taken by surprise. He felt in such situations that he had no control over what was happening. He felt helpless, and this feeling of helplessness was also intolerable to him. He would rather die in charge of the situation than let a coronary attack happen, with him being completely passive, even though he knew he could very likely recover from the coronary. He tried to kill himself to avoid dying. For him dying was far more frightening than death. There are others who can bear dying quite well but are terrified of death. I would like at this point to quote e. e. cummings, who is most eloquent on this point.

> dying is fine)but Death
>
> ?o
> baby
> i
>
> wouldn't like
>
> Death if Death
> were
> good:for
>
> when(instead of stopping to think)you
>
> begin to feel of it,dying
> 's miraculous
> why?be
>
> cause dying is
>
> perfectly natural;perfectly
> putting
> it mildly lively(but
>
> Death
>
> is strictly
> scientific
> &artificial&
>
> evil & legal)
>
> we thank thee
> god
> almighty for dying
>
> (forgive us,o life!the sin of Death)

Another patient once consulted me because she wanted me

to promise her that should she be deathly ill, I, or a doctor she was also fond of, would sit by her bedside, even if she were totally unconscious, until we were absolutely certain of her being dead. To her the most frightening aspect of dying was the loneliness of dying all alone. Also, she had the thought that if I were there, I would protect her even in death. I would somehow look after her, take care of her, see to it she had a good death, and would help her meet nice people in her after life. Above all, she could not bear the aloneness that death signified to her. Her history revealed that for her, death remobilized her separation from her mother, who died when the patient was five. If I would promise to see her through her dying and death she would do all right. It was like accompanying her to the scary kindergarten class the first day of school as her mother had done shortly before she had died.

Another typical obsession about death is the fear the person will not be completely dead and will be buried or cremated alive. How often have I heard the plea, "please, doctor, be sure I am dead, I am horrified at the possibility of awakening in a coffin, suffocating, or in an oven burning." Again the major fear is dying and not death. To be realistic about such obsessions, not that it helps the patient, and I hate to sound cold blooded, but facts are facts, by the time you get into the coffin or oven, even if you are not totally dead, consciousness is practically completely extinguished and there is no sensation.

Some people can't bear the idea that if they are dead they will be unknowing of what is happening in their outside personal world. They dread unconsciousness and equate it with being left out of all the exciting events, an emotional state that goes back to the time when they were children and left out of the adult's fun, especially the "fun" in their parents' bedroom. A patient jokingly said to me: "I don't mind dying, just as long as you keep in touch with me."

There are people who dread death because it means to them a time for receiving punishment. They fantasy unconsciously how they will be at the mercy of God or demons who will punish them for their secret transgressions, and they will not be in a position to defend or excuse themselves, attitudes they maintained all their lives. Usually these people are loaded with *unconscious* death wishes, especially for those close to them. It is the punishment for their unconscious death wishes which makes them dread death. I have said on an earlier occasion: "A conscious death wish a day (without guilt), keeps the analyst away."

Finally there is a vast group—most of us to some degree—who dread death because it is something unknown. We cannot know what we have never experienced, and none of us has ever been dead and if we have for short intervals, we didn't know it, or experience it. There are some people who were temporarily "declared dead"—but all they recall is the nothingness, or the peace of a deep dreamless sleep. Yet for people who have been terrified of the new, the strange, the different, all their lives long, the new experience of death is terrifying and not just unpleasant.

## The Love of Death

A professional young man came to see me several years after he had made an almost fatal suicide attempt. On the fifth anniversary of his mother's suicide he became overwhelmed by his sense of personal emptiness and worthlessness. She had been the only person who was really close to him, understood him, admired him, and had enjoyed him by playing four-hand piano duets, etc. This was the most happy experience of his life. No human being approached her in virtue, charm, and kindness. This was my patient's original version of their relationship. Later it turned out his mother was a controlling, sweet sounding, obsessional, dominant woman. His new wife was eager to provide him with a good life, but her very sincere efforts only highlighted the uniqueness of his *fantasied* symbiotic closeness to his mother. He became furious with God, which horrified him; he had been brought up in a very religious environment (by his mother). He felt mistreated by God, angry at fate, fed up with his wife and children, and disappointed in his profession and his sexual competence. In this state of mind he increasingly began to visualize his saintly mother as though she were waiting for him, smiling down at him from heaven. He decided one day when the entire family was out, to join her. He undressed himself naked, lay down in his bathtub (his mother had been very neat), and meticulously cut his throat and his wrists. For him, death meant meeting his idealized dead mother in a blissful reunion. He told me that the sensations of the blood flowing out of him and the slow dimming of consciousness was like falling into a peaceful, ecstatic sleep.

I saw a skinny nineteen-year-old boy who had recovered from jumping from a ten-story building while under the influence of LSD. He was eventually able to recall his feelings very precisely. After swallowing the LSD he first had magnificent sensations of colors and texture, very rich and voluptuous. It seemed as if someone were feeding this opulent sensory experience into his eyes and he felt for the first time in his life, powerful, unafraid, and omnipotent. This was in marked contrast to the paranoid, fearful, degraded state of mind he was usually in. In his newly discovered state of omnipotence, he decided he would take on the world, no longer would he hide, in fact he would challenge God and even death, he was fearless. He felt convinced he could jump from the roof of the building and be unharmed. After months of hospitalization he slowly realized he was still the skinny frightened paranoid boy. His leap was an attempt to prove that he was "really" unafraid and not skinny. It was a counterphobic act. The drug had temporarily changed his real identity into a counterfeit identity. Unfortunately, he hit the ground with his real self. Hospitalization and psychotherapy helped him get rid of his false self and the need for LSD.

Children who have been rebuked by their parents will often think of killing themselves. They enjoy seeing their parents' shock, grief, and remorse and sorrow at the sight of the child's dead body. I have seen similar behavior in grown-ups, particularly after a lover's quarrel. In such situations, one of the lovers represents a parent and the other a child. Such suicide attempts are attempts to gain revenge against the cruel depriver of love, but above all, it is an attempt to gain pity, and often piety as well.

The largest group of death-lovers I have encountered are those who seek partial death. They are the searchers for bliss, peace of mindlessness, an end to fears, uncertainties, insecurities, and feelings of unlovableness. I have the impression that this group may make up a very high percentage of people in this country. It may well represent the average American citizen. They are tranquilizer poppers, they have a pill for everything, even the slightest discomfort. Their medicine cabinet would put a drugstore to shame, and they prescribe promiscuously for friend and stranger alike. They mistrust doctors and call them only for refilling their old prescriptions. They are also the people who need two double scotches to face their family in the evening and need three more doubles to face going to sleep. These people are also the television addicts who can only bear living by living vicariously. Their main objective in life is to kill time. Some of them are addicted to making money or being social successes. Their name in the paper is more important than their relations to their husbands or their children. I would call most of these people the "undead set." Part of them is unalive and they want it so. They don't come for psychotherapy. They function effectively in certain local areas of their life, they go to work (joylessly), have sex (promiscuously and joylessly), they can even talk animately to people—but they usually are people they don't care about personally, the hairdresser, salesmen, strangers, etc. They have allowed the intimate, sensitive, imaginative part of themselves to wither away and die. The "undead" sleepwalk through life. This type of person seems to be becoming more prevalent. They are only partially alive, they seek oblivion, they try to push the hours away, they sleep as long as possible and hate mornings. They are running away from their inner awareness, anxieties, and depressions and above all, they are avoiding their fantasies and imagination. Partial death is preferable to a rich life which includes some conflict and misery.

I must add a group of people who have sexualized and libidinized guilt, anxiety, and suffering. They are essentially masochists and often belong to clinical groups we classify as perverts. Weisman has pointed out that in people with perversions, there is a high degree of suicide, which is a combination of revenge, hatred, homicide, and complete submissiveness. The accident-prone people share some of these traits.

Another small group is represented by people whose main reason for living is their hate for a particular person or group. I know of one instance when two neighbors lived side by side hating and bedeviling each other for over thirty years. Both were unmarried, neither thought of moving. When one of the neighbors died, the other committed suicide, she had no further reason to live. Ironically, in the small village they lived in, they were buried next to each other.

Finally I should mention a group in whom the search for death is not irrational. Some people are subjected to so much pain and humiliation and they are truly helpless against them. I speak here of people suffering from incurable painful physical illnesses, people in concentration camps, and prisons, and people with incurable mental afflictions. In these people there is an all-pervading sense of hopelessness, and it is realistic. I believe under such conditions, seeking death is rational, even courageous, it means an end to pain and terror.

## Summary

I have tried to explain in this paper why man behaves and reacts so paradoxically and contradictorily about death. Part of the difficulty stems from the fact that we have never experienced death and tend to be frightened of the unknown. Furthermore, everybody is convinced of his own immortality *in his unconscious* and irrational mind, no matter how logical, reasonable, and scientific he may be on a conscious level. Another complicating circumstance is that death arouses in man simultaneous and contradictory impulses and attitudes. This results in a state of fascination with death so that man is partly terrified and attracted to it at the same time. These factors may be some of the reasons it has taken us so long to scientifically study death and suicide.

These same elements may also be the underlying causes of why we are so inept in dealing with war and violence. This symposium, however, indicates that now we may be making some progress.

# 16 Boredom, American Style (1971)

*Hildi Greenson finds it interesting that someone who was so rarely bored and certainly never boring, should choose to speak on this subject yet again. He had dealt with that "painful state of mind" as he called it, some thirteen years earlier in "Apathy, Boredom, and Miltown." He found it to be not only an individual symptom but also an expression of cultural malaise.*

*Greenson felt that boredom is basically a state of mind that results from blocking thoughts and fantasies that would otherwise lead to recognition of conflict, frustration, or unhappiness. He discussed the many faces of boredom, including its "3 R's": routines, recipes, and rituals; the pursuit of trivial pleasures; the search for intensity and meaning; the drug-taker's search for oblivion, mindlessness, and death; and un-American boredom, the mutant hippie strain. In studying his patients, Greenson found that chronic and severe boredom is a defense against an underlying deep-seated depression. Such patients try to avoid the depression by plunging impulsively into a variety of intense activities or by regressing into persistent lethargy.*

*The antidote for boredom, according to Greenson, is to plunge into life, which includes dealing with painful conflicts and being willing to suffer. Suffering is preferable to boredom; at least it has the potential advantage of leading to purposeful reflection or action. His argument was passionate.*

> *I believe that life is to be lived and to live a life of meaning we have to contend with the painful aspects of our human existence. By that I mean that within the limits of our abilities we should try to face the realities of our internal and external worlds. All people are full of loving and hateful impulses. . . . If we face our conflicts and are willing to endure some suffering, we shall be able to love and work with our fellow man, we may often be unhappy, but we shall never be bored.*

## Introduction

Boredom is a painful state of mind which occurs in different forms and disguises throughout the world. I have decided to write on this subject because it seems to be increasing alarmingly in all sectors of our society. Boredom afflicts the rich more than the poor, the grown-up more than the child, and the so-called healthy more than the neurotic. I shall explain these apparent contradictions later on. In its benign and harmless form, it is felt as a transitory state and can be readily relieved by a variety of diversions and distractions. In its more severe forms it is usually covered over by behavior patterns which make the bored person *seem* to be unusually energetic and impulsive or remarkably relaxed to the point of lethargy or apathy. Most people are reluctant to face the fact they are chronically bored and this affliction only comes to light when the disguises of their boredom fail them. Boredom itself is rarely felt as a symptom, as something foreign to the self. It is usually attributed to the external world. *I* am not bored, but one's hometown, one's friends, one's husband or wife, or one's job is boring. The mechanism of projection helps one feel that one is the victim and *not* the cause of one's boredom. There are boring people and situations, but frequent boredom, from whatever external cause, is an indication of some internal emotional aber-

---

Presented to the Reiss-Davis Child Study Center, Women's Division, Los Angeles, April 21, 1971.

ration. This becomes evident in people who, despite frequent changes of cities, husbands, wives, friends, and jobs, nevertheless remain bored.

Let me try to describe boredom. It is a state of dissatisfaction accompanied by a feeling of longing and an inability to designate what is longed for. There is a sense of emptiness, frustration, and restlessness, but at the same time, one also feels essentially passive. The bored person waits expectantly for someone or something in the external world to provide the stimulus, the solution. If such people could or would talk, they would say, "I am restless, fidgety, or stirred up, please tell me what I would like to do." The sad part of the story is that even when some activity is attempted, it rarely turns out to be satisfying, it ends up as merely a time killer. This is characteristic of boredom, time seems to stand still—it does not pass. The German word for boredom is *langweile*, which translated literally means, "long time." The activities of bored people serve the purpose of killing time—and sufferers from boredom eagerly squander their time. Their immediate objective is to make the hours, days, nights, and weeks go by. Their actions are diversions and distractions, i.e., they are evasions of what they really long for *but* are afraid of.

I have found it useful to distinguish between two major kinds of boredom, agitated and apathetic. Boredom, American style, is of the agitated, frantic type. The European variety is more languid and phlegmatic. In some European circles, boredom is even a sign of sophistication, it is the "in" thing to be. I should add that we have Americanized a great deal of Europe, particularly with the advent of television, and you can see a good deal of turbulent nothingness going on all over Europe. Analogously, some sections of the American scene still find it posh to imitate European high society, and you will find members of the international set conspicuously displaying their boredom with life in America. They wear it as a badge of arrogance indicating their superior sensitivity and our inferior culture. Actually, sensitive and cultured people are rarely bored. They are far more likely to be depressed or miserable, but not bored. There is also an "un-American" subtype of boredom, to be found primarily in many of the dissident youths of today, which has both apathetic and agitated phases. It is not pure boredom, but is shot through with anger, depression, and contempt.

## Some Theoretical Remarks

Before I go on to some clinical examples, let me outline for you the dynamics of boredom. The state of boredom is based on a damming up of instinctual drives *plus* the repression of the instinctual aims and objects. The bored person is not only instinctually frustrated, but he does not know what kind of instinctual activity he seeks and with whom he desires it. The usual neurotic is also blocked in his instinctual outlets, but he knows or surmises what he wants. It is guilt, shame, and fear which keep him from attaining satisfaction. The neurotic does not feel empty but full, in fact, weighted down with the misery of guilt, anxiety or depression, a very different state of affairs.

The sense of painful emptiness characteristic of the bored, stems from the fact that a major part of their fantasy life is repressed or inhibited. Their imagination is stultified or blacked out in regard to major areas of their life. They would rather feel empty than miserable. It is for this reason that they turn to the external world, hoping someone will "guess" what they want. A typical statement of a bored person is: "I can't get with it, I am nowhere, I am out of it." In this way his language indicates that he is out of touch with his *emotionally* meaningful fantasies, thoughts, and imaginings. People who are severely and chronically bored and who are aware of it suffer great pain.

Many years ago I treated a patient who made a serious suicide attempt because of her unbearable boredom. In the hospital and during treatment she felt quite depressed, which she found to be a welcome relief from her intolerable boredom. In studying such patients it became apparent that chronic and severe boredom is a defense against an underlying deep-seated depression. They attempt to avoid the depression by plunging impulsively into a variety of intense activities or regressing into a persistent lethargy. These solutions are never truly satisfactory. The reasons are as follows: As long as there is an inhibition and blocking of fantasy, thought, and imagination, there are no connecting links between instinctual drives, emotions, and human relations. These people may go through the motions of living and loving, but it is essentially a charade, or a desperate search for something from the outside which can only be found inside a person and then only after suffering through a depression.

Boredom also may have an adaptive function, particularly when it is recognized as boredom and is only temporary. It is a kind of local anesthetic, dulling the pain in a particularly sensitive psychic area while natural healing takes place. Any change of routine, like a weekend away from home, a poker game, talking seriously with one's wife, or skiing, may be sufficient if the underlying conflicts can be faced consciously. Sometimes boredom may also serve as a period of germination before the birth of creative ideas. When the pathology is more serious, then boredom becomes a form of hibernation, a kind of self-preservative trance-like state, an attempt to wait out or ward off the stormy depression which howls below. I have seen such apathetic states in prisoners of war who survived years of imprisonment in World War II.

Boredom, per se, is not a sickness, but it is also not a wellness. It is a signal, an indication that the conscious self has lost contact with the deeper levels and structures of the mind. If boredom lasts for any prolonged interval, the reasonable self usually attempts to search out and at least approximate an understanding of the underlying painful conflicts. Then boredom is replaced by suffering. *Suffering has the advantage of leading to potential purposeful reflection or action. In fact, it can be said that suffering is the specific antidote for boredom.* That is why the poor, the persecuted, and the disenfranchised, those who battle for their very existence, are so rarely bored. That also holds true for the neurotic who struggles against his fears, his depressions and guilts. Boredom is an affliction of the successful, the affluent, and the pseudonormal characters, all of whom make up a high percentage of our current population. I would hazard a guess that there are several millions of these American-style boredom types walking, or rather, running around this country today. These people attempt to conceal their boredom from themselves and the world at large. To them, obvious boredom would signify failure, unhappiness or neurosis. *They hide their boredom in activities which are potentially more dangerous than the underlying unhappiness.* I propose that we now look at some of the typical disguises characteristic for those who suffer from boredom, American style. A precautionary note: everyone of us will think he sees himself or someone he loves in these clinical vignettes. This is not intentional but it is unavoidable.

## The Many Faces of Boredom

### *Routines, Recipes, and Rituals: The 3 R's of Boredom*

Bored people try to escape their internal emptiness and loneliness by establishing routines. Married couples who have blocked out their marital misery will schedule social events months in advance because they have a horror of a free evening. They would then have to face each other and conversation might upset their precarious equilibrium. By calling long in advance they also ensnare people who would otherwise claim to be busy. A full calendar proves to them they are popular, well-liked, and a social success. They have long lists of people to chose from because they do not discriminate among friends, acquaintances, relatives, enemies, business contacts, and strangers. Guests are chosen according to certain tried and tested recipes containing various social ingredients. One couple may be picked because they are, at the moment, socially prominent and will impress another couple who have recently slighted the host and hostess. Then come the couples one "owes" a dinner party to. To this group one usually adds other couples who are fillers, people whose function is to add social bulk to the room. To this concoction one may add a dash of spice in the form of an entertainer, a black couple, or a psychoanalyst. If this melange is placed into a crowded room, served strong drinks quickly, and delicate, puny hor d'oeuvres, the noise and confusion gives the appearance of cheerful and interesting goings on. Dinner is only served when people have to eat ravenously in order not to pass out from the alcoholic intake or from pure hunger. The food is praised because the guests can no longer taste, and they are also grateful for having been saved from paralysis. Having overeaten, the guests are too tired to leave early and linger on until the early morning hours, all of which proves the party was a smashing success.

The hostess notes the dates each person was invited because most of them belong to the "You remember what's-his-name" group. The guests are rotated regularly, new names added after a few drinks at someone else's party, and no one is dropped unless they committed some deadly sin like spilling red wine on the expensive tablecloth or accidentally telling a painful truth to the hostess under the influence of alcohol.

The sex life of people who cannot stand not standing each other, is also ruled by routine and recipe. One does not have intercourse spontaneously on the spur of the moment. (At least not with one's husband or wife.) Spontaneity and improvisations might break through the protective wall warding off the underlying miseries. Marital sex is carefully placed into a groove or rut and is scheduled for a certain day. In this way, neither person has to take the initiative and run the risk of being rejected. If Sunday night is scheduled, then Sunday night is the time that intercourse shall take place. The sex act is usually performed without much eagerness or passion and usually follows a set pattern, using a previous recipe that turned out well. The blacking out of all fantasy may force such couples to use artificial aids like marijuana, pornographic magazines, or motion pictures in order to facilitate and heighten sexual excitement. If that is beyond their financial means, one of the participants will tell details of lurid sexual adventures taken from his collection of obscene literature. In recent years certain mechanical gadgets have been added to the formula. Vibrators, Jacuzzi baths, and water beds, plus pot, add spice to the usual menu. Under such conditions, both partners may become so immersed in the movie, the story, or the strange sensations, that they are often startled after orgasm to see who is actually in bed with them.

Bored people are often promiscuous because they keep searching for ways to fill up their internal emptiness. They are not able to love because they are unable to communicate intimately either verbally or emotionally. They use physical contact and sensations as a substitute for meaningful human relatedness. They are alienated from a vital part of themselves and hope that physical contact with a new person will give them the feeling of being whole or in touch. Unfortunately, as marvelous as orgasm sensations can be, it is no substitute for either love or intimacy.

Such sexual affairs do not last long and have no important emotional repercussions. These people continue to remain on each other's guest lists, they meet as though nothing happened, and, sadly enough, they are right.

### The Pursuit of Trivial Pleasures: Favorite Pastimes of the Bored Set

I am referring here to a vast number of people who spend a great deal of their time seeking superficial satisfactions. There are women whose major delight is shopping, without any specific need or objective. They will even accompany a friend on a shopping tour when they themselves have nothing to buy. They do this as other women might go for a walk, or have a cup of coffee in order to talk. The advantage of shopping is that it makes it impossible to engage in any serious or meaningful conversation and their fantasy and imagination is safely walled off. These same types of women are terribly dependent on beauty parlors, visiting them with the same regularity neurotic women go to their psychotherapists. They study their faces in the mirror every morning very carefully and for long periods of time. They usually use a magnifying mirror so as not to miss any wrinkle, blemish, or extraneous hair. They are equally scrupulous about the state of their figures and know their measurements to the last decimal point. These women get facial massages, hot packs, ice packs, and body manipulations of different kinds. In addition they have their hair washed, dyed, curled, and set. This is very time-consuming and these ladies come home exhausted. At bedtime they put on a variety of facial creams, body oils, hair nets, eye shades, and skin dewrinklers. If they only spent a similar amount of time looking inward instead of outward, their faces might look less artificial and strained. But to look inward means to be willing to suffer and perchance to cry, and this might produce bags under the eyes, so they stay with the beautician, the hairdresser, and the masseur. Often they talk so much to these people that one has the impression that the hairdresser serves as a shrink who is safely inept. These ladies talk a lot, mostly trivia and gossip, and their phone bills are enormous.

The male counterparts of the women above are the country club addicts. The bored rich play golf daily, then have a massage and a sauna bath. After that they play cards until they are late for dinner. They often have dinner at the club; in fact, they spend more time at the club than at home. They remain members of the golf club long after they have given up golf. In a sense, most country clubs serve as a camouflaged sanitarium for the rich. Those who have to work for a living stop off at a bar for a few drinks with the "boys". *Boys* refers to chronic acquaintances of approximately your own age, who you n ever really get to know because you only meet in crowded bars where the din is so loud you have to shout to be heard, and the smoke is so thick you can barely recognize one another. There is much verbal horseplay which is unrepeatable at home because it turns out to be nonsensical when sober. These men prefer the company of men, feel very masculine with men, and often consciously admit they dislike women. They are unaware of the fact that actually they are afraid of women. The typical boast of the barroom: "I can lick anybody in this room," is not an indication of pugilistic prowess, or even of aggression, it is a slogan used to bolster one's doubts about one's masculinity.

### *The Search for Intensity: The Bored Person's Search for Meaning*

There are people who never seem to have an ordinary experience. Whatever happens to them, according to their accounts, is the greatest, the best, the worst, the most awful or horrible or wonderful. In any case, it is the "most." Some of them do their best to create these situations. They are the life of the party, or the death of it. They are cut-ups, jokesters, story-tellers, or confessors. Interestingly, they can admit in a group what they cannot say in private. They laugh loud and long and they cry copiously and noisily. They often confuse loudness with sincerity, tearfulness with intimacy, and obscenity with passion. These people love crowds, it gives them the illusion that they are "in," that they belong. At parties they overdress, overeat, overdrink and overtalk. They reach home exhausted, which they misinterpret to mean they are satisfied. Actually they are in that uncomfortable position of feeling depleted and still discontent.

These frantic people try to work up emotional and instinctual intensity of all kinds in order to cover up their inner isolation and their loneliness. They are unable to communicate intimately because their fantasy life is inhibited, and they hope the "great" party will hide their internal silence.

A recent addition to this forlorn group of intensity-seekers may be seen in the encounter groups, touch therapy, and nude therapy groups. They hunger for contact and warmth and hope it can be achieved by artificial togetherness. This is doomed to fail because if one is unable to make contact with one's own inner feelings and thoughts, one cannot do so with an outsider.

### *The Drug Takers: The Search for Oblivion, Mindlessness, and Death in the Bored*

Here I am referring to a diverse group of people. This subgroup is enormous and complex, and I cannot do justice to this important topic. Nevertheless, I do want to sketch some of the outstanding characteristics because drug taking is so widespread, involves every age group, and is definitely on the increase.

Alcohol makes time pass, it is one of the great time killers. The temporary synthetic elation and good mood is a palliative for the monotony and loneliness of the drinker's life. In sufficient dosages, alcohol also makes such people temporarily gregarious, hale and well met. Alcohol, however, can also break the defensive barrier around the depression, and destructive brutality can emerge as well as terrible sadness. If taken quickly enough, or long enough, it eventually leads to oblivion and unconsciousness, which superficially resembles sleep, but is more like a coma than normal sleep.

Sleeping pills, tranquilizers, and sedatives are sold in such abundance both legally and illegally that it is impossible to estimate how much is being consumed. The highest percentage of all prescriptions filled in pharmacies are for this group of drugs. Their overall function is to do chemically what boredom does psychologically; namely to repress and inhibit the fantasy life and imagination. Sleeping pills block out a high percentage of night dreams. The tranquilizers and sedatives dull awareness and produce a state of mind which is actually more of a peace of mindlessness. In recent times sedatives are also used as "downers," a means of counteracting the ill-effects of such stimulants as the amphetamines, Dexedrine and Dexamyl. The latter are euphoriants, which means a producer of a temporary synthetic good mood or elation. If taken to excess they produce extreme motor restlessness, agitation, irritability, palpitations, and insomnia. Hence the vicious cycle. What is basic for our discussion, however, is that these people cannot face their conflicts and miseries and resort to artificial means for temporary and illusory relief.

Marijuana, or pot, is also a euphoriant, but it acts differently inasmuch as it does stimulate the imagination and permits some repressed fantasies to break through into consciousness. It is this fact which makes it appealing to the bored person. It also enhances certain perceptions, sound for example, and if taken in groups, as is customary, gives a feeling of belonging. There is an illusion of closeness, but it is only an illusion. The physical proximity and the communal use of pot, does not break down the real isolation each person in the group feels. Sexual capacity seems to be enhanced, but that too is an illusion. The number of orgasms in women is high but the quality of the orgasms go to pot with pot. The most outstanding difference between alcohol users and marijuana users is that alcohol makes people prone to violence, while pot makes people good natured and lovers of loud music. Cocaine is now "in." It also produces a synthetic good mood which often leads to sleep. Not much is known about this drug at this point.

LSD is the most dangerous drug of the lot. It can produce psychotic breakdowns which may be irreversible. It is appealing to those who search for new and vivid sensations because the old have failed to give them pleasure and satisfaction. It also is a way of daring to face death or insanity, a form of playing "chicken," and it attracts people who are actually phobic about madness or death.

Television. I put television in the category of drugs because it is habituating and addictive, it dulls the intellect, it artificially stimulates certain senses while it blurs the identity. All bored people are drawn to the "tube" and are prone to take overdoses. The fascination of television is complex, but for those with an inhibited fantasy life, here they have ready made fantasies, even in color. They do not have to imagine, it is done for them. The unfortunate side effects of television are that it makes real life seem even more drab for the bored person. I know of people who put the TV on the first thing in the morning and shut it off only when ready for sleep. It is essentially an oral activity, people eat or drink constantly while watching television.

### *Boredom, Un-American Style, or the Hippies: A Mutation of Boredom*

Drugs and television prompt me to say a few words about the question of boredom in the youth, the dissident youth of today. Hippies hate television. They hate it because so much of it is false, synthetic, and distorting. They do not buy the cut-rate justice or the superficial problem solving TV portrays. I feel many of them were robbed of their childhood by being placed in front of television sets when very young, and, further, were robbed also of their parents who were television watchers. The instantness of television interfered with the development of fantasy life and the ability to be patient, to wait.

Many of the teenagers take pot, some to escape boredom, but many more to escape the meaninglessness of their lives as they see it. The majority of them are more depressed than bored. Most of them do not expect to live to reach forty. I think you should know that 6 percent of suicides are of youngsters between the ages of thirteen to nineteen. From 1968 to 1969, there has been a rise of 100 percent in the suicide rate of people between the ages of thirteen and twenty-nine years of age. Incidentally, the most prevalent instrument was not drugs, but guns.

As I see it, the hippies, or the dissident youth of America, yearn for life and are faced with war, imprisonment, or engulfment in the establishment they despise. They cannot conform because they cannot bear the hypocrisy of those who waged war all their life long and yet make pompous speeches about loving peace and virtue. The dissidents waver between depression, aggression, apathy, and boredom in a world they never made. For them, boredom is a temporary armistice from war, death, or surrender.

### The Cure and Conclusions

I hope that I have made it clear that boredom is a state of mind which is the result of blocking the thoughts and fantasies that would otherwise lead to the recognition of conflict, frustration, and unhappiness. On occasion we all may need some boredom as a respite from struggle and misery, but it can become a serious problem when distractions and diversions replace the basic elements of life. I believe that life is to be lived, and to live a life of meaning we have to contend with the painful aspects of our human existence. By that I mean that within the limits of our abilities we should try to face the realities of our internal and external worlds. All people are full of loving and hateful impulses. That is the human condition and is as true for the rich as for the poor, the black and the white, the Americans and the Chinese. To know ourselves we must be willing to face and acknowledge our strengths and weaknesses. To form meaningful and enduring relationships we must be willing to share this awareness with those who matter to us. Honesty and humility are prerequisites for relating in any substantial and significant way. We change and the world changes, too. It is painful to find oneself old or out of step or ignorant or weak. Yet, if we want to be part of the world, we must face these eventualities. If we do, and are willing to endure some suffering, we will be able to love and work with our fellow man, we may often be unhappy, but we will never be bored.

# 17 A MCP Freudian Psychoanalyst Confronts Women's Lib (1972)

*This lecture was given as a fund-raiser for the Reiss-Davis Clinic in Los Angeles. Hildi Greenson relates how a German television crew set up their cameras in an adjoining room at the Century Plaza Hotel, with interpreters standing by. They were confident that Dr. Greenson would agree to an interview. He did not disappoint them; he only surprised them by discussing the complicated subject of women's liberation completely in German!*

*Greenson catalogued the myriad ways women are subjugated and exploited in our society: in the family; religiously; legally; in the arts, business, and the professions; as housewives; in medicine, education, and the advertising media. He confessed to the audience that he was guilty of "having been unaware of the enormity of this tyranny until recently and I am grateful to women's liberation for educating me."*

*After quoting at some length from both the moderate and radical literature of the movement, Greenson asked the following questions: Why is there so much hostility between men and women? Why do men dominate and oppress women? Why have the majority of women accepted this?*

*It was clear to him that men who were contemptuous of women actually envied and feared them. Although men are physically stronger and more prone to violence and aggression, they still unconsciously envy the emotional strength of women (dating from the mother–child dyad) and are far more uncertain of their masculinity than women are of their femininity. "Patriarchy seems to work as a screen for aggression, envy, and fear."*

*He dealt with some of the misconceptions regarding penis envy and the controversies about clitoral versus vaginal orgasm and closed the lecture with the following plea:*

> *The women's liberation movement is a potentially valuable source of starting major and much needed changes in the relationship between men and women. Great gains have been made in awakening the hearts and minds of men and women to the terrible injustices perpetrated against women the world over, but women's lib has failed to reach the poor or the nonwhite minorities. Is it going to remain a middle-class white movement? And don't men need liberation too? It is disturbing that many of their members seem to be interested in gaining vengeance rather than deliverance. Unless feminist women recognize and control their hatred of men and of those women who are happy with the male-dominated standards of today, they will unleash a terrible backlash that will ultimately destroy all progressive women's movements.*

## Introduction

I have chosen the subject of women's liberation for discussion and exploration for a variety of reasons. First, I believe the movement, if it continues to grow, has great possibilities for righting the myriad of wrongs perpetrated against women ever since the dawn of recorded history. In addition, I consider myself an intellectual and progressive human being and therefore feel it is my duty to speak out on issues dealing with injustice and oppression, particularly when those issues are in the forefront of the news and thought of the day, and are the source of heated controversy.

---

Presented at the Reiss-Davis Child Study Center, Women's Division, Los Angeles, April 26, 1972.

Third, I feel guilty that I have unknowingly played along with the oppression of women, despite the fact that in a Freud lecture in 1966 I had written that "women are the largest underprivileged, victimized group in the world." I have enjoyed many of the advantages of a male-dominated society without realizing the degree of subjugation and enslavement of women which exists in our present day world. I think Kate Millett is right when she says: "Groups who rule by birthright are fast disappearing, yet there remains one ancient and universal scheme for the domination of one birth group by another in our social order [and that] is the birthright priority whereby males rule females." Finally, I felt impelled to speak out on women's liberation when I discovered that many of their most articulate members are not only seeking deliverance from male tyranny, but are bent on venting their vengeance on men in general, on women happy with their lot, and on Freud and psychoanalysis. I can illustrate this last point by translating the title of my talk. According to the language of the women's liberation movement, I am a male, chauvinist, pig. Terms used so frequently by them that they only use the initials, MCP. The subtitle of this talk is: "Women's Liberation—Deliverance or Vengeance."

In this presentation I shall limit myself to only a brief description of the multiple ways women are subjugated and exploited in our society because of their sex, their being female. Then I shall turn to a brief examination of the women's lib movement and quote some of their characteristic views. My next task will be to try, from a psychoanalytic point of view, to explore such questions as: Why is there so much hostility between men and women; why do men dominate women; and why have the vast majority of women accepted this so submissively even until now? Finally, I shall also examine such issues as, why do the women libbers so vehemently reject Freud and especially such Freudian concepts as penis envy and the vaginal orgasm? Limitations of time will make my explorations brief, which I do regret. The subject deserves careful and lengthy consideration. Nevertheless, I would rather be short than silent. I would rather be attacked than ignored, because I believe that women's lib and psychoanalysis might learn from one another, to the advantage of each.

## Examples of the Subjugation and Exploitation of Women

The fundamental instrument and the foundation of male domination is the typical family and the roles it imposes. As cooperation between the family and society as a whole is essential, else both would fall apart, the fate of three patriarchal institutions are interrelated: the family, society, and the state. This concept has generally been granted religious support such as the Catholic precept that "the father is head of the family," or Judaism's delegation of quasi-priestly authority to the male parent. Secular governments also confirm this, as in census practices of designating the male as head of household. Female heads of household tend to be regarded as undesirable; it is a sign of poverty or misfortune. Women's chattel status continues, however, in their loss of name, their obligation to adopt the husband's domicile, and the general legal assumption that marriage involves an exchange of the female's domestic service and sexual services in return for financial support.

Gregory Zilboorg, the brilliant analyst and medical historian, hypothesized that when man began to use woman to satisfy more than his immediate sexual needs, she became the first piece of property in the truest sense of the word. Freud himself recognized the fact that woman was, in a sense, man's property, and in a paper on the taboo concerning virginity, said the following: "The insistence on virginity before marriage is, after all, nothing but a logical consequence of the exclusive rights of possession over a woman, which is the essence of monogamy."

The different religions which flourish in Western European civilization have not been kind to women. The Jewish tradition, for example, is heavily masculine. The Old Testament devotes inordinate space to the listing of long lines of male descent, to the point where it would seem that for centuries women "begat" nothing but male offspring. The true spirit of the tradition is unabashedly revealed in the prayer men recite every day in the synagogue: "Blessed art Thou, O Lord . . . for not making me a woman."

In the Catholic Church women have no position of power, even though Mary is the mother of God and was eventually raised to semidivine status. Yet the same religious men who sang Mary's praises continued to fulminate against women in general. St. Thomas, writing at the height of the Virgin cult, called woman "defective and accidental . . . a male gone awry."

The traditional Protestant denominations are only slightly better. For example, the United Methodist Church gave women full rights to clerical appointment in 1956 but in 1970, there were only 322 women among the 34,722 clergy. The Presbyterians have ordained only a few women, but the United States Episcopal Church does not ordain any women priests. The Jews are no different. Reform Judaism has only a handful of female *cantors* (singers) and this year they will have their first woman rabbi.

In the law, according to Blackstone, "Husband and wife are one person in the law; that is, the very being or legal existence of the woman is suspended during the marriage." Of the fifty states only eight accept the idea of community property. In no state does the law credit a wife with income for the household work she does for the family. The laws which are supposed to protect the fragile female forbid her to serve in restaurants late at night when the tips are higher and the work load is lighter. However, these fragile ladies are permitted to scrub floors in office buildings until 2 to 3 o'clock in the morning. There is not, nor has there ever been a woman nominated for Justice of the Supreme Court and only one Justice, Thurgood Marshal, has a female clerk.

In the arts, although 75 percent of art students are women, few make it big in the major galleries or museums. Among all the important art galleries across the nation, only 18 percent display works by women. Of the 1000 one-artist shows at the Museum of Modern Art, only five were by women. At the Los Angeles County Museum, of the fifty-two one-artist shows in its history, none has been by a woman. It is hard to believe that women are as untalented as these statistics imply.

In business and the professions today, 44 percent of all women over sixteen work outside the home as compared to 27 percent in 1940. There is a shocking double standard in pay scales and promotion opportunities. A federal survey shows that the average woman employed in a full-time job earns only $3 for each $5 paid to a man with a similar job. When the National Organization for Women picketed San Francisco's Crocker Bank over promotion opportunities, bank officials announced that the secretaries of its President and Chairman had been appointed "Assistant Vice Presidents." The promotions were counterfeit, both women, in fact, remained secretaries.

The work of housewives is unsalaried and thus not counted in the U.S. gross national product. Based on the usual wage rates of housekeepers, cooks, dietitians, practical nurses, and other persons who get paid for doing wifely chores, Chase Manhattan Bank estimates that the U.S. housewife holds the equivalent of a 99.6-hour-a-week job, paying $13,391.56 per year. After working full time for years raising children, women today, when they try to enter the labor market at midlife after a decade or two of absence—or after never having worked at all—find that employers consider them qualified for only the lowest jobs. The skills and knowledge that they acquired in college or in a few years of work before marriage have become obsolete.

"Medicine is a man's world, and only recently have women received any encouragement to enter it as doctors instead of nurses." All medical schools have had a quota system which limited the number of women, Jews, blacks, and other nonwhites. This has recently changed markedly for the better in regard to Jews but a "decade ago women accounted for just 6% of the nation's 260,000 doctors; today they are 7.6% of the 345,000 practitioners" (*Time*, March 20, 1972).

In education, in the past, male-dominated societies permitted only occasional and minimal literacy to women, and we often forget how recent an event higher education is for women. In the U.S. it is barely one hundred years old; in many Western countries, barely fifty. Oxford did not grant degrees to women on the same terms as to men until 1920. In Japan and a number of other countries, universities have been open to women only in the period after World War II.

In elementary education, 85 percent of the schoolteachers are women, but only 21 percent of the principals. In high schools, the percentage of female principals drops to 3 percent. And, if a woman wishes to become a college president, she is advised to become a nun; almost all of the meager 1 percent who make it are heads of Catholic institutions.

The female as a commodity in the advertising media: Germaine Greer, author of *The Female Eunuch*, said in an interview in *Playboy* (January 1972) that *Playboy* and American advertising display women's bodies as though they were things to be bought, sold, or exchanged for newer more fashionable models. "What does this do to the man who looks at them? His wife's legs have been ruined by childbearing or her bum sags. Thanks to your youthful image of female sexuality, he's not expected to have sex with his seamy old wife anymore. No one blames him for not doing it."

Greer goes on to say that any repulsive, scrawny, half-wit little man feels he can go up to every woman on the street and proposition her. You give the illusion that fifty-year-old-men are entitled to fornicate with fifteen-year-old-girls, while fifty-year-old women are too repulsive to be seen with. You display your girls as if they were a commodity. Why can't their bodies just be an extension of their personalities, the way a man supposes his body is?

A forty-three-year-old woman expresses a similar point of view most eloquently in the very title of her essay, "It Hurts To Be Alive and Obsolete: The Ageing Woman."

> The mass media tell us all day and all evening long that we are inadequate, mindless, ugly, disgusting in ourselves. . . . Don't tell me that it is human nature for women to cease to be attractive early. Black women are more oppressed on the job and in almost every other way in this society than white women, but at least in the ghetto men go on assuming a woman is sexual as long as she thinks so too. . . . Think what it is like to have most of your life ahead and be told you are obsolete! To be, in other words, still a living woman, and to be told every day that you are not a woman but a tired object that should disappear [Zoe Moss in *Sisterhood Is Powerful*, Edited by Robin Morgan].

I believe all the examples I have cited, and they are but a tiny fraction of what I had collected, convincingly demonstrate man's subjugation and oppression of women. I plead guilty to having been unaware of the enormity of this tyranny until recently and I am grateful to women's liberation for educating me.

### The Women's Liberation Movement

The New Feminism is a cultural, social, and psychological phenomenon. Women's liberation, "the movement," is composed of some twenty different organizations from moderate to extreme radical.

On the local level, the movement flourishes in eclectic profusion. Los Angeles boasts 100 women's groups working on issues as broad as hiring practices and as narrow as do-it-herself auto repair classes. For all this purposeful activity, the heart of the women's liberation movement consists of small groups of women meeting informally to discuss shared problems. Most of the groups are formed, meet for a while, and are disbanded, with no one outside the principals, not even organized feminist groups, aware of their existence. Yet, it is in the catharsis of consciousness raising that most women find their identification with women's liberation.

The goals of the movement range from the modest, sensible amelioration of the female condition to extreme and revolutionary visions. The first camp includes the likes of Betty Friedan, Midge Decter, Gloria Steinem, and Germaine Greer who emphasize an egalitarian society: equal pay for equal work; a nation in which women are not blocked from access to education, political influence, and economic power; sterner enforcement of equal employment practices under the Civil Rights Act of 1964; and federally funded child care centers.

The more radical wing of the movement would not be content, however, with such prosaic gains. They call for a drastic revision of society in general. In their view, the sexual roles must be redefined so as to free both sexes from the stereotypes and responsibilities that have existed for ages. They oppose the family, marriage, and even sexual relations with men. On its most radical level, the New Feminism at times seems to constitute an assault—sometimes thoughtful, sometimes emotional and foolish—not just on society but on the limitations of biology.

Let me give some examples of the various views from moderate to radical extreme. Gloria Steinem stresses the importance of consciousness raising in women, and its economic and political possibilities.

Germaine Greer in *The Female Eunuch* emphasizes the need for change in the institution of marriage, sex, and the family: "Speaking to quiet audiences of provincial women decently hatted and dressed, I have been surprised to find that the most radical ideas are gladly entertained, and the most telling criticisms and sharpest protests are uttered. Even the suffragettes could not claim the grass-roots support that the new feminism gains day by day."

Kate Millett viciously attacks the role of Freud and psychoanalysis. Toward the end of her diatribe she manages to make a milder statement:

> In America, the influence of Freud is almost incalculable, and America, in many ways the first center of the sexual revolution, appears to have need of him. Although generally accepted as a prototype of the liberal urge toward sexual freedom, and a signal contributor toward softening traditional puritanical inhibitions upon sexuality, the effect of Freud's work, that of his followers, and still more that of his popularizers, was to rationalize the invidious relationship between the sexes, to ratify traditional roles, and to validate temperamental differences.

Another view, this time from a female psychiatrist of women's liberation orientation:

> Freud's theories of feminine psychology have been by now well documented, and also well criticized. Yet it is necessary to call attention again, quite briefly, to Freud's basic theories about women. His major great contribution was recognition of woman's dual sexual role. In a biologic sense, it is woman's first task to attract and have a sexual relationship with a man. The second task is that of producing children and assuming the mothering role. One must agree with Freud that to some extent, anatomy is destiny. Yet this is an oversimplification. As we have become removed from simple earthy ties, and freed from haphazard and continuous reproduction, women are also freed to utilize their resources in more complicated ways [Natalie Shainess, M.D., *Sisterhood Is Powerful*].

It is startling to contrast this view with those in Susan Lydon's essay on *The Politics of Orgasm*:

> Freud's insistence on the superiority of the vaginal orgasm seems almost a demonic determination on his part to finalize the Victorians' repression of feminine eroticism, to stigmatize the remaining vestiges of pleasure felt by women, and thus make them unacceptable to the women themselves. With the clitoral orgasm, woman's sexual pleasure was independent of the male's, and she could seek her satisfaction as aggressively as the man sought his, a prospect which didn't appeal to too many men. The definition of normal feminine sexuality as vaginal, in other words, was a part of keeping women down, of making them sexually, as well as economically, socially and politically subservient.

I shall close this section with a quote from a women's liberation organization called SCUM (Society For Cutting Up Men): Excerpts from The Manifesto by Valerie Solanis: "Life in this society being, at best, an utter bore and no aspect of society being at all relevant to women, there remains to civic-minded, responsible, thrill-seeking females only to overthrow the government, eliminate the money system, institute complete automation and destroy the male sex."

And from *Sisterhood Is Powerful*:

> It is now technically possible to reproduce without the aid of males (or, for that matter, females) and to produce only females. We must begin immediately to do so. The male is a biological accident; the Y (male) gene is an incomplete X (female) gene, that is, has an incomplete set of chromosomes. In other words, the male is an incomplete female, a walking abortion, aborted at the gene state.

This brings to an end what I believe to be a fair sample of the literature put out by women's liberation.

I want to turn now to the three questions I raised in my introductory remarks: (1) Why is there so much hostility between men and women? (2) Why do men dominate and oppress women? (3) Why have the majority of women accepted this? These questions are extremely complex and interrelated. I shall have to limit myself to what I consider the essentials.

Men and women are different both biologically and psychologically. By biological differences I am referring to anatomy, physiology, and hormonal factors, those elements which determine a person's sex, male or female. These are genetically determined. The psychological differences refer to those qualities we group ordinarily under the heading of masculinity and femininity, or a sense of maleness or femaleness. Most of these differences are learned, some are biologically determined, and some differences can be seen too early to have been learned. I shall not debate here what is genetic or what is acquired by learning, there are enough "cultural universals," a phrase of Margaret Mead's, to justify the assumption that males and females differ significantly from one another no matter in what culture they are raised.

As a general rule the male is physically and muscularly stronger than the female. In terms of simple brute force he can subdue the female. Although physical violence is not a prevalent or acceptable mode of expression in many sectors of society, I believe that the male's physical superiority and his potential for using it does play a significant, if unconscious, role in man's dominance and woman's submission to it.

The male's superiority in physical strength goes along with the male's greater propensity for violence and aggression. In all cultures I have read about, the male is more prone to brutality, crime, and war than the female. The greater aggressivity can be seen in boy babies in all societies and even in the baby chimpanzee, the animal which most resembles man biologically.

If the male is physically stronger and also more aggressive, it is not surprising that he will tend to translate these primitive drives into more "civilized" forms like taking possession of the power positions in religion, politics, law, business, and even in the family and in bed. The situation is complicated and compounded, however, because men also envy and fear women.

There is a tendency in human beings to be fascinated, i.e., attracted and frightened by all beings who are different from them. This can be seen in the fear of the stranger and the ambivalence among different nationalities, races, and religions. Similarities tend to make for familiarity and security but they also lead to boredom. Differences evoke excitement and fearfulness which may eventuate in sexual activity or aggression or a combination of both.

It is fairly typical in our society for men to display contempt for women. This contempt is obviously inappropriate and irrational because it is not based on evidence or fact. The most nondescript of men will speak of outstanding women in slurring terms and even talk of their wives or lovers as "juicy morsels," mere sexual objects. All of this is a symptom of prejudice. Let us reflect upon prejudice for a moment. All prejudiced people feel contempt for those they hate and fear. If one examines the content analytically, one finds that beneath the contempt lies unconscious envy. This is true for all irrational contempt. The white man who consciously despises all black men, unconsciously envies their imagined strength and their potency. The Gentile who has contempt for the Jew envies his supposed cleverness. I believe one can find in all prejudice the surface facade of contempt and the hidden, unconscious envy, hate, and fear. On the basis of this reasoning, it would appear that men, contemptuous of women, actually envy and fear them.

I was first made aware of the possibility that man's envy of women was more widespread than I had anticipated by some clinical experiences that I had at the Gender Identity Research Clinic at the UCLA Neuropsychiatric Institute. In that Clinic we see patients who desire a surgical change of gender. People come there who believe they are "really" a man in a woman's body or a woman in a man's body, or who simply insist they cannot live in their assigned gender and want an anatomical, surgical readjustment. Incidentally, these patients are clinically not psychotic. My theoretical training had led me to expect that, on the basis of penis envy, most of the patients would be women hoping to achieve a male habitus. To my surprise, two-thirds of the patients were men desiring to be transformed into women. The wish in men to be a woman is far more widespread than the conscious attitudes of men and women indicate, and more than the psychoanalytic literature would lead one to expect. Incidentally, transvestism, masquerading in the clothes of the opposite sex, only occurs in men, not in women.

This leads to the question, what is it that men envy in women?

It is a characteristic of human behavior to envy, to want to possess for ourselves alone that which is precious and valuable which someone else possesses and we lack. This is the very essence of envy. If we now go back to the earliest relationship of infant to mother, it is not hard to imagine that the helpless infant must eventually react with envy in regard to the mother's job and security-giving capacities. Envy of the mother's various abilities, faculties, and body must exist in all infants and must undergo changes in the course of development like all other instinctual impulses and all other ego attitudes. (The penis envy of girls, which I will talk about later, is just one variety of envy, and a late one at that.) There is no doubt in my mind that men ultimately, unconsciously, envy women's capacity to bear children. Man's urge to be creative in other ways is eloquent testimony to that fact. The same is true of childless women, who are far more creative than childbearing women in their childbearing years.

Envy is a special form of hatred, and hatred, especially repressed hatred, is closely related to fear. Repressed hatred causes fear, and fear again mobilizes hatred. The male child's repressed envy of the mother combines with other repressed hostile feelings toward mother and later female figures. In societies like ours where mother tends to be idealized and desexualized, men displace their anger and contempt upon non-mother-like women. In addition, such men tend to project their hostility and consequently develop a dread of the instinctually aroused woman. The vulnerable intimacy of sexual relations tends to bring forth great anxiety in men who cannot cope with their deep-seated fear and hatred of women. As a result, men will have potency difficulties and then will doubt their maleness. No man can feel securely masculine if he doubts his ability to satisfy a woman sexually. He will tend to withdraw or to overextend himself sexually in order to protect or to assert his maleness. In either case he will resent and envy the female who is sexually eager.

There are additional factors which undermine men's sense of gender identity, men's sense of maleness. Margaret Mead has pointed out that in our modern society men constantly have to reearn, reestablish their masculinity. The success or failure of their latest venture determines the strength of their feelings of maleness. The enormous complexity of present day business and science and women's burst of psychological independence have compounded men's sense of uncertainty and anxiety. In addition, the very origin of the sense of maleness in men is far more precarious than the sense of femaleness in women. It is my contention that women are far surer of being female and feminine than men are of being masculine.

In infancy, perception and identification and imitation are inseparable. What the child sees and hears, he imitates. Since almost all children are raised by women, all children tend to take on some of the mother's characteristics. Girls, therefore, learn "femaleness" as they learn to talk and walk. The boy has to find another model in order to learn how to be male. He has to shift his identifications from mother to father, and fathers are not nearly so available. Furthermore, the mother has to encourage the boy to identify with father. This does not happen if mother loathes or despises father. As a consequence of these vicissitudes, men are more uncertain about their masculinity than women are of their femininity. This is confirmed, I believe, by the striking fact that men in our society prefer stag parties and bachelorhood. A woman tends to feel at her most feminine in the company of men. Men tend to feel most manly when they are with other men. If a woman wants a man to feel relaxed, she has to act and dress boyishly, or maybe girlishly, but certainly not womanly. I believe these are all indications of uncertainty among men about their masculinity.

What I have described, I think, explains the major reasons men are oppressive and tyrannical toward women. Physically stronger, more prone to violence and aggression, men also envy women unconsciously, and are far more uncertain of their masculinity than women are of their femininity. Patriarchy seems to work as a screen for aggression, envy, and fear.

If we now turn toward the female and ask why has she submitted to the role of the second-class sex, several answers come to mind at once. Women's compliance is partly due to fear of the physically stronger and more violent male. Another obvious factor is that most women identify with their mothers who behaved submissively, which is considered the traditional feminine role. Even in the radical leftist movements women were given the menial tasks by the men, and most of them submitted. Those who did not, left to form or enter the various women's liberation groups.

In the middle and upper economic social classes many women prefer the chivalry paid them by men to the responsibility of being an equal, and many of them live parasitically on their husband's status, prestige, or financial success. Some women are willing to be a junior partner to a big man, they enjoy vicariously their husband's accomplishments, and feel their job in life is to facilitate his success; they do not consider this demeaning. Many women give the appearance of submissiveness while they actually make all the important decisions. Their skill lies in the ability to give their husbands or lovers the impression that he is the dominant one when, in fact, it is she who covertly rules the roost.

At this point I would like to turn to the unconscious sources of women's hatred for men. Here it is pertinent to bring up penis envy which I believe exists in every woman, despite the vehement denials of women's lib. I shall try to describe how a modern psychoanalyst thinks penis envy arises and what happens to it. When a little girl gets to be two, three, or four years old and sees a little boy's penis for the first time, she has the feeling that his genital organ is superior to hers. Why? It protrudes, it is something more, something extra, and he can urinate through it and manipulate it far easier than she can her own genital and urinating apparatus. It is as elementary as that. When she becomes aware of pleasurable sexual sensations in her clitoris she imagines the boy must have even more pleasure. At any rate, once the little girl has seen it, she wants it for herself. Have you noticed how frequently little girls try to urinate standing up like boys, and how the reverse never occurs?

Freud said anatomy is destiny and I agree with him. I would modify his early concept of penis envy by emphasizing the importance of the girl's personal experiences in her family and in her social sphere. The mother's attitude toward the girl's genitals and the mother's own resolution of her penis envy will determine whether the girl will be warped by penis envy, become a penis hater, become ashamed of her sexual organs, or whether she will overcome her penis envy and be able to enjoy a man's penis and enjoy her own sexuality as well.

The earliest relationship to her mother will in part determine the intensity of the girl's penis envy. The more unresolved her envy of her mother, the greater will be her penis envy. For example, all little girls envy the mother's breasts. Some of them learn quite early that someday they too will have such beautiful and joy-giving organs. These girls will have less intense penis envy than those who believe they will never become the equal of their mother. Furthermore, girls who feel loved by their fathers in the early years, will feel their body is lovable, including their genitals. They too will have less intense penis envy in later years. In healthy women, penis envy is resolved by a satisfying sex life and a feeling of being loved and respected by the people she loves. In any event, unresolved, strong penis envy can contribute to feelings of inferiority and lack of self-esteem. This in turn makes women more dependent, timid, and submissive and hateful toward men. It also tends to turn their aggressive and sadistic impulses against the self, in the form of masochism. Many women accept male tyranny because they have learned to enjoy it masochistically.

To summarize: women have been raised in a society in which men have most of the power and influence. They learn early in childhood that males are physically stronger and are prone to violence. They are raised by mothers who for the most part act subservient toward the father and other males. Then comes the experience of penis envy, the awareness of the anatomical differences between the sexes, which they may take as another sign of female inferiority. The teachings of religion, experiences of being discriminated against in school and work, contribute to her lack of self-esteem, her frustration and her hatred of the oppressor. Add to this the barrage of the advertising media where she is made to feel she can only be lovable by use of artificial aids and only as long as she remains or gives the appearances of being youthful, beautiful, dry, and odorless. Her main hope for salvation is to marry a man whose success she can live off of and hope he will not notice that she grows older day by day. Or perhaps he may be that rare creature who will love her and enjoy sharing physical, emotional and verbal intimacies with her as they both get older. Most women feel trapped by their inadequate training for emotional, sexual, and financial independence. They submit to the male's domination because it is better than being alone. In our society a woman over thirty-five without a man is considered a failure unless she has an outstanding career, or great wealth, *plus* a cause she ardently believes in and a few people who truly care about her and need her.

### Why Does Women's Liberation Attack Freud and the Concepts of Penis Envy and the Vaginal Orgasm?

Freud was the product of a Jewish middle-class Victorian upbringing. Genius though he was, he did share the prejudices of his day, namely the belief that women were not as trustworthy as men, not as high-minded nor as creative. Nevertheless, he did recognize that women and girls were capable of sexual satisfaction, although in assigning the main cause of penis envy essentially to anatomy, he erred in not also attributing the resultant difficulties to social experience. However, it should not be forgotten that Freud and psychoanalysis accepted women into their profession when most of medicine and science was closed to them.

I feel impelled to state that Freud founded psychoanalysis, but he is not all of psychoanalysis. Why does women's lib ignore those Freudian psychoanalysts like Jones, Fenichel, Benedek, Greenacre, Jacobson, Zilboorg, Gillespie, Heiman, and a host of others who have corrected Freud on his conception of penis envy? Freud himself admitted he based his theories on only a few cases and the future would have to decide if he were right.

I have the impression that many followers of the women's liberation movement cannot bear admitting that penis envy is a normal developmental phase of girls, because women have been forced to be silent so long about so many other male advantages in our society. The issue of penis envy seems to be related to the question of clitoral or vaginal orgasm.

Let me begin by admitting that Freud was unclear and misleading in his writings on the subject. He did state in his paper "Female Sexuality" in 1931 that in order to mature, the female had to change her leading sexual zone from the clitoris to the vagina, and must renounce active sexual aims for passive ones. However, he did maintain that the clitoris retains the function of transmitting sexual excitement to the "adjacent sexual parts."

Freud never used the terms *vaginal* or *clitoral orgasm*, but it was implied, and some of his followers insisted on the vaginal orgasm being the sole criterion for sexual maturity in women. The major difficulty in Freud's formulations and those of other analysts was their failure to distinguish (1) the sexual area which is stimulated to induce the orgasm; (2) the location of the orgasmic experience; (3) the anatomical and physiological changes which occur during orgasm.

Masters and Johnson found a basic pattern of anatomical and physiological changes common to all women during orgasm and always including vaginal contractions, independent of the area of stimulation, with marked variations in intensity and duration. Their work is inconclusive about correlations between observable physiological reactions and the area stimulated. There is great variation in the location of the orgasm experienced, it need not be at the site of stimulation. It should not be forgotten that during orgasm there is a state of diminished ego perceptivity so that the subject is not fully aware or is not interested in observing her reactions. Furthermore, in the sexually highly aroused female, clitoris, vulva, and the lower third of the vagina become like a single sexual entity. Sheffry states there is absolutely no difference in the response of the pelvic viscera to effective stimulation, regardless of the source of psychic or physical stimulation. In other words, an orgasm is an orgasm, although one may differ from another in degree, completeness, or in the emotional satisfaction that accompanies it. To put it briefly, the vaginal orgasm experience is no myth. It is only difficult for many women to distinguish it from an orgasm clitorally experienced. I do believe, however, that one criterion for healthy sexuality is for a woman to be able to feel sexual sensations in the vagina exactly as I would expect a healthy male to feel sexual sensations in his penis.

I have found that women who have experienced orgasms both clitorally and vaginally find the vaginal orgasm more satisfying. I am not alone in this belief. Germaine Greer says: "It is nonsense to say a woman feels nothing when a man is moving his penis in her vagina; the orgasm is qualitatively different when the vagina can undulate around the penis instead of a vacancy. . . ." In addition, there are many experienced psychiatrists, gynecologists, psychologists, and lay people who can verify this point. The reason for Freud's insistence on the woman's ability to achieve vaginal excitability was not to make women dependent on men but was the result of finding, as many of us do today, that the inability to feel the vagina as a sexual organ indicates an inhibition of psychosexual development.

Despite the value of Masters and Johnson's research work, I believe they have come to some misleading conclusions. In their laboratory experiment women were photographed with motion picture cameras while masturbating and having intercourse, and were quoted as having had more intense orgasms from clitoral masturbation than from intercourse. Is it not likely that the presence of cameras would cast doubt on the validity of the experiment and their reactions? I have the impression that Susan Lydon reveals the real reason for denying the existence of the vaginally experienced orgasm when she states that men believe in it to keep women dependent on the male's erect penis. Here I believe she and those who go along with her thinking, are missing the point that the erect penis and the aroused vagina are admirably suited to gratify one another. They seem to have been made for each other. All other stimulants of either organ are poor substitutes, though I agree that sometimes a substitute is better than nothing.

The vaginal orgasm is no myth, but I do believe that the current multiple orgasm fad comes close to being a myth, and it has become an obsession. Masters and Johnson, using the women their research project described above, found that some of their "laboratory women" could have multiple orgasms, up to fifty or more, from clitoral stimulation alone. This has given rise to the myth of the sexually insatiable female. What kind of sexual experience is a woman having masturbation in front of a motion picture camera? How terribly impersonal, how much like a pornographic public exhibition is this kind of procedure. Simple organ pleasure is only part of the orgasm experience. I doubt that such orgasticlike responses are as satisfying as an orgasm, single or multiple, clitoral or vaginal, in private, with passion, and with someone you care about. Incidentally, in both of Masters and Johnson's books, comprising over 820 pages, the word *love* is not to be found in the index.

My own clinical experience, and this can be confirmed by others, is that many women who generally have multiple orgasms are usually unconsciously afraid of a single large orgasm. They are afraid of the loss of control a strong orgasm induces. One patient I analyzed, tried to restrain her tendency to have many small orgasms but when she approached the peak of a strong orgasm, bit her sexual partner so severely he needed medical attention. It seemed clear to us both, multiple small orgasms were a defense against the frightening single strong orgasm.

Let me now turn to other misleading information given out by women's liberation. I want to mention how Kate Millett distorts the writing of authors like Henry Miller, Norman Mailer, and D. H. Lawrence. She does so by deleting all those phrases and sentences in the passages she quotes which show the authors cared for and were concerned about their sexual partners. Mailer's book, *The Prisoner of Sex*, gives startlingly clear and abundant examples of this. It is, in my opinion, another demonstration of women's hostility and revenge, not their quest for liberation. The same is true for statements in the feminist leaflet stating that sex in marriage is legalized rape, nor can I condone this quote: "We can't destroy the inequities between men and women until we destroy marriage. We must free ourselves. And marriage is the place to begin." To me, this is an irresponsible statement. Our present system of marriage and our traditional family structure, I believe, needs modification. There are far too many unhappy marriages, people living together as fellow borders because living alone is worse, and there are far too few happy families.

Before destroying marriage and the family we ought to try, in some experimental form, to correct the two major sources of hostility: (1) Some new arrangement must be found for doing the despised household chores. Payment for the household worker or perhaps alternating the tasks between husband and wife. (2) Sexual equality for women is essential, no double standard. Perhaps open-ended marriage or marriage contracts or communal marriage will be an answer for some. I believe in experiments of this kind on a trial basis before we try to destroy the institution of marriage and traditional family life. I do make a plea, however, that such experimentation be done before there are children involved or after the children have reached the fourth year of life. Then, at least, we can hope the children will become healthy neurotics and not psychotics, borderline cases, addicts or delinquents who are almost untreatable. (3) We need men's liberation and not only women's liberation in marriage and family life.

I feel I must comment on the often heard suggestions of raising baby girls and boys as if they were identical. I believe this is artificial and unnatural. The notion of a unisex society is abhorrent, boring, and potentially pathogenic, in my opinion. Boys and girls are equal but not identical. There is a great deal of latitude as to what is masculine and what is feminine, but let us not blind ourselves to the real qualities in the individual child, genetic or acquired. For those eager to experiment, fine, but please, not with my grandchildren.

All of these deliberations lead me finally to make these closing statements. The women's liberation movement is a potentially valuable source for starting major and much needed changes in the relationship between men and women. Great gains have been made in awakening the hearts and minds of men and women to the terrible injustices perpetrated against women the world over, but women's lib has failed to reach the poor or the nonwhite minorities. Is it going to remain a middle-class white movement? And, don't men need liberation too? It is disturbing that many feminists seem to be more interested in gaining vengeance rather than deliverance. Unless the feminist woman recognizes and controls her hatred of men and of those women who are happy with the male-dominated standards of today, they will unleash a terrible backlash that will ultimately destroy all progressive women's movements. None of us has all the answers, humility and not arrogance is in order. We have much to learn from one another.

# 18 Sophie Portnoy Finally Answers Back (1972)

Portnoy's Complaint *by Philip Roth had been reviewed extensively, and the neurotic Portnoy was discussed, laughed about, and analyzed at cocktail parties. Hildi Greenson remembers how "Romi, whose mother had died the year before, felt Portnoy's mother, Sophie, deserved understanding and empathy and it was time to desist from making mothers forever culpable."*

*Greenson related to his audience his mixed feelings upon reading* Portnoy's Complaint. *He enjoyed it as a reader, but resented it as a psychoanalyst. Portnoy was at once terribly funny and at the same time unbearably narcissistic. In particular Greenson resented Roth's picture of the Jewish mother and his portrayal of his nonanalyst analyst, Dr. Spielvogel. So Dr. Greenson daydreamed about how he would have analyzed Portnoy, which led to the idea of writing a letter to Alexander Portnoy from his mother Sophie. Greenson's hilarious Sophie turns the tables on her complaint-ridden, self-absorbed son, reminding him that he too was a player in the drama and must take some responsibility for his problems. Her letter ends with a demonstration of Greenson's playful wit and sense of irony:*

> *So I will now end the letter. Yes, I helped make you a neurotic, thirty-five-year old bachelor. I admit it. But Alex Portnoy, you are not a dope addict, nor are you a homosexual, nor are you psychotic and in an insane asylum, so I really have little to complain about. I feel, sincerely, despite all my weaknesses and wrongnesses and badnesses which you so beautifully described in much detail, that I did pretty well. Please make sure you eat the proper food, and be careful with Gentile girls and I'm not going to remind you that I would like you to get married and have children so we can be grandparents. Listen, I know that's all up to you. Don't worry about your poor mother and I am sorry about the splotches on the paper, but they are only from my tears. The tears of an old Jewish mother who is crying with pleasure and pain about a book, a best-seller yet, and even a movie, that her marvelous son wrote about her. All my love and kisses to you. Take care of yourself and don't worry, no matter what happens to me.*

*It's possible that some of the popularity enjoyed by* Portnoy's Complaint *derives from the hostility and envy men feel toward women so clearly described in Greenson's lectures.*

One of the most difficult demands psychoanalytic therapy makes on the analyst is that he empathize with his patient, i.e., make partial and temporary identifications with him, crawl under his skin in order to feel how he feels. The task then is to crawl back and become the objective analyst observer, assess what is going on in the patient, and what should be pointed out, keeping in mind how much insight the patient can bear. Very frequently the analyst can only tell part of his insights at a given time, more would be too painful, traumatic. So, as a result the analyst is often left frustrated, because his impulse was to say more, not only in the service of therapy, but because the patient's behavior arouses emotional reactions in the analyst, which he must control.

When I first read *Portnoy's Complaint* I had mixed feelings. I enjoyed it as a reader but I resented it as a psychoanalyst. I found Portnoy terribly funny and pathetic but also almost unbearably

---

Presented June 17, 1972, at the Founder's Dinner, Center for Early Education, Los Angeles.

narcissistic. In particular, I resented his picture of the Jewish mother and his portrayal of his nonanalyst analyst, Dr. Spielvogel, whose only words after Portnoy's complaining for 274 pages are: "So, now vee may perhaps begin. Yes?" That was the last straw, so I began to daydream how I would have analyzed Portnoy. I even thought of writing Philip Roth a letter but realized that would be ineffectual and irrational. When I heard that the movie was going to be made, I was again stirred into action and finally came up with the idea of writing a letter, not to Philip Roth, but to Alexander Portnoy, and writing not as a psychoanalyst but as Sophie, Alex's mother, albeit with some analytic insight. So the actual title of my paper should be: "Sophie Portnoy Greenson Finally Answers Back." Herewith the letter.

May 14, 1972
Mother's Day

Dear Alex:

I have just finished reading your book and I must tell you how proud I am of you and the fact that the book is a best-seller. Everyone is talking about it and I am glad for you, no matter what it does to me. After all, what are mothers for? You yourself said so in your book. We should enjoy, particularly for our children, even if it kills us. I must say, Alex, although you called yourself in the book Portnoy, I have the impression that maybe you should have chosen another name. I know I am not a writer, but I am the mother of a writer, so let me have my little joke. Maybe you should have called the book "Alexander Oy-oy's Complaints." Your book is so full of grumblings, and reproaches, mostly about me, but also your father, and all the girls you sleep with or don't sleep with. You complain about the Jews and the Gentiles . . . in fact your whole life seems to be nothing but one gigantic accusation, a continuous "oy, oy, oy," and little else.

But I do want to have a chance to answer some of the complaints you make against me. Not just because they are against me, but they are also against Jewish mothers. I know it is very fashionable today to make fun of and to complain and to have contempt for Jewish mothers, and mothers in general, Gentile ones even. I do think sometimes a mother ought to have a chance to say something back. Even if she's not Jewish, or even if she's not a mother.

I'll start with complaint number one, which in your book is on page 15, this is what you wrote, Alex: "Then there are the nights I will not eat. My sister, who is four years my senior, assures me that what I remember is fact: I would refuse to eat, and my mother would find herself unable to submit to such willfulness—and such idiocy. And unable to for my own good. She is only asking me to do something for my own good—and still I say no? Wouldn't she give me the food out of her own mouth, don't I know that by now?

"But I don't want the food from her mouth. I don't even want the food from my plate—that's the point.

"I just don't want to eat, I answer.

"So my mother sits down in a chair beside me with a long bread knife in her hand. It is made of stainless steel, and has little sawlike teeth. Which do I want to be, weak or strong, a man or a mouse?

"Doctor, why, why oh why oh why oh why does a mother pull a knife on her own son?"

OK, Alex, I plead guilty to what you have just described in your book, I plead guilty by reason of my own neurosis, my personal "mishegass." However, I do think there are some extenuating circumstances, certain things you ought to know about eating and food, which you don't seem to have mentioned in your book. You were born, it was 1932, and this was at the height of the depression and the depression continued for the first ten years of your life. I think you ought to have mentioned in your book that there were many hungry people in those times. There were lines of people waiting to get some hot soup or a piece of bread or a free meal. Food was terribly important because we had very, very little money and your father worked very hard, no matter what you think of his job, he did work hard.

I think you also ought to have mentioned that both of us came from very poor people in Poland and I don't think you know how much poorer a poor Jewish person is in Poland than whatever you can imagine about the poor Jews in America. There's even more to the story, yes I did say to you, "eat, eat for me, eat from me," but I think you ought to know, after all you're a very intelligent boy, a man by now, that it is quite typical for mothers, and it is very motherly, to feel that if a child does not eat, will not eat, the child is really rejecting the mother. Yes, the child is really rejecting the mother's body. After all, where does the first food come from anyway? It doesn't come from the store, it comes from the breast, from the mother's body, the same place a baby is born and first grows up in. So, I begged, I pleaded, I screamed and I even threatened, because I somewhere knew your not eating was basically and essentially a rejection of me. What was wrong, was the way I tried to get you to eat.

The knife part was crazy, silly, hysterical. I admit that. But, you know, Alex, you were six or seven years old, by that time you should have understood the difference between a real threat and a pretended threat or a hysterical threat. I'm only a Jewish mother, but I've got common sense. And sometimes I know when a knife is a knife and when a knife is not a knife, and I also know that when you are afraid of your *mother's* knife it is not because *she* has a knife, but perhaps maybe you ought to ask Dr. Spielvogel more about that.

Complaint number two begins on page 44 and goes on. This is when you complain about my getting dressed or undressed in front of you:

"While I crayon a picture for her, she showers—and now in the sunshine of her bedroom, she is dressing to take me downtown. She sits on the edge of the bed in her padded bra and her girdle, rolling on her stockings and chattering away. Who is Mommy's good little boy? Who is the best boy a mommy ever had? Who does Mommy love more than anything in the whole wide world? I am absolutely punchy with delight, and meanwhile follow in their tight, slow, agonizingly delicious journey up her legs the transparent stockings that give her flesh a hue of stirring dimensions. I sidle close enough to smell the bath powder on her throat—also to appreciate better the elastic intricacies of the dangling straps to which the stockings will presently be hooked (undoubtedly with a flourish of trumpets). I smell the oil with which she has polished the four gleaming posts of the mahogany bedstead, where she sleeps with a man who lives with us at night and on Sunday afternoons. My father they say he is. On my fingertips, even though she has washed each one of those little piggies with a warm wet cloth, I smell my lunch, my tuna fish salad. Ah, it might be cunt I'm sniffing. Maybe it is! Oh, I want to growl with pleasure. Four years old, and yet I sense in my blood"—uh-huh, again with the blood—"how rich with passion is the moment, how dense with possibility."

Yes, Alex, your description of what I did was accurate. I did get dressed and undressed in front of you, but I would like to ask you a few questions. Alex, would it have been better to hide from you? Would it have been better for you if I had acted as though my body was bad or ugly or mysterious or dangerous or terrifying or forbidden, so forbidden that I have to hide it from you? Alex, you make it very plain that you have a lot of trouble with women, you not only love so many women, but you also have sex with many women, would it have been better for you to be disgusted or frightened by women, to find them frightening or awesome or repulsive? Would it have been better if you found men attractive? Okay, I was guilty. I stirred up your feelings of attraction for a woman's body, but I don't think that was the worst thing that could have happened to you.

On page 50, you describe another incident in which you felt terribly humiliated by me. Let me remind you what you wrote:

"We are in my Uncle Nate's clothing store on Springfield Avenue in Newark. I want a bathing suit with a built-in athletic support. I am eleven years old and that is my secret: I want a jock. I know not to say anything, I just know to keep my mouth shut, but then how do you get it if you don't ask for it? . . . 'What's your favorite color?' Uncle Nate asks—'maybe you want it in your school color, huh?' I turn scarlet, though that is not my answer. 'I don't want that kind of suit any more,' and oh, I can smell humiliation in the wind, hear it rumbling in the distance—any minute now it is going to crash upon my pre-pubescent head. 'Why not?' my father asks. 'Didn't you hear your uncle, this is the best.' 'I want one with a jockstrap in it!' Yes, sir, this just breaks my mother up. 'For your little thing?' she asks, with an amused smile.

" 'Yes, Mother, imagine: for my little thing.' "

Yes, Alex, I did say it was little—it was—that was real—a

fact of life. I did not say it with contempt, I did not say it with disgust, you yourself admit I said it just with amusement. Alex, part of growing up is learning the painful facts of life. You were, at that time, a boy with a boy's penis. Your father was the man in the house and he had the big penis. Is that wrong? I know it hurts your feelings to face that but realizing where you belong in life, what your place is in life, hurts sometimes, but it is real. Little boys are little and big men are big. Or at least they ought to be. When you were being so upset about your little thing, as you call it, or as I called it, do you realize a war was going on? A huge, terrible, world war—men with their big penises were being killed by the thousands. Little boys with their little things were home safe with their mothers. At least in this country. How come, Alex, you never mention any of this in your book?

You also describe somewhere in the book, my terrible fear of Gentiles, which is also true. I was afraid of Gentiles. In fact, I have to admit, I still am somewhat afraid of them. But do you know in my youth there was a Hitler, and that he and his friends murdered six million Jews? Destroyed them, burned them, incinerated them. Maybe there are still reasons to be afraid of Gentiles. Do you think Israel is so beloved in the non-Jewish world, let's not just talk of Arabs, let's talk about Gentiles. Do you think anti-Semitism is really dead? And I'm not speaking only about Egypt, or Germany, or Russia. I'm speaking about America. Are you so sure there is no reason to be afraid today? Are you comfortable with blacks or they with you? And with Mexicans. I won't go on. Yes, Alex, I did many things wrong, but, with good heart, with good intentions. Or shall I say it in your language, with good motivation.

Another point: you seem to forget all the joys. Only rarely, rarely do you ever mention any of my good points, and when you do it turns out that my virtues are something to complain about. So, let's turn now to complaint number four. On page 11, you describe a failing of mine which you describe as, I was "too good."

"She could make jello, for instance, with sliced peaches hanging in it, peaches just suspended there, in defiance of the law of gravity. She could bake a cake that tasted like a banana. Weeping, suffering, she grated her own horseradish rather than buy the pishachs they sold in a bottle at the delicatessen. She watched the butcher, as she put it, 'like a hawk,' to be certain that he did not forget to put her chopped meat through the kosher grinder. She would telephone all the other women in the building drying clothes on the back lines—called even the divorced goy on the top floor one magnanimous day—to tell them rush, take in the laundry, a drop of rain had fallen on our windowpane. What radar on that woman! And this is before radar! The energy of her! The thoroughness! For mistakes she checked my sums; for holes, my socks; for dirt, my nails, my neck, every seam and crease of my body. She even dredges the furthest recesses of my ears by pouring cold peroxide into my head. . . . She lights candles for the dead—others invariably forget, she religiously remembers, and without even the aid of a notation on the calendar. Devotion is just in her blood. She seems to be the only one, she says, who when she goes to the cemetery has 'the common sense,' 'the ordinary common decency,' to clear the weeds from the graves of our relatives."

I was not only devoted, but you also insist that I was moral, I had a sense of right and wrong and then you turn this also into a complaint, into a badness, not a virtue, not a goodness. Just take a look at your fifth complaint on page 124 of your wonderful book:

"Because to be bad, Mother, that is the real struggle: to be bad—and to enjoy it! That is what makes men of us boys, Mother. But what my conscience, so-called, has done to my sexuality, my spontaneity, my courage! Never mind some of the things I try so hard to get away with—because the fact remains, I don't. I am marked like a road map from head to toe with my repressions. You can travel the length and breadth of my body over superhighways of shame and inhibition and fear. See, I am too good too, Mother, I too am moral to the bursting point—just like you! Did you ever see me try to smoke a cigarette? I look like Bette Davis. Today boys and girls not even old enough to be bar-mitzvahed are sucking on marijuana like it's peppermint candy, and I'm still all thumbs with a Lucky Strike. Yes, that's how good I am, Momma. Can't smoke, hardly drink, no drugs, don't borrow money or play cards, can't tell a lie without beginning to sweat as though I'm passing over the equator. Sure, I say fuck a lot, but I assure you, that's about the sum of my success with transgressing. . . ."

Yes, I was devoted and moral and you have managed to make this into a complaint, a badness, a weakness, a deficiency, a wrongness in me. I admit, Alex, I did it. I gave you a conscience and as a result you now tell me you are a sick man, you are a neurotic. But you know something Alex? It wasn't all me, nor your father, or your sister, or just we Jews, or Jewishness. There's a whole world of people who believe there is such a thing as right and wrong, and who try to live by it, as strange and as warped as it may seem to you. There are workers, teachers, housewives, doctors, professors, even businessmen and sometimes politicians who believe in this. But, I must also tell you something as you yourself must know by now, that there are some people who don't truly believe in what they say, don't live by it, but just talk it, and lie and cheat and are hypocrites. You know something, their children don't even get to be neurotics. They become something worse, delinquents or drop-outs, or addicts or alienated, I think you call them.

You know something else, Alex, there is also you. Alex, so-called, Portnoy, you too. You were not just a passive recipient of what happened in your life and to you. Certainly by the time you were seven or eight or nine, you were not just an innocent victim who had no resources, no brains, no muscles, no strength, no will, nothing. You went along with everything that was happening because you must have gotten some pleasure, some satisfaction, some gain from all of it. You know, Alex, you can't blame television, the radio, or the comic book, because there comes a time when one is able to shut off the television, and the radio, and close the comic book. There are some kids who do and there's some kids who don't. You are not just a helpless martyr in the world, you who was picked to play a part in all of it. You, Alex Portnoy, were a person, a human being, already when you were three and four years old. Even then you began to have a certain individuality of your own, and you have to take over some of the responsibility, some of it anyway, for what happened to you, certainly by the time you were ten, eleven, or twelve, and absolutely by the time you were twenty-five, twenty-six, or thirty-five.

I am tired of blaming you, just as much as I'm tired of everybody blaming all the failures on the mothers of the world, especially the Jewish mothers. I'm just as tired of giving mothers the credit for all the goodness, the virtues, and all the accomplishments and successes. You know something, Alex, we mothers are neither angels, nor saints, nor are we devils. I don't want all the credit, nor do I want all the blame. I only want to be remembered for what I really was and am, a mother with good and bad qualities, who tried, sometimes successfully and sometimes unsuccessfully, to do her best for her family and for herself.

So I will now end this letter. Yes, I helped make you a neurotic, thirty-five-year-old bachelor. I admit it. But, Alex Portnoy, you are not a dope addict, nor are you a homosexual, nor are you psychotic and in an insane asylum, so *I* really have little to complain about. I feel, sincerely, despite all my weaknesses and wrongnesses and badnesses which you so beautifully described in such detail, that I did pretty well. I only want you now to take care of yourself. Please make sure you eat the proper food, and be careful with Gentile girls and I'm not going to remind you that I would like you to get married and have children so we can be grandparents. Listen, I know that's all up to you. Don't worry about your poor mother and I am sorry about the splotches on the paper, but they are only from my tears. The tears of an old Jewish mother who is crying with pleasure and pain about a book, a best-seller yet, and even a movie, that her marvelous son wrote about her. All my love and kisses to you. Take care of yourself and don't worry, no matter what happens to me.

Your Jewish mother,
Sophie Portnoy

# 19 Jealousy, Envy, and Possessiveness (1973)

*This lecture evolved out of an article on jealousy that Greenson had written some years earlier for* Look *magazine. He described for his audience how jealousy and envy are two of the most painful and destructive emotional states experienced by human beings. However, he pointed out, they are present to some degree in all normal people, in fact, their total absence indicates something pathological. Furthermore, there is no love without jealousy, and there is no ambition without envy. He chose to discuss these emotions because of his feeling that, especially in our country, jealousy, envy, and possessiveness tend to be either dangerously high or damagingly absent, and, above all, unrecognized for what they are by the vast majority of the people who suffer from them. Greenson clarified how the common ancestor of envy and jealousy is possessiveness. He usefully differentiated between envy and jealousy, both normal and pathological, and suggested some measures that may prevent or at least curb the most hurtful forms of these states of mind.*

## Introduction

Jealousy and envy are two of the most painful and destructive emotional states experienced by human beings. They are present to some degree in all normal people, their total absence indicates something pathological. There is no love without jealousy and there is no ambition without envy. Yet pathological jealousy has ruined what might have otherwise been good marriages, and irrational envy has been the downfall of many a promising career. I have chosen this subject matter for discussion because especially in our society, jealousy, envy, and possessiveness tend to be either dangerously high or damagingly absent, and above all, unrecognized for what they are by the vast majority of people who suffer from either of these conditions. Destructive jealousy, envy, and possessiveness are essentially unconscious in such people. The matter is further complicated by the finding that these three emotional states also have an important positive value in forming highly desirable traits.

In this presentation I shall try to explain the complex and contradictory ingredients which go into the make-up of envy and jealousy by first briefly exploring their common ancestor: possessiveness. Then I shall go on to describe and then differentiate between envy and jealousy, normal and pathological, and finally, I shall suggest some measures which may prevent or at least curb the most hurtful forms of these three states of mind. Restrictions of time will make my presentation little more than an outline.

## Possessiveness

To possess means to own, to have as a property. Possessiveness is the excessive concern or desire to own things as property, as one's own, as possessions. Greed is nothing more than generalized possessiveness. It means to be acquisitive beyond reason, insatiable, gluttonous. Of all character traits, people seem more ashamed of greediness than any other, therefore, awareness of its existence is usually repressed.

---

Presented at the Reiss-Davis Child Study Center, Women's Division, Los Angeles, February 7, 1973.

If we probe a bit deeper into the psychology of possessiveness we come upon the fact that the earliest method of possessing anything was to take it into one's body, things were taken into the mouth and swallowed. In the child, the first concept of self is the body. The child learns eventually that there are desirable things which cannot be swallowed and taken inside the self. They are called "mine." Mine means basically, symbolically, I'd like to take it inside of me and swallow it but I know I cannot, it is outside of my body. "Mine" refers to things outside the body which one would like to put inside one's body or are felt to be *symbolically* inside.

All treasured possessions are personalized and individualized by the child, they are charged with "ego quality." I have even heard adults do the same thing. A woman I knew was once house hunting. She arrived breathlessly one day, enthused and ecstatic saying, "I have found it, it's *the* house, it's not just beautiful, it is mine, it is *me*!"

The first possession a child gets is the breast or bottle. It must be remembered, however, that in the early months of life, the child cannot clearly differentiate between self and nonself. This develops gradually and only starts to become clear between six months and one year. In other words, in the first months of life the infant cannot differentiate whether the breast is "mine" or "me." For the infant the breast is his exclusively and forever, while he is sucking it. The possession of the breast is not only joyous to the infant, it makes him feel loved and powerful and full of goodness inside.

Children who are not given enough milk and sucking pleasure and the loving emotional warmth and skin contact that should accompany feeding, feel unloved, frustrated, and enraged at the mothering person. Such children tend to become depressed, pessimistic, insatiable, and greedy. They later try to overcome such feelings by becoming acquisitive, possessive. They become takers and not givers because they feel an inner emptiness, and an inner badness which comes from the absence of a giving mother and their rage at the depriving mother. Orally gratified babies, if life is reasonably kind to them later on, tend to become optimistic, cheerful, and generous, they get genuine pleasure in giving.

Right after World War II, Anna Freud and her staff worked

with six children from ages two-and-a-half to three-and-a-half who were taken from their parents at birth and were raised in a variety of concentration camps. They came to England speaking only German. Within seven weeks they understood English and spoke enough to make themselves understood. By the end of the year they could no longer understand German and would laugh at that strange language. The only German word they retained was the word *meine*, the German word for "mine," which they used with affection, like "meine" dolly, or "meine" Anna.

The first possession the child *knows* is his, loves dearly, and which is regularly taken away from him, without his consent, is his bowel movement. For the baby, feces is a valuable possession but it is losable. More than that, the environment often reacts to it as if it were dirty and disgusting. If children are toilet trained too early, which means, deprived of their anal pleasures too soon, before they are ready to go on to other pleasures, they tend to become retentive, constipated, sadistic, and spiteful. There is also an accompanying sense of worthlessness and dirtiness. In later life they often become stingy, sometimes to the point of miserliness which is often hidden by pseudogenerosity, big public donations, and chintzy tips to waiters. They also become conspicuously neat and orderly, on the surface. Such people adore money, have a pathological desire to amass wealth, become compulsive collectors of things, or acquaintances, and are never satisfied because of their basic lack of genuine self-esteem.

I ran across this item concerning the life of a prisoner of war in Vietnam a few days ago in the *Los Angeles Times* of February 3, 1973, which confirms the relationship of possessions to the sense of being a person, an individual, in some severely regressed, deprived adults or children. Here are the words of a returned POW:

> I save things, too. I hate waste. In prison, we saved everything—rocks, nails, pieces of wood. You'd never use them, but it gave you a feeling of ownership, of having something.
>
> Now I hate to use paper towels or tissues for anything. When you're through, you have to throw them away.I'd rather use a rag. You can wash that and use it again.

It seems to me that as a POW he felt in danger of being considered disposable and would rather be a rag than disappear totally. To possess something served a vital purpose for the POWs.

People who have been either orally deprived or anally frustrated in childhood, or who have later life experiences which recreate this situation, tend to feel internally empty, bad, worthless, dirty, and unlovable. Later in life such people in an attempt to compensate, tend to measure what they have and another has, and if the other has more, or something better, they are plagued by a terribly painful urge to get it for themselves—a state we call envy.

All of us went through a period of life, no matter how short, when we felt the breast was ours exclusively and our bowel movements belonged to us and were controlled by us. All of us experienced to some extent the disappointment that "real life ain't so," and all of us have some degree of possessiveness and envy, both of which have the ultimate aim of recapturing those delightful old times of having exclusive possession and power to decide what I can keep for myself and for how long. People who have never experienced these delights of childhood are not possessive, envious, or jealous. They are apathetic or in deep despair; many of them die in early childhood. Possessiveness, if controllable in intensity, and also tamed and sublimated, can lead to desirable traits like the wish to possess knowledge, the wish to possess so that one can care for somebody or something, and even the wish to share and to be generous.

## Envy

Envy is an angry, hateful emotional reaction toward another person based on the feeling that the other person possesses something desirable which one would like to possess for oneself. In envy there is the urge to take that thing away from the other, or at least to spoil it or damage it. Envy exists between two people. This is one of the major differences between envy and jealousy. Jealousy always involves at least three people, it is essentially a triangular situation. There are other differences which I shall take up later.

Envy may be conscious, unconscious, or both. It begins early in life, once the child can comprehend the concept of "mine." From then on the child will react with envy if someone else seems to have something more desirable than what he or she has. I believe it is clearly visible from age one to one-and-a-half onwards. It becomes accentuated or diminished in different phases of early development and by certain life experiences. But first let me describe the many components which go to make up envy.

In addition to angry feelings, an envious person hates the one he envies. Hate is a durable and personal reaction and not as transient as anger or rage. It develops later in life. We usually hate people who are meaningful to us or who we consider superior in some way, whereas we can become enraged with unknown inferiors. The hatred and rage in envy can reach violent, even murderous, proportions as exemplified by the bloody riots in our large cities in the sixties. The have-nots, in those recent instances, the blacks, expressed their envy of white affluence by looting, robbing, and even killing. It still goes on in the sporadic killing of the police, who are envied and loathed for many reasons, but above all, because they are the supreme symbol of the white man's misuse of power.

Envy also indicates a discontent with oneself, one's self-esteem is low, there is a lack of healthy narcissism. When the low self-esteem is irrational it can lead to unrealistic and usually intense envy, often unconscious and disguised. One of the most deceptive masks of unconscious envy is contempt.

I believe the most widespread example of this is the male's contempt for the female. Despite all of the male's advantages in our society, men envy women's certainty about being feminine. Girls just have to get older to become feminine, while men have to continue to prove their masculinity. Every failure is felt as emasculation. I also believe men envy women's capacity to bear children. All of the male's creativity pales when it is compared to carrying and giving birth to a healthy baby. The story of God creating Eve from Adam's rib was obviously written and approved of by a group of envious males. The little girl's envy of the boy's penis is well known, especially since it has been so severely and publicly attacked by women's lib. However, one only has to observe the behavior of little boys and girls, between the ages of two to five, to see that it really does exist. In part it is based on the fact that the penis is a conspicuous organ, it looks like it is something more than what the girl has, and it is far more accessible and manageable for urinary purposes and for pleasure. Penis envy never would reach such intense proportions in many girls and women if our society did not give boys and men far more rewards and prestige in a variety of other ways. I should like to add a small consolation for women; there is also penis envy in men. I refer to men who feel they have a little penis and envy those with a large one.

Men and women envy others if they feel the other is superior in strength, beauty, intelligence, potency, power, prestige, and, above all, in our society, in wealth. We live in a world which prizes a person's possessions above all else. It is a sad commentary to note that the average man is more upset by the relatively few wealthy persons in our society than by the hundreds of thousands of poor people around us. Our society is characterized by the prestige it accords acquisitiveness.

I shall turn now to an important agency in our society whose aims are to make us acquisitive and envious. Most, if not all, advertising has the aim of making people discontent so that they will feel envious and will go out and try to possess and thus to equal or excel the person in the ad. For example, this girl can't get a date, and this means you, the TV watcher, and do you know why? It is because your teeth are not pearly white. Now, this other girl, the "nonyou" in the commercial, she is surrounded by boys. Why? She uses "Extra White" toothpaste. You are not going to let her get more dates than you, so go out and buy "Extra White." Another example: do you know why you are not married? It is because you have dandruff. Get this shampoo and in a matter of days or weeks you will be tripping down the matrimonial aisle. You are embarrassed in front of your date when your car stalls. Get this special gas and you will no longer be embarrassed. You are humiliated before your guests when your dishes have spots on them, you could die! Now, get our spot remover and become a social success. Do you feel insecure in public? Buy this deodorant and you will be full of self-confidence and will become the life of the party. You must not have any individual odor if you want to be popular, but you must smell as Mr. Gillette, Madame Chanel, or

Mr. Brut commands you to smell. And you may not sweat. In fact, you may not even perspire; that is vulgar, only for peasants or foreigners. So, dry up those armpits and other more unmentionable places, even if it is physiologically wrong. Do you want your children to love you? Then buy this special brand of peanut butter. I could go on and on.

Implied in all of this is that other people know these secrets and have achieved these successes. They are far ahead of you. Such advertising is nothing more than envy evoking. You are persuaded to feel that you are lacking or missing something valuable which you might and should possess. The response they want from you is to go out and buy it. Attractiveness, popularity, self-assurance, social grace, love, and even marriage are obtainable if you just buy, buy, and buy. Intelligence, sensitivity, warmth, honesty, humor, and decency are trivial. The keys to success are to look sparkling clean, odorless, and dry and use the right brand of detergent or peanut butter, and you will live happily ever after—until the next commercial, anyway. The worst offender in this group is TV advertising. It makes it all so vivid and concrete and it is so repetitious that it works almost like hypnosis.

This touches on another quality inherent in envy. There is also admiration for whomever one envies. Unfortunately, the admiration is usually clouded by the hateful components. Happy and contented people, especially a happy couple, are among the most envied and unconsciously hated people in our society, especially by the unhappy and discontented majority. It even happens that very wealthy people will, on occasion, envy the less affluent because their wealth has not brought them happiness or peace of mind. The middle class is just as unhappy with their lot as the wealthy, only more uncomfortable. The supposed simplicity of the life of the poor is true because most of their waking life is devoted to fighting off starvation and eviction. Many of the wealthy and the middle class have free time which they fill with trivial distractions in order to hide their internal emptiness. The poor are full of the misery of chronic hunger, frustration, and fatigue. There is no energy or time for boredom. Combatting poverty is a full-time job.

Envy is a miserable state of mind—especially when it is irrational and intense. It can lead, when it is camouflaged, to violence, self-hatred, and depression, which often manifests itself in intense and persistent rivalries, compulsive acquisitiveness, and, above all, in the pathological, compulsive or addictive urge to amass wealth.

Envious people have to possess the best or be first in their group in everything they want that is meaningful to them. For example, it is not sufficient to be successful. In men, their wives must be the most beautiful and conspicuously so, and if and when her beauty begins to fade, the man, driven by envy, has to dispose of her for a newer, more flashy model, in order to be envied by all his friends. In business, depending on his circle, he must get the highest salary or become the owner or president of his company or of other companies or conglomerates and so on. He is never contented if he is not on top. Envy of his rivals gnaws at his insides and literally consumes him, eats him up, often leading to psychosomatic disorders like ulcers of all kinds, chronic restlessness, hypertension, and insomnia. After all, to such a man, sleep is just a waste of time.

In women, irrational envy shows itself in her competitiveness with other women in her group. She has to be the most attractive, the best dressed, have the best and latest plastic surgery, in order to make the best conquest, and keep him.

Should the man fail, or not continue to be the *top* dog, she will lose interest in him, feel contempt, dispose of him and go on the prowl for a better trophy to show off to her little world.

Another possibility, and a more morbid one, is that she, and her husband too, will deflect their envious impulses onto their children and demand of them to be the best, the smartest, the most attractive, the most popular, etc. Such children have to make up for their parents' deficiences. Other sad examples are mothers and fathers in middle age who become envious when they are excelled by their children's greater beauty or intelligence or success. Instead of enjoying their children's achievements, they begrudge them their success and become belittling, cold, feel mistreated, unappreciated, and depressed.

In recent times, children of successful, acquisitive, envious and competitive parents have rebelled against these qualities in their parents and have become hippies, freaks, or drop-outs; renouncing all material possessions, turning to a life of asceticism, fanatical religiosity, communal nonpossessive sexual relations, and extreme antiviolence and antimaterialistic attitudes toward the establishment, be it the government, the family, or the so-called norms of society. Basically that is their revenge against their parents and a society who treated them, behind all their moralistic rhetoric and verbal hypocrisy, as possessions, things, or commodities. Their lives were expendable in Vietnam, for example, for what was called "Peace with Honor." Yet envy, like possessiveness, if it is limited in degree and aimed at worthy goals can lead to laudable ambition, industry, and achievement.

## Jealousy

Jealousy is another torturous state of mind which is compounded of love, hate, depression, envy, grief, and rivalry. Jealousy is always triangular: it contains the jealous person, a desired person or personalized thing, *and* a rival. For example, a man may be jealous of another man or his wife's love of painting or golf. The crucial elements which differentiate jealousy from envy are the following: in jealousy one wants to be loved and one fears his rival is loved more. There is a fear of losing the loved one and there is also envy toward the more successful rival. This fear of loss may be real or fantastic.

Jealousy begins in childhood, later than possessiveness and envy. I would say usually around two, three years of age. It is often hard to distinguish envy from jealousy because jealousy contains envy—the jealous person envies his more successful rival. It is a normal reaction if it is proportionate and realistic to the situation which evokes it, and if it can be overcome in a reasonable period of time.

There is no love without some jealousy, because all love, especially romantic love, contains a degree of possessiveness. There is sadness and grief in jealousy, particularly in childhood. The boy who loves his mother and wishes to possess her for himself wants to get rid of his major rival, usually his father. This hated rival, the father, however, is also beloved and so the boy is sad and guilty at losing his loving feelings for his father and finding himself full of death wishes, etc. This triangular situation is an inevitable development in children raised in our society with one father and one mother at a time. I am sure most of you know Freud called this the Oedipus complex. It is far less intense in societies where children are raised with multiple mother and father figures all living in the same house, or within walking distance. Margaret Mead described this in Samoa some forty years ago. If a child was unhappy with his parents, he just moved his belongings across the hall or road to some other family he knew and who accepted him. Interestingly enough, such children never developed the capacity for strong romantic love in later life, had practically no neuroses or psychoses, and were also very uncreative. We pay a high psychological price for romantic love and creativity.

Jealousy is a natural outgrowth of the experience of having once been loved exclusively, no matter how briefly and inconsistently. There is an urge to reexperience it that remains throughout life—although it diminishes with emotional maturation. A fully adult person is quite satisfied to have the feeling of exclusively possessing and loving a person on occasions, providing it is reciprocated, and providing he has and receives other loving feelings from the loved person, like emotional warmth, compassion, friendship, respect, affection, and fun, in the intervals between passionate sexual possession or other emotional fusings with one another.

Jealousy exists among siblings in the family and peers in later life. There is the wish to be the favorite and one's rivals are jealously hated. You can see this in a temporary form when a celebrity enters a home where a group of ostensibly good friends are gathered. While the celebrity is there, you may well see a flare-up of the old urge to be the favorite, the special one, and good friends become cunning and hateful competitors, and are devastated if they fail. Black-tie charity dinner dances are excellent opportunities to collect data on the different techniques for capturing the interest of the best, the richest, or the most beautiful someone or other.

Parents sometimes become jealous of their children, not just envious. In other words, a parent can unconsciously fall in love with a child and, for example, a father will become jealous of a daughter's boyfriends and later her sweethearts and lovers. This usually becomes pronounced when a man and woman are middle aged and begin to doubt their own competence and sexual attractiveness. They then find fault with most of their child's suitors, especially the most attractive and successful ones. The parents are not conscious of their jealousy and find a variety of reasons they prefer their child to marry someone "safe," rather than someone the son or daughter loves. This is a rationalization, a desire of the parent to remain *the* only beloved of his child.

Even in good marriages, jealousy will arise on occasions. No man or woman is immune from polygamous impulses which often break through at social events, especially when under the influence of alcohol or other intoxicants. These flirtations may remain superficial and temporary, but they can evoke intense jealousy in the mate. In good marriages this will be talked out and worked through and resolved. In marriages which look good, but are actually chronic housekeeping arrangements between two people who are afraid of change or loneliness, such trivial flirtatiousness can give rise to intense and prolonged jealousy leading to violence, divorce, murder or suicide. The pathology of such reactions can be best demonstrated when the occasion is trivial or even nonexistent. A husband will be furiously jealous because he believes he saw a look, a glance, his wife gave a certain man, or vice versa. This kind of reaction is most likely to occur when the other party involved is a good friend and/or an attractive one, like one imagined oneself to be in the past.

This points to the *unconscious* love a man or woman has for the friend of the same sex, an unconscious homosexual love. Often pathological jealousy is an indication of paranoid suspiciousness, which we know is based, to a great extent, on repressed homosexuality.

There is an interesting point about jealousy which fits in here. There is a linguistic obscurity in the use of the phrase, "I am jealous of." You can say with equal correctness, "I am jealous of my wife who is flirtatious," or, you can also say, "I am jealous of my rival." This ambiguity confirms the dual love objects which is especially pronounced in pathological jealousy. It is quite clear this is a carry over from the oedipal triangle of childhood. Example: Who do you kill if you find your wife in bed with another person? Your wife? Your rival? Yourself? Or all three? Read the daily papers for the possible answers.

Jealousy seems to be far less prevalent in today's "modern" society. The easygoing "instant sex" without passion in the young indicates there is not much love, passion, or possessiveness present. The wife switching and swapping of older people, which is fashionable in some circles, also proves that the capacity to love sensually is becoming extinct or is warped in a perverse direction.

The differentiation between normalcy and pathology in jealousy can be determined by the following factors: (1) Is there a realistic basis for believing the person you love, prefers another? If so, intense jealousy would be expected; absence of jealousy would be a sign of abnormal love or no love. I have seen husbands who supposedly loved their wives, and practically push their wives into the arms of other men. I have known of men who enjoy watching their wives having sex with other men or women and are not jealous but get sexually excited from it. These men are voyeurs, peeping Toms, at least unconsciously, and/or are repeating scenes from childhood when they wanted to, but were forbidden to, enter the parental bedroom. It is a form of belated revenge because it degrades the woman.

2. When jealousy is intense and leads to rage and violence, and the event provoking it was slight, then we are dealing with pathological jealousy. Very often a man will be "insanely" jealous of his wife because he is projecting his own repressed wishes to be unfaithful, either heterosexually or homosexually. *He* wants the infidelity—*unconsciously*, for himself.

3. If a past experience of jealousy is remembered for years and years, far in excess of what one would expect, you can be sure that event has become unconsciously connected to an event from childhood. A man married more than twenty years, from time to time would upset his wife and himself by reminding her of an experience when he found his wife, then seventeen and not his wife, hugging and kissing his dearest friend. You would imagine after twenty years of a predominantly happy marriage, a good sex life, three children and fidelity on both sides, this twenty-three-year-old experience would be a dead issue. It was not for him because, as analysis revealed, it was a screen memory for an experience that was much more painful. It covered a repressed memory, uncovered in his therapy, of unexpectedly finding his

mother hugging and kissing his father's closest friend. After this insight, the twenty-three-year-old flirtation of his wife became a joke.

Jealousy within limits makes you treasure a loved person and exerts a force and zest to love and sex. Passionate and romantic love always has a potential for jealousy. Sex without passion, communal love, and sexual promiscuity only occur when there is an absence of jealousy.

## How Does One Prevent or Cure Pathological Possessiveness, Envy, or Jealousy?

As I have stressed, all healthy people are born with a tendency to possessiveness which leads to the development of envy and jealousy. The absence of possessiveness or envy indicates apathy, despair, boredom, or autism. The absence of jealousy indicates the absence of a meaningful love.

To keep possessiveness within normal limits, the parent has to develop the feeling that the child is not merely his possession, but has a right and a need for his own separate feelings, values, temperament, and, above all, independence. The child should be loved and admired even if he does not resemble you or your family. If you treat him as a person, if you treasure people above things, value warmth, intelligence, sensitivity, imagination, and joy above money; if you have as friends poor people as well as rich, if you show concern and care about humanity in deeds and not just in speeches or conspicuous donations; your child will learn that material possessions are not the greatest joy producers in life. To the contrary, he will learn that possessions make a slave of the possessor.

To prevent pathological envy and jealousy, one has to begin with one's children. When your child evidences these emotional states, do not squelch him as though he were doing something horrible or morbid. He has to be shown that such emotional reactions are understandable and human and painful, but one has to learn to control and direct them. Children have to be allowed to struggle for control over the intensity and aims coming from their envy and jealousy without crushing it in them. You can help by acknowledging that there are occasions when you, too, feel envious and jealous, and you will be all the more effective, the more honest and perceptive you are about yourself. One should not forget that children are influenced by your behavior far more than by your words. Above all, remember envy and jealousy are also a cry for more love and you should give it, within reasonable limits. That means your child should be given enough love, warmth, and affection to feel worthwhile, loved, accepted, and, above all, lovable, but it would be a grave error to give so much love and affection that might be seductive and fixate the child forever to the old longings of being loved exclusively, as he or she once felt as an infant. The child has to learn that sharing can also be pleasurable. To share means to have the capacity to wait and that requires trust; trust in the pleasure and security-giving parents.

In adults, pathological envy and jealousy should be opened up for honest discussion in a marriage and even among close friends. If it persists and recurs, then psychotherapy is indicated. It is unfortunate that we live in a society where possessions, wealth, competitiveness, and being number one are so highly prized and publicized, while love, friendship, loyalty, and contentment are considered boring. It is sad to live in a country that would rather be envied, feared, hated, and admired as the number one power, rather than admired and envied as a land of freedom, justice, and contentment. We have more millionaires and more poverty, more affluence and more boredom, more violence and more apathy, more possessiveness and more envy than in any other society I know of. Wouldn't most of us here in this audience be happier with less money, fewer cars, fewer clothes, and gadgets and more peace, tranquility, and justice? We should not try to totally repress possessiveness, envy, and jealousy because the result would be living without zest and eagerness, merely being passive and vegetating. Perhaps we ought to rethink what is truly worth possessing and envying.

# 20 Crisis in Adult Life: Prevention and Survival (1974)

*Hildi Greenson writes in her notes that this paper was reworked and edited from taped transcript and that the subtitle, "Prevention and Survival" was added later by Greenson. "A poignant change. At age 63 he had already sustained the loss of many friends and colleagues. Coming home from a funeral he would comment, 'We have to learn to live better.' For Greenson, this meant to enjoy intensely his family, friends and all the activities he loved, but, above all, to allow himself the time for quiet work."*

*Greenson anticipated a whole new theoretical movement in contemporary psychology, psychiatry, and psychoanalysis. Life-span or life-cycle psychology, particularly with a new interest in adult development, has emerged as an important heuristic set of ideas and concepts in current behavioral science theory and clinical practice. Many multidisciplinary efforts are now under way to raise understanding of the second half of the life cycle to the sophisticated theoretical level enjoyed by students of the phenomenology of childhood.*

*Greenson recounted how Freud and his followers described in great detail the psychological development of the child from birth through adolescence. However, maturity was minimized and only touched upon, characterized simply as that stage of life achieved when one had the capacity to achieve sexual satisfaction by the "union of the genital organs with a loved person of the opposite sex." Freud also claimed, in another famous statement, that the secret to maturity was to know how to work* (arbeiten) *and love* (lieben). *Subsequently Erik Erikson, the father of psychoanalytic life-cycle psychology, had limited himself to describing only three stages in adulthood proper.*

*Then Greenson outlined for his audience five stages or phases in the development of the adult. He organized these stages around universal crises, the decisive moments or issues that become turning points in the lives of individuals. At such points one either progresses, stagnates, or regresses, depending on how the situations are dealt with. The five phases are: getting married; becoming a parent; reappraisal of one's way of life (or sleep-walking through the remainder of it); unmistakable aging (acceptance or denial); old age (liveliness or hibernation). Greenson integrated the stages in a coherent pattern of adult life and witnessed,*

> *It takes courage, honesty and modesty to grow old with joy and dignity. Yet for life to be rewarding one must develop and retain a certain playfulness. Man is the only animal who still enjoys playfulness in adult life. To be able to have a sense of fun gives one a quality of youthfulness, no matter what age. To laugh, to have a sense of humor and above all, the ability to laugh at one's self will either minimize the crises of adult life or at least help you survive them.*

## Introduction

Man's development from birth to death is continuous, both physically and psychologically. As a psychoanalyst I shall limit myself essentially to man's *psychological* progressions and regressions including his emotional reactions to physical changes. From Freud we learned that the normal child goes through various typical developmental phases from birth to adolescence, and which Freud and his followers described in great detail. Developmental progressions and regressions are selective and uneven and may be temporary and partial. Every phase of

---

Presented to the Reiss-Davis Child Study Center, Women's Division, Los Angeles, February 20, 1974.

development carries with it normal vestiges of earlier phases, and even the most mature person can temporarily regress. We see that every night in the dreams of sleep, under the stress of illness, and the ecstasy of sexual excitement. Prolonged regressions or stagnations, which we call fixations, indicate sickness. Precocious development may also indicate that such unusual achievement was purchased at the price of some part of necessary childhood having been skipped.

For example: A thirty-five-year-old, brilliant physicist is so outstanding in his field that he becomes a full professor at an important university. He is cultivated, well read, politically astute, socially adept, but he is unable to marry or live with a woman he loves. He has sexual relations successfully but he is afraid of prolonged physical intimacy. All love relations ultimately wither away and he lives alone, self-sufficient superficially, but basically depressed. It seems clear that this man has achieved many qualities indicating maturity, but he failed to have successfully gone through a period of happy and secure bodily closeness with his mother or nurse and has remained fixated to a period of his early years where prolonged physical intimacy was essentially more painful and frightening than satisfying. All lovers made him regress to this time of childhood when he felt helplessly needful, dependent, and neglected. All his other mature functions coexisted with this infantile fear and drove him eventually to seek help.

I have used this example to illustrate the unevenness and selectivity of progressions and regressions. Although Freud and his followers described in great detail the psychological development of the child from birth through adolescence, maturity was neglected and only touched upon by stating that this stage of life is characterized by having developed the capacity to achieve sexual satisfaction by "union of the genital organs" with a loved person of the opposite sex. Erikson limited himself to outlining three stages of adulthood, but they are only the merest sketches. Thérèse Benedek felt there should be a special phase of adulthood designated as parenthood. Other writers mention only briefly one or other aspect of adulthood, with the exception of Gould who studied carefully, but not in depth, several hundred patients and nonpatients and described five separate detailed phases of adult development from age twenty-two to sixty. It was his paper that prompted me to pursue the question: Are there distinct phases of adult life?

The enormity and complexity of this subject forces me to present to you only an outline of what I consider to be typical and decisive for the five phases of adult life I believe I can distinguish. My approach has been to focus on the crises, the decisive moments or issues which become turning points; one either progresses, stagnates, or regresses, depending on how one deals with these situations.

## Adulthood: Phase 1: Getting Married

I am referring to marriage here not merely in the legal sense. A real marriage in the psychological sense means the following: I have built a relationship with a person I love so much I want to live with him or her. She, or he, is more important to me than my family. I now prefer to live separately from my parents and siblings and make a place for ourselves to live in which will feel homelike. I expect to enjoy intimacy with my spouse physically, emotionally, sexually, and intellectually—most of the time.

The big accomplishment here is the separation from the family. Bachelors or spinsters who live alone are still living *unconsciously* with mother, or their security blanket, and will not let that be interfered with by a spouse. They are fixated to this early phase of childhood and are terrified of changing it. The thirty-five-year-old bachelor belongs here.

People who fall in love and marry and then find, to their dismay, that once married and living together, the spouse has lost his or her attractivenes, have unconsciously turned the spouse into a relative. "I know you intimately" has been demeaned into, "I see you in the early morning without makeup, I hear your toilet noises, see the food particles collecting in the corners of your mouth at dinner, smell your body odors, see your soiled underwear—all of which means you remind me of home, mother, father, sister and brothers and that is unattractive." People in such a marriage have to go outside of home to find another romantic and sexual involvement and often end up in divorce.

### Phase 2: Becoming a Parent

The birth of a child is a turning point in the lives of a married or unmarried couple. It either brings them closer together by having a new love and interest they share, or it becomes like cement that glues them suffocatingly together out of a sense of responsibility or guilt. There is a third possibility: it tears them apart because one or the other feels he or she wants to be the only baby, a fact they were unaware of until the baby was born. Frequently you get mixtures of all three. The baby is a joy, an enrichment of their lives. Then there are times when the child is a burden, an interloper in their honeymoon-type life. Or, the baby is a rival. The husband cannot wait to rush home to hug and kiss and fondle his beloved—baby—not his wife, like he used to do. Or, the wife cooks for, cleans, caresses, fondles, and plays with the baby endlessly. The baby's vomit is met with sympathy, his poopoo is cute, and a great "jobby," his diapers and shirts are washed with gaiety and song, while the husband's socks and underwear are repulsive and his breath smells bad. By now the wife is too tired and "turned off" sexually, and he is impotent with jealous rage.

These reactions are equally true for both sexes. The point is: I was once the favorite, the beloved, and now the baby is. A further issue that may arise is that your young lover is now a mother or father and you are unable to get passionate and have sex with somebody's mother or father, that is incest and forbidden. Such occurrences lead to infidelity, boredom, resentment, and either divorce or resignation to a boarding-house type of existence. We eat and sleep in the same house but for fun and games we look elsewhere. The crux of the matter is whether the baby or babies are predominantly an enrichment of one's life despite the worries, frustrations, and burdens, or does being a parent essentially constrict and impoverish the life of the couple as individuals or as a pair.

There have always been people who voluntarily decide not to have children. The causes are many and varied. Sometimes it is a realistic appraisal of their inability or unwillingness to cope with the stresses that children bring into the life of a more or less happily married couple. Sometimes it is an indication of despair about the state of the world we live in.

## Phase 3: Reappraising of One's Way of Life—or, Sleepwalking Through Life

Sometime between the end of youth and before the menopause, in early middle age, usually between thirty-five to forty-five, people go through a period of seriously examining the basic components of their life. They ask themselves such questions as: Is this the best way for me to live? Is this the best wife, husband, job, career, geographic area, friends, set of political beliefs, etc., for me? Do I want to live this way for the rest of my life? I am getting older, but am still capable of real change. There is enough time left for change and a realistic hope for a new beginning. I want to emphasize that this question of changing and hope for new beginnings at this time is different from earlier youthful impetuosity where action is a substitute for thought, when faith, enthusiasm, and intensity cover up one's lack of self-confidence. It is also different from the changes sought by older people desperately trying to deny the fact of aging. I shall speak of those later.

The people I am referring to are at the end of youth and just beginning middle age; they may be youthful in certain ways and in some of their activities, but they now know there are limits physiologically, physically. They are aware of other limitations in what they can do, have already done, what they might have done, what they have experienced or avoided and missed. There are certain events which trigger this reappraisal, agonizing reappraisal, if you will. I shall mention some, even if briefly, to illustrate my points.

### *Success as an Anticlimax*

Nothing brings one so abruptly to self-appraisal as a success one had expected to bring triumph or ecstasy and instead it brings disappointment—a "so what," "blah" feeling. G. B. Shaw said: "There are two tragedies in life. One is to lose your heart's desire.

The other is to gain it." He was referring, I imagine, to the man or woman who falls in love and marries the most beautiful, intelligent, charming, compassionate, sensitive person they ever met, only to discover after some seven to fifteen years of marriage that all beauty fades, what seemed to be great intelligence was glibness and a magnificent verbal virtuosity, charm turns out to be an animated mask changed for each occasion. Compassion is really grandiosity, one plays the rich man giving a few pennies to the poor and sensitivity is revealed as a narcissistic wish to be in on everything. When this happens one has to ask oneself, are my perceptions accurate, or are they projections of *my* loss of self-esteem? And, if I am right, have I caused these changes? Do I exaggerate them? Are they changeable? Am I? Can I do better with someone else or alone?

The same kind of self-appraisal occurs when you have achieved a great success professionally. A forty-year old physician was appointed to a full professorship in a prestigious university. After a night of champagne and exhilaration he fell into a severe depression. He felt he was a fraud, had not earned the honor bestowed upon him, was tempted to resign, or to kill himself. I worked with him for a while and his depression lifted when he recognized that all his life he had unconsciously been in deadly rivalry with his father, a general practitioner he dearly loved. He had learned much from that man who had never reaped the academic rewards my patient had. Once he overcame his depression and his guilt-provoking rivalry, however, he began to question whether he really wanted to be a full professor, or did he prefer the hurly-burly of private practice, working with patients both rich and poor, and not just giving a few lectures, writing papers, and seeing a few patients in consultation. He also wondered whether his social circle was composed of friends or of people who would advance him academically. He decided finally to ask for a part-time professorship so he could do the work he loved most, working with patients. He also decided to stop playing golf, resigned from the country club, worked more in his garden, and went fishing with his wife and children.

It is worth noting that people who are insatiable, be it about money, millions upon millions are not enough, or sexual orgies with the most beautiful and sensuous sexual partners who leave them unfulfilled, or devourers of the most succulent foods and rarest wines that leave them still hungry—all these people can never get enough because what they are getting is *not* what they truly want *unconsciously*. The money, sex, and food are only poor substitutes.

### *Failures, Too, Set Self-Reappraisal in Motion*

You have all heard of stories of a young millionaire who lost all his money at forty and instead of committing suicide, or becoming a criminal to make another million fast, or becoming a politician, decided, along with his wife and kids, that maybe they might find a happier way of life away from the jet set, in the country, or a small town or even in a small apartment in the city, and it turned out to be true. The same is true of farmers who failed, went to the big city, and found a far better life.

Sexual failures, impotence, or failure to achieve orgasm can also trigger soul searching reappraisal. What is wrong, who is wrong, my spouse, my health, our social life, or all of us and to what degree, and what do I, we, do about it? The loss of physical beauty or strength can also do the same thing.

### *Serious Illness Can Also Be the Instigator of a Careful Reassessment of One's Life*

A coronary heart attack from which you recover makes you ponder and reevaluate what in life is precious to you; what are you willing to give up; what have you almost missed; what can you change. Should you change? What is important to you and what is trivial? What gives you the greatest pleasures? What things are you not willing to give up, even though there is some risk, etc. People come up with different answers. I have known some physicians who continued to smoke and overeat despite their knowledge of the dangers. Some become so frightened of exertion they renounce all sport, even sex, and live in a monastery of terror. Others, previously undisciplined, follow strict medical rules and yet find time and energy for exuberant love and hard work, within limits. I know several people who have said they have led a far happier and more productive life after their coronary than before.

The same can be said of people in this age group who survived cancer, tuberculosis, Hodgkins disease, and severe physical trauma. Almost losing your life gives food for thought and sound reasons for reassessing what makes life worth living, what are my priorities for a good life.

*A Death in the Family*

A death in the family, usually of one or both parents, or an older sibling or dear friend usually occurs for the first time during the years thirty-five to forty-five. The first death in the family has a special and powerful impact. It is the first time one has to experience as an adult the enforced separation from a loved one; it revives old feelings of loss, longings, helplessness, and sadness which we call grief. In addition, it is also a forceful reminder of the inevitability of one's own death. We and all our loved ones are not immortal. Birthdays no longer signify how long you have lived, but also make you wonder how long you still have to live. At this age one is usually not desperate, but it gives impetus for asking oneself those same questions: Do I want to spend the rest of my life this way? How can I increase my pleasures? Enrich the quality of my life, get more satisfaction from those I live with? Is this work going to be my life's work? What should I change, can I change? What can I change in myself and in the world around me? There is still time for a better life, a new beginning. Life and time become more precious as we realize life is transient.

*Loss of Beauty*

The loss of beauty, especially in women, in our male chauvinistic society, is not an illness, but it is not a wellness. For some women it is the cause of great mental anguish, particularly when it is remarked upon or reacted to by one's husband or lover. The face, neck, eyes, breasts, and buttocks can be made more youthful by successful plastic surgery. But this raises several questions. Does this synthetic rejuvenation feel genuine, suit you physically and emotionally, or make you feel fraudulent? Does it change for the better the way your loved ones, lovers, children, and friends react to you or was it all in vain? Are you more attractive to yourself? Has it improved your self-esteem, your self-confidence, or are you still treading on eggshells, still on trial? Perhaps the surgery should have been amputation of the spouse? At this age a woman or man ought to be accepted and loved for what they are, not for what they were or should have been. A different man or woman may find an older woman or man very attractive physically as well as mentally. It is now well known that women are more sensuous between thirty-five to forty-five than in their earlier years. Men at this age should be accomplished lovers and accomplished in other endeavors. Before surgical change one should consider the possibility of other changes. Even psychological changes in oneself.

### Phase 4: Unmistakable Aging—Denial or Acceptance

Most people between the ages of forty-five and sixty go through a normal developmental phase which is called, in ordinary language, "the change of life." Medical terminology had labeled *menopause*, a female term, because only recently was it discovered that men too go through such a phase, but in them it is less acute and less conspicuous physically. In women the menopause is the result of the decline of certain ovarian functions. It may start abruptly or gradually, may last a few months or many years. The outstanding clinical signs are a decrease and finally a cessation of menstruation, hot flashes, chills, and fatigue. In men the decline of testicular function is more gradual. The physical manifestations are balding, loss of body hair, increase of fatty tissue around the breasts, in the pubic area, and prostate enlargement. In women sexual desire and capacity for orgasm does not necessarily diminish and may even increase. In men there is usually a gradual decrease in sexual desire, but there are exceptions due to constitutional, physical and emotional factors (see Kinsey et al. for the enormous variety of sexual responsiveness of men and women of all ages).

The emotional responses to the awareness of the decrease in the function of the sexual glands initiates and may dominate the clinical picture. People undergoing the change of life can be divided into three major groups:

1. Those who consider aging a catastrophe. Some attempt to deny this by resorting to plastic surgery, flamboyantly youthful clothes, change of wife for a younger woman, or change of husband old enough to make you feel young. Others resort to alcohol, gambling, pot, and hallucinatory drugs. Then there are those who resort to a variety of therapies: glandular therapies, cells produced from unborn pigs, urine of pregnant women (fashionable in Europe). Then there are the psychotherapies, especially quick, "primal" therapies, nude encounters, marathons, group sex, and only on rare occasions psychoanalysis. Some of these attempts make some people feel younger, temporarily. Most result in disappointment, smoldering rage, and agitated depression covered over by frantic running around, frequent infatuations, addictions, etc.

2. The second group react to the cessation of gonadal function with a burst of creativity. Some of the great works of art, literature, and science were done by men and women in these years. I think offhand of Michaelangelo, Freud, Madam Curie, and Margaret Mead. Others react to the change of life by falling in love or trying to become great sensualists, using their creativity in this sphere, a creativity which has lain dormant until then. This is not necessarily hurtful if it is combined with thought, discrimination, and is not destructive to oneself or others. Above all, it must be recognized as an attempt to fulfill one's life, to fill in something lacking, not to deny the process of aging.

3. There is a third group who react to the change of life by making no drastic changes. These people accept menopause or testicular decline as part of the process of living. Yes, one is getting older and death is closer, but if one's way of living has the basic ingredients of a good life, they feel no urge for radical change. True, one tends to read the obituary columns more often, but that serves as a spur of getting as much and more out of the good things one has and can do. One becomes more selective but one does more of what is enjoyable, productive, and worthwhile. These people treasure their loved ones more, work more effectively and also do good for others because there is a greater aware-

ness of all of us being part of the brotherhood of man and after all, death is the great equalizer.

Crises at this age are also brought about by other factors than the reaction to aging as a catastrophe. Some people cannot bear feeling unneeded by their children. They have not made the step of having an adult relationship with their offspring. Such parents treat their adult sons and daughters as children by trying to control them, demanding submissiveness and conspicuous love and devotion. At the same time, such parents belittle and find fault with the spouses, friends, habits, customs, dress, and style of life of their offspring. They refuse to let go of them, and as a result are hated consciously or unconsciously, avoided, or they have grown-up babies of thirty to forty years of age and not adult offspring.

You do not have to be needed if you are willing to be liked and sometimes loved by your children. But, this is only possible if you respect the differences between you. If you admit the likelihood you made serious errors in their upbringing and your generation also made grievous errors in handling the world situation, then one also has to admit to oneself one's envy of their youth, vigor, zest, and stamina. Above all, you will be liked and wanted by them if you have a sense of playfulness, a willingness to laugh at yourself, and if you are an interesting person. Who wants to spend time with a fifty-year-old man who is genetically one's father, but is a snoopy, critical, stuffed shirt, who is fault finding, joyless, and boring? He may be father, but no friend.

Another crisis producing factor at fifty is having parents still alive but deteriorating. Here the issue is, are you doing all you reasonably can to make their lives comfortable? Do you do enough, with good will, not essentially out of guilt, which usually produces righteous feelings of resentment, or do you avoid the parents and suffer from guilt consciously or unconsciously? We all have limitations in dealing with such situations, but we ought to recognize them and try to handle them fairly and intelligently within our limitations.

In the forty-five to fifty-five-year old group the same events which precipitated self-reassessment ten years earlier now evoke the specter of one's own death and the reactions I described earlier. Death of relatives, siblings, and friends produces sadness, guilt, anxiety, and depression. The same may occur in response to a serious physical illness in oneself or someone close. Successes and failures may evoke the unexpected reactions I described earlier.

Becoming a grandparent usually occurs for the first time at this age. This event may have many salutary effects. There is a natural tendency to identify with one's son and daughter and relive vicariously the joys of new parenthood via grandparenthood. There are special joys in being grandparents because one can love and be loved by little children, and yet one does not have the major responsibilities. Easy access to grandchildren who like you is a bonus of aging. On the other hand, it is especially bitter when the grandchildren are kept away from you and you are unable to rectify the situation. All one can do is to try to sublimate the urge to love and be loved by little children by becoming involved in little children who are outcasts by their own parents, the orphans, or those who are case out of ordinary society by disease, congenital or acquired. One can become a surrogate grandparent by contributing time, attention, and money to their welfare. It is amazing how often one hears the cry of affluent people: "Nobody needs me." The world is so full of needful people, but unfortunately many people are so limited by whom they care to be needed by. It is a poor substitute for loving grandchildren, but it is far better than nothing. Even in good relationships with children and grandchildren, one should expect to be misused occasionally as baby-sitters, which can be a great joy and also very exhausting.

## Phase 5: Old Age—Hibernating or Being Lively

From age sixty onwards, the idea of death is a steady companion. The decrease in physical stamina and strength, forgetfulness, absentmindedminess, a slowing down of certain mental functions, physical aches and pains are constant reminders that old age is here. I want to stress that there are youthful as well as fossilized sixty-, seventy-, and eighty-year-olds. You can ignore one's breathlessness or grab frantically at your pulse, or just stop jogging, or yell for a doctor. But at this age one does not have to bemoan all one's losses, one can also enjoy the benefits of old age.

Certain traits of character which were once considered obnoxious are now looked upon more benignly, as mere eccentricities. People tend to allow old folks greater latitude in breaking the standards of convention which were expected of them in the fifties. You can leave any boring gathering early and are excused because you need to conserve your energies. You can be brutually frank and it is forgiven as one of the peculiarities of old age. And then there is the general tendency to attribute wisdom to the whiteharied one. If you now think slowly it is considered careful pondering, if your answers to the major questions of life are vague and obscure, many will consider you profound and even philosophical.

The crucial issue of old age is whether you are going to face the day with all the zest, vigor, and vitality at your command, not necessarily loudly or intensely. It can be done quietly and determinedly, but above all, in contact with people in reality or fantasy. Or, are you going to hoard your energies and spend them stingily and reluctantly, usually alone, in order to postpone death? The error in the latter course is that such living is already half-dead, only the person doing so does not know it. The sixties, seventies, and eighties is the time to take up all those activities you longed for but never tried before because you were too busy. This does not mean discontinuing those activities you enjoy and do well. Retirement from activity is foolish, depressing, and unhealthy. This is a great time to explore new potentials, new areas of endeavor, of inquiry, new areas of pleasure. I have been impressed by the paintings of a senior citizens cultural center in Venice, all by people who never painted before seventy. I was moved to see women over seventy taking classes in rhythmic dancing and yoga. They were touching and beautiful in their seriousness and their grace, despite their fingers gnarled by arthritis, their lips bluish from heart impairment, and their wrinkled skin. In her seventies, my mother became an expert on Freud's life and lectured on Jones' three-volume biography and also on recent fiction until a week before she died at eighty-three. I may add she always attended my evening lectures (she was too busy during the day), but was not a severe critic. She had two typical responses: (1) It was the greatest, or (2) it was great but not the greatest.

One cannot leave old age without mentioning the vitality, creativity, and youthfulness of such great people as Picasso, Casals and Chaplin, Eleanor Roosevelt and Anna Freud, Picasso and Chaplin fathered babies in their sixties and seventies, Casals married at seventy-five and lived to ninety-two.

## Conclusion: Prevention and Survival of Crises in Adult Life

Throughout this presentation I have mentioned different attitudes and approaches to each of the five phases that will prevent or help you survive the different crises each presents. Lest these points be lost in the mass of material let me outline the major points.

The first major task facing the human infant and which persists in various forms throughout life is separation and individuation. That means in infancy the newborn has to give up his sense of symbiotic fusion with mother and learn that the blissful oneness and fusion he feels with mother is illusory. He must learn to distinguish inside from outside, self from others. An essential prerequisite for this is trust in the mothering person, i.e., I don't have to be physically joined with you to know you will be there when I need you. The other essential step, a later one, is learning to trust one's body functions. I can walk away and return to you; I can leave you and still maintain contact by speaking; I can give up my bowel movements and more will be made and I will not be left empty and vulnerable and helpless. Throughout life man is torn by the urge to return to different forms of loving and safe fusion and the drive to individuate and develop an independent self. In healthy people we see both aspects satisfied in loving relationships and the capacity to work effectively and be alone.

I can put it in another way. As much as man wants variety, he is afraid of change. Yet change is inevitable and has to be met with a willingness to risk pain, fear, and defeat and endure it. The alternative is an ever-increasing anxiety or withdrawing, denial of reality by false enthusiasm, or turning to magic and mysticism rather than reason and vitamins. Man is born unfinished and needs to develop himself to cope successfully with himself, his fellow man, and the world around him. To do so, it is necessary to be honest with oneself, about one's abilities, capacities and limitations. For me, it is better to try and be a first rate Greenson than an imitation Freud. It takes courage, honesty and modesty to grow old with joy and dignity. Yet, for life to be rewarding one must develop and retain a certain playfulness. Man is the only animal who still enjoys playfulness in adult life. To be able to have a sense of fun gives one a quality of youthfulness, no matter at what age. To laugh, to have a sense of humor, and above all, the ability to laugh at oneself will either minimize the crises of adult life or at least help you survive them.

Finally, we have to recognize that it is not the goals achieved that matter as much as the process of striving for them. In this light then the framers of the Declaration of Independence were perhaps wiser than they knew when they proclaimed an inalienable right, not to happiness, but to the *pursuit* of happiness; a right to a means and not to an end. To cite Shaw again: "Folly is the direct pursuit of happiness, happiness is always a by-product."

More generally, the attainment of ends is only satisfying when those ends enlarge the scope for further activity. Unfortunately, most ends (if attained) would narrow or restrict this scope. Perhaps we should be grateful for the unvarying bungling with which most of us pursues his presumed goals.

Complexity and richness, not tidiness and order, are man's natural habitat. The basic questions which have animated man's best activities in the past—regarding justice, beauty, wisdom—thus have, and can have, no answers. The value lies, not in the attainment of answers, but in the quest for them.

# 21 The Devil Made Me Do It, Dr. Freud (1974)

*The lecture with this wonderful title was a hellfire and brimstone parody given at the Leo Baek Temple. Later, Hildi Greenson notes, it was reworked and shortened for* The Saturday Review of Literature *where it appeared under the title "A Psychoanalyst's Indictment of* The Exorcist."

*Greenson chose to speak about the Devil and how psychoanalysis understands that phenomenon, because it was becoming apparent to him that there was a growing tendency at the time for people of all ages, economic groups, and intellectual levels to be swept back toward a belief in demons, the occult, the mystical, and the supernatural. The immediate stimulus for the talk was the motion picture* The Exorcist *and the harmful effects the film had on the public at large and for the medical profession in particular.*

*Greenson read the book and saw the movie and found that they upset him in several ways. First, they were so unashamedly exploitive, so obviously an attempt to stir up people's most primitive sensual and brutal impulses. His indictment was as follows: "It is to my mind, unquestionably the most shocking major movie I have ever seen. Never have I seen such a flagrant combination of perverse sex, brutal violence, and a vicious misuse of religion. In addition there was a degradation of the medical profession and psychiatry."*

*He quoted from a study done by Georgetown University psychiatrists who found that seeing the film was harmful to young people and to people of precarious emotional balance. To some it seemed to be a traumatic shock leading to acute hysteria, a return to childhood phobias, acute psychotic episodes, acute obsessional states, insomnia, and nightmares. "The Devil made me do it . . . is the total explanation the film offers." Romi reminded his audience that witchcraft and demonology represent a very persistent and insidious movement that had been around for hundreds of years and seemed to be going through a revival.*

*Prophetically foreshadowing the satanic cults, astrological fervor, etc., of today, Greenson said that mysticism, supernaturalism, transcendentalism, and occultism flourish when many people are disillusioned by the deterioration of moral standards, social and economic inequities, excessive permissiveness and punishments, and the hypocrisy and the corruption of people in high places. He felt that this "makes people feel disoriented, rootless, without goals or standards, and tempts them to regress into mysticism to gain instant power or a sense of belonging, and bliss. We see this in the emotionally sick, the drop-outs, the disenfranchised and the hard-drug users, among others." Addressing the collective conscience, Greenson closed this lecture about morality, or lack of it, this way: "Demonology blames the world via the Devil. We could blame Watergate, Vietnam, the atom bomb, etc., but horrendous as they may be, they are no excuse for our self-centeredness, greed, and immorality."*

## Introduction

I have chosen to speak about the Devil and how psychoanalysis understands this phenomenon because it is becoming very apparent that there is a growing movement at this time in which people of all ages, economic groups, and intellectual levels are being swept back into a belief in demonology, occultism, mysticism, supernaturalism, and spiritualism. Through-

---

Presented at the Leo Baek Temple, Los Angeles, as one of four lectures on aggression, March 21, 1974.

out history, Satan and his demonic disciples have always been depicted as hateful, vicious, and yet also quite human at times. I have also been struck how often the true believers in God and Christ and their followers have misused their religiosity to perpetrate the worst crimes in the name of getting rid of evil. These points, interesting as they may be in relating aggression and the Devil, were not decisive for my selection of this topic. The crucial factor, the trigger event which prompted me to speak out on this subject, was the motion picture *The Exorcist* and the harmful effects this picture has had on the public at large and on the medical profession.

I was aware that there was something extraordinary about this movie because of the long lines of people surrounding the theater in Westwood and the impossible traffic congestion for blocks in that vicinity. Then, some two months ago, I was called by an intelligent, stable social worker almost begging me to see her as quickly as possible, she was in a state of sheer panic. I saw her at my home and she told me, shivering with fright, that her husband had persuaded her to see *The Exorcist* the other evening and since then, she has had a return of intense fears and phobias she could only dimly recall from her early childhood. She is now afraid to be alone, to go out, to be in the dark, to be in another room from her husband, etc. It was easy to make her aware that the movie had remobilized the fear of the Devil with whom she had been threatened in her early childhood. This insight was partially helpful, and I arranged to send her to a colleague for further psychotherapy.

A week later, I saw a young university professor in an emergency consultation, who had to see me in order to let the devils inside him come out. He chose me because he felt I would not be killed by his devils. I had to see him three times in one day to allow him to rave, rant, cry, beg, stamp his feet, and bang his fists, until he became exhausted. During the third visit, when he was relatively coherent, he told me that he had felt he had a psychotic core deep inside him, a devil, and it was the movie, *The Exorcist*, that convinced him of it. I also sent him for further therapy.

At this point, I asked my colleagues at UCLA and in private practice, if they were seeing patients who were having acute neurotic and psychotic reactions to *The Exorcist*. They all confirmed this.

I decided to read the book and see the movie, and also to do some reading on exorcism and demonology in general. First, I looked up exorcism in *Webster's Unabridged Dictionary* and found it to mean driving the demoniacal spirit out of the human soul. It is considered a somewhat disreputable professional pursuit today. It was practiced by the Indian medicine man, the shamans, the witch killers of Salem, and the mob who burned Joan of Arc. Even those therapists in ancient Egypt who split open the skulls to allow evil spirits to escape were exorcists, but they had, at best, modest success, because though they may have driven out the Devil, their patients died in the process.

I found Blatty's book, *The Exorcist*, easy reading, slick, synthetic, but interesting because it described aspects of demoniacal possession with which I was not familiar, and the Catholic exorcism rite, of which I was totally ignorant. I was taken aback, however, by the mixture of sexual sadism, masochism, brutality, perversity, and religion. It took me longer to get in to see the picture than to read the book, but I was determined because I could not believe they would dare to show this type of behavior on the screen.

The movie, *The Exorcist*, did upset me in several ways. First of all, it seemed to me to be so unashamedly exploitive, so obviously an attempt to stir up people's most primitive sensual and brutal impulses. It is, to my mind, unquestionably the most shocking major movie I have ever seen. Never have I seen such a flagrant combination of perverse sex, brutal violence, and a vicious misuse of religion. In addition, there was a degradation of the medical profession and psychiatry. Finally, the audience was the most noisy, unruly group who laughed, giggled, talked, and yelled throughout. I was not aware of anyone fainting, but the floor was slimy and I had no inclination to investigate it more closely.

At Georgetown University, where this movie was shot, Dr. Richard Steinbach, head of the Department of Psychiatry, said in the *American Medical News* of March 4, 1974, that the staff resented the effects the picture had on suggestible people. One survey reported an average of six men fainting and six women vomiting at every showing. Georgetown psychiatrists testified that, in their opinion, the pornography in *The Exorcist* makes *The Last Tango in Paris* seem tame. I would say *The Last Tango* is a Strauss waltz in the Vienna Woods by comparison. They found it to be harmful to the youth and to people of precarious emotional and mental balance. To some, it is a traumatic shock leading to acute hysteria, a return to childhood phobias, acute psychotic episodes, acute obsessional states, insomnia, and nightmares.

I resent most of all that the movie depicts a twelve-year-old child, Regan, who is responsible for three deaths, untold suffering upon everyone near and dear to her, who shamelessly exhibits bloody vaginal masturbation with a crucifix, among other sexual perversities, and the movie ends up with the girl represented as merely a poor innocent victim of demonic possession. The Devil made me do it, that is the total explanation the film offers. Regan is not only innocent, says the movie, she has no memories or any other scars from the experience, and no inner conflicts.

So, I return to my title, "The Devil Made Me Do It, Dr. Freud," i.e., I am not liable for my actions, I am pure, innocent, and without any responsibility and guilt. For 400 years, science, and later the medical profession, especially psychiatry, fought the belief that devils or evil spirits or witches caused mental and physical illnesses. Now *The Exorcist* proclaims that the Devil does exist, can take possession of you, and you are merely the helpless victim. Both book and picture further degrade the medical profession by implying we are unwilling or unable to handle patients who feel they are possessed by the Devil or anything else. All the hospital or sanitarium scenes show physicians to be callous, brutal, and ineffectual. One of the bloodiest scenes in the movie is when the girl is given an arteriogram in the hospital and a huge quantity of blood is gushing out of her neck across the screen.

It is claimed that *The Exorcist* is based on a true story of a fourteen-year-old boy, but this has not been substantiated. All of us psychiatrists have seen patients who had one or another of the symptoms that plague Regan in the movie, but I do not believe any of us have seen any single patient who had all the bizarre and savage symptomology the girl in the movie exhibits. It is my conviction that *The Exorcist* was contrived to appeal to a huge audience, to fascinate, i.e., to frighten and attract troubled and disoriented people, to appeal to their voyeuristic impulses, their sadism and masochism, and to titillate them by making fear sensations sexually exciting. Those in the audience who did not break down may have gotten a vulgar thrill or a feeling of machismo, "I can take this shocking stuff," which is a counterphobic reaction. Besides, it is also a shameless degradation of women's sexuality and will appeal to all women haters.

I am told *The Exorcist* will earn more money by far than any previous motion picture. I have read it has been nominated for ten Academy Awards by the Academy of Motion Picture Arts and Sciences. I believe *The Exorcist* is a menace to the mental health of the community and I believe the public should be warned about it. I think Mr. Blatty, the author, and Mr. Friedkin, the producer, should ask themselves if they should not take some responsibility for the harm they are doing. I also wonder whether the Academy should not do some soul-searching about the reasons for finding *The Exorcist* worthy of ten Oscar nominations.

The *American Medical News* of March 4, 1974, headlined their story about this movie with:

> *"The Exorcist" Haunts MDs at Georgetown*
>
> Because of this movie, the rising epidemic of cases of possession will find its natural explanations in brain disorders, hysterical phenomena, disassociated mental states, and just plain psychoses. Freud and Jung, where are you when we really need you?

The same seems to be true over the rest of the country. The *AMA Journal* of March 4 stated editorially:

> "The Exorcist" is heady stuff. Men and women, having seen it, or part of it, leave because they cannot tolerate it; they faint, they vomit, they are consulting physicians in the belief that they or their children are "possessed."
>
> Other examples of the phenomenon are in the news: "Do demons possess; do humans succumb? Do theologians or psychiatrists have an answer? Comments are invited by those who have read Blatty's novel or who have seen Friedkin's cinema.

This indicates the degree of concern this movie has elicited, and I feel a psychoanalyst should respond. How would Dr. Freud, i.e., psychoanalysis, respond to such phenomena?

Freud was interested in the fact that the old belief in the Devil, witches, angels, and good and bad gods, had never died out, it only went underground, and was repressed in the unconscious mind while being repudiated by man's rational mind. In all of us, the spirit of heavenly goodness or hellish evil persists. We see it overtly in psychotics, and covertly in neurotics and other emotionally infantile characters. We also find it in the dreams of normal persons, especially in nightmares as well as in "daymares," the frightening conscious fantasies. When the times in which we live become chaotic, unpredictable, corrupt, violent, and we feel relatively helpless, people regress to believing in God and the Devil, at least temporarily.

In 1923, Freud wrote, "A 17th Century Demonological Neurosis," about an Austrian painter, Haizmann, whose case history could be gained from his diary and the records kept by monks in a nearby village. The painter, depressed to the point of melancholia and unable to work, had seizures, visions, fell unconscious, and bled from nose and mouth. He later confessed that he had made a pact with the Devil. Freud felt the Devil represented the patient's bad and reprehensible wishes, derivatives of instinctual impulses that had been repressed. He projected his wickedness onto the demon which was typical for the Middle Ages, when demonology flourished. Today, said Freud, we recognize such fantasies as having their abode in our internal mental and emotional life.

The painter had entered the pact with the Devil and had given up his immortal soul because he believed he would receive wealth, security, power over mankind, magical abilities, and especially the enjoyment of beautiful women. It did not work for Haizmann. He got even more depressed to the point of a paralyzing melancholia. Freud believed that the feeling of being possessed by the Devil stems from the fact that the Devil is a substitute for the father. Haizmann's father had died shortly before he became possessed. (Regan, too, lost her father, by divorce, in the movie, *The Exorcist*.)

The Devil, Satan, and God, said Freud, are all derived from

the father. God, as he is perceived by little children, is an exalted father figure. Religious people call God "our Father" and call themselves "His children." This primal image of father survives in all of mankind. It is ambivalent, it contains love and hate simultaneously, a longing to please and submit, along with spite and defiance. Some part of it may be conscious, but in most rational people, it is predominantly repressed and unconscious.

Hence, the good loving father is God, and Satan is created out of the hateful impulses of the child to the terrible, wrathful, and punitive father. Father is the prototype of both God and the Devil. Religions teach that God created man in His image. Psychoanalysis, on the other hand, shows that the child created God out of his primitive perceptions of his father and projects his own feelings and impulses onto his ambivalently loved God. When a man loses his father whom he loved consciously, he mourns and grieves. When he loses a father whom he hated consciously and loved unconsciously, he cannot mourn or grieve, he develops a chronic depression or melancholia.

Man finds it hard to deal with his unconscious love for his father, it makes him feel passive, submissive, and feminine. To love father, for men with *unresolved* conflicts of love and hate, means, I must castrate myself so as not to compete with him. Sometimes, the conflict is resolved by both men and women, by loving father consciously and letting oneself be entered into and possessed by the Devil.

In a paper on "The Uncanny," Freud pointed out that events are felt as uncanny when what occurs coincides with something one believed in as a child and then relinquished as false. For example, you suddenly think you see someone whom you know is dead, and you have an uncanny feeling. The childish idea that the dead can return momentarily seems to be real and results in this feeling of uncanniness. Unexpected coincidences, about imagined events, also give you a feeling of the uncanny when they suddenly do take place. The widespread belief in the evil eye belongs in this category. The secret intention of doing harm, most frequently out of envy, can be frightening and guilt-producing if something should befall the victim of one's evil eye. Superstitious people blame misfortunes on having been victimized by the evil eye.

Animism, magic, sorcery, and the omnipotence of thoughts

(i.e., everything is personified and thoughts and wishes are all-powerful) preceded religion, and still exist in primitive societies. Spirits, witches, demons, and sorcerers could only be protected against by magic, man's first technology. By making certain signs, gestures, sacrifices, and thinking certain counterthoughts, etc., one could fight the evil spirits. This persists to this day in the form of superstitions, obsessions, compulsions, and in certain religious rituals.

It is also to be found in our literature, even our great literature, the Old Testament and the New Testament, Dante's *Divine Comedy*, Milton's *Paradise Lost*, and Goethe's *Faust*, to mention just a few, are full of demonology. The concept of God and Devil is most fully developed in Hebrew and Christian theology, but it can be found in the religious beliefs of the Babylonians, Egyptians, Greeks, Hindus, and Zoroastrians.

The Reformation took the Devil very seriously, and it is said by historians that Protestant zealots may have executed 3 million people in Europe and America between 1450 and 1750. Contemporary Protestants disavow a literal interpretation of Satan, and the Jews have had only a modest range of devils like the Dybbuks.

One cannot leave the subject of the Devil and demoniacal possession without mentioning that witchcraft and demonology is a very persistent and insidious movement, which has gone on continually for hundreds of years, and seems to be going through a revival today. I refer you to Norman Cohn, who described the ups and downs of these phenomena in his classic work *The Pursuit of the Millennium*. Cohn maintains there is a hidden continuity between the medieval revolutionary messianism of Europe that recurred through the Middle Ages and was based on the social and economic inequities of medieval times. The instability of the social structures like church, state, government, convention, law and order, provoked the outbursts of revolutionary and anarchic millennialism, and is at least partially responsible, in his opinion, for both Bolshevism and Hitlerism.

People who are prone to such beliefs are the poor, the disenfranchised, and the disorganized. Under the influence of a prophet or messiah, they feel themselves "chosen," at one with God, and go forth to do battle with evil, the clergy, the wealthy, the Jews, the gypsies, and the intellectuals. In destroying them they hope to establish a Golden Age of wealth, peace, and joy that would last 1000 years. Does this have the ring of one of Hitler's speeches?

A final word on being possessed: Today mysticism, supernaturalism, transcendentalism, occultism are flourishing because many people are disillusioned by the deterioration of our moral standards, the social and economic inequities, the excessive permissiveness and punishments, the hypocrisy and the corruption of people in high places. This makes people feel disoriented, rootless, without goals or standards, and tempts them to regress into mysticism, to gain instant power, or a sense of belonging, and bliss. We see this in the emotionally sick, the drop-outs, the disenfranchised, and the hard-drug users, among others.

Being possessed is not only a negative force; sometimes people are possessed by feeling states which give them great power and great creativity. Hypnosis can give a frail woman strength enough to carry three grown men. Think of Beethoven's frenzied periods of creativity. Not to be forgotten is that most powerful sensation of being possessed, which endows one with great strength, which is the feeling of righteous indignation. We would attack a giant to protect a child of ours who was being mistreated. Many of us have discovered endurance we never knew we had when fighting against injustice or illness.

In conclusion, I hope I have demonstrated that aggression, violence, and even primitive love exist in the realm of demonology. Now the question arises, what can we do about it? I have only few and inadequate answers.

We must not absolve people of responsibility for their actions. To kill or maim or steal, no matter what the psychological explanation, is wrong and calls for punishment of some kind. If not, people will feel free to transgress or else surrender to feeling guilty. The only cure for guilt is to suffer pain and make reparation. The point is, the punishment must not only fit the crime, but the person—it should make him a better human being. Demonology blames the world via the Devil. We could blame Watergate, Vietnam, the atom bomb, but, as horrendous as they may be, they are no excuse for our own self-centeredness, greed, and immorality.

There must be limits to permissiveness and explanations.

There is a place for punishment, but humane and intelligent punishment. We must all assume some responsibility for the horrors of this world from Bangladesh, Vietnam, Watergate, to the famine in India. We are all part of the brotherhood of man, whether we like it or not. We can and must do more to help our fellow man. Otherwise, we will become not just a sick society, but worse, a morally corrupt one.

# 22 You Only Live Twice (1975)

*Mrs. Greenson painfully recalls the 1970s as a very difficult time for the Greenson family because those years were punctuated with Romi's many hospitalizations. As we have recounted, after a pacemaker implant in 1975, Romi suffered an embolus to the brain with resulting aphasia. She tells how "his determination 'to overcome' and regain his most precious gift was an inspiration to all who knew of his struggle."*

*In this very personal lecture, Greenson shared some of his feelings and experiences following his original heart attack in 1955. He said, "Before 1955, I lived in an age of innocence, blissfully unaware that I would actually die. I knew intellectually that I was mortal, but I had put my own death way off in the hazy, distant future . . . like in Freud's great 1915 essay "Our Attitude Towards Death" . . . at the bottom no one believes in his own death . . . in the unconscious every one of us is convinced of his own immortality."*

*Greenson conveyed to his audience his transition from emotions of anxiety and rage, following his near-death experience, to a feeling of being very lucky indeed.*

*I was stricken with a coronary and I went through the various emotional phases that people who physically survive their first coronary usually follow. My belief in my immortality had disappeared . . . as time goes on, and if you have no physical complications and have a loving, nurturing environment, you begin to feel as physically well as before, but more important, you begin to feel that you have another chance to live. Not only another chance, but a chance to live a richer and fuller life. I am not only speaking for myself, but people who have tasted death, if they survive physically and emotionally, they will feel life is very precious and want to make good use of every moment.*

## Introduction

I want to explain to you the origin of my enigmatic title, "You Only Live Twice." Before 1955, I lived in an age of innocence, blissfully unaware that I would actually ever die. I knew intellectually that I was mortal, but I had put my own death way off in the hazy, distant future. As a physician, I had become acquainted with death, but those deaths concerned strangers and, though I grieved for them, it had only temporarily upset my attitude toward my own death. Even the death of my father, for whom I had mourned, did not make me consciously think about my own mortality. I was a good example of what Freud had in mind when he wrote in 1915 about "Our Attitude Towards Death." "It is indeed impossible to imagine our own death; and whenever we attempt to do so, we can perceive that we are in fact still present as spectators. Hence the psycho-analytic school could venture on the assertion that at bottom no one believes in his own death, or, to put the same thing in another way, that in the unconscious every one of us is convinced of his own immortality. . . ."

Then in 1955, I was stricken with a coronary and I went through the various emotional phases that people who physically survive their first coronary usually follow. My belief in my immortality had disappeared. One wonders if one will wake up dead or alive. Coronary patients feel vulnerable and fragile at first and, at odd times, they can disavow their fears and their morbid thoughts.

---

Presented at the Reiss-Davis Child Study Center, Women's Division, Los Angeles, October 6, 1975.

It is quite frequent that coronary patients, and other seriously ill patients, can deny their anxieties and replace them with anger, resentment, and envy, culminating in the phrase of, "Why me, of all people?" After some months, one will strike up a bargain with God, or Fate, or the Doctors, that if I am "good" I will survive. As time goes on, and if you have no physical complications and have a loving, nurturing environment, you begin to feel as physically well as before, but more important, you begin to feel that you have another chance to live. Not only another chance, but a chance to live a richer and fuller life. I am not only speaking for myself, but for people who have tasted death, if they survive physically and emotionally, they will feel life is very precious and want to make good use of every moment. You feel lucky to be alive. That is when, and why, I coined the phrase: "You only live twice!" I shall later explore the mechanisms that made this outcome possible. What is of crucial importance is the transition from the emotions of anxiety, rage, and depression, to the feeling of being lucky.

There has been a great deal of emphasis in the psychiatric literature lately on how people tried to cope with the dying or death of people other than themselves. A few days ago, I received a notice from the UCLA Extension of a course given for one weekend only by Dr. Shneidman on "Life, Death and the Dying Person." In the bibliography he cites, there is an amazing plethora of books on dying. To mention only a few: Edwin S. Shneidman, *Deaths of Man*; Geoffrey Gorer, *Death, Grief and Mourning*; John Hinton, *Dying*; Elisabeth Kübler-Ross, *On Death and Dying*; Herman Feifel, *The Meaning of Death*; and Jacques Choron, *Death and Western Thought*. It is striking, however, that the literature on one's own death is so sparse. I shall give examples of the way people handle or cope with the inevitability of dying. I want to stress that the human being has certain options, not unlimited options, but there are choices if one is resourceful, creative, has the ability to regress flexibly and selectively, and has some good luck.

Let me give you some clinical examples: Many years ago, a thirty-three-year-old, very rich young man was sent to see me by his internist and cardiologist; I shall call him Mr. A. He complained that, for the last three years he had suffered from attacks of pain in his midsternal region, which occasionally radiated to his left arm, and made him feel weak, dreadfully tired, and woefully depressed. These attacks varied from once a day to four or five times daily, and varied in length from a few seconds to several hours. A whole battery of tests were done during the period of one year and all proved to be negative. His condition was diagnosed as angina pectoris of unknown origin. A trial with nitroglycerine tablets was of no help, neither were mild sedatives, strong sedatives, hypnotics, or tranquilizers. Mr. A's attacks of chest pains persisted and with it a feeling of impending doom. He was quite sure he was going to have a fatal coronary attack. He often begged for hospitalization, sometimes as an emergency late at night, but despite giving in to his requests, nothing definite was ever found to explain his symptoms on an organic basis (medicine was not as advanced in the fifties as it is now). They suggested his seeing a psychiatrist several months before his seeing me, but Mr. A only wanted quick relief and went to a hypnotist, which helped him not at all.

Mr. A was an intelligent man, supposedly happily married, with two small children. In his desperation to get over his feelings that death from heart disease was imminent, he agreed, despite his severe resistances, to see me for exploratory psychotherapy. In about one and a half years, he had improved sufficiently to have gotten over his fear of impending death. He still had occasional mild heart pains, but was resigned to them. Mr. A decided to interrupt his treatment, notwithstanding my urging that there were still important psychological conflicts which warranted exploring. He was satisfied to live with the resigned attitude that sooner or later he would die, but it was no longer so obsessive and menacing.

The special reason for telling you about this case is that Mr. A was so frightened about dying from a coronary attack (and it is possible he may have had a mild one), that before and during treatment with me, he made several half-hearted attempts at suicide. What was more terrifying than dying, to Mr. A, was that death would take him by surprise, it would seize him unaware. Even in sleep, he was vigilant, he could not bear to really relax despite heavy doses of sedatives. Finally, I was able to show Mr. A that death to him meant that a devil would suddenly seize him and crush the life out of his heart. This aspect of his anxiety was based on the fear of a devilish father-figure of his childhood years. Slowly the story unfolded of the beginning of his coronary illness. It started when the patient was thirty and rich and his ambivalently loved and hated father died, drunk and penniless. Once Mr. A realized this interrelationship, he was able to sleep.

The crucial point in this example is that once Mr. A felt he had tasted death, and after failing to be reassured by his doctors, he had thought of killing himself as a way of coping with his fears. He was so afraid of his own passivity and also so guilt-ridden, he felt unconsciously he deserved to die. I was able to alleviate some of Mr. A's fears of passivity and his wish to punish himself. But, once Mr. A felt no chest pains or heart symptoms, and the fear of sudden death abated, he wanted to stop treatment. He had no wish for a better life—he only wished that I let him vegetate in peace. He never made the step to wanting a second chance for a better life. He regressed to living in an "air-raid shelter" type of existence. Security above all else was his motto—a form of attenuated, slow dying.

I would like to contrast this case with a young doctor whom I had known personally from my early childhood years. Before forty, he had a severe coronary. Later, he suffered from occasional heart pains. He took nitroglycerine for his heart pains and was also placed on anticoagulants, told to lose weight, stop smoking, and watch out for high cholesterol foods. Later, Dr. B and I talked about each other's heart condition and our changed life. We both agreed that the life after the coronary (which we abbreviated to B.C. and A.C., before the coronary and after the coronary) was by far the better one. For the most part, we both stopped feeling anxious or angry, depressed, or envious over the condition of our hearts. We had many attitudes in common and decided the best way to live longer was to recognize that time was precious, to follow the physician's orders as much as possible, and to make for ourselves a happy life. Dr. B loved the practice of medicine, loved music and was a bridge nut, a fishing addict, and an avid sports fan. But, he also loved to eat and smoke. When we talked about the fact that I was able to give up smoking and overeating, he said, "That may be fine for you, but I refuse to do it. I like it too much and it would make my life too frustrating." For close to twenty years, we argued in a friendly fashion, and then, one day, some twenty years after his coronary, he suddenly died. His death occurred during a vacation with his wife and a few doctor friends. Dr. B had gone deep-sea fishing in the morning, snorkling and spearfishing in the afternoon; after a hearty dinner, they had begun to play bridge, drinking and smoking on the side, and suddenly after an exciting hand, he, for some "unknown" reason, dropped dead. There were doctors at his side, but he was dead the moment he closed his eyes. His wife said that was the way he wanted to go. After his coronary, he felt he had earned the right to a joyous life and he had achieved it.

I have no intention of focusing my remarks solely on coronary disease but hope to cover "death-tasting" events in women and those experiences with death we all go through when we get older. At this point, I want to contrast Mr. A and Dr. B.

What I learned from Mr. A was that his major interest in life was making money. Coming from a poor family, a brutal father, raised in the school of hard knocks, he believed in the power that money could give him. It enabled him to combat and surpass his father, and with it he suffered from unconscious guilt feelings. He wanted to be secure for the rest of his life. But he paid a high price for it. He only respected financial success and was willing to sacrifice his scruples for better business deals. In the end, his *unconscious* scruples proved to be his undoing. He was terrified by the devil he had created within him, modeled after his father, but projected and magnified by his own hatred for his father. The devil he feared was his own creation who made his life a mass of terrors.

Dr. B loved people, his profession, music, fishing, and sports. His parents were educated and decent people who cared about the suffering that seemed to be man's lot. Their family life was stimulating, characterized by lots of warmth and intellectual fighting. As an adult, Dr. B cared about his patients, he worried about them, studied them, and made sure they followed his advice. He was a kind of benevolent dictator. This did not diminish after his illness, he worked just as hard, but it was a work of love. He did manage to take an extra half-day off, and took up golf which he played atrociously but with gusto. He played the violin in a chamber music quartet with whom he now met twice a week instead of once, since he had more free time. He became the first violinist because he had fellow musicians who were easily intimidated and though they were better musicians, he was able to take over. One was a shoe salesman and a fine cellist, one a monument engraver and an excellent fiddler, and the violist was a watchmaker. They all suffered from either an inferiority complex or extreme submissiveness. What they played and the tempo and phrasing was determined by Dr. B. At times, when I visited him in his mid-Western city, I was allowed to play second violin. I told him quite frankly that he played too loudly, too fast, and out of tune. Dr. B looked at me smilingly, he did not refute me, but he said serenely, "When I play, I hear Heifetz!" He looked at me as if to say, "Poor man, no imagination." Yet, I was amazed at the increase of his musical knowledge. Relatively untutored, he gave his young son (born A.C.) cello lessons which he accompanied on the piano. It was a joy to behold.

Dr. B had the capacity to laugh at adversity. This is a form of negation and denial. What it means is that yes, I can die at any moment, but there is nothing I can do or am willing to do, so why worry about it. He took some reasonable precautions and instead of bemoaning his fate, he laughed at it and at himself. He always had the knack of making something negative or frightening into a positive activity, even a happy one.

He died a few years ago and as I tell this story, I feel tearful and yet the memory of him is accompanied by merriment.

I would now like to go into detail about the most important mechanisms we have had through the ages in combatting the fear of death. I believe it is the main function of all orthodox religions. Freud talks about it in his paper, "The Future of an Illusion" (1927). Here are a few of his main points:

> And thus a store of ideas is created, born from man's need to make his helplessness tolerable and built up from the material of memories of the helplessness of his own childhood and the childhood of the human race. It can clearly be seen that the possession of these ideas protects him in two directions—against the dangers of nature and Fate, and against the injuries that threaten him from human society itself. . .

Freud goes on to say that religion reassures us:

> Over each one of us there watches a benevolent Providence which is only seemingly stern and which will not suffer us to become a plaything of the overmighty and pitiless forces of nature. Death itself is not extinction, is not a return to inorganic lifelessness, but the beginning of a new kind of existence which lies on the path of development to something higher. . . . In the end, all good is rewarded and all evil punished, if not actually in this form of life then in the later existences that begin after death. In this way, all the terrors, the sufferings, and the hardships of life are destined to be obliterated . . . they are illusions, fulfillments of the oldest, strongest and most urgent wishes of mankind. The secret of their strength lies in the strength of those wishes. As we already know, the terrifying impression of helplessness in childhood aroused the need for protection—for protection through love—which was provided by the father (parents), and the recognition that this helplessness lasts throughout life made it necessary to cling to the existence of a father, but this time a more powerful one. . . .

It is important to remember that I am by profession an analyst, and also a Jew, so I could not resort to a belief in the hereafter as a source of comfort. When I say you only live twice I am referring to people who have tasted death and yet feel they have the possibility of improving their lives here on earth.

Therefore, we have to face the question, what can man and woman do to help them cope with the harsh reality which sets in, after they have first tasted death? We have to use primarily a defense mechanism which is often in ill-repute, a mechanism called denial, a disavowal of reality. We have to give up our reality testing to some extent. We can be realists in our profession, our business dealings, even in the death of others. But about our own death, and of those very close to us, we deny the reality and the finality of it. We may mourn a beloved and yet as we talk about them, they are very much alive. Freud said, in order to maintain a semblance of a happy life, we must believe in an illusion of immortality. This is not an all or nothing situation; we believe in our immortality unconsciously, but we consciously can allow this illusion to come and go.

Mr. A was a sick man, not because he had chest pains, but because he could never disavow them, he was obsessed with his own death. Dr. B had anxiety in the hospital at first, but made sure he got the best medical care, and despite feeling vulnerable and weak, had managed a perhaps overly strong belief in medical science, and that helped him cope with his anxiety. The belief in the omnipotence of one's doctors is, in my opinion, somewhat more realistic than a belief in God's benevolence. Mr. A was tormented by a harsh conscience while Dr. B had a more reasonable conscience, modeled after his parents' basic human decency to him and others.

Another way of handling one's fear of death is to displace it on to something less important. Dr. B was furious with the fact that he was given large amounts of sedatives. He wanted to be fully conscious and his "stupid" doctor believed he was too excited and ordered more sedation every time he complained or enjoyed something. Yet I believe he protested too much; it was less strenuous not to be too alert, and a comfortable haze punctuated by frequent naps made the crucial first three days go faster.

After the critical period, when Dr. B felt well again, he began to act as if nothing very serious had happened. Sometime later he went fishing for marlin, a very strenuous sport, as if to say, I am in such good health, I am not about to die. It is a counterphobic attitude. He overdid every activity, from his practice, to his music, which I believed signified, I am not only unafraid of exertion, I love it, I seek it out. The zest covers the underlying fear.

I am reminded of Freud's ideas about "transience." He was walking during the summer with a young poet who was disturbed by the thought that the beauty of the scene around them was fated to extinction. He complained that all the beauty and splendor of man was doomed by its fleetingness. The poet said, "No. It is impossible that all this loveliness of nature should fade into nothingness." But Freud realized this was another form of the wish for immortality, a wish that goes back to childhood. Freud felt that all the beauties of life are enhanced by the scarcity of time. Limitation in the possibility of an enjoyment raises the value of the enjoyment. I believe that having tasted death can make life all the more precious.

Another clinical example is about a woman I saw in extended psychotherapy. Mrs. C came because her adult children were aware that she was going through a sudden and destructive change in her behavior. Mrs. C, age fifty-five, had been divorced for some fifteen years, and until recently had seemed to have led an interesting and productive life. She had been a good mother, a devoted grandmother, an interesting friend, until about six months earlier. Then fate took over. Mrs. C was told that she had developed some undiagnosable tumors and she would have to undergo a hysterectomy, a complete removal of the uterus. The tumors were not cancerous. From the time of her recovery from surgery, Mrs. C's behavior changed. She began to drink to excess, became promiscuous with, above all, younger men. Then she experimented with drugs, with grass, cocaine, even a touch of LSD. In this condition, her children persuaded her to go see a psychoanalyst.

From the ensuing therapy with Mrs. C, I want to highlight what has relevance to my theme, "You Only Live Twice." The removal of her uterus was for Mrs. C the kiss of death. It meant to her that her life was all over. I told her I found her recent behavior smacked of a secret suicide pact. It seemed to me that her previous life had been irrationally transformed and that her new behavior was a mass of betrayals. Now, to add insult to injury, she must feel that her own body had let her down, and she began to regress destructively. Mrs. C partially agreed, but added that her children and grandchildren no longer needed her. Her friends were uninvolved with her. Why not hurry up the process of dying. I am not afraid of death, she maintained, I am a surplus commodity and serve no useful purpose. I cannot bear slowly withering away to nothingness.

First it was my task to help Mrs. C return to her normal sense of self-esteem and to build up her sense of personal worth. The hysterectomy had made Mrs. C face the fact that she was mortal and she confused it, out of guilt, with being in imminent danger. I reassured her this was not a punishment for her divorce, and not malevolent fate punishing her for her occasional love alliances. She had been faithful to her children, to her grandchildren, and to her friends. I also pointed out that her children needed her as a model on how to grow old with dignity and joy, and for her grandchildren she was an important human being as well as proof of life's continuity.

The patient had had a good life, and with psychotherapy she was able to put the hysterectomy in its proper perspective. Mrs.

C's surgery no longer stirred up her irrational guilt feelings and feelings of inferiority. Mrs. C once again joined the healthy, happy life she had before the hysterectomy. She too found "You Only Live Twice," and the second time around can be even better.

What I have said to Mrs. C applies to those people who are finally convinced they are past the middle age of life and have indisputable signs that they have joined the legions of the elderly. You can try to hide this by marrying someone twenty-five years younger, you can get a hairpiece to cover the baldness, or a facelift to cover the wrinkles. But, they are only masks, and you cannot fool yourself for very long. The defects in memory or speaking ability can be cute to those who love you, but they are also a reminder of the brain's shrinking ability to remember or speak as sharply as we did in our youth. One's stamina is not all it used to be, either physically, mentally or sexually. True, these declines are selective and not total. It is not total amnesia nor total impotence, but the signs are unmistakably there. You can also, in the ensuing years, get smarter, wiser, particularly if you chose to reexamine your values and priorities. Nevertheless, you are getting older, and how does one cope with that? Each day you are subliminally aware that the end of your life is approaching. You notice that friends of yours are dying, even some who are younger than you are. When any celebrity dies, you find yourself searching for his age and you feel good that he was older than you.

Let me quote again some excerpts from Freud about "Our Attitude Towards Death."

> Our habit is to lay stress on the fortuitous causation of the death—accident, disease, infection, advanced age; in this way, we betray an effort to reduce death from a necessity to a chance event. . . . It is an inevitable result of all this that we should seek in the world of fiction, in literature, and in the theatre compensation for what has been lost in life. . . . In the realm of fiction, we find the plurality of lives which we need. We die with the hero with whom we have identified ourselves; yet we survive him, and are ready to die again just as safely with another hero. . . .

That is why tragedy has a hold on us.

To achieve any semblance of a happy life, to fill one's life with wit, humor, and courage, one has to have the capacity to deny, or at least minimize that some day we all have to die. Once you are at all aware of that harsh reality, the denial, or partial denial of it can make life still enjoyable, zestful, and even more bearable. When one has tasted death, above all, tasted one's own death, one has to use healthy denial, denial in the service of the ego. To be constantly aware that one is mortal and can die at any moment would tend to make a person develop hypochondriacal ideas, an obsessional neurosis about death and dying. Some people like Mr. A and Mrs. C tried to pursue death actively by suicide in order to avoid dying. The search for security and the search for love are in conflict, in many ways.

To go all out for security means instinctual starvation, and such people develop obsessions regarding atomic war and global starvation, without realizing that they have projected their inner hunger upon the world at large. To love, not just romantically, but to love ideas or a cause, means taking risks, but that gives living a zest. Many men risk their lives for people or causes they really love. It is only great love that can neutralize fear and morbid depressions.

For a meaningful existence after the middle years, one has to reassess one's values and try those talents one had to forego when one was young and had other problems. I think Feifel put it well when he said:

> One leitmotiv that is continually coming to the fore in work in this area is that the crisis is often not the fact of oncoming death per se, of man's unsurmountable finiteness, but rather the waste of limited years, the unassayed tasks, the lost opportunities, the talents withering in disuse, the avoidable evils which have been done. The tragedy which is underlined is that man dies prematurely and without dignity, that death has not become really "his own."

The capacity to handle one's own death, even in the face of one's organic adversities, is to use one's own capacities creatively, even the ones that have been neglected. To do this, one has to stop feeling sorry for oneself and one has to rid oneself of an irrational sense of guilt or masochism. One has to continue to risk doing or thinking about something new, and not dwell only on one's past. At times remembering can be the adversary of a rich fantasy life.

People who are prone to use the mechanism of denial become dreamers and, if talented, become artists or poets. I would like to add to that list the gifted actors and skillful psychotherapists. A recent study of creative people done by Goodman in Jersey City revealed that highly creative artists and scientists who have lived fully, are not as afraid of death as those who lack imagination. The ability to say "no," to assert one's independence of perception of reality when this is warranted, is essential to the development of what we commonly call firmness of character. It may seem paradoxical to propose that the capacity to deny reality, which so often is overdeveloped in our sickest patients, should also be implicated as essential to the ego's strength. I knew of a man who suddenly became aphasic. The first word he was able to say was "no." I believe characters who have this kind of firmness can be either stuffed shirts or healthily stubborn. A dash of denial makes for a richer and more interesting character structure.

### To Sum Up

The patients I have described had options, tried to cope within these options and some succeeded more or less. A man with heart trouble can feel fate has dealt him a terrible blow, and he is now obsessed over the loss of his good health. Another man in that position may feel how lucky he is to have survived his first coronary. You can look at a half glass of wine and say, "Too bad, it is half empty," or, "How great, it is still half full."

"You Only Live Twice" is based on how lucky we are to have the bottle half full of wine. I will savor it even more than the first half.

Gensundheit and Shalom!

# 23 Beyond Sexual Satisfaction . . . ? (1976)

*Greenson's last two public lectures were given in San Diego. They were to benefit both the San Diego Psychoanalytic Institute as well as the Hanna Fenichel Nursery School. These performances were truly remarkable because they followed his struggle with aphasia and are a testimony to his enormous courage and burning desire to study and share what he had learned.*

*In the first of them, Greenson returned to one of his favorite themes: true versus false emotional involvement. This time he addressed it in the context of the so-called sexual revolution. As he looked at his clinical practice he was finding that the notion of sexual satisfaction with someone for whom one cares, with whom one gives and receives pleasure, was viewed by a growing number of people as rather "straight" and somewhat old-fashioned if not quaint. "They seem to want super-sex, superorgasms, as quickly as possible. Intimacy and mutuality are not important. In fact, they are a hindrance."*

*Greenson felt that efforts to go "beyond" sexual satisfaction (meaning beyond intimacy and mutuality) were in fact retrogressive. The attitudes and practices he was encountering seemed to him to be primarily narcissistic, wrapped up with pathology and addiction. The interest in supersex and multiple orgasms was really a form of compulsive masturbation, with a human partner or a gadget, expressing a pathological narcissistic orientation toward relationship. "This new generation has become less aware of emotions and conflicts in depth, and thinks only in conscious and superficial terms. Self-actualization or the new ethos of 'being oneself' in a standardized, postindustrial society may well be the new grand illusion. This notion is merely a new kind of narcissism."*

I shall begin by explaining the strange title of my talk, "*Beyond* Sexual Satisfaction . . . ?" In recent years I have found many people are not content to be sexually satisfied. They are searching for something more, and better. *Mere* satisfaction is not enough! There is a very apparent contradiction between *mere* satisfaction and *beyond* sexual satisfaction. My own clinical experience and observations of the social scene is that sexual satisfaction with someone one cares for, that gives mutual pleasure, is considered old-fashioned, straight, if not quaint. The more one looks at the social and sexual mores in the seventies, it is apparent that people are not interested in intimacy and mutuality. They seem to want supersex, superorgasms, as quickly as possible. Intimacy and mutuality are not important. In fact, they are a hindrance.

I believe that this trend toward supersex goes hand-in-hand with the use of drugs, group sex, vibrators, promiscuity, and pornography. Supersex confuses sexual satisfaction with an ecstatic high. It is more like a religious experience, like a hallucinatory happening, than a sexual experience. In fact, is it not merely a coincidence, supersex and the growth of newly founded religious experiences seem to be on the rise!

In psychoanalysis we learn that a truly satisfying *genital* experience includes intimacy and mutuality. Now we seem to neglect genital sexuality. In fact, a new operation has been discovered: the genital bypass. It is like the heart bypass because it cuts the heart out of the orgasm.

---

Lecture for the Hanna Fenichel Nursery School, University of California, San Diego, Extension Division, 1976.

*Beyond* sexual satisfaction is, in fact, a retrogression. It is primarily narcissistic. It seems to contain elements of pathological narcissism, perversion, and addiction. Let me give some clinical vignettes as illustrations.

## Clinical Material

A few years ago I saw a forty-five-year old man, Mr. A, successful both artistically and financially, who complained about his sexual potency. In the past, he had always been able to satisfy his wife and himself but, recently, the situation had changed. For some unknown reason, his wife was no longer satisfied with a single orgasm. She wanted multiple orgasms; at least five to ten. The patient felt his wife got this notion from reading books like Masters and Johnson, and Germaine Greer's *The Female Eunuch*, etc. My patient tried valiantly to satisfy her, but after forty minutes to an hour he was limp, with or without an ejaculation. His wife, Mrs. A, could not be dissuaded, and went merrily on her way to get further gratification by rubbing against his thigh. The poor man stated that he felt he was being used and demeaned, like a sexual thing and not a man, and he was very depressed over this state of affairs. I sympathized with him and tried to find out more about the situation.

"Yes," he said, "they had had a good sex life, he thought." I quickly intervened when he said, "he thought." I wanted him to explain why "he thought" and did not *know* about his wife's sexual satisfaction. The patient then told me that when he first met his wife she was a young virgin. He had been raised in the streets of a big city and was already twice divorced. Mr. A gradually taught his wife all she had to know about sex. She was a willing partner and, soon after, they married and had a child. Ten years later, Mrs. A became interested in women's lib, the pill, equal rights, astrology, and, eventually this spurred her on to see a psychologist. But when his wife began to see the psychologist, all hell broke loose. "Hell" being her demand for multiple orgasms with every sexual contact.

What had driven Mrs. A to see a psychologist, apparently, was her *chronic* complaint that her husband preferred being with "the boys" rather than having female companionship. He loved to watch football games, horse racing, and to play gin rummy. Mr. A could not stand the blandness nor the bitchiness of women, especially when they began to talk about sex and used the same four-letter words men use. He had contempt for women and yet was in awe of them. His wife's acute complaint was his negative attitude toward her desire for multiple orgasms. Yes, the husband admitted, he was a male chauvinist. He was repelled and felt humiliated by his wife's demands for equal rights, especially in the sexual sphere. It made him feel put down, on the defensive, and as a result, he had diminished sexual desire, at least for his wife. In the past, Mrs. A had reacted as though he were the greatest lover in the world. Now she was telling him in four-letter words, that he was a sexual underachiever.

I do not want to make this a lengthy case history, so I will only tell you the highlights. After seeing Mr. A several times, I asked if it were possible to see his spouse. Mrs. A, with her psychologist's consent, agreed to see me in her husband's presence. She was extraordinarily pretty and naive-looking, younger than her age of thirty-five. True, she said, she had learned about sex from her husband. But, in recent years, Mrs. A could not bear the double standard with which he ruled the house. He was free to come and go as he pleased, whereas she had to stay at home or account for where she had been. When her friends began talking about women's lib, she realized that she was not alone. She then read Friedan, Greer, Millet, and Masters and Johnson, and was determined to see a male psychologist to determine what she could do about her situation.

The psychologist, who was mainly a psychological tester, and not a therapist, listened to her story and told her she had every right to do the same kinds of things her husband did. "Yes," the psychologist told her, "multiple orgasms are better than one," and also agreed that "smoking pot before sex makes it easier to achieve multiple orgasms." I must say that I had not heard from Mr. A about the pot smoking. He shamefacedly said he had "overlooked" telling me that. The wife asked, "Did you tell about going to parties with Hugh Hefner and his bunny girls to which I was not invited?" The husband said he had "neglected" to mention this. It had "slipped" his mind.

After several consultations I was able to show Mr. and Mrs. A that the wife's desire for multiple orgasms was basically a form of revenge. It was her way of getting back at her husband's tyrannical behavior. Mr. A had been proud of his sexual prowess. Now she had turned their sex life into a battlefield, and *she* was the victor, after having been an apprentice and in second place in most areas of their lives. Her orgasm hunting was not primarily a sexual pleasure but an "ego-trip" for her and a humiliation for her husband. She was now in the driver's seat.

I recommended to the couple that each one get into psychotherapy with a competent psychoanalytically trained person. She did. He felt too humiliated and vengeful, and so decided to quit the marriage. Now they are more-or-less happily divorced.

Another clinical demonstration is the case of Mrs. B. A few years ago a forty-year-old woman came to see me about the deterioration of her sex life and romance with her lover, a surgeon, Dr. X. Mrs. B had lost her husband some five years earlier in an automobile accident. She took care of her two children dutifully, if not cheerfully. Then, one-and-one-half years ago, she fell head over heels in love with Dr. X. He was divorced and had several children whom he completely ignored. Mrs. B was delighted to have a man all to herself. They very quickly had a sexual affair and, although Mrs. B thought she had had a good sex life, her lover told her she was just a beginner. He moved into her house and began to introduce her to new varieties of sex.

Dr. X liked reading hard core pornography before and during sex. At first Mrs. B found it exciting when she could have multiple orgasms. Somewhat later, she admitted she was finding this kind of sex boring and her lover introduced her to sex with a vibrator. But Dr. X found this dull and suggested "tripling"; sex with a third person, male or female, it did not matter. Mrs. B did not dare complain because she knew that if she did he would want something more outlandish which, eventually, he did. He wanted group sex, marathon sex, and "daisy chains" with or without pot. Slowly, Mrs. B watched the disintegration of her love life, sex life, and even the care of her children began to suffer. Her children felt neglected, jealous, and also envious of her lover.

I decided Mrs. B needed psychoanalytically oriented psychotherapy. I had, in the meantime, discovered that during the first years after the death of her husband, Mrs. B had tried existential therapy, then yoga, transcendental meditation, Reichian therapy, and rolfing. Basically, Mrs. B was quite depressed and infantile. She had never succeeded in having a core identity, no object constancy, and tended to be polymorph perverse. This was the name Freud gave to infants who could enjoy all forms of sensual feelings, no matter what part of the body was touched or fondled, and the character of the person giving the pleasure played no role. She would start doing what her sex partner wished, could enjoy it up to a point, and would then find it boring. It took quite a few years for Mrs. B to reveal and finally get over a traumatic childhood. She had been raised by nurses who cared little for her welfare. Eventually, she was able to rid herself of her lover, and enjoy a stable and continuous relationship with someone she cared for and who also cared for her.

These are two clinical examples but they illustrate how four people who got involved with supersex are essentially both perverse and narcissistic.

## Some Definitions and Formulations

I do not believe I am a moralist, though perversion hints at something wicked or evil. It has become an old-fashioned word, even though perverted behavior is gaining prominence in the sexual sphere.

I agree with the formulations and definitions of Robert Stoller. First we have to distinguish between a variant form of sex and a perversion. A variant form of sex is an abberation but it is within the person's conscious control, it is not obligatory, and it does not harm or dehumanize or desecrate the partner.

A perversion is a compulsory activity, contains a goodly amount of hostility, and intends to dehumanize and humiliate the partner. The hostility can be done in daydreams, in conscious or unconscious fantasy, and in actuality. Often it is in the form of revenge, in people who were severely traumatized as children. The naive-looking Mrs. A, I mentioned earlier, was not only revenging herself against her tyrannical husband but also revenging herself against her loving but antisexual father.

In her childhood she never saw a trace of affection or tenderness, let alone sexuality, pass between her father and mother. The story of Mr. A was replete with sexual promiscuity, "gang-busting," group sex, and the like. He put his wife on a pedestal, an idealization, essentially nonsexual, keeping her a prisoner of his childhood dreams.

Mrs. B, however, had never built up a core identity. Her mother was very rich, and she was brought up by a succession of maids, and was repelled by her father's grossness and alcoholism. Mrs. B knew at an early age her father was unfaithful to her mother, and had conscious fantasies of having sex with him, but in disguise. We were able to reconstruct that, in Mrs. B's early childhood, her father used to exhibit himself before her. She was fascinated by sex with a powerful, hateful person. One of her major fantasies was of a harem where the dreadful Sultan preferred her to all the rest. Dr. X I only knew from the stories about him, but I believe he is a walking textbook on perversions.

Stoller believes that all of perversion can be explained as an erotic form of hatred. We have to know the conscious or unconscious fantasies of the person performing the perverse act.

For example, the compulsive need to read hard core pornography. There is always a victim; no victim, no pornography. There is always voyeurism, which is a safety device. *I* did not harm anyone, *I* only watched. In this way guilt is reduced. Hard core pornography in magazines and movies is obviously a revenge against women. The male watcher is the victor; but, it can be turned around, and you can identify with the woman, the temptress, the phallic woman. The victim and the victor become one.

One man's excitement is another man's boredom. People tend to get bored when doing repetitious acts. Sexual boredom is the greatest cause of promiscuity. In order to create more excitement there must be an element of risk taking. (This is true of all perversions, and of all normal, happy sex, as well.)

Pornography is essentially bisexual; you can identify with the aggressor or the victim. (I remind you of the case of Dr. X and Mrs. B. They "tripled" and it did not matter what the gender of the third party was.) He not only takes the woman heterosexually, but he even puts himself into her skin, gets into her boots, to feel what she is feeling. Women seem to be less influenced by pictures of naked men. Men are mystified by the sex life of women and women are not mystified by men. There are few Peeping Tom women.

I want to say a few words about the vibrator since we had mentioned it. "Plain Talk About the New Approach to Sexual Pleasure," by Claire Safran, from the respected journal, *Redbook* magazine, March 1976:

> The vibrator, which began as a gadget made by fly-by-night companies in places like Taiwan, is now being made by solid corporations in places like New Jersey.
>
> Sex therapists, however, consider the vibrator to be more than a device. In fact, it has been hailed as the only significant advance in sexual technique since the days of Pompeii. (Perhaps they thought of Mt. Vesuvius!)

Margaret Mead is less enthusiastic about the vibrator. Americans prefer having machines do everything. Machines alienate people from their bodies and their emotions. In the same issue, Virginia Johnson said that women who use the vibrator for long periods of time have lost the richness of the sexual, sensual, fantasies, daydreams, and thoughts.

Now I would like to turn to the pathological narcissism in supersex. Part of the sexual revolution is based on the quest of sexual egalitarianism, but the answers are too easy, too empty, and lead to emotional impoverishment. In an article by Tom Wolfe (1976) which he called: The "Me, me, me and only me" phenomena, he condemned the sexual revolution. He found it composed of pseudo supersex and pseudo theology, destructive of the nuclear family, promoting violence, delinquency, and other sundry vices.

The pathological narcissistic interest in supersex, multiple orgasms, is a form of compulsive masturbation with a human partner or a gadget. When I question women who are *addicted* to multiple orgasms, they say that it does not matter who the partner is. They prefer someone they know, but it is their fantasies that matter. Actually, their sex life is promiscuous even though they may use the same partner. The same holds true of men and women who use other perverse behavior. There is no intimacy nor mutuality. Its purpose is to satisfy "me, me" and only "me."

Recently I received a letter from an editor of a very prestigious journal in sociology and economics, which touches on our topic. Let me quote:

> We are preparing a study dealing with the current popularity of pornography and the profitability of pornography as a business.
>
> We have found that one extraordinarily successful magazine, *Hustler*, which is considered hard core in the industry, is expected to earn $13 million this year. This is 5 times more than the entire Playboy Enterprises, more than the *Boston Globe*, double Doyle, Dane, Bernbach's earnings and three times more than the net income of Esquire, Inc. *Hustler* does this with an editorial staff of 12.

I find that some of my answers to that letter are pertinent to my current theme. Let me quote some of what I said:

> Pornography differentiates itself from other perversions in that someone else's fantasy is being used; it is prepackaged. The pornography reader is only an observer. This attempts to get rid of guilt feelings. But it is not pornographic without the *observer's pornographic fantasies.* In my professional role as physician and psychoanalyst I see, and I look upon, hard core pornography as though it were a primitive anatomy lesson; a brutally childish imitation of sex. There is no sexual excitement as long as I maintain that professional role. From my clinical experience, I realize the pornography addicts are trying to cure themselves of sexual trauma, real or imagined, by performing their rituals. It is important to recognize that hard core pornography, like *Hustler*, is tremendously and obviously sadistic, masochistic, masturbational, full of defecation and urination as sexual acts, etc. *Hustler* outdoes *Playboy* and *Penthouse* by its accent on sadomasochism, blood-thirstiness, lesbianism, and all kinds of triangular bisexual arrangements.

Why has normal sexual activity become boring for many who look to pornography for excitement?

1. Many people are too timid to do anything "extraordinary"

with their spouses. They save that for a "hooker" or an "affair."

2. Others have been traumatized in childhood and, instead of developing polite neurotic symptoms like phobias, depressions and obsessions, they let it "all hang out and do their own thing," etc.
3. The influence of television, publications such as *Hustler*, and drugs, all share a common popularity. Although it is true that while under the influence of such drugs as LSD, pot, cocaine, etc., colors, music, and sex can be beautiful. Nevertheless, it withers the real person inside. All these stimulants harm and deform the core identity.
4. We live in a culture that idealizes our "me"-ness. We seem to be following our own uniqueness to a ridiculous extent. It leads to emotional apathy toward other human beings. It is essentially narcissistic.
5. The other side of the coin is self-abnegation, leading to faith in phony gurus, the so-called "Jesus people," and other devout followers of deviant gods.

This leads me to my last theme of this talk. Let me simplify: The late fifties and early sixties were the days of protest against racial discrimination: Martin Luther King and "We Shall Overcome" days. People dropped out of school to march in Alabama. They were the days of the hippies, the Jesus people, and flower children. The late sixties were characterized by pot, LSD trips, assassinations, and the beginning of Vietnam. In the seventies we see the results of Watergate, the FBI and CIA scandals; shell-shocked from the war in Vietnam, disillusioned by crime ini high places, people are hungering for something to believe in. They do not want specific remedies. It ends up with an emphasis on "Me"-ness—me, me, me, "*uber alles*"—narcissism.

California leads the rest of the nation with its hippies, communes, drugs, and the quick and easy therapies. A businessman's or housewife's special: For $220 a week you can go to learn about yourself; loosen yourself up, wriggle your fanny a bit, and a variety of marathon encounters. People are encouraged to bare their souls and to strip away their defenses, similar to the old-fashioned games at Synanon and the new ones at EST. The basic idea is simple: Let's talk about *ME*. No matter what the outcome is, *ME* is the subject of the group. We have to find the *REAL ME*.

I am paraphrasing Tom Wolfe: Group therapy leads to primal scream, to encounter marathons, and turns to Oriental meditation religions. Communes began to enroll thousands of students. A new assumption was formulated: All men possess *conscious energy* paralleling the physical world, and this mysterious energy can unite the universe. The only difference is that it happens so quickly, almost instant conversion, and it is basically, "*LET'S TALK ABOUT ME.*"

In the "Me" generation, every man or woman is worth instant analyzing and agonizing over. What it had been for him or her once, sex had now become a religious experience. The orgasm had been transformed into a spiritual ecstasy.

This is a combination of pathological narcissism and sexual perversion. The people I am describing not only believe in supersex, in charismatic gurus, but talk a different language. I am quoting John Wykert, in *Psychiatric News*, 1976, who quotes R. D. Rosen about "Psychobable"—the new "in" thing:

> It seems that almost everybody belongs to the Cult of Candor these days, and that everyone who does speaks the same dialect. Are you relating? good. Are you in touch with yourself? Fine. Gone through some heavy changes? Doing your own thing? (or, are you by some mistake doing someone else's?) Is your head screwed on straight?

I have had patients who said to me in their first interview, they are trying to get their shit together. I was startled. They looked upon me with condescension. The same held true when they reported a conversation between friends, using phrases like: Are you mind-fucked, or just engaged in mental foreplay? Very often the young people call me by my first name—and I just became a senior citizen. Peculiarly enough, I am getting used to this kind of talk and sometimes find it refreshing.

This new generation has become less aware of emotions and conflicts in depth, and thinks only in conscious and superficial terms. Self-actualization or the new ethos of "being oneself" in a standardized, postindustrial society may well be *the new "grand illusion."* This notion is merely a new kind of narcissism.

I am reminded of a Freudian philosopher, Paul Pruyser, who said that the games people play and roles they "transact" are superficial indicators of what the internal relationships are. There is a world of difference between "being yourself," or "knowing yourself," and "doing your own thing." A neurosis, on the other hand, is not a trick but a costly price one pays for the suppression of drives in order to become civilized. Quick therapies, I have mentioned earlier, treat all patients alike.

I believe the therapy should fit the patient, not the therapist, his theories, or his institution. The best therapies are humanistic as well as scientific. Freud's theories are, to my mind, the ones which take the individual seriously, with so much respect for his assets and liabilities, with so much reverence for the depth of his predicaments. To work well as analysts, we need compassion, empathy and zest, but with a goodly amount of craftmanship.

The Freudian analyst is aware of omnipresent ambiguity and ambivalence. He does not sacrifice deep truth or experience to elegance of formulation or phony ease in living. He avoids promises he cannot keep and, therefore, promises little. He aims at open-mindedness, open-endedness, and tolerance. He has grave doubt about those formulations which come off too neatly, too orderly, too understandably. They are usually empty. Today it is very difficult to value psychoanalysis because the marketplace puts great emphasis on cheer, faith, optimism and quickness.

Psychoanalysis demands humor too. Precisely that humor which can keep the image of man rich though somewhat sloppy, complex though somewhat inelegant, close to those disorderly facts of experience that make life worth examining and worth living.

# 24 People in Search of a Family (1978)

*In Greenson's last public lecture, the theme of obstacles and barriers to true intimacy and mutuality is explored further. Hildi Greenson feels that this lecture "concerned a need Greenson found in his patients which echoed his only partly unconscious desire to make people he cared about a member of his family. It was his foster-home fantasy of a haven where all hurts are mended." Greenson described a number of clinical situations involving grown people who have difficulty in setting up a new family, or in remaining with a new family, or are compelled to have many new families. He addressed many confusing contemporary psychosocial phenomena, including the turn to gurus or strange religions, teenage suicide, and the need for communes, and related them to the search for family security. In his conclusion he was again and forever the developmentalist: "People who search for families try to undo the effects of a bad family life. It is an acting out, to replace the unhappy past with a happy future. It is an attempt to ameliorate the unhappiness of the original family life. Sometimes it works and sometimes it fails. On an optimistic note, I can add, family life is good for your health. You live longer, both men and women. . . ."*

## Introduction

The topic I would like to discuss with you seems deceptively simple. Yet as psychoanalysts we know not to trust the obvious. We know that part of growing up is finding a new family to replace the old one. Men and women get married, or live together, with the hope of having children. Yet there are people who do not want to get married, or to live together, or have children. And there is the man of fifty, presumably happily married, with pleasant children, who suddenly divorces and then marries a twenty-five-year-old bride. We have so many contradictory urges; it is hard to be human and happy. Think a moment. We humans start life being part of the mother, and then highly dependent on father, siblings, and peers. Then we strive for independence and attain it to a degree; only to desire and achieve another form of symbiosis in sexual intercourse.

My subject "People in Search of a Family" has to do with grown people who have difficulty in setting up a new family, or in remaining with a new family, or are compelled to have many new families. There is a great deal about this subject that I cannot answer. Perhaps the panelists and audience can help me out.

## Clinical Material

### *Case 1*

A young man, Mr. P, came to see me. He is a thirty-year-old lawyer doing his clerkship with a judge. He was sent to me by a psychiatrist in Chicago with the statement that this intelligent and sensitive young man was very hard to diagnose. He is depressed and yet outgoing. He meets people easily. He gets involved with women who mistreat him. Although he is aware of this, he is drawn to such women. Mr. P tells me that he has come to see me because he recently fell in love with a young lady who, once again, often mistreats him. True, she seems to care for him, but her caring is tainted with teasing, making fun of him, and at times

---

Presented to the San Diego Psychoanalytic Institute, October 6, 1978.

humiliating him. Many times when they have a date, she fails to show up, and when he goes to her home or calls her, he finds out she has gone out with somebody else. Mr. P says he likes the girl and she likes him; he feels that they have a very good relationship. They are very friendly and intimate with one another, despite the fact that they do not have a very good sex life. They pet and neck and often masturbate each other. At times, when she is in good spirits or has used pot, they may have intercourse. As much as he likes intercourse, he prefers to feel that she loves him. She delights in telling him about her sexual experiences with other men. Mr. P is jealous, yet he eagerly listens.

Slowly something else proved to be significant. This came to light gradually when they quarreled. The patient told me he got up early in the morning, went to her house, and drove her to work. (This was his usual procedure.) After Mr. P finished his work, he picked her up, and drove her back from work, even though they did not talk with one another. When she breaks a date with him and goes out with other people, he unexpectedly appears at her parents' home. He says, "Here I am. Is anybody home?" Yes, the mother is home, the father is home, her brother is home, and he has no trouble spending the evening with her family. They talk or watch television or play cards.

I could hardly believe my ears. After a quarrel he gets up early in the morning to take her to work. And, after a full day's work, exhausted, he brings her home without exchanging any words. I realize this was not the usual romantic couple. But the answer evaded me for the time being.

I questioned him about his jealousy: he is jealous but he gets so much joy out of being friendly with her family. I asked him how things were in his own family. Mr. P started out superficially, telling me that his parents and sisters live together, but they are not very close to one another. In fact, his mother was closer to her own mother than she was to him, his sisters, or their father. Now the situation with Mr. P became clear to me.

I brought out that he is attracted to women who are similar to his mother, because they offer him a chance to redo the past. He wants to become a member of a happy family; a family not like his own. Mr. P is not mature enough to establish his own family.

*Case 2*

A young woman, Mrs. T, who was in analysis with me had had two divorces and was now in her third marriage. She came for analysis because she suffered from many phobias. Her most severe phobia was that going from a known place to an unknown place brought about very intense feelings of anxiety. The patient was a middle child. Her father died when she was five years old in a train accident. Mrs. T was brought up by a very strict mother who told the nurses to toilet train each child by the time they were nine months old. I reconstructed with the patient that when she was put on the toilet before she was able to get on or off by herself, she needed help. The transition from being helpless to being helped, or being mobile to being immobile, played an important role in all her phobic reactions, and also her reactions to her family.

When my patient decided to divorce her first husband, her greatest concern was how her in-laws would react. Mrs. T actually spoke to them about the possibility of a divorce to insure that they would not hold it against her. In addition, Mrs. T's own mother tried to make sure that a divorce would not interfere with the relationship between herself and her daughter's mother-in-law and father-in-law. When the patient divorced her second husband some three years later, she and her mother repeated precisely this conduct.

This need to maintain an in-law family structure for the patient and her mother had its origin in some added details of their common history. Mrs. T lost her father when she was five years of age due to an accident; her mother remarried some thirteen years later. In the meantime she suffered from the fact that she did not have a father. She was taunted at school, "You don't have a father, you don't have a father." Now she tries to make up for this by having many fathers, stepfathers, and fathers-in-law. Also, my patient's mother had lost her father at an early age and had a bad relationship with her mother. Therefore, she too was very keen on having an extended family. When my patient's mother died (before she began analysis) her stepfather remarried soon thereafter. The new stepmother had many annoying traits, but my patient felt instantly close to her, called her mother as well as by her first name.

Some adults, when they get married, find it easy to call the in-laws "mom" and "dad," while others find it difficult or even impossible. This latter group finds it easy to call their in-laws by their first names. Parenthetically, one can call a mother-in-law "mother" or "mom" but never the original words you called your own mother. A good example is a Swiss woman who could call her mother-in-law "mom" but never "mutti" which she called her mother in her own mother tongue. The same holds true for fathers and fathers-in-law. The people who cannot make that switch seem to be saying, "I have only one set of parents and they are irreplaceable and untouchable."

Let us return to Mrs. T who did not have many friends, but about each friend she always said, "I feel attached to her. I feel she could live with me, like a member of my family." This was in contrast to how she felt about her own brothers and sisters. She could be utterly frank with her friends, while it took her quite awhile to achieve this with her latest husband, although she loved him dearly. Mrs. T had been happily married for eight years; yet she lived in constant fear as though on probation, that someday he would say, "I'm sorry, you have failed me. Pack up and get out." This was by far the best relationship she had had with a man; but it was still lurking in her mind that she would be abandoned by him. And all the while she was buttressing herself with in-laws and friends who became part of the family. Thus when the need for a family had not been met during the growing up years, one may spend the rest of one's life not running away from home, but running toward home.

Family intimacy is not as intense as intimacy on a one to one basis. Mrs. T was partly a "loner." She treasured being alone at times, but it was only possible after she had touched "home base" with friends, or if she knew exactly when her husband would return.

*Case 3*

A young man, Mr. O, marries a woman five years older than himself. They have a stormy marriage, but they are willing to go on. Slowly a rift seems to be developing. They begin living in separate places. One lived in the city and one lived in Palm Springs. What had happened?

The wife's father died and then her mother. When his in-laws died the husband was ready to leave his wife. He had married a difficult woman because he loved her family. He wanted to become their son, not just their son-in-law. The marriage was his way of becoming a member of the family. His original family was killed by the Nazis when he was very young.

*Case 4*

A former prisoner of war in Germany, Mr. B lives unhappily with a married brother. He tries to get a job and fails or is fired. He is only happy when talking with old buddies about the war, above all, with those who were prisoners of war. One day Mr. B robs a liquor store without any disguise. Instead of leaving with the small sum he had stolen, he drove around and around in his car, even after the police arrived. Finally the police stopped him. He is brought before the store owner who recognizes him because he is wearing his Army jacket, and he is arrested. Once again he is a prisoner.

His brother asked me to see Mr. B in jail, which I did. He is apathetic, talks mournfully about the good times in Stalag 14, how marvelous it was being a prisoner of war. However, he hates this jail because here is no communication in the county jail. He rarely talks about his preprisoner of war days. I question him about getting a job in a veterans' hospital helping the paraplegics and he agreed. When the storeowner heard about his willingness to work with paralyzed people, he dropped the charges.

This is a man whose happiest days were being a prisoner of war. What he missed was the camaraderie. When he began working at the VA Hospital he was happy.

My experience, and the experience of others, confirms that many people do not want to leave jail. When released they will do something to get themselves arrested again.

The patient had volunteered for the Air Corps when his mother and father had killed themselves. The POW camp was, for him, a group of many more siblings than in his ordinary life. The authorities treated him fairly well. Obviously they were his parent figures.

## Return to Religion

In the last ten years there has been a turning to religion. It has been observed that God may be dead, but Jesus remains. While the traditional God has been intent on being glorified by men, Jesus is "the man for others." While the traditional God has come to seem absent, gurus are present, you can see them. In fact, they make themselves highly visible.

The Hare Krishna and the "Moonies" behave as an extended family. All orthodox people are united by a common faith which is much stronger than reason. (This is true for certain psychological groups too.)

This indirectly brings me to the formation of another group. People who were disappointed in their own family, try to become members of an exalted family. It may be led by the rich and the famous. It is another chance to act out the family romance, which is well known in Freudian literature.

## Teenage Suicide

The adult rate of suicide has remained constant for almost fifty years, but the rate of young people who suicide *has nearly tripled* in the last twenty years. The major cause may be drugs combined with rejection by their girlfriends/boyfriends or peer group. Many of today's teenagers do not have a family to fall back on. When today's parents loosen the reins, the kids often feel that as *not caring*, rather than as a sign that they are becoming more grown-up. Again, these are partial answers but they are relevant to my subject.

## The Need for Communes

There is a search for an extended family and communes as one approaches middle-age, and certainly when you get to retirement age. I see in friends of mine, and in myself, how one hates to be alone. Your parents have died, your friends die, the idea of dying alone is terrible. In a strange way you find yourself running toward home. It is odd that the communes did not fare well for young people. They proved to be unstable, use drugs, were promiscuous, and often became destructive. A glaring example is the Manson Family.

The Kibutzim, I believe, represent a successful commune. Perhaps the reason for this is that they have people of all ages and a common purpose. It has the special advantage of furthering communication with all generations and age levels.

## Some General Points

How often in a marriage, when children are born, do husband and wife begin to call each other "dad" or "mom"? They seem eager to have another mommy and daddy. They prolong the joys of childhood, or they attempt to improve on the deficiencies of past parenting or both. These are the kind of parents that tell their children to call grown-up friends "uncle" and "aunty."

The family one is born into is irrevocable—even a black sheep remains part of the family. The new family has the advantage of being the family one has chosen, and one can get rid of it, one can get divorced. As the French say, "A family is a group of people condemned to live together." The second family has the advantage of avoiding incest and committing incest.

In any family the wife or husband may resemble the parents, or be so different to insure that they are not the original parents. This may break down, for example, when a first child enters the family picture. Now the wife and husband have become parents. This breaks the incest barrier and the wife or husband is no longer a sexual person, they lose the "turn-on appeal." As clinicians we hear very often, "We had a great sex life until we got married, or until we had children."

Sometimes you hear of husbands who on their way home from work have to stopn off at their mother's house. Mahler and her co-workers have pointed out how children who just are learning to walk (from 10 months to 18 months) go through a refueling phase. They love to leave the mother, but then have to return to her for a brief period, and then are able to leave her again. I think grown-ups do this by different varieties of "touching home base"—like Mrs. T. Nobody is completely autonomous!

I cannot finish a talk on people who need families without mentioning the great hostility that goes on between in-law parents and children. People who tend to idealize their parents usually hate their in-laws. This is also true for stepmothers, stepfathers, and stepchildren.

## Conclusion

People who search for families try to undo the effects of a bad family life. It is an acting out, to replace the unhappy past with a happy future. It is an attempt to ameliorate the unhappiness of the original family life. Sometimes it works and sometimes it fails. On an optimistic note, I can add, family life is good for your health. You live longer, both men and women. Perhaps, it may only seem longer.